Wider War

The Struggle for Cambodia, Thailand, and Laos

DONALD KIRK

PRAEGER PUBLISHERS
New York · Washington · London

PRAEGER PUBLISHERS
111 Fourth Avenue, New York, N.Y. 10003, U.S.A.
5, Cromwell Place, London S.W.7, England

Published in the United States of America in 1971
by Praeger Publishers, Inc.

© 1971 by Praeger Publishers, Inc.

Library of Congress Catalog Card Number: 70–76790

Maps by Karen Ewing

Printed in the United States of America

To My Parents,
Rudolf and Clara Marburg Kirk

Contents

Maps

Preface

The American public, as well as most of the rest of the world, has long harbored the illusion that the Vietnam conflict is an isolated struggle rather than a phase of a regional war. This illusion should have been shattered in 1970 by sudden expansion of the fighting across the Cambodian frontier, but Americans still seem to view that event as only an episode, a "happening," an interlude, as it were, amid the battles in Vietnam.

This book, therefore, is an attempt to delineate the "wider war" for Indochina—the contest that began long before the entry of the first U.S. combat troops into South Vietnam, much less Cambodia, and promises to go on for some time after the Americans have left. Because so much has already been written on Vietnam, this study emphasizes the three remaining theaters of the conflict: Cambodia, Thailand, and Laos. The purpose is not only to outline events and trends in each of these countries but also to relate them as facets of the same over-all struggle. In that context, U.S. and South Vietnamese incursions into Cambodia and Laos appear only as illustrations—dramatic examples, perhaps—of the long-range confrontation of forces in the region.

In forming this general view on the Indochinese conflict, I am indebted, first of all, to some of my professors and lecturers at the University of Chicago and Columbia University—notably John Luter, coordinator of the Ford Foundation's international reporting program at Columbia; Tang Tsou, who advised me on my master's thesis on North Vietnam's relations with China and Russia; and Roger Hilsman, in whose seminar I enjoyed many stimulating discussions and debates. Since arriving in Vietnam in September, 1965, just as the first U.S. combat troops were plunging into the jungles, I have talked to hundreds of diplomats, politicians, officials, students, soldiers, and many others from the warring countries. It would be impossible to list all of those who have provided me with valuable information and insights.

For their assistance on this book in particular, however, I am grateful to two journalists and a scholar. Arthur Dommen, of the *Los Angeles Times*, not only read the manuscript but gave useful advice on research and writing. Sam Jameson, of the *Chicago Tribune*, kindly shared with me the results of his exhaustive reporting on Cambodia. David Chandler, of the University of Michigan, also reviewed the manuscript and offered many helpful comments, notably on Cambodia.

Finally, my special thanks go to two women whom I met during my year at Columbia. My editor, Mervyn Adams, first suggested that I write this book and then prodded, encouraged, and directed me toward its completion. My wife, Susanne, my constant companion in our six years of nomadic existence in Southeast Asia, has patiently borne many of the inconveniences and hardships of producing a book—and contributed directly to the project by reading the manuscript at various stages and compiling the Bibliography.

Majestic Hotel, Saigon
March, 1971

I

Introduction to Conflict

"We shall avoid a wider war, but we are also determined to put an end to this war."

—RICHARD M. NIXON
Address on the
Southeast Asia situation
April 30, 1970

The Indochinese Peninsula

I

The Setting

Contest for the Mekong

The Mekong springs from the Tibetan plateau, fed by Himalayan snows, pours through the southwestern Chinese province of Yunnan between high canyon walls, and then, in the mountains of northern Laos, assumes the appearance of a great river. At Luang Prabang, the royal Laotian capital occupied more than six centuries ago by the first king of Lane Xang ("kingdom of the million elephants"), the river, several hundred yards across, swirls below the white-walled royal palace and a succession of Buddhist temples before disappearing into the mountainous jungle. Small boats float serenely near the banks, some of them pointed downstream toward Vientiane, the political capital, which is only 150 miles south by plane but several days away by water, past an enormous curve in the river.

The boats, powered by Japanese-built motors, tend to travel in convoys after they leave the relative security of the town. The boatmen, one hears, are afraid of the Pathet Lao—meaning "Lao Land," the name the First Resistance Congress adopted for the indigenous Communist movement at a 1950 meeting somewhere in these same mountains. Guerrillas collect money as well as rice bags or whatever else a boat may carry and sometimes open fire from ambush positions. Even in convoys, a local official told me, the boats are never entirely safe.

By the time the Mekong passes Vientiane, Savannakhet, and Pakse, the main towns of Laos, it is vast—half a mile wide in the dry season and always in danger of overflowing its banks during the monsoon. The river, dividing northeastern Thailand from Laos, is traversed by small motorboats, sampans, and canoes but is almost empty of the larger craft that once carried such foreign im-

3

ports as liquor, cigarettes, automobiles, light machinery, and weapons from the delta region of South Vietnam. The towns of Pakse and Savannakhet, once essential river ports, no longer have the docks or other facilities for this kind of traffic.

Guerrillas rarely harass river traffic through the lowlands, home of two thirds of the country's 3 million inhabitants, but the slow decay of towns still reflects the ravages of the Indochina war. Sporadic fighting, from the Mekong delta region of South Vietnam to northern Cambodia, has blocked the river to normal commercial traffic among the riparian nations of Thailand, Laos, Cambodia, and South Vietnam. North Vietnamese troops seized the main towns on the Mekong in northern Cambodia within two months after the overthrow, on March 18, 1970, of the "neutral" chief of state, Prince Norodom Sihanouk. South Vietnamese Navy vessels, supplied by the United States, patrol the Mekong as far as the Cambodian capital of Phnom Penh, but the river to the northeast is a no man's land, in which boats operate strictly at their own risk. American planes, which refrained from bombing Cambodia during Sihanouk's rule, conduct day and night raids on small craft suspected of carrying enemy arms. North Vietnamese troops, which, under their unwritten agreement with Sihanouk, limited their activities in Cambodia to the South Vietnamese border region, now waylay traffic on the Mekong and its tributaries in northern Cambodia and threaten to extend their control to the center of the country.

The contest for the Mekong in Cambodia is itself a manifestation of the larger struggle for the region. Pursuing his goal of independence and neutrality, Sihanouk formed diplomatic ties with both North Vietnam and the National Liberation Front of South Vietnam, the powers he was certain would eventually rule all Vietnam and exercise life-or-death influence over his own people. The prince often indicated his displeasure with the continuing presence of Communist troops in the jungles near the Vietnamese borders but made clear that he regarded that phenomenon as preferable to the introduction of American and South Vietnamese armies and expansion of the fighting to the rice-rich Cambodian heartland. The result, he predicted, would be the destruction of Khmer—Cambodian—civilization and culture.

Indicative of the Mekong's importance in this struggle is that, well before Sihanouk's fall, the river served military as well as commercial purposes. Downstream from Phnom Penh, the Mekong and its tributaries provide ideal routes for slipping Communist weapons to storage areas, from which they are carried to Vietnam on foot or else on any of the tiny canals and waterways that lace the countryside. When it reaches South Vietnam, the Mekong is an even greater factor in the conflict. Navy boats, far more numerous than on the Cambodian side of the frontier, ply the many branches of the delta and the small streams and canals in between them. The waterways also carry motorized sampans, fishing boats, and other small vessels, still engaged, in the midst of war, in normal commerce.

Twisting 1,000 miles from the Chinese border to the South China Sea, the Mekong roughly bisects the oblong peninsula that juts southeast off the Asian mainland, bounded on the northeast by the Gulf of Tonkin and on the southwest by the Gulf of Thailand. The Mekong irrigates and drains the center of the peninsula, from the Annamite Cordillera paralleling the Vietnamese coastline on the northeast to the Cardamon Mountains, running along the Thai and Cambodian coasts on the southwest. On either side of the peninsula, 500 miles wide between the ports of Kompong Som, formerly Sihanoukville, on the Gulf of Thailand, and Da Nang, on the South China Sea, are two other principal waterways. The Red River, almost paralleling the Mekong in its southeasterly flow from Yunnan Province, fans out in a fertile delta around the capital of Hanoi before emptying into the Gulf of Tonkin near the port city of Haiphong. Then there is the Chao Phraya River, flowing from the mountains of northern Thailand and irrigating the plain around the flourishing capital of Bangkok.

The geographical opposition of the centers of Thailand and North Vietnam, separated by the plains and forests of northeast Thailand, the Mekong lowlands, and the mountainous jungles of Laos, epitomizes the most crucial aspect of the Indochinese conflict. It is the rivalry between Thailand and Vietnam for control of the Mekong—or, more specifically, suzerainty over the river states of Laos and Cambodia—that led Thai and Vietnamese armies to wage a series of wars before the rise of French colonialism in the last century. It was, in fact, French espousal of "the incontestable rights of Annam," the colonial name for central Vietnam, that provided the pretext for France to colonize all of Laos, most of which was already controlled by Thailand, up to the banks of the Mekong. Thailand finally succumbed to military, diplomatic, and propaganda pressure and gave up its claims to both Laos and Cambodia in separate agreements signed with France in 1904 and 1907.[1]

Historical Background

As Prince Sihanouk's diplomacy demonstrated he was well aware, Cambodia would not have survived as an independent country if France had not in effect "rescued" it from its hostile and much stronger neighbors to the east and west. Cambodian nationhood dates from approximately A.D. 600, but Khmer civilization did not reach its height until the reign of Jayavarman VII, who ruled from 1181 to 1219. Jayavarman VII put down a civil war and ordered the construction of thousands of monuments, temples, and other structures. Many of these memorials to Cambodian greatness still stand today, but the kingdom itself entered a period of irreversible decline after Jayavarman's death.

The empire's main competition was the fledgling state of Siam, as the territory to the west of Cambodia was known from the 1300's until it changed its name to Thailand, or "land of the free," in 1939. Angkor, the seat from which Jayavarman VII had ruled his kingdom—stretching from, in the north, almost as far as Vientiane, across the Mekong delta and the kingdom of Champa, to the South China Sea—succumbed for the first time to Siamese invaders in the mid-fourteenth century. The Siamese retreated after six years only to return and sack the city a second time a few years later. By the close of the sixteenth century, after a series of raids and invasions back and forth, Siam controlled Cambodia, whose rulers then set the precedent of playing Vietnamese against Siamese power. A forerunner of Sihanouk's independent course, Chey Chetta II, who ascended the throne in 1618, renounced the subservient relationship to Siam, defeated the Siamese troops, married a Vietnamese princess, and called on the Nguyen rulers in Hue for support.

The entry of the Vietnamese into the southern part of what is now South Vietnam had begun, at least on a significant scale, with the defeat of the dying Champa kingdom in 1471. After the final conquest of Champa—a twelve-century-old empire that once extended from north of Hue to Cam Ranh Bay and westward across the mountains to the land of the Khmer—Vietnamese soldiers, officials, peasants, and their families streamed still further south into the Mekong delta region. Long before the rise to power of the Nguyen rulers in Hue in the late sixteenth century, Vietnamese were ready to join with the Thai to threaten from both sides the last vestige of precolonial Khmer independence. The Nguyen, resisting the authority of the Trinh regime in Hanoi, desperately needed more land on which to develop and enrich their own newly acquired power.[2]

For more than 100 years, from the mid-seventeenth century, Vietnamese armies waged almost constant, and generally victorious, war against Cambodia. The Vietnamese and Siamese competed for the remnants of Cambodia for most of the eighteenth century, with Vietnam establishing an unshakable grip over the Mekong delta region and Siam dominating the Khmer rulers, who still clung to their northern territory. By the end of the century, when Vietnam was again roiled by rebellion, Siam had gained control of not only the northernmost Khmer provinces, some of which it still holds, but the western provinces of Battambang and Siemreap, which includes the entire Angkor complex. In the early 1800's, after Emperor Gia-long had risen to power over a reunited Vietnam, enervated Khmer rulers in Phnom Penh decided it would be wise to pay tribute to both Siam and Vietnam. For the next forty years, Siamese and Vietnamese troops clashed intermittently in Cambodia, each group promoting its own puppet regime. Finally, in 1845, they agreed that both sides would "protect" the Cambodian king.

The loss of Cambodian integrity to Vietnamese and Thai neighbors accounted for the peculiar attitude of Prince Sihanouk, who demanded statements of "recognition and respect" from every nation with which he maintained diplomatic relations. In the immediate regional struggle, however, Sihanouk minimized the danger posed by North Vietnamese and Viet Cong troops in Cambodian jungle sanctuaries, evidently in hopes that the Vietnamese would reciprocate by disappearing after winning the war to communize South Vietnam. Indicative of his deepest fears was his maintenance of 20,000 troops, two thirds of his armed forces, along Cambodia's Thai, rather than Vietnamese, frontier.

Cambodia in effect constituted a buffer between renascent Thai and Vietnamese ambitions. In the same sense, Laos also served as a buffer, but the analogy does not extend to the manner in which Laotian leaders reacted to threats from across the Mekong, on one side, and the Annamite Mountains, on the other. Laos had been hopelessly divided, in terms of territory and leadership, since the end of World War II, but Cambodia did not fall apart until after Sihanouk's March, 1970, ouster. Sihanouk set up a rebel "government in exile" in Peking in May, whereas the Pathet Lao had supported opposition fronts in Laos since at least 1950. Like Sihanouk, Prime Minister Souvanna Phouma, the most successful Laotian politician, viewed "neutrality" as the only policy by which he could possibly ensure his country's survival.

Unlike Cambodia, however, Laos, before post–World War II attempts to unify it, was really what foreign diplomats in Vientiane described privately as a "noncountry." The first king of Luang Prabang who was capable of uniting several Lao states was Fa Ngum, a fourteenth-century protégé of the dying Khmer empire. Laotian power reached its short-lived zenith three centuries later under King Souligna Vongsa, whose land stretched from the Annamese Mountains, across the Mekong River lowlands, and over most of what is now northeastern Thailand. But the death of the king in 1694 left the country open to the same intrigues and rivalries that divide it today. The king's nephew, supported by Vietnamese troops, seized power at Vientiane, letting that part of the empire fall under Vietnamese domination. In 1707, one of the king's grandsons established a separate independent government at Luang Prabang. And, in 1713, a brother of the Vientiane king set up still another state, the principality of Champassak, in the south.

The division of Laos in the early eighteenth century also marked the beginning of the Thai-Vietnamese struggle for the kingdom, which persists to this day. For most of the century, the Vietnamese increased their control and influence over the Vientiane region, including territory across the Mekong once ruled by King Souligna, but Siamese troops marched into Vientiane in 1778 in the midst of civil war in Vietnam. For nearly fifty years, Vientiane survived between great powers to the south and east by the traditional expedient of paying tribute to both of them. But, in 1829, after the prince of Vientiane attacked Siam in order to obtain independence for his own vassal state, Siamese troops conquered, looted, and burned Vientiane. Siam, approaching the period of its greatest strength, then gained control of the Mekong lowlands as far south as Cambodia and deported thousands of Lao across the river into what is now northeastern Thailand. Siam's aims were to fragment the threat posed by the Lao princes, ensure the security of the rising power of Bangkok, and blockade the Vietnamese advance across the Annamite Mountains into the great valley of the Mekong.[3]

The current war for Laos, then, is the logical successor to a previous series of conflicts. Just as Vietnamese Communist troops have rampaged over large swaths of Laotian jungle in alliance with Lao rebel leaders, Thailand since World War II has supported right-wing generals and politicians in Vientiane. Conservative

rulers in Bangkok, allied with the United States, viewed Vietnamese Communist activities in Laos with much the same hostility
as their predecessors had displayed toward their Vietnamese enemies in previous centuries. The historical analogy even extended
to conflict in Thailand itself, where cadres from North Vietnam
organized guerrilla bands and led them on acts of terrorism similar
to those in Laos and Vietnam.

The revolt in Thailand began in the early 1960's but was not
really declared until 1965, when Ch'en Yi, the foreign minister of
Communist China, at a diplomatic reception in Peking told a
Western ambassador, "We hope to have a guerrilla war in Thailand before the year is out."* The implications were plain enough.
If Thailand could not defend itself against this type of warfare, its
northern and northeastern provinces might turn into battlegrounds
and eventually fall to Communist—Chinese or Vietnamese—invaders.

The Siamese, whose ancestors originally migrated from Yunnan,
the southwestern province of China, have gained, lost, and regained much territory since the birth of their country in the Chao
Phraya River valley some seven centuries ago. The pattern of advance and retreat may be all too familiar in Southeast Asian history, but Thailand has one distinction that sets it apart from the
other countries. At no point in the era of colonialism—beginning
with the arrival in Asia of European missionaries and merchants
in the sixteenth and seventeenth centuries and continuing into the
heyday of British imperialism in the eighteenth and nineteenth
centuries and the entry of the French into Indochina in the nineteenth century—did Siam fall under the rule of a foreign power.
The reasons for this phenomenon lay in Siam's position as a geographic buffer between French Indochina and British-ruled Burma,
in the negotiating abilities of the Siamese rulers, and also, to some
extent, in the country's unity and strength.

Illustrative of the great Siamese tradition of balancing foreign interests was a series of negotiations in the early seventeenth century
between the court of Siam and all the European maritime powers.
The court, entertaining overtures from British, Dutch, and Por-
tuguese envoys, arrived at a number of favorable agreements for
trade without permitting these countries to establish colonies from
which they might have extended their authority over the entire
country. In the same century, the court acquired its first truly in-

* This remark was reported privately by diplomatic sources. It was not
broadcast or published by Peking.

fluential foreign "adviser," a Greek named Constantine Phaulkon, who had been a mate on a British ship before entering the service of the king in 1680. Phaulkon rose to become *de facto* foreign minister and almost steered the country into an alliance with France, partly because of his hatred for British merchants and officials whom he had regularly cheated when he was in their employ. But he was executed, and the French garrison was withdrawn in 1688 in a violent reaction against foreign influence.[4]

Thailand escaped the first real threats of the colonial era, but it was not until the nineteenth century that it encountered its most serious problems. Britain and France, having reduced their dealings with Siam for more than a century, now slowly encroached upon the kingdom's sovereignty from adjoining possessions to the north, south, east, and west. The expansion of British interests in Burma and Malaya and the conquest of Indochina by the French conflicted directly with Thailand's own pursuit of territory and power. Under the Anglo-Siamese treaty concluded in 1904, Siam acknowledged British rights over four Malay states encompassing 20,000 square miles. The southern borders established by that treaty remain in effect today.

The difficulties vis-à-vis the Malay states were relatively minor, however, in comparison to the threat posed by France in Indochina. The French exposed the essential weakness of the Siamese Army and Navy in 1893 by sending gunboats up the Chao Phraya River to Bangkok and occupying towns along the Mekong. The Siamese, who had counted on the British to fend off the French for them, had to cede to France all the land along the Mekong in what is now Laos and northern Cambodia. Finally, in the treaty of 1907, France regained for the colonial state of Cambodia the two western provinces of Battambang and Siemreap. The value of Siam as a buffer state was demonstrated, however, by the Anglo-French agreement of 1896, in which the two countries guaranteed the neutrality of the fertile plain around Bangkok, the home of most of the country's population. While the British were not willing to defend Siam's Indochinese frontiers, their presence was enough to keep the French from advancing into the nation's heartland.

Although Siam had suffered enormous losses, it was undoubtedly more unified and easier to govern than it might otherwise have been. Moreover, it had preserved its essential integrity and did not enter the postcolonial era with the same sense of injustice and grievance that afflicted most of the other Asian and African powers. But it was not merely the desire of Britain and France to maintain Siam as a buffer state that accounted for the preservation of its independence, while the countries around it were slowly crumbling. One must also credit Siamese leaders with having neutralized internal quarrels and rivalries that might have provided European powers with a pretext for sending in armies to preserve order and security for their interests and with having attempted to modernize its political, legal, and educational institutions. If Siam had been upset by constant civil strife, as were other countries before their fall to colonial intervention, then both Britain and France might have pursued more aggressive policies than either of them finally adopted.[5]

The absolute power of the Siamese monarchy was broken by a bloodless *coup d'état* in 1932, but Thai leaders still maintain the Chakri dynasty that rose in 1782 from the disorder that followed a series of battles with Burmese troops in and around the old capital of Ayudhya. The dynasty reached its height under King Mongkut, crowned in 1851 as the fourth Chakri ruler, and his successor, Chulalongkorn, both of whom employed European technicians and advisers. During their reigns, the Chakri dynasty appeared to have struck a balance between the ideal of complete freedom from foreign influence and the reality of colonial mercantile ambitions. The same approach guided the country's nationalist, militarist rulers when they moved closer, economically and diplomatically, to the rising power of Japan in the 1930's and finally allied with it against the United States and Britain in World War II.

They recognized that they could not oppose Japan militarily, any more than they could have opposed Britain or France in the nineteenth century, and they also were enticed by the promise of regaining territory ceded to France and Britain nearly half a century before.

From Past to Present

The struggle among powers external to the region still dominates the regional conflict. Thailand, demonstrating the pragmatic enlightenment that has characterized all its recent history, sided with the United States after World War II and has profited since then from American aid, advice, and private investment, just as it benefited from foreign assistance in the last century. The city of Bangkok today reflects the country's success in blending Western acumen with Thai culture. Alone among the capitals and ports of the region, Bangkok is truly a national center, the product not of colonial rule but of the cultural, political, and economic drives of a dynasty of Siamese kings. Ornate temples, dominated by enormous statues of Buddha, crowd for space in teeming commercial and shopping districts. The halls of government, often somewhat bleak and dingy, overlook wide streets jammed from dawn to dusk with buses, trucks, cars, and motor scooters. The construction of the city demonstrates the skill of foreign architects and merchants, but, despite its helter-skelter confusion, its jumble of signboards and lights, its towering new hotels and stilted wooden shacks, the capital remains uniquely Thai.

The experience of foreign influence has also shaped the attitudes and ambitions of Thailand's traditional competitor, Vietnam, but in a very different manner. Vietnam, finally united and stabilized under the Emperor Gia-long in the early nineteenth century, was partitioned into three distinct regions, Cochinchina in the south, Annam in the center, and Tonkin in the north. The process of empire-building, beginning with the French conquest of Cochinchina between 1858 and 1862 and culminating in the occupation of Tonkin and Annam in 1883, brought an end to a sense of national drive built up over more than twenty centuries, the last nine of which the Vietnamese had spent on expanding geographically, economically, and culturally, after finally winning their freedom from the Chinese. The Vietnamese rulers were at least as sophisticated and ambitious as the Thai, but their subjection to the French fragmented their sense of purpose, splintered their countrymen into dozens of regional and political groups, and completely shattered the traditional social and economic structure.

Nor did French rule result in significant social reforms or a greater sense of equality among Vietnamese. Instead, a new class of extremely wealthy landowners developed, especially in the south, sharpening the contrast with the mass of poor peasants, and few local citizens were trained for more than petty positions in the colonial bureaucracy. The country was modernized to fit the commercial and political purposes of the colonialists, but the average Vietnamese could certainly not identify with the construction of roads and railroads by foreigners, as they had with their own push south and west centuries before. Those Vietnamese who went to France for education or training, moreover, often returned to Indochina imbued with European liberal, leftist, or Communist ideas.

The French, employing harshly repressive methods, might have clung to their hold over Indochina if the Japanese had not finally dislodged them toward the end of World War II. The hiatus in French influence before the final surrender and withdrawal of the Japanese gave the Vietnamese nationalists the chance they needed to campaign openly, to publicize their programs, and, in the case of the Communist Viet Minh, actually to seize power in Hanoi. Whereas Thailand had, if anything, gained unity during the colonial period, Vietnam seemed to have been hopelessly divided. In the kaleidoscopic range of Vietnamese reactions to French rule, however, there appeared to have developed two fundamental opposing groups. On the one hand, the era had produced a "new" mandarin middle class of well-to-do businessmen, landowners, and other officials who relied utterly on the West for inspiration and direction. On the other hand, there were the vehement nationalists, epitomized by the Viet Minh, who not only detested Western imperialism but were driven even harder than their ancestors to unite and expand their country's influence.

The dichotomy in Vietnamese national prototypes was dramatized, of course, by the 1954 Geneva agreement in which Vietnam was divided at the 17th parallel between the North, governed by the Communists under Ho Chi Minh, and the South, ruled by a conglomeration of anti-Communists, some of them refugees from the North, who often were more prone to fight among themselves than against Communist guerrillas. Ngo Dinh Diem, a northern Catholic mandarin, emerged as the most powerful leader and ruled the government of the South in Saigon until his assassination in 1963 in the first of a series of *coups d'état* by discontented politicians and generals. The struggle between the North and the South was characterized by contrasts. The North was united, while the South was divided. The leaders of the North seemed incorruptible, while those in the South profited off American aid, the gold and opium trades, and private enterprise. The northern government appeared efficient, dedicated, and extremely harsh, as exemplified by the ruthlessness with which it carried out its land reform program in the late 1950's; the southern regime was erratic, indolent, and afraid to try to extend its control over the countryside.

The interests of the great powers were grafted onto the struggle for Indochina after 1954 as surely as they had ever been during the colonial era. The great-power contestants in the postcolonial period were the Communist nations, notably China and the Soviet Union, and the United States. China and Russia, despite their own worsening ideological differences and frontier problems, strongly supported North Vietnam and the Communist guerrillas in South

Vietnam and Laos with arms and ammunition. The United States at first supplied only arms, ammunition, and advisers to the anti-Communist governments in South Vietnam, Laos, Thailand, and Cambodia. As North Vietnam prosecuted the war for Vietnam more fiercely, however, the United States in 1965 introduced regular combat troops. Major foreign powers, if anything, were now more deeply involved on the Indochinese peninsula than any of the mercantile Europeans had been at the height of the colonial drive.

In view of the native aggressiveness and intelligence of the Vietnamese, as well as their history of conquest in Cambodia and Laos, one might suppose that a divided Vietnam would increase the national security of Thailand, Laos, and Cambodia. Prince Sihanouk's military commander, General Nhiek Tioulong, now living in exile in France, told me, on November 6, 1968, that he preferred "a Vietnam divided not in two but in three parts." Prince Sihanouk's great-grandfather, King Norodom, had also welcomed French "protection" in 1863 to counter both Siam and Vietnam, to both of which he had to pay obeisance and tribute. Sihanouk himself, despite his renunciation of American and South Vietnamese ties, often expressed alarm before his downfall at the prospect of a Communist victory in South Vietnam. He recommended that American troops remain in the countries whose governments wanted them— for example, Thailand and the Philippines—to counter the threat of a united Communist Vietnam.*

Culturally, Cambodia and Laos seemed to have had more in common with Thailand than with Vietnam. In the centuries in which the Lao, Khmer, and Thai had settled over the Indochinese peninsula, they had merged in physical appearance and mannerisms. All three groups were characterized by round faces, flat noses, and, as foreigners have often observed, pleasant smiles and easygoing manners. All three countries were dominated by Theravada Buddhism, which was spread over Southeast Asia in the early centuries of the Christian era by Indian traders and scholars, who also introduced forms of medicine, government, law, and language. Vietnam, on the other hand, was infused with Mahayana, or Greater Vehicle, Buddhism, propagated by the Chinese, as well as

* Prince Sihanouk offered this opinion in a series of press conferences and impromptu interviews between November 1 and November 15, 1968, during which he permitted Western journalists, including this writer, to visit his country, which he normally closed to all but a handful of correspondents from France and from Communist countries.

Confucianism and Taoism. The Vietnamese, reflecting ten centuries of Chinese rule ending in A.D. 939, also adopted the Chinese mandarin system, certain Chinese words and customs, and even, it seemed, aspects of the Chinese physical appearance. They had narrow, slightly slanting eyes, high cheekbones, and hard mouths that seemed to smile in nervous flashes, not openly and easily in the style of the Thai, Lao, and Khmer.

It is an interesting commentary on the current struggle for the Indochinese peninsula that great foreign powers more than 2,000 years ago were implanting their interests and their culture among the people of the region. The Thai and Vietnamese, with Cambodia and Laos divided between them, would almost certainly oppose each other today under any circumstances, but their own differences sometimes seem secondary to the problems introduced by the foreign powers. All the Indochinese governments have revealed grave suspicions about Chinese intentions, especially after China vociferously declared its support of "wars of liberation" against non-Communist regimes while opposing all movements toward compromise in Vietnam itself. Similarly, all the countries, including those most dependent on aid from the United States, expressed doubts about the Americans, whose economic and cultural influence represented as much a threat, a challenge, and a temptation as did that of ancient India or Europe.

The countries of the Indochinese peninsula, as their historical backgrounds have shown, were interested first in their own survival, then in independence, and, finally, in expanding their territory and power. Cambodia, Thailand, and Laos, in pursuing these goals, have had to tread very carefully between overlapping regional and great-power rivalries. Their leaders have reacted in many different ways, depending on historical fears, geographic considerations, international response, and a host of other factors, with widely varying degrees of success and failure. The conflict is likely to go on long after the present foreign powers have departed or a new set of ideologies and interventionist regimes have replaced them, for the struggle is rooted deep in history, and its principal participants are not the transient foreigners but the inhabitants who till the soil, meet at the temples and market places, sit in the offices of government, fight in the jungles and rice paddies—and eventually must learn to live with each other.

2

Vietnam

The Nixon Doctrine

Since the end of the Korean War in 1953, American leaders and diplomats had paid at least lip service to the concept that Asians should live as they wish—and fight their own wars. It was partly because of national aversion to further fighting in Asia that the United States became involved in the Vietnam conflict through a series of half steps. First, there was the shipment of arms to the French, then, the commitment of military advisers for Saigon government forces under President Ngo Dinh Diem, and, finally, the introduction of American combat troops in 1965.

By 1969, after the inauguration of Richard Nixon as President, American involvement in Asia again had crested and begun a slow decline. Nixon's predecessor, Lyndon Johnson, had ordered the cessation of the bombing of North Vietnamese factories, supply depots, and roads in 1968, and Nixon continued this trend by beginning the gradual withdrawal of American combat troops. Nixon had signaled his future policies in *Foreign Affairs* in October, 1967. "One of the legacies of Vietnam almost certainly will be a deep reluctance on the part of the United States to become involved once again in a similar intervention on a similar basis," wrote Nixon, who had traveled widely since his first campaign for the Presidency in 1960. "The war has imposed severe strains on the United States, not only militarily and economically but socially and politically as well."[1] The *Foreign Affairs* article provided the substructure of thought and ambition upon which Nixon was, within a relatively brief period, to build his intricate policy of reduction of American force combined with massive military aid and training for South Vietnam.

"The central pattern of the future in U.S.-Asian relations must be American support for Asian initiatives," wrote Nixon in the concluding section of the article.[2] The words "South Vietnamese" might have been substituted for "Asian," for South Vietnam was certainly the place where the aspiring President planned to put his theories into practice. Six weeks after his inauguration, he sent his defense secretary, Melvin Laird, to Saigon specifically to discuss with Vietnamese officials and American field commanders the possibility of a massive infusion of American arms and materiel into a South Vietnamese military establishment totaling well over a million men. "One of the high priority items is to put the money in the budget for the Vietnamese armed forces," Laird told correspondents in Saigon on March 8, 1969. "One of the amendments [to the budget] I will propose is money for the upgrading of and modernizing of ARVN [the Army of the Republic of Vietnam]."

The complexities of Nixon's policy were apparent from Laird's remark, in the same briefing, that "we have got to be planning that we might not have success in Paris," where talks had been initiated in 1968 among negotiators for the United States, South Vietnam, North Vietnam, and the National Liberation Front (NLF), or Viet Cong. From Laird's comment, it was clear that American strategists had no real expectation that the talks would produce meaningful results, much less a "settlement." At the same time, President Nixon, although he had not yet ordered the first withdrawals of American troops, realized the political necessity of scaling down the commitment, in terms of American men and lives, if not money, in Vietnam. Therefore, in a televised "Report to the Nation" on May 14, 1969, he declared that "apart from what will develop from the negotiations, the time is approaching when South Vietnamese forces will be able to take over some of the fighting fronts now being manned by Americans."[3]

By July, 1969, after he had announced the first withdrawal of American troops from Vietnam, Nixon was ready to expand his thoughts on the future role of the United States in Asia into a full-blown "doctrine." The President introduced this doctrine on July 25 at a briefing for correspondents on the island of Guam before flying to Manila on the first leg of a tour of Southeast Asia, followed by visits to India, Pakistan, and Romania. The mood was triumphant and expectant. Nixon had just watched the splashdown in the South Pacific of the Apollo 11 astronauts. Now he was off on his first round-the-world trip since his election. He intended to persuade the leaders of Southeast Asia—and also the American public—of the wisdom of his policies. Since Nixon has subsequently referred to his policy on Asia as the "Guam, or Nixon, doctrine," it would seem appropriate at this stage to single out, precisely, some of the statements he made at the Guam briefing.

"The United States is going to be facing, we hope before too long—no one can say how long, but before too long—a major decision," said the President. "What will be its role in Asia and in the Pacific after the end of the war in Vietnam?" Nixon answered this question in part by averring that he was "convinced that the way to avoid becoming involved in another war in Asia is for the United States to continue to play a significant role." At the same time, the President noted "a very great growth of nationalism" combined with regional pride. "Asians will say in every country that we visit that they do not want to be dictated to from outside," he explained. "Asia for the Asians. And that is what we want and that is the role we should play. We should assist it, but we should not dictate." Vowing to "keep the treaty commitments that we have," Nixon then declared, "We must avoid that kind of policy that will make countries in Asia so dependent upon us that we are dragged into conflicts such as the one that we have in Vietnam."[4]

It was never certain, as Nixon began to try to apply these thoughts to the realities of the Vietnam conflict, to what extent he had succeeded in convincing South Vietnamese leaders of his ideas. President Nguyen Van Thieu had refused at first to endorse the final halt in the bombing of North Vietnam on October 31, 1968, and had repeatedly expressed his skepticism about the wisdom of further troop withdrawals in the absence of a response in kind by the North Vietnamese.

The decision for Nixon's program, however, was irrevocable. Despite reservations among some American officers, "progress" was the official "line" in discussions on the South Vietnamese forces. A colonel advising a South Vietnamese division or regimental commander could hardly afford to talk in pessimistic terms when every American official, from President Nixon to Secretary Laird to the American commander in Vietnam, General Creighton Abrams, was citing South Vietnamese achievements. The popular catchword for Nixon's policy, as applied specifically to Vietnam, was "Vietnamization," a term that seemed insulting to Vietnamese officials but still was useful in selling the program to the United States. In a major television address of November 3, 1969, Nixon insisted that the program was a success.

"The Vietnamization plan was launched following Secretary Laird's visit to Vietnam in March," said Nixon, noting that the "primary mission" of American troops now was to "enable the South Vietnamese forces to assume the full responsibility for the security of South Vietnam." The President pointed out what he knew his listeners wanted most to hear—that "we are finally bringing American men home," that, by December 15, 1969, "over 60,000 men will have been withdrawn from South Vietnam, including 20 per cent of all of our combat troops." Then he buttressed this summary of recent events by presenting the underlying rationale. "The South Vietnamese have continued to gain in strength," he said. "As a result they have been able to take over combat responsibilities from our American forces." The United States and South Vietnam, he went on, had worked out a plan "for the complete withdrawal of U.S. ground combat forces and their replacement by South Vietnamese forces on an orderly scheduled timetable."[5]

Nixon's logic was founded not entirely on political considerations. It was indeed true, as he indicated, that enemy activity had declined since the attacks on cities and towns during the Tet, or lunar new year, holidays in early 1968. Despite threats in regions once patrolled by Americans, the roads were now largely open, and rice and other products were again moving freely to the markets. South Vietnam, in fact, was stirring almost with a sense of relief, a sensation not experienced since the period of relative peace that followed the signing of the Geneva agreement in 1954.

Protracted War

It was not, however, a sense of victory that permeated the atmosphere in Saigon at the end of 1969—nor was it a question of revulsion or reaction against the Viet Cong or renewed confidence or devotion to the Saigon government. It was, rather, a brief respite—a break in which millions of Vietnamese, from officials to peasants, could relax for a moment before bracing for the next series of upheavals. For the Communists, despite a long period of relative quiescence since the end of their last major offensive in February and March, 1969, had made indelibly clear that the war was far from over. In the delta, two North Vietnamese regiments had infiltrated into desolate swamp and mountain base areas, and two more regiments were already moving south through eastern Cambodia to join them. Previously, the South Vietnamese had only had to contend with the Viet Cong in the delta, while the North Vietnamese focused on all the other regions.

Perhaps the most significant indication of Hanoi's intentions,

however, was the presence of four North Vietnamese divisions anywhere from 50 to 150 miles from Saigon. These divisions—the 1st,
5th, 7th, and 9th—had withdrawn most of their forces into Cambodian base areas early in 1969, but elements of them had returned
in the summer and fall. As if the physical presence of the enemy
were not enough, the Communists had revealed their basic reasoning and strategy in a morass of orders, reports, and propaganda
documents picked up by American and South Vietnamese troops
on operations throughout the country. Notable among them was
a ninety-page "resolution" adopted by the Central Office for South
Vietnam, the top-level headquarters, referred to as COSVN by
American officials, for the Viet Cong's National Liberation Front
and the Provisional Revolutionary Government. "The U.S. is
bogged down in the most serious strategic crisis and is trying to
de-escalate the war by 'de-Americanizing' it," said the resolution,
drafted in July, 1969, at the "ninth conference" of Viet Cong
military and political leaders summoned to their jungle headquarters across the Cambodian border some 100 miles northwest of
Saigon.*

"Due to the collapse of their will of aggression," the resolution
went on, the Americans "could not continue the present war of
aggression for a long period of time." The Viet Cong conference,
dominated by representatives from Hanoi rather than the NLF,
produced a remarkably accurate appraisal of the aims of the Nixon
Administration. "Their plan is to 'de-Americanize' the war step
by step and de-escalate gradually," said the resolution. "They are
de-escalating while maintaining manpower and material resources,
especially the U.S. potential." The resolution was larded with
propaganda, but it showed clearly enough how the Communists
planned to combat American strategy. "Strategic offenses" in the
"cities, the rural and the mountain areas" would parallel diplomatic
activity.

Besides preparing for military campaigns in the midst of the
lull, North Vietnam and the Viet Cong carefully supported a
South Vietnamese "third-force" political movement as a bridge to
coalition and Communist rule. One aim was to isolate the Thieu
government not only from leftists but from anti-Communist intellectuals and professional men who wanted some form of reconcilia-

* A copy of the ninth conference resolution, marked "top secret," was captured by American troops three months after it was written. Contents of the
resolution were disseminated by American and South Vietnamese officials in
Saigon. The Viet Cong did not publish or broadcast it.

tion to end the fighting. The resolution, however, indicated some of the weaknesses and fears that pervaded much of the Communist structure after the disastrous losses suffered in the Tet, May, and September, 1968, offensives. Viet Cong leaders no longer proclaimed "victory." Nor did they overemphasize the theme of popular uprising, as they had during their costly military campaigns. Communist strategists appeared to realize that victory, if it were to be achieved, would require much more time, and perhaps a more subtle approach, than they had anticipated at the beginning of 1968.

Some analysts in Saigon attributed further changes in Communist—both Viet Cong and North Vietnamese—strategy in part to the death, on September 3, 1969, of Ho Chi Minh, for the Communists had fought to attain victory in his lifetime. The Party secretary, Le Duan, who emerged as the most powerful North Vietnamese leader after Ho's death, elaborated on the new approach to the war in a lengthy article published in February, 1970, in which he advocated any method that could effect the "greatest victory allowed by the balance of forces at a given moment." It was just as serious a mistake not to "carry out military struggle when it is needed," he said, as it was to go ahead "with the military struggle when conditions are not ripe."[6]

Le Duan's article was, in a sense, a political and theoretical elaboration on a military treatise published in December, 1969, by General Vo Nguyen Giap, the Communist military commander since the closing days of World War II. Perhaps the most important point in Giap's essay was the emphasis on the strategy of "protracted war." In general, said Giap, "the process of a protracted struggle is that of successively attacking the enemy, gradually repelling him, partially overthrowing him . . . and moving toward defeating him completely."[7] This definition represented a departure from Giap's previous view, expressed in the book *People's War, People's Army*, published in 1959, of the war as a series of phases culminating in the inevitable overwhelming defeat of the enemy.

The shift in Hanoi's approach reflected acute economic problems in North Vietnam as well as the realization that immediate victory in the South was an unattainable goal. The extent of North Vietnam's difficulties was always subject to widespread speculation —and exaggeration—but Giap himself admitted that the country had lost more than half a million young men in the war. Lack of manpower, combined with the effects of four years of American

The answer, as he saw it, was to bypass French-trained provincial bureaucrats and inculcate a sense of nationalism, together with some rudimentary skills, in village leaders who tended to dislike both the Viet Cong and the government. Garbed in black uniforms, some 50,000 students a year attended courses ranging from two to six weeks at which they studied such subjects as "how to stage demonstrations" and "how to apply for government funds." Whether or not these lessons really applied to individual situations was a matter of debate, but even Colonel Be's critics praised the program for its propaganda value.

In a ten-day drive around the Mekong delta region in November, 1969, with Paul Vogle of the English-language *Vietnam Guardian*, we found American officials almost euphoric about progress in pacification since Tet, 1968. John Vann, in charge of American pacification efforts for the region, estimated, on November 8, that half the Viet Cong leadership had been broken or destroyed in the sixteen delta provinces. "The situation was badly deteriorating before the Tet offensive," said Vann, often a sharp critic of American policy in Vietnam. "Tet antagonized much of the population against them. There's no question the enemy can make limited gains, but, whenever he sticks his head out, he gets shot at." U.S. and South Vietnamese officials in 1970 believed the government controlled or influenced at least 5.5 million persons in the delta—twice as many as it had in February, 1968, the month of the Tet offensive. Conversely, the Viet Cong by 1970 controlled only 500,000 persons as opposed to 2 million in 1968. The number under government control in the delta represented approximately nine tenths of the populace of the region. The American "Hamlet Evaluation Survey," never regarded as a truly accurate guide but perhaps the best educated guess available, revealed the same percentage for the entire country.

Against this picture of progress, however, observers emphasized the skepticism of the majority of peasants regarding the Saigon government. "You get the impression they don't want the VC to rule them, but they don't like the government either," explained an American who had traveled extensively through the region. "You ask a farmer what he wants most, and almost inevitably he'll answer, 'peace.' " A general complaint among farmers was the spiraling inflation, renewed in late 1969 by a set of "austerity" taxes imposed by Thieu. The price of rice rose between 20 and 50 per cent on the retail market, and the cost of some commodities, such as tools and clothing, more than doubled. Officials hoped eventually to balance the effects of inflation by vast increases in rice production, thanks both to military security and the success in some areas of new strains of "miracle rice."

The difficulty was that the progress recorded in the pacification effort after the 1968 Tet offensive was often much too thin and superficial. "You get the feeling one good crisis could wipe it out," observed an American scholar who had lived in Vietnam a number of years. "This emphasis on the village is a kind of a fad," the American went on. "They should have recognized the importance of the village in Vietnamese society ten years ago." Pacification officials hoped to solidify and improve on some of the gains they had made since Tet, but they were impeded by the lethargy of national leaders too embroiled in power struggles to involve themselves in the problems of the countryside. Perhaps the most self-defeating contradiction in Saigon politics was the underlying question of whether the government should remain in power or yield to new leaders, who would then enter into some kind of agreement with the National Liberation Front.

Saigon Politics

The catchwords "coalition" and "neutrality" dominated Vietnamese politics in 1970-71 as never before. To President Thieu, the words were traitorous reflections of the Communist campaign to undermine the fragile structure of government that had risen in Saigon in the five years since the overthrow of General Nguyen Khanh, in February, 1965. To Thieu's non-Communist political opponents, the words pointed the way to reconciliation and compromise in a conflict that might otherwise go on indefinitely after the withdrawal of American combat troops. To the Viet Cong, they represented a vital step toward the twin goals of communization of South Vietnam and reunification of North and South.

In a society fragmented for decades, with wildly differing political and religious groupings, the will of the majority might be impossible to determine. Professional men in Saigon, as much as peasants in the countryside, often gave the impression that they supported neither Thieu nor the Communists but simply wanted "peace." It was to appeal to this sentiment that politicians and religious leaders, some of them obviously far to the left, proclaimed their support of a third force between the extremes of the Saigon regime and the Viet Cong. The rise of the third force presented Thieu with his most severe political challenge since his election as President in September, 1967. The question was whether or not his non-Communist opponent could somehow force his downfall before the next regular election in the fall of 1971.

If the government were to fall, either before the election or as a result of the voting, the Communists could collaborate with some of Thieu's non-Communist opponents on a compromise. The result might be a face-saving way out of the war for all participants—or the final failure of America's policies in Vietnam. In the campaign to force Thieu out of power, dissident monks, laymen, and students emerged in 1969 and 1970 as a strong, provocative force for the first time since the bloody Buddhist uprisings in the spring of 1966. The monks, headquartered at the An Quang Pagoda in Cholon, Saigon's Chinese quarter, did not necessarily criticize Thieu by name but claimed that they were "working for peace" despite the "new imperialists" who wanted "foreigners to enslave the country."

The An Quang Pagoda provided the spiritual and political inspiration for a movement that encompassed former generals, students, politicians—even members of the National Assembly and government ministries supposedly controlled by Thieu's allies. Beneath an appearance of impartiality toward the country's warring factions, the monks and students nevertheless gave a clear impression that they would gladly align with the Communists if it appeared politically expedient.

Despite government attempts at intimidation, the third-force movement appeared to have gained respectability among politicians and officials who might have disavowed it in 1967 or 1968, including two of Vietnam's most famous personalities, General Duong Van Minh and Senator Tran Van Don, a retired lieutenant general. "Big" Minh, stocky, bluff, often smiling, had led the 1963 coup against Ngo Dinh Diem and then headed a military junta for three months until he was overthrown and exiled to Thailand by Nguyen Khanh. In a gesture that American diplomats mistakenly believed would enhance the chances for political unity, Thieu persuaded Minh to return from Thailand in late 1968. The talk for months was that Minh would head a council of advisers, but gradually it became clear that neither Thieu nor Minh had any intention of cooperating with each other.

"I was a military adviser to President Diem," Minh told reporters at a reception proffered by Senator Don on October 31, 1969, the eve of the sixth anniversary of the coup against Diem. "I don't want to go through that again." The mere presence of Minh in Senator Don's villa seemed to confirm suspicions that the pair were aligning with each other as well as with the An Quang monks and other antigovernment forces. At the same time, Don appealed for An Quang support by declaring that the future of Vietnam was "neither left nor right but just between the two worlds" of capitalism and Communism.

In an interview in his own home two weeks after meeting with reporters in Don's villa, Minh left no doubt as to his political ambitions. "I have never intended to be President," he declared, in the time-honored fashion of a candidate for office, "but if something ought to be done to save the country, no citizen has the right to run away from his duty." Nor did he leave any doubt as to where he expected to obtain the support he needed to return to power. "The government stands on one side and the Viet Cong on the other," he said. "Both only succeed in gathering a minority as the majority of the population remains uncommitted."[8] Against the eroding effect of Minh's influence, President Thieu attempted to tighten his control and campaigned, almost desperately, against those who advocated neutralism or any other change in government.

He shrewdly solidified his position in August, 1969, by a cabinet shake-up in which he appointed his powerful minister of interior, General Tran Thien Khiem, as Prime Minister in place of the popular but ineffective Tran Van Huong. He also appointed several former Diemists and anti-Communist Catholics to the cabinet in an obvious attempt to organize a machine that would not buckle or falter under militant Buddhist and student pressure. Beyond his government, Thieu's only sure allies were northern Catholic refugees, approximately 800,000 in number, whose leaders demanded prosecution of all of those who had opposed Thieu's strongly anti-Communist position. Thieu tended to regard most of his political opponents as pro-Communist conspirators who should be either intimidated or jailed. Nor were his suspicions necessarily unfounded. It was inevitable that many of Thieu's enemies, if not Communists themselves, should have friends and relatives working for the Viet Cong. It was equally inevitable that the Communists should try to exploit them. For Thieu, the cruelest irony, however, was the conviction at the end of November, 1969, of four government officials charged with spying for the Communists. Two of these men had previously had entree to the palace and had often met with Thieu.

The most celebrated case was that of the assembly deputy, Tran Ngoc Chau, arrested and convicted in February, 1970, for having failed to report his meetings with his brother, jailed eight months before as a North Vietnamese spy. The case seemed to galvanize public opinion to the point at which students, despite police reprisals and torture, had the temerity to express themselves more openly than ever before. The students were particularly incensed by the comment of U.S. Ambassador Ellsworth Bunker, who remarked during a visit to the United States in May, 1970, that some of them were influenced by Communists. Charging Bunker with "interference" in South Vietnamese affairs, they demonstrated in front of the National Assembly, the U.S. Embassy, the palace, and other symbols of established power. The National Students Union, on June 22, 1970, denounced government leaders as "American puppets" who had failed "to heed the aspirations of the people."

Bunker's remark may have seemed to be a diplomatic blunder, but it dispelled, at least temporarily, some of the widespread Vietnamese rumors that the United States was planning to turn against the Saigon government and install a regime acceptable to the Communists. Bunker managed to maintain the respect and trust of Vietnamese Government leaders, despite their disappointment over the cessation of the bombing of North Vietnam and the withdrawal of American troops. One reason for Bunker's rapport with Thieu, Vice President Nguyen Cao Ky, and other members of the ruling elite was that he conveyed the impression he was essentially in sympathy with them. He assured Thieu that the United States would, as Nixon had said, "honor all its commitments."

Vietnamese of all political persuasions seemed to trust the word of the silver-haired ambassador, who, on April 25, 1967, at the age of 73, had succeeded Henry Cabot Lodge. The question many of them asked, however, was how much longer Bunker would remain on the job. There were reports throughout 1970-71 that Nixon's chief foreign-affairs adviser, Henry Kissinger, would just as soon have Bunker returned to America "for reasons of health." Vietnamese believed that Bunker's removal, for whatever reasons, would mark a major U.S. step away from the Saigon government. The United States might then feel free to bargain secretly with the enemy on the formation of a new government—and withhold material support from Thieu after the withdrawal of American troops. Since the Communists under no circumstances would accept Thieu or Ky, the Americans could turn against the two and overtly support some of their "neutral" opponents.

Then there was a corollary question: What if the Communists won significant military victories, possibly in the northern provinces, where the South Vietnamese Army faced its greatest threat since the allied intervention in Cambodia, which had reduced

enemy capabilities around Saigon and the Mekong delta? Might
Hanoi and the NLF combine success on the battlefield with
political chaos in Saigon? On the answers to such puzzles rested
the political future of South Vietnam at the opening of the 1970's.

Vietnamization

"Troop replacement" was the term American leaders seemed to
favor for the assignment of South Vietnamese forces to "areas of
responsibility" once patrolled by Americans. The impossibility of
real "replacement" of American with South Vietnamese troops,
however, was apparent to observers who visited the Demilitarized
Zone (DMZ), the Central Highlands, and the provinces northwest,
west, and south of Saigon.

After the withdrawal of the 22,000-man 3rd Marine Division
from below the DMZ in November, 1969, for instance, the Communists carefully began to rebuild the guerrilla infrastructure on
which they depended to infiltrate populated areas. Enemy squads,
once blocked by aggressive marine ambushes, patrols, and air and
artillery fire, were again traversing jungle regions. American advisers lavishly praised the South Vietnamese Army's 1st Division,
totaling 16,000 men, but the division commander, Major General
Ngo Quang Truong, admitted that his troops could not possibly
patrol the entire area once covered by the marines. "My concept
is to keep some key bases and protect the population by mobile
operations," said General Truong, pointing to a map in his headquarters in the Citadel, the "imperial city" of Hue built by Vietnam's nineteenth-century emperors and ravaged during the 1968
Tet offensive. Truong promised that his troops would fly into the
mountains to rout out the enemy, just as the marines had done for
four years in the northern provinces.[9]

The general answered "no," however, to the question of
whether his division, regarded by American military advisers as the
best in the South Vietnamese Army, could survive against attack
by 50,000 Communist troops stationed immediately across the
nearest borders in Laos and North Vietnam. "Then I hope the
marines would come back," said Truong, explaining that his division would not, in fact, "replace" the marines on most of the fire
bases below the DMZ. "We do not even plan to move another
regiment to the marine area of operations," he added. The inevitable result, in the opinion of many military analysts, was that
the North Vietnamese, within another year or two, would rein-
filtrate the mountains and force the South Vietnamese into de-

fensive positions on the long, low-lying coastal plain. This prediction was borne out in 1970 and 1971 as North Vietnamese troops, despite persistent American air strikes, gradually increased their activity in the region to the highest level since the middle of 1968.

The strength of the South Vietnamese would probably always lie to a large extent in quantity as opposed to quality. In late 1970, the 1.1 million-man South Vietnamese defense establishment, according to U.S. and South Vietnamese officials, included 375,000 in the regular army, more than 500,000 in the regional and popular forces, another 100,000 or so in the national police, and the remaining 125,000 in the air force, navy, and marines. The South Vietnamese forces, in fact, were so large that their leaders, lacking administrative and logistical experience, were hardly able to handle the influx of new equipment, ranging from M-16 rifles to riverboats, tanks, and helicopters. The American command launched what it called a "logistics offensive" to enable South Vietnamese forces to cope with the bulk of their supplies, but South Vietnam still counted on American planes to ferry most of its materiel, just as it needed them to defend troops in battle.

American plans called for training enough Vietnamese for all critical fields in the following few years, but senior advisers admitted in 1969 that they did not envision the day when South Vietnam could bear the burden entirely on its own. "We've got to keep at least 100,000 men here for some time," an American experienced in both military and civilian phases of the advisory effort told me in September. "We'd be lucky if we could just train and equip all their ground troops and then share the other assets, including helicopters and airplanes." Advisers often complained that officers were lethargic and that enlisted men deserted at the rate of three or four per cent a month. Still, the armed forces were sending more than 400,000 men in 1970 through everything from basic infantry training to officer candidate school to English-language study. The number of trainees in South Vietnam in 1969 and 1970 almost equaled that in the U.S. Army in the same two-year period.

One problem, according to Americans, was that the Vietnamese had been "under French influence for so long that they still use methods obsolete by our standards." The Vietnamese lectured "hour after hour," said an adviser, "instead of letting a man take a weapon apart, put it together again, and fire it." Another problem was that many instructors lacked battlefield experience. "Often we depend on aspirants—sublieutenants just out of officer candidate school—to do the job," the adviser went on. A corollary factor was that of nepotism and social favoritism. The sons of diplomats, politicians, and wealthy businessmen, if they went into the armed forces at all, often were among those chosen for study in the United States, flight training, or other glamorous assignments. In order to attend officer candidate school, a man generally needed the equivalent of a high school diploma—a requirement that disqualified many combat-hardened sergeants who might have proved superior to educated, urban youths.

The greatest single difficulty, in the opinion of many advisers, was the absence of a sense of urgency. "It's apparent they're getting a little bit concerned now that the Americans are pulling out their troops," a senior officer noted in 1969, "but they'll still lock up headquarters at noon on Saturday. It's no secret that many of their top officers look after outside interests such as real estate and import-export." The lack of urgency among senior military officers pervaded the lower levels as well. Enlisted men in 1970 deserted at the rate of 3 or 4 per cent a month, sometimes so they could re-enlist in units near their homes or delay their entry into combat by going through another training cycle.

Senior American advisers were more confident in 1970 than in 1968 or 1969 of the fighting capabilities of regular South Vietnamese divisions but admitted that the over-all records of these units were "extremely spotty." One way by which the Americans hoped to train them was to team them with U.S. units on operations. This approach was doubtless worthwhile, but Americans were likely to go on the riskiest phases of an operation, while the South Vietnamese provided "blocking forces" and depended on their U.S. advisers to coordinate air power and artillery. Some critics, after witnessing these and other operations, questioned whether the United States should have emphasized highly sophisticated forms of warfare in training the South Vietnamese. Perhaps the Vietnamese forces would have progressed more smoothly on a program that stressed lengthy field operations with basic but modern weapons—and not complicated tactical maneuvers requiring American-style mobility and firepower.

The Vietnamization program, in fact, appeared in some respects as an overreaction to the period, before the 1968 Tet offensive, when the United States supplied the South Vietnamese with World War II–style rifles, machine guns, and other such materiel, while American troops did most of the fighting. One of the gravest mistakes of American conduct of the war, in the opinion of many military advisers, was the failure to begin arming and training the

South Vietnamese with the best basic weapons—the American equivalents, at least, of Chinese-made rifles, machine guns, and rocket-launchers carried by the North Vietnamese—well before sending in large American combat units. Similarly, the Americans may also have erred, after recognizing the enormity of their neglect, in reversing themselves after the Tet debacle and supplying the South Vietnamese with equipment that was far too sophisticated for them to use effectively.

The Cambodian Campaign

One factor that entered into all discussions of the Vietnamization program was that it rarely had to face real tests of its efficacy. American airpower and artillery were almost always available to stave off complete disaster, as nearly happened in the case of North Vietnamese attacks on isolated fire bases. It was extremely difficult, then, to reach any conclusions as to whether or not these scattered battles were real tests of the success or failure of the program. For this reason alone, it was not surprising that South Vietnamese and American military leaders were impatient to enter the enemy's Cambodian base areas, where they were sure they would encounter enough opposition to reach some conclusions about the merits of Vietnamization.

There was little doubt that South Vietnamese soldiers from time to time strayed into Cambodia, sometimes on special missions, but by and large, until 1970, American and South Vietnamese troops observed the "sanctity of the border." The feeling among American diplomats and policy-makers, if not the generals in the field, was that it would be wiser to cultivate the confidence of Prince Norodom Sihanouk, who was already deeply concerned about the presence of the Vietnamese Communists in his country, than to inflame his anti-American sentiments. Sihanouk, who had broken off diplomatic relations with the United States on May 3, 1965, had re-established them in July, 1969.

In Vietnam, at the same time that Sihanouk was receiving a new American chargé d'affaires in Phnom Penh, intelligence sources predicted only "high points" of activity until the North Vietnamese and Viet Cong had regained the level of strength they had reached before the 1968 Tet offensive. The rate of movement down the Ho Chi Minh trail in southern Laos had set new records in the dry season from November, 1969, through April, 1970, but analysts doubted if the North Vietnamese would launch a major series of attacks until 1971. Communist troops in the meantime were expected to follow the hit-and-run approach of "protracted warfare." Small units, sometimes highly trained "sapper squads," would continue to set ambushes, invade, and possibly besiege small bases and would fire occasional rockets and mortars into cities and towns.

It was often remarked, however, that the truly greatest events in the Vietnam war were totally unpredictable. Who in 1962, for instance, would have forecast the 1963 assassination of President Diem? Despite widespread indications of a country-wide build-up of Communist troops, no one imagined that the enemy would mount attacks on every major city and town during the Tet holidays in early 1968. It seemed logical—in hindsight, that is—that the next major event of the war would also escape the advance notice of sensitive political- and military-intelligence analysts.

That event was the overthrow, on March 18, 1970, of Prince Si-hanouk, who had seemed so firmly entrenched that no responsible analyst would even have listed this possibility among the wildest contingencies in the Indochinese conflict. Two days after his ouster, the first South Vietnamese troops had crossed the Cambodian border on the southern side of the "Parrot's Beak," the part of Cambodia that extends into South Vietnam some 40 miles northwest of Saigon. The South Vietnamese, on .this particular operation, did not range more than 2 or 3 miles inside Cambodia and coordinated their activities with nearby Cambodian military outposts. Before the end of the month, however, the South Vietnamese had launched a series of small-scale incursions across the frontier in the delta region and the Parrot's Beak.

Then, in the middle of April, 1970, some 1,800 troops drove across the northern side of the Parrot's Beak, in the area known as the "Angel's Wing." Villagers at the town of Bavet, the Cambodian checkpoint on Route 1, the main road from Saigon to Phnom Penh, reported that American advisers were with the South Vietnamese, but neither South Vietnamese nor Americans would admit any cross-border operations. There was no doubt about what was happening, however, especially since American troops formed blocking forces on the Vietnamese side of the frontier to prevent Viet Cong or North Vietnamese from attempting to flee into South Vietnam. American artillery and airplanes, which had not operated regularly against Cambodia before Siha-nouk's fall, supported the South Vietnamese.

U.S. diplomats had expressed some reservations to the South Vietnamese about these operations, but Ambassador Ellsworth

Bunker was said to have favored them, just as he had favored, privately, cross-border operations into Laos and northeastern Cambodia after the 1968 Tet offensive. General Creighton Abrams, the American military commander, thought the South Vietnamese understood the "realities" of the situation and the limits of their capabilities. Like Bunker, however, Abrams was enthusiastic about carefully timed and planned incursions to clean out the sanctuaries and also, not incidentally, to support the anti-Communist Cambodian Government, whose forces had suffered a series of military defeats at the hands of the North Vietnamese and Viet Cong since the beginning of April.[10] Thus, by the last week of April, Abrams was prepared to recommend a full-scale military campaign in Cambodia for the dual purpose of denying the Communists their sanctuaries and buttressing the faltering Phnom Penh regime of General Lon Nol.

In view of the over-all Nixon doctrine of granting Asian nations the initiative to decide their own future, it was fitting that the first formal announcement of American or South Vietnamese operations in Cambodia should emanate from South Vietnamese, not American, sources. On the night of April 29, the defense ministry in Saigon issued a communiqué disclosing that South Vietnamese troops had launched an operation in the Parrot's Beak "with American logistical and combat support." A total of 15,000 South Vietnamese troops entered the Parrot's Beak from north, south, and east, while still more crossed the border below that area. By the night of April 30, the South Vietnamese, riding tanks and armored personnel-carriers, had pushed some 21 miles from the border as far as the town of Prasaut, from which the North Vietnamese had driven Cambodian troops two weeks before. The South Vietnamese encountered only scattered resistance from the Communists, who adopted their usual tactic of retreating rather than resisting a momentarily superior force.

Then, on the morning of May 1—the night of April 30 in the United States—President Nixon, in a nationwide television address, innocuously billed in advance as a report "on the situation in Southeast Asia," announced that American combat forces were also entering Cambodia. The President was careful to emphasize the South Vietnamese role above that of the Americans'. "A major responsibility for the ground operations is being assumed by South Vietnamese forces," he said, citing the forays into the Parrot's Beak. "There is one area, however, where I have concluded that a combined American and South Vietnamese operation is

necessary. Tonight, American and South Vietnamese units will
attack the headquarters for the entire Communist military operation in South Vietnam. This key control center has been occupied by the North Vietnamese and Viet Cong for years in blatant
violation of Cambodia's neutrality."[11]

The headquarters to which Nixon referred was generally believed
to have been located in the salient of the Cambodian frontier,
known as the "Fishhook," that juts into South Vietnam some 80
miles north of Saigon. American intelligence analysts portrayed it
as a complex network of bunkers containing all the facilities for
COSVN, the Central Office for South Vietnam, which directed
Communist military and political activities in the southern half
of South Vietnam. Besides smashing COSVN, American and
South Vietnamese officers hoped to destroy the Communists' logistical and storage depots, where they were certain the enemy had
stored enormous caches of arms and ammunition. At least three
North Vietnamese divisions were known to have based for several
years in the Fishhook and the Parrot's Beak, and still more North
Vietnamese units were encamped in the Cambodian highlands to
the north and the Mekong delta to the south.

Nixon's announcement was so unexpected that many observers
concluded that the United States would fight the North Vietnamese in Cambodia just as it had in South Vietnam. The territory
that the war might encompass seemed suddenly to have doubled.
In fact, however, the President attempted to set the entire Cambodian campaign in the framework of the Nixon doctrine, which he
had first enunciated on Guam in July, 1969. Ten days before his
April 30 address, he had announced his decision to withdraw 150,-
000 more American troops from Vietnam within a year. American
troop strength in May, 1971, according to this program, would be
approximately 284,000—a reduction of 265,000 from the number
in Vietnam before Nixon's inauguration in January, 1969. The
precise rationale for American involvement in the Cambodian campaign, as stated by Nixon on April 30, was "to protect our men
who are in Vietnam and to guarantee the continued success of our
withdrawal and Vietnamization program."

The first argument—"to protect our men who are in Vietnam"
—was entirely for domestic American consumption. North Vietnamese and Viet Cong diplomats had made amply clear that they
would not menace American troops if the United States acquiesced
to an orderly program of immediate withdrawal. The second argument—"to guarantee the continued success of our withdrawal and

Vietnamization programs"—was the one that counted from the viewpoint of all that had happened in Vietnam since the 1968 Tet offensive. The Cambodian campaign, if at all successful militarily, would deprive the North Vietnamese of at least six months' worth of arms and ammunition. In the meantime, the South Vietnamese forces, whose quality was always a doubtful quantity, could "progress" to the point where they could bear the primary burden of the war. Thus, in theory, it would be a simple matter—or simpler than before—to continue to withdraw American troops without jeopardizing security and stability.

Bearing these objectives in mind, the President, under severe criticism from Congress and segments of the American public, limited the scope of the Cambodian campaign several days after it had begun. All American troops, he said, would withdraw from Cambodia by June 30. No Americans would venture further than 35 kilometers—21.7 miles—inside Cambodian frontiers. Only 31,-000 troops, less than 10 per cent of the total number of Americans in Vietnam at the time, ever were involved in the Cambodian campaign. They concentrated on the Fishhook and parts of the Parrot's Beak (except for a one-week foray into a base area in northeastern Cambodia), while the South Vietnamese focused on the Parrot's Beak and the delta. Some 40,000 South Vietnamese troops entered Cambodia before the onset of the summer monsoon in late June, 1970. Many of them, besides attacking the sanctuaries, defended Cambodian towns, roads, and rivers as far as Phnom Penh and Kompong Cham, 45 and 35 miles, respectively, from the border at its nearest points.

American commanders were impressed by the South Vietnamese performance but still ambivalent as to its value as a test of Vietnamization and the Nixon doctrine. The South Vietnamese, said General Abrams at a dinner with correspondents on May 26, 1970, had had "a relatively good time of it" during the operation. "They understand that the enemy hasn't really been able to stand and fight," Abrams explained—confirming the prediction that South Vietnamese troops would remain in Cambodia on a limited basis but hopefully would not overextend themselves. The general also indicated that American planes would continue to bomb North Vietnamese supply lines in Cambodia and provide limited air support for South Vietnamese, and possibly Cambodian, troops after the Americans had returned to Vietnam.

It was not difficult to rationalize all these activities as examples of the Nixon doctrine in action. The picture of South Vietnamese and Cambodians fighting for themselves, provided only with American "support," and of the United States offering diplomatic, political, and material assistance while withdrawing its troops, all fit into the conceptual framework so carefully explained to both correspondents and the American public. Like most such theories and doctrines, however, President Nixon's ran the grave risk of foundering on imponderables and losing all meaning amid numerous exceptions and distortions to suit unpredictable circumstances. Perhaps the least predictable variable was the Cambodian Government and Army. How long could the anti-Communist regime survive in Phnom Penh? Could the army ever develop the strength to face the North Vietnamese and Viet Cong on its own? What if the North Vietnamese overran the entire country, reinstalled Sihanouk as chief of state, and then presented a threat more severe than ever before against a crumbling South Vietnamese Army and Government?

The answers to these questions were far from clear. Nixon, however, was determined to apply the same over-all policy to Cambodia as to South Vietnam. "The United States, as I indicated in what is called the Guam, or Nixon, doctrine, cannot take the responsibility and should not take the responsibility in the future to send American men in to defend the neutrality of countries that are unable to defend themselves," he said in a press conference on May 8, 1970, by ironic coincidence the sixteenth anniversary of the fall of Dien Bien Phu. Cambodia, it seemed clear, would present an even more complicated test of the Nixon doctrine than South Vietnam. A non-Communist government might survive in Saigon, in one form or another, for years, but the immediate question was how long the regime in Phnom Penh could last beyond the period of American—and South Vietnamese—intervention.

Beyond that question was the ultimate issue of whether the Cambodian Government, if it did survive over an appreciable period, would only exist in a kind of a limbo while North and South Vietnamese troops rampaged over much of the rest of the country. Phnom Penh might veer from *de facto* alliance with Hanoi to *de facto* alliance with Saigon, but basically Cambodians were hostile toward all Vietnamese. While the Nixon doctrine might work in a relatively limited context, it might prove of considerably less validity in terms of Cambodia's long-range struggle for survival.

II
Cambodia: From Peace to War

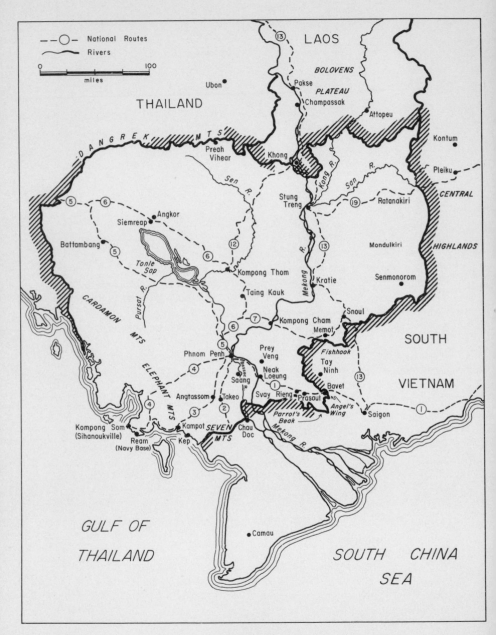

Cambodia

3

Price of Peace

Sihanouk and the Nixon Doctrine

Prince Norodom Sihanouk, before his downfall in March, 1970, had come to be regarded by American officials as almost a prototype for the Nixon doctrine—an independent statesman who would attempt to stand on his own amid conflicting forces. He did not welcome foreign troops—American, North or South Vietnamese, Thai, Chinese, or whatever—inside Cambodia's frontiers, and he 'wanted foreign aid only if offered without preconditions. He had, to be sure, broken off diplomatic relations with the United States nearly five years before, but lately the pendulum appeared to have been swinging in the other direction. Although powerless to prevent Vietnamese Communist troops from basing in Cambodia, he had finally conceded their presence and begun expressing serious alarm in 1969. Thus, it was not surprising that he agreed, in mid-1969, to resume ties with the United States. American diplomats were so heartened by signs of reversal in Sihanouk's policy—and so convinced of his control over his own government—that his overthrow caught them entirely by surprise.

"Our initial response was to seek to preserve the *status quo* with regard to Cambodia," said President Nixon in a 7,000-word statement released from his residence at San Clemente, California, on June 30, 1970, the day the last American troops were withdrawn from Cambodia at the end of their two-month campaign against Communist base areas. Nixon explained that American policy throughout the war had been to refrain from moving against the Communist sanctuaries in Cambodia "in order to contain the conflict." The United States, said Nixon, had "recognized both the problems facing Sihanouk and the fact that he had exercised some measure of control over Communist activities, through regulation of the flow of rice and military supplies into the sanctuaries from

41

the coastal ports. We considered that a neutral Cambodia out-weighed the military benefits of a move against the base areas."[1]

Sihanouk, in 1968 and 1969, had begun to reflect and reciprocate the U.S. attitude, as summarized by Nixon. Perhaps the most significant manifestation of his ambivalent, if delicate, position was an article written by the prince shortly before his departure in January, 1970, for health treatment in France. The greatest internal menace, wrote Sihanouk, was the "Red Khmer," or Cambodian Communists, who had "organized bands which are increasingly supplied with modern weapons." Sihanouk predicted that the period after the Vietnam war would see "without any doubt, the reinforcement of these anti-national elements not only in Cambodia but also in the whole of the Indochinese Peninsula."[2] In the same article, which was not published until the month after his overthrow, Sihanouk made plain that the "foreign masters" whom he most feared were the Viet Cong and North Vietnamese, "several tens of thousands" of whom, he said, had "infiltrated large border areas of Cambodia, promising to leave 'at the end of the war.' "[3]

Against this threat, the prince fully appreciated the advantages of "American 'imperialism,' " which, he said, had "involuntarily and indirectly . . . done us a service, be it only in creating grave difficulties for our neighbors."[4] Although Sihanouk did not allude specifically to the Nixon doctrine, he clearly had Nixon's 1969 statements in mind when he asked the question, "Will the Americans, as President Nixon has implied, progressively disentangle themselves from Southeast Asia?" Sihanouk's answer: "My personal opinion is that they will not be able to do it if they do not want the 'domino theory' . . . to apply to themselves." Nor, in fact, did Sihanouk appear unhappy with the prospect of continued American involvement in the region. It was "permitted to hope," he reasoned, "that to defend its world interests (and indeed not for our sake), the United States will not disentangle itself too quickly from our area."[5]

The tenor of Sihanouk's article, his last major policy statement before his fall, indicated that he and Nixon shared the same outlook. Even if the two leaders had not corresponded directly, their views seemed to mesh. Each seemed to understand the other's problems in the region. Neither wanted such a close relationship as to involve the United States in a war in Cambodia. Sihanouk indicated that he favored the *status quo* of large-scale American presence in Thailand and South Vietnam to balance the alarming activities of

Vietnamese Communist troops on his own soil. Nixon, while embarking on a new policy of American "withdrawal" from South Vietnam, wanted to maintain the *status quo* in Cambodia. Careful limitation of Communist use of Cambodia as a "base area" seemed preferable to a wider, generalized war across the heart of Indochina.

One reason, perhaps, for the curious understanding between Sihanouk and Nixon was that both of them were highly sensitive to the background of U.S.-Cambodian relations since World War II. Sihanouk, during his country's struggle for independence from France and later in talks with the American secretary of state, John Foster Dulles, had gained the impression that the United States viewed Cambodia only in the context of America's "global," or at least Southeast Asian, interests. Nixon, who had been Vice President from 1952 to 1960 while Dulles was secretary of state, was intimately familiar, as both an observer and sometime adviser to Dulles and President Eisenhower, with the evolution of American policy during the period of the first Geneva conference and the formation of the Southeast Asia Treaty Organization.

Toward Neutrality

From the beginning of his relations with the United States, Sihanouk had sensed that America was not sufficiently concerned with Cambodia, home of only 7 million persons scattered over a land of forests and rice paddies approximately the size of Missouri, to want to risk vast quantities of arms and men in a possibly climactic struggle against the Vietnamese Communists or even the Chinese. In Sihanouk's mind, the United States had always been as unreliable and ambivalent in its approach toward Cambodia as he had appeared to American leaders.

The history of Cambodia's strained relations with the United States had begun with what Sihanouk regarded as a highly symbolic snub. The U.S. State Department in April, 1953, sent the undersecretary of state, W. Bedell Smith, to meet him when he arrived in Washington seeking American diplomatic support for Cambodia's liberation from France. Sihanouk, whom the French had installed as king in 1941 at the age of eighteen, headed a government still controlled essentially by French administrators who could veto internal decisions and were entirely responsible for national defense and foreign policy. Nonetheless, Sihanouk believed that Washington, if it had sympathized with his cause, would have accorded him the honors normally due a national leader.

"For you, the chief of state of Cambodia is on the same level as the undersecretary of state," Sihanouk remarked to American correspondents more than fifteen years after his 1953 visit. "A few days after my arrival in Washington," added Sihanouk, in a characteristic mood of argumentative reminiscence, "I saw a Negro Prime Minister from Africa, and he was received by Dulles."[6]

The sensitivities of young Sihanouk, who was thirty years old in 1953, were not soothed during his conversations with Dulles. On the one hand, wrote Sihanouk, Dulles realized that France "ought to accord independence more rapidly to its former 'protégés,'" while, "on the other hand, he was far from sharing my conviction that the Indochinese Peoples, completely liberated from the French protectorate, would be capable of checkmating Communism by opposing it with the force of their Nationalism." Sihanouk, who had been rebuffed by the French President, Vincent Auriol, shortly before departing from Paris for Cambodia and the United States, noted that "a fundamental difference existed even then between the point of view of Mr. Dulles (that is to say, of the American Government) and mine." For Cambodia, he said, "Independence was in a way the 'oxen' that alone would pull the 'plow' of pacification and success against the Viet Minh and Communization. For Mr. Dulles, it was just the opposite: The oxen could only be the French Army, war materiel, and American money. Each of us was convinced that the other was putting the plow before the oxen."[7]

The disappointing conversation between Sihanouk and Dulles may have been the first step on the way to the total break in Cambodian-American relations twelve years later. The significance of this meeting was obscured, however, by an interview published in the *New York Times* on April 19, 1953, in which Sihanouk said that Indochina would "be joined to the Communists" if France rejected his demands. Sihanouk, certain that only national independence would give his people the will to fight the Viet Minh guerrillas who had been in Cambodian jungles since World War II, claimed that the interview alarmed the French authorities into inviting his representatives in Paris to participate in fresh negotiations, which led to full Cambodian independence seven months later.[8] At the Geneva conference in 1954, Cambodia again sought American support. As representatives of a newly independent non-Communist nation already endangered by Vietnamese Communists, Cambodian diplomats hoped to persuade the United States to guarantee the defense of their country against foreign attack.

Again Sihanouk had reason to be impressed with Washington's lack of interest in Cambodia's future, for American diplomats carefully refrained from offering any real defense other than the "umbrella of protection" afforded by the embryonic Southeast Asia Treaty Organization (SEATO). The ostensible reason for the American diplomatic position was that a specific military commitment to Cambodia would violate assurances by both Britain and China that Cambodia would remain neutral, but the United States basically was afraid of overextending its interests in Southeast Asia.[9] The SEATO treaty, signed in Manila seven weeks later, on September 8, 1954, offered scant encouragement, with its protocol designating Laos, Cambodia, and South Vietnam as states worthy of defense by the SEATO alliance of Thailand, the Philippines, Australia, New Zealand, Pakistan, Britain, France, and the United States. Cambodian leaders surmised that America and its allies would defend Cambodia only when it suited their—and not necessarily Cambodia's—best interests.

Cambodia, then, had to solve a problem: how to ensure national security and still avoid the kind of holocaust that threatened the other former French Indochinese colonies.

The solution seemed to lie in the policy of neutrality. Sihanouk, who the French had thought would prove a malleable figurehead when they chose him over his uncle, next in line of succession to succeed his grandfather, King Sisowath Monivong, was much too shrewd to call for diplomatic neutrality if such a policy failed to suit his or his country's best interests. Sihanouk even argued that Cambodia might remain in the French union, just as the former British colonies had maintained their ties with the commonwealth. But, by the end of 1954, after having received in Phnom Penh Indian Prime Minister Jawaharlal Nehru, noted for his advocacy of neutrality, Sihanouk was convinced that national salvation for Cambodia lay in following a carefully demarcated middle course among the great powers. Dulles might rail against the "immorality of neutrality," but those were empty words when measured against Cambodia's urgent national interests.

In the same period in which the United States was demonstrating an essential lack of concern for Cambodian security, China was executing a *volte-face* in its own outlook. Both China and the Soviet Union had at first supported demands of the Democratic Republic of Vietnam—North Vietnam—for a separate place at the Geneva conference for the clandestine "resistance government" of the Cambodian Communists, sponsored by the Viet Minh. After

Moscow and Peking dropped their support of the Cambodian Communists, however, Hanoi had no choice but to follow their lead. All three Communist powers agreed at the conference on withdrawal of "foreign troops" (that is, the Viet Minh) remaining in Cambodia because they, like the United States, did not want to overextend their interests.[10] Moscow and Peking both seemed to have sensed that it might be wise to support the Vietnamese Communists in Vietnam and possibly Laos but to try to maneuver Cambodia into a neutral position.

It would be simple to compare America's lack of interest in Cambodia with the attitude of the Soviet Union and China and conclude that all three countries were adopting essentially the same approach. The difference, however, was that the American position was discouraging to Cambodia, which had negotiated at Geneva for the right to enter into defensive alliances supported by foreign bases on its soil, while the Communists' was encouraging. The opportunity the United States missed in mid-1954 to win a potentially valuable ally in Indochina was matched by subsequent efforts of the Communist countries, particularly China, to gain Sihanouk's confidence by diplomacy. The setting for Peking's first significant overtures to Sihanouk was the Asian-African conference, held in Bandung, Indonesia, in April, 1955, and attended by senior statesmen and diplomats from twenty-nine countries.

At Bandung, Sihanouk first met the Chinese Premier, Chou En-lai, who headed the Chinese delegation. Chou's aim at the conference was to convince Asian and African nations of China's friendly intentions by espousing the concept of neutrality, which was also loudly publicized by Indonesian President Sukarno as a prelude for drawing former colonial countries out of the Western orbit. Virtually all nations represented at the conference, except for those already allied with the United States, indicated their sympathy with Chou's foreign policy by expressing their support for *Pancha Shila,* the five principles of peaceful coexistence enunciated by Nehru and Chou in the Sino-Indian agreement of 1954, in which India had recognized the legitimacy of China's conquest of Tibet. The principles included mutual respect for territorial integrity, nonaggression, noninterference in the internal affairs of other countries, reciprocal equality, and peaceful coexistence.

The Bandung conference did not solve the real problems of Africa or Asia, and it did not produce a united bloc of like-minded nations. But it did evince the "spirit of Bandung"—a sense of brotherhood and purpose among some of the former colonies—

and it also engendered in their leaders a certain confidence in their ability actively to assert independence from their former colonial rulers and the United States, already accused of "neocolonialism" and "imperialism" in its foreign policy. Although unproductive of concrete results, Bandung represented a new style. Sihanouk's sojourn in Bandung marked the point at which he seriously committed himself to the policy of neutrality as a principle that would guide him until he was removed from office and completely aligned himself, in exile, with China and North Vietnam.

Sihanouk's adherence to what he called "strict neutrality" in foreign affairs was born of the hardest practical considerations. The awareness that the United States would probably not support Cambodia, militarily, in a struggle with China or North Vietnam was always paramount in his thinking. If the United States was determined to ally with Thailand and South Vietnam, while neglecting Cambodia's best interests, then, in Sihanouk's view, he was all the more obligated to seek the friendship of countries whom he could balance against what he regarded as the immediate predatory menace from both west and east. The United States might not openly defend the interests of Thailand and South Vietnam against Cambodia, but American military and civilian aid inevitably strengthened the mechanisms with which these countries could harass Cambodia's frontiers or support political enemies whom Sihanouk had defeated or driven into exile.

The most offensive of all the anti-Sihanouk forces were the Khmer Serei, or Free Khmer rebels, organized in Thailand and South Vietnam for the purpose of conducting raids across the frontiers and broadcasting propaganda against the government. The radio propaganda in particular struck one of Sihanouk's most sensitive nerves, for the Khmer Serei leader was Son Ngoc Thanh, a once popular nationalist who had risen to power under the Japanese and then challenged both Sihanouk and France after World War II. Sihanouk was convinced that Son Ngoc Thanh's activities were financed by American funds, channeled through the Central Intelligence Agency. The extent of CIA involvement in Thanh's machinations against the Prince has never been clear, but some of Thanh's troops in Vietnam were armed and trained by the U.S. Army's elite Special Forces, popularly known as the "green berets." The duty of the Vietnamese Khmer Serei ostensibly was to prevent infiltration from Cambodia into South Vietnam, but not infrequently they themselves infiltrated the other way into Cambodia.

Symbolic of Sihanouk's deepest fears was the occupation by Thai troops in 1956 of the temple of Preah Vihear, built by the ancient Khmer in the Dangrek Mountains along the present Thai-Cambodian frontier. To Sihanouk, this action signaled Thailand's intention of encroaching across Cambodia's entire western border with the aid of Khmer Serei troops. Thailand and South Vietnam both closed their frontiers to traffic to and from Cambodia for several weeks in March and April, 1956, in order to demonstrate Cambodia's economic, if not political, dependence on its neighbors. Imbued with the "spirit of Bandung," Sihanouk followed a delicate, sophisticated line of diplomacy that surprised his adversaries and the United States.

Although he had signed a military assistance agreement with the United States in mid-1955, he had begun in 1956 to accept some of the overtures made earlier by Chou En-lai at Bandung. First, he spent five days in Peking in February, 1956, and, then, prodded by Chou's questions as to how he could claim to be neutral while accepting aid only from Western countries, he signed an economic assistance agreement with China in April. In July, little more than two months after having signed the agreement with China, Sihanouk journeyed to Moscow, where Soviet leaders offered him technical and economic assistance and pledged to respect Cambodia's independence. Then, in November, 1956, Chou En-lai paid his first visit to Phnom Penh, at the end of which he signed a communiqué reiterating the five principles of peaceful coexistence. Chou also was careful to allay Sihanouk's fears that China would attempt to rule Cambodia indirectly through the influence of the country's Chinese population, totaling some 400,000, and including economic leaders and merchants in every city and town, by urging them to demonstrate their loyalty to Cambodia rather than China.

Chou En-lai's advice did not, however, mean the end of Peking's efforts at influencing the Cambodian Chinese. While accepting more and more Chinese aid and technical advisers, mainly to design and build small factories in such fields as textiles, glass, and cement, Sihanouk was disheartened by Peking's continuing efforts at financing the country's Chinese-language press and handing out funds to local Chinese who were supposedly unemployed. China also antagonized Cambodian authorities by vying for political control of the Chinese community through the five "congregations"* into which the French had assigned the Cambodian Chinese for

---

* The French divided the Chinese into congregations according to main place of origin—and dialect—in China. The Chinese administered the congregations, which served social and economic functions, as well as political aims.

administrative purposes. The Cambodian Government, in May, 1958, a year after the Chinese technicians had arrived, abolished the congregations in hopes of limiting Peking's influence and governing the local Chinese on the same basis as the Khmer.

In the interests of his nonalignment policy, Sihanouk was still inclined to give Peking the benefit of the doubt. So confident was he of the good faith of the economists and technicians who had arrived from China that he agreed, in July, 1958, to open diplomatic relations with Peking, which promptly reciprocated by promising him more aid. The act of extending formal recognition to Peking might appear of only routine importance in retrospect, but, in 1958, it was regarded as open defiance of Sihanouk's main Western benefactor, the United States, then determined to rally international support for the Nationalist Chinese regime on Taiwan.

The Break with Washington

Sihanouk was not yet prepared to turn against the United States, but he was in no mood to show a charitable attitude toward Thailand. Shortly before establishing relations with Peking, he and Bangkok had begun negotiating the Preah Vihear temple controversy. There was little doubt among diplomatic observers, as well as Thai officials, that Sihanouk had timed the resumption of relations with China to prove to Thailand that he had a powerful potential ally in case the Thai attempted to support their claim to the temple with an invasion on Cambodia's western front. Just as the temple debate symbolized traditional hostilities between Thailand and Cambodia, so the quarrel between the two countries was turning into a symbol of the larger Sino-U.S. confrontation. As long as the United States shielded Thailand behind a military alliance, China was bound to support Cambodia, whose leader had long since lost confidence in American diplomatic efforts to dissuade Thailand from staking its national prestige on possession of the temple. Indeed, American officials merely infuriated Sihanouk by their "nonaligned," conciliatory position in the dispute.

The negotiations on the temple led to a total break in diplomacy between Thailand and Cambodia on November 28, 1958. Prince Sihanouk, who had explained that relations had been compromised by criticism in Thai newspapers, agreed to re-establish diplomatic relations on February 20, 1959, after mediation by Baron Johan Beck-Friis, special representative of the United Nations Secretary-

General. Essentially, however, the differences between Sihanouk and the Thai Government, under Field Marshal Sarit Thanarat, were beyond repair. In the midst of acrimonious exchanges and demands, both governments had increased their border guards. Sarit, besides matching Sihanouk's troops with an equal number of Thai, fully endorsed Son Ngoc Thanh's plan to organize units of ethnic Khmer living in Thailand. The number of Khmer Serei in Thailand now reached 3,000.

Perhaps the most bizarre example of hostility between Thailand and Cambodia was what Sihanouk called the "Bangkok plot" of March, 1959, in which General "Dap" Chhuon Mochulpich, governor and military commander of Siemreap Province, was accused of conspiring to overthrow the government. Sihanouk charged that Dap Chhuon's main allies were Son Ngoc Thanh and Sam Sary, a former adviser to Sihanouk who had lost influence and prestige in a power struggle with other advisers and ministers. The Thai, according to Sihanouk's account, had provided the funds for sending Khmer Serei troops into Siemreap, but Sihanouk also implicated the South Vietnamese Ambassador to Cambodia and the CIA. The former was accused of having paid large bribes to Dap Chhuon and the latter of having provided communications facilities linking all the diffuse elements in the conspiracy. Sihanouk's charges were never verified, but they provided an excellent excuse for him to smash Dap Chhuon's forces, regardless of whether or not they were really Khmer Serei troops. Dap Chhuon himself was shot and killed in a forest near Siemreap.[11]

That both Son Ngoc Thanh and Sam Sary, whatever their roles may have been, were assured of safe havens in Thailand and South Vietnam seemed to prove Sihanouk's contention that both of these countries wanted to overthrow him. Thailand and Cambodia papered over some of their differences with the signing, on December 15, 1960, of a set of accords, mediated by U.N. representatives, in which the two nations promised, among other things, not to violate each other's borders and not to exacerbate tensions with hypercritical propaganda attacks. Within a fortnight, however, both sides charged each other with violations of the accords. Finally, on October 23, 1961, Sihanouk broke off diplomatic relations with Thailand. Sihanouk charged that Thailand was threatening to attack Cambodia with its American-supported army, and Sarit retorted that Cambodia was cooperating in a Communist plan for the conquest of Southeast Asia.

The *coup de grace* for any hope of resumption of relations between Thailand and Cambodia was the decision by the International Court of Justice at the Hague on June 15, 1962, in favor of Cambodia in the Preah Vihear temple dispute. Thailand, under U.S. pressure, finally abandoned the temple, but Thai leaders had no intention of seriously renewing negotiations with Sihanouk, who by now was firmly embarked on a foreign policy of "strict neutrality," as he put it, or of pro-Communist anti-Americanism, as it was widely interpreted. In this spirit, Sihanouk also entered into bitter debate with the South Vietnamese Government of Ngo Dinh Diem, who refused to relinquish any of his country's claims to two off-shore islands, already populated and governed by Cambodia, as well as several disputed villages along the frontier. To Sihanouk, such irredentist claims symbolized Saigon's desire to overrun Cambodia from the east. A series of incursions by South Vietnamese troops pursuing the Viet Cong across the Cambodian frontier were immediately responsible for Sihanouk's decision, on August 27, 1963, to sever diplomatic relations with Saigon.

Sihanouk, at this point, seemed to have manipulated his country, diplomatically and militarily, into an impregnable position vis-à-vis his neighbors. It was true that Thailand and South Vietnam could have squeezed Cambodia out of existence in a pincers movement, but the United States exercised restraint on both of them. U.S. diplomats hoped to improve relations with Cambodia, despite Sihanouk's increasingly acerbic attacks, while continuing to support Thailand and South Vietnam as allies not against Cambodia but against the Communists. From the U.S. Government viewpoint, the historic feud between Cambodia, Thailand, and Vietnam was a petty irritant in which all the participants had shown a disconcerting lack of interest in the global issues of the cold war.

Unlike many American leaders and diplomats, however, Sihanouk was finely attuned to the forces at work in Southeast Asia. He was now entering the period in which his country, under the guise of neutrality, was, in effect, to align itself with the Communist powers, notably China and North Vietnam. Sihanouk fully understood the perils of this course. In fact, he did not wish to support China and North Vietnam to such an extent that they might really replace Western influence in Cambodia. Rather, so long as the United States was not willing to defend his immediate territorial interests, he viewed the policy of leftist neutrality as the most expedient method with which to counter his neighbors' ambitions.

The United States was caught almost unwittingly in the vortex of Cambodia's struggle with Thailand and South Vietnam. American officials carefully earmarked arms, ammunition, and advisers for South Vietnam's fight against the Viet Cong, but it was inevitable, as the war slowly expanded, that the fighting should boil over into Cambodia. And it was equally inevitable that Sihanouk, fearful of losing his territory under the force of U.S.-made arms and U.S. troops, should accuse the United States of fomenting deliberate violations against Cambodia, particularly in view of the Khmer Serei's inflammatory broadcasts and small-scale incursions from Thailand and Vietnam. The prince was incensed, moreover, by charges in the American press that Cambodia had wasted American aid, which had totaled slightly more than $400 million, far more than the amount supplied by any other country, in the first decade of Cambodia's independence.

"We Khmer cannot endure for long this unjust and scandalous condemnation," he declared in 1953. "When Thai, South Vietnamese, and others shamelessly stuff their pockets with American aid dollars without incurring the least reproach, we who are *incontestably the most honest of the 'assisted'* undergo *permanent injustice from the 'free' world,* which makes of Cambodia the most incapable and the most corrupt of the beneficiaries of American largesse."[12] Sihanouk retaliated against such criticism by accusing American contractors of slipshod practices in constructing the showpiece of American aid, the Cambodian-American Friendship Highway, running 232 kilometers from the new port of Sihanoukville on the Gulf of Thailand to Phnom Penh. Sihanouk claimed that Cambodian crews later had to repair much of the highway, inaugurated on July 22, 1959, but American officials replied that it was built across extremely porous terrain and would have required constant maintenance under any circumstances. Sihanouk's complaint, whether or not it was really justified, signified his desire to show that Cambodia did not need American aid and could rely on its own resources or look elsewhere for assistance.

It was in this spirit that Sihanouk, on November 21, 1963, asked the United States to cancel all economic and military programs. "U.S. aid has brought Cambodia enough humiliation," the New China News Agency, in a dispatch from Phnom Penh, quoted Sihanouk as having said. "It is to kill the Communists who did not menace us at all that the U.S. gave arms to us, the 'neutralists,' " Sihanouk was reported to have complained. The prince was then quoted as having alleged that the Americans, whose military assistance and advisory group in Phnom Penh had swollen to 150 officers and men from a total of 30 in 1955, had discouraged him from turning his U.S.-made equipment against "Cambodia's real enemies," the Thai and the South Vietnamese.[13] The New China News Agency might have exaggerated somewhat the tone of Sihanouk's remarks, but the prince, hypersensitive to distortion about him in the press, raised no objections. In fact, Sihanouk enlarged on the same theme in a series of three articles written for the Khmer magazine Le Nationaliste and then incorporated in a pamphlet entitled "Le Rejet de l'Aide Américaine."

The "mercenary armies" of South Vietnam and Thailand have "overwhelmed us with their contempt and their sarcasm, making murderous incursions on our territory with impunity," said Sihanouk in one of the articles. The prince accused Thai and South Vietnamese ships and planes of "systematically violating our territorial waters and . . . air space" and portrayed Cambodia as a helpless victim. "We can only lower our heads in shame and impotence," he said, "bound by our poverty, always enchained by restrictive clauses conceived to keep us forever in a position of inferiority and ineffectiveness in the face of our mortal enemies." The "restrictive clauses" Sihanouk mentioned were stipulations in the military assistance agreement with the United States that U.S. arms would be used only to defend Cambodia against internal revolt or Communist aggression. Henceforth, Sihanouk made plain, he would "solicit military aid from People's China and, depending on the circumstances, diplomatic aid from the Soviet Union."[14]

Despite Sihanouk's remarks, it was still conceivable at this time that relations with Cambodia and its neighbors, as well as the United States, might have improved. One factor was the odd chance that the leaders of South Vietnam, Thailand, and the United States all died within six weeks of each other. Diem was overthrown and assassinated by a military junta on November 1, 1963. John F. Kennedy was assassinated on November 22, 1963, the day after Sihanouk had asked the United States to cancel its aid program. Then, on December 9, 1963, Sarit died in Bangkok after a prolonged illness. The emergence of three new administrations could have provided opportunities to relax tensions. The new government in Saigon, for instance, might have abandoned some of its territorial claims, while Thailand might have gracefully conceded that Preah Vihear rightfully belonged to Cambodia. And the United States might have persuaded both governments to cease supporting Khmer Serei broadcasts and armed incursions.

The deaths of Diem, Sarit, and Kennedy, however, had no real effect on the policies of their countries vis-à-vis Cambodia. One reason, perhaps, was that Sihanouk did not hesitate to disguise his joy at Sarit's passing. He promptly ordered national celebrations, which some observers regarded as the reflection also of his true feelings about the deaths of Kennedy and Diem. All four governments were committed to their policies and were not at all disposed to consider any change. The new American President, Lyndon Johnson, retained Kennedy's secretary of state, Dean Rusk, and committed the United States, perhaps more firmly than Kennedy would have done, to Saigon and Bangkok. The Saigon government, despite a series of coups and other changes over the next year and a half, followed precisely the same foreign policy as had Diem. The Thai Government ruled just as it had while Sarit was alive.

Although the deaths of Diem, Sarit, and Kennedy were not reflected in attitudes toward Cambodia, it was still possible that the United States might have averted the total collapse of its aid program by bargaining with Sihanouk rather than immediately agreeing to his request for the program's termination. The United States responded as it did partly as a matter of national pride. U.S. diplomats were convinced that it was pointless to endure further attacks from Sihanouk. Some of them believed that polite and immediate agreement on termination of U.S. aid might "call Sihanouk's bluff" and persuade him eventually to soften his attitude. Sihanouk, who had signed a "friendship treaty" with the Chinese President, Liu Shao-ch'i, during Liu's visit to Phnom Penh in early May, was not so easily intimidated. Instead, on November 24, 1963, he proposed to the Soviet Union and Great Britain, as cochairmen of the 1954 and 1961–62 Geneva conferences, that they call another conference to guarantee Cambodia's neutrality.

Sihanouk's proposal proved that, even if he had rejected U.S. aid, he still was not willing to place his faith entirely in China or the other Communist powers. Sihanouk hoped at this point to extract from his neighbors, as well as the United States, China, the Soviet Union, and other nations with substantial influence on Cambodia's welfare, a treaty guaranteeing his country's neutrality and territorial integrity. The Soviet Union, on January 18, 1964, proposed to Britain that a conference be held the following April, but Britain replied ten days later that all participants should first reach an understanding on its purpose. Sihanouk was also amenable to a four-power conference of representatives from Cambodia,

Laos, Thailand, and the United States, but he was infuriated by the U.S. proposal that such a conference establish a commission to determine the exact frontiers, which Sihanouk had never regarded as subject to negotiation.[15]

Throughout the period in which he was pursuing the idea of a conference—to consist of either all the signatories to the Geneva agreements or the four powers—Sihanouk was threatening to enter into military alliance with China and to open diplomatic relations with North Vietnam. These suggestions constituted a form of diplomatic, if not psychological, warfare by which Sihanouk hoped finally to persuade the United States to change its policy and support him against all acts of aggression. Sihanouk's ultimate hope was that Washington would side with him on his border disputes with Saigon and Bangkok rather than lose all influence in Phnom Penh. To dramatize this hope, Sihanouk staged demonstrations outside the U.S. and British embassies and information centers on March 11, 1964, the day after the army commander, Lon Nol, had left Phnom Penh on an arms-buying mission to Peking and Moscow. Mobs of students and workers, marshaled by the government, attacked and looted British and U.S. facilities.

The riot, despite the publicity it received, had little immediate effect. Washington did not change its policy regarding Thailand and South Vietnam. Britain did not support the Soviet suggestion for a conference. Although no Geneva-type conference was held, Sihanouk did not enter into an alliance with Peking. If nothing else, however, the incident epitomized the over-all breakdown of Cambodia's ties with the west. The only Western country with which Sihanouk seemed interested in improving relations was France, with which he had negotiated a military assistance agreement the previous January. The French military aid program was smaller than those of the United States, the Soviet Union, or China, but some analysts interpreted the agreement as proof that Sihanouk wanted insurance against total dependence on the Communist powers. The French President, Charles De Gaulle, in turn, wished to maintain French economic and cultural influence in Cambodia while opposing American involvement in Indochina and appearing sympathetic with some of the aims of Hanoi and Peking.

While cultivating France, Sihanouk was fortified in his strategy of strengthening relations with China, which had always supported his proposals for "neutralization" of not only Cambodia but all of Indochina. Communist leaders in general—despite ideological differences—welcomed Sihanouk as a potential ally in their diplomatic campaign to undermine the alliance between the United States and South Vietnam. The effect of Sihanouk's policy was such that Seymour Topping, Southeast Asian correspondent of the *New York Times*, described Cambodia in late 1964 as "a showcase for Peking-style coexistence." Before Sihanouk's decision to refuse U.S. aid, wrote Topping, "a United States diplomatic, economic, and military mission of nearly 300 people was assigned to this country. Today the shell of the United States Information Service Library, which was wrecked by demonstrators, deserted military quarters, and unfinished economic aid projects testify to Prince Norodom Sihanouk's abrupt rejection of the nation that Cambodia once regarded as one of her best friends."[16]

Implicit in Sihanouk's position, however, was the understanding that he would again seek the favor of the West if Communist troops threatened his country. In the meantime, hope had vanished for an immediate U.S. Cambodian rapprochement. Diplomats from both countries met for two days in New Delhi in December, 1964, but broke off the talks after failing to reach any agreement on the problem of Cambodia's frontiers.

In view of Sihanouk's anger about what he regarded as the hostile policies of South Vietnam, Thailand, and the United States, it was no surprise that he sympathized with the Vietnamese Communists, despite their record of having sponsored guerrilla units in Cambodia. Sihanouk's support of North Vietnam, the NLF, the Pathet Lao, and Communist China was demonstrated at the Indochina People's Conference, held in Phnom Penh in March, 1965, the month after President Johnson had ordered the regular bombing of supply routes and military storage areas in North Vietnam. Chou En-lai, in a message to the conference delegates, set the tone for the conference by charging that the "U.S. imperialists," in bombing North Vietnam, were "extending the war flames step by step beyond South Vietnam and posing a grave threat to peace in Indochina and Southeast Asia."[17] The conference gave delegates the chance to discuss the next phase of the Indochinese struggle. They could not be sure that Johnson's decision to bomb North Vietnam would mark the beginning of large-scale American involvement in the war, but they sensed the necessity for cooperation and coordination.

As might have been expected, however, Sihanouk was less pliable than some of the delegates would have liked. First, he miffed the Vietnamese Communists by insisting on seats at the conference for the Khmer Krom, the Cambodian minority in South Vietnam, for whose rights the NLF had shown as little concern as had the Saigon government. Then, he demanded genuine neutrality for South Vietnam and advocated formation of a neutral bloc of nations between India and China.

Neither the Vietnamese nor the Chinese Communists displayed the least interest in these ideas. The final communiqué, published on March 9, 1965, supported Sihanouk's demands for a new Geneva conference to recognize Cambodia's neutrality and territorial integrity but overlooked Cambodian proposals for a negotiated settlement leading to neutralization of South Vietnam. Instead, it called for withdrawal of American troops and "liberation" of the country.

The conference still enabled Sihanouk to press his demands for recognition of Cambodia's frontiers. Sihanouk may also have viewed the gathering as a final warning to the United States, which he was convinced, following a series of border incidents, wanted South Vietnam to overrun Cambodia. Sihanouk was now waiting for a significant U.S. concession—or sufficient pretext for breaking off relations altogether.

Two incidents provided all the pretext that Sihanouk needed for the break. The first was the publication in *Newsweek*, on April 5, of an article impugning the integrity and morals of Sihanouk's mother, Queen Kossamak, the first lady of the kingdom and one of the country's most revered figures. The article, by Bernard Krisher, the magazine's Tokyo correspondent, who had just spent several weeks in Cambodia, noted "an undercurrent of criticism leveled by young intellectuals at Sihanouk's private life and at his mother who is said to be money-mad and reportedly runs a number of concessions in town plus a string of bordellos at the edge of the city." The article added that nearly "everyone who can afford it from the prince on down has one or several concubines, which is one reason why the royal family is so large and why there are so many Cambodian princes."[18]

The article gave Sihanouk a perfect excuse to encourage a demonstration on April 8, 1965, in which students again mobbed the American embassy shouting, "Go Home," "Down with the Free World," and so forth. Then, on April 28, 1965, four South Vietnamese Air Force Skyraiders bombed and rocketed two Cambodian border villages, killing a thirteen-year-old boy and wounding three others. No amount of apologies or explanations that the raid was an accident, that the South Vietnamese had thought that they were firing on a Viet Cong base, that the Americans did not condone such attacks on civilian populations could dissuade Sihanouk from ordering, on May 3, 1965, the closure of the U.S. Embassy in Phnom Penh. Cambodia now appeared to alarmed and angry State Department officials to have aligned itself, formally and permanently with the Communist camp.

Phnom Penh and Peking

The relationship between Cambodia and China seemed to have reached its warmest point during the prince's visit to China in September and October, 1965, when he toured ten provinces and major cities and attended China's sixteenth National Day ceremonies in Peking. Praising China as Cambodia's foremost friend, Sihanouk gave the clear impression of favoring Peking against Moscow in their ideological dispute by warning against the futility of compromise with Washington and its Southeast Asian allies. Moscow was not long in retaliating against this reflection of Chinese charges that Soviet leaders were pursuing a revisionist, conciliatory policy vis-à-vis the Americans. In the North Korean capital of Pyongyang, which Sihanouk visited after China, the Soviet Ambassador informed the prince that high-ranking Soviet officials would be "too busy" to receive him on a trip he was planning to Moscow and Eastern European capitals. Insulted, Sihanouk canceled the remainder of his tour.

Thus, before the end of 1965, China had Sihanouk's support in its struggle against its main enemies, the United States and the Soviet Union. Cambodian-Chinese friendship, symbolic of China's growing power among the nonaligned countries, emerged as a major theme in Chinese propaganda. In Indonesia, Sukarno promoted the concept of an axis formed by drawing a line from Pyongyang through Peking, Hanoi, and Phnom Penh to the Indonesian capital of Jakarta. The abortive Communist coup in Jakarta, staged on the night of September 30, 1965, while Sihanouk was meeting with Chinese leaders in Peking, may have reminded the prince of the dangers of steering too closely to the Chinese line. The stubbornly pro-Communist Sukarno, whom Sihanouk had visited on the occasion of Indonesia's twentieth National Day ceremonies in August, 1965, was forced, in March, 1966, to sign over his power to General Suharto, who officially succeeded him a year later.

Even during Cambodia's most anti-American period, in fact, Sihanouk never overlooked the dangers of Communism, especially when fostered in his own country by Chinese or Vietnamese agents. Seymour Topping, the first U.S. journalist to visit Cambodia after Sihanouk had closed his country to the Western press in May, 1965, reported "authoritatively" in October that an "avenue is carefully being left open for eventual re-establishment of diplomatic relations between Cambodia and the United States." At the same time, Topping noted that China would remain Sihanouk's closest friend, "unless Peking overtly encourages the incipient left-wing Marxist movement in Cambodia to revolution."[19]

Although China and North Vietnam shared similar interests in Cambodia, they inevitably played considerably different, if directly interlocking, roles. North Vietnam was charged with prosecuting the war in South Vietnam and desperately needed base areas and supply routes. Chinese officials, while recognizing this need, were most concerned, on a daily basis, not with fighting the war but with providing weapons and propaganda support. In addition, Peking was anxious to assert its influence over Moscow's in Indochina, if not all of Southeast Asia, while Hanoi viewed the rivalry between the two Communist superpowers as a complication best solved by remaining nonaligned. Thus, China was more likely than North Vietnam to express itself openly in Cambodia. Besides, North Vietnam was always sensitive to the dangers of arousing traditional Cambodian antipathy against the Vietnamese.

The relationship of both North Vietnam and China to Cambodia was further complicated by the presence in Cambodia of some 400,000 residents of Chinese descent and some 600,000 of Vietnamese descent. Both sizable minorities provided a base for political and military activities. Chinese officials had steadily solidified contacts with the Chinese community since the arrival of Peking's first aid mission in 1957. These activities, like those of Chinese missions in other Asian countries, had aroused widespread suspicion by the time that local Chinese schools introduced the teachings of Mao Tse-tung in the early 1960's.

The Chinese in Cambodia, as in the other Southeast Asian nations, formed an economic elite whose members often allied, for mutual benefit, with Cambodian princes, politicians, and generals in business enterprises. Beneath the Chinese were the Vietnamese, a third of whom were crowded into Phnom Penh, where they flourished as small-shopkeepers, artisans, craftsmen, tailors, and the like. Vietnamese also lived as fishermen by the rivers and lakes and worked on large rubber plantations still owned by French interests on or near the Vietnamese border. Many of the Vietnamese had migrated from South Vietnam during the period of French colonialism and had very mixed feelings about the struggle for their country. The ideal solution was to ignore that struggle and make the most of life in Cambodia, but the Vietnamese Communists, as the war intensified in the 1960's, began taxing them and propagandizing among them. Many Vietnamese, particularly those living near the frontier, could not avoid or ignore this type of pressure.

In late 1965, both China and North Vietnam, despite the difference in their specific roles in Indochina, might have been content with their relationships with Sihanouk had it not been for a combination of events far beyond Sihanouk's—or Cambodia's—control. The bombing of North Vietnam, followed by the introduction in mid-1965 of the first American combat forces into the South, necessitated the rapid expansion of North Vietnam's involvement in the conflict. Hanoi, which had previously counted on the Viet Cong to topple the faltering Saigon government, soon was sending its own troops to the South. As the Americans began mounting large-scale operations in previously inviolate base areas in South Vietnam, the Communists expanded their bases in Cambodian jungles. The Chinese, at the same time, increased their own commitment, in terms of propaganda and the consignment of modern small arms, ranging from AK-47 automatic rifles to B-40 rocket launchers to machine guns, mortars, small cannon, and the like.

Sihanouk responded to Communist pressure in a number of ways. First, he was adamant in his opposition to local Cambodian Communists, who often were supported and encouraged by Chinese and Vietnamese residents. In February, 1966, for instance, Sihanouk ordered the arrest of a number of members of the Prachachon, or People's Party, a pro-Communist front. The revival of armed Communist opposition, related directly or indirectly to the struggle of the Vietnamese Communists, marked the beginning of Sihanouk's gradual disillusionment with Communist diplomacy. At the same time, he was not at all inclined to change his policies vis-à-vis the countries whose friendship he had sought in order to protect himself from U.S.-supported armies in Thailand and South Vietnam. He was still far more afraid of invasion by the anti-Communist powers than he was of attack by the Red Khmer, or Khmer Rouge, as the local Communists were known in Phnom Penh.

The prince was remarkably consistent in his refusal to receive U.S. officials as long as American or South Vietnamese forces occasionally fired across his frontiers. In mid-1966 the American journalist Robert Shaplen, who covered Southeast Asia for the *New Yorker*, interviewed Sihanouk and conveyed a personal letter from President Johnson's roving ambassador, Averell Harriman, requesting the opportunity "to resume amicable conversations to which I have always attached the greatest interest." Sihanouk graciously replied that Harriman would "be welcome in Cambodia on a date of your choosing."[20] The visit was scheduled for early September, 1966, after De Gaulle's departure, but, on July 31, U.S. planes attacked the village of Thlok Trach, just inside the Cambodian border. Then, on August 2, 1966, while foreign diplomats and military attachés were touring the village, U.S. helicopters and planes twice attacked nearby homes.

An old woman and two children were killed, but Sihanouk might not have canceled the talks with Harriman if the U.S. apology, transmitted after Western diplomatic reports had verified the incidents, had not claimed that the village was in South Vietnam, not Cambodia. "This touched Sihanouk on the raw," reported Shaplen, "and he angrily declared that there was no sense in holding any talks because 'the United States must first recognize that Cambodia is a country that has frontiers.' "[21] Thus, by the autumn of 1966, the prince was sedulously maintaining his anti-American policy while also opposing the Communists at home.

At this stage, the Chinese Embassy—and the local Chinese community—might have done well to follow the example of the Vietnamese Communists, who deliberately remained aloof from any activity in Cambodia that was not directly related to the prosecution of the war in South Vietnam. The local Chinese, however, were caught in the maelstrom of their own Cultural Revolution and were apparently under orders from Peking to spread it in Cambodia, as they had attempted to do in Burma and other countries in the region. Peking in 1967 recalled its ambassador to Cambodia, Ch'en Shu-liang, as part of the general diplomatic retrenchment that accompanied the Cultural Revolution. Although Peking had recalled most of its ambassadors, Ch'en's departure still surprised diplomatic observers, because he had been on particularly good terms with Sihanouk and had painstakingly fostered warm relations between the two countries. Local Chinese and Cambodian Communists, after Ch'en's departure, openly spread Maoist propaganda material, published some of it in local newspapers, and handed out Mao buttons.

Sihanouk, giving Peking every benefit of the doubt, tried to exonerate China while blaming local Chinese. He not only expelled Chinese merchants convicted of smuggling rice to the Viet Cong (and thereby avoiding government taxes) but also closed a number of Chinese schools and undercut Chinese influence in the youth movement by inveighing against "any support of any foreign country." The government also banned films and magazines from China, just as it had earlier forbidden the sale of such "capitalist" publications as *Time* and *Newsweek*, and forebade all Cambodians to attend parties given by foreigners unless they had special permission.

In the midst of his anti-Chinese campaign, Sihanouk began his diplomatic offensive in search of a separate statement from each country with which Cambodia had relations that it would respect "the neutrality, independence, and territorial integrity of Cambodia within its present frontiers." Sihanouk had first appealed for such recognition in January, 1966, after the failure of his efforts to persuade Great Britain and the Soviet Union to agree on convening another Geneva conference. The Vietnamese Communists were the first to perceive the enormous advantages of mollifying Sihanouk with simple statements. On May 31, 1967, the NLF, asserting its propaganda position as the representative of the people of South Vietnam, issued a declaration supporting all of Sihanouk's frontier claims. On June 6, the Soviet Union, stealing a march on China, offered its own statement of recognition and respect. North Vietnam's declaration was issued on June 12. China did not release a similar statement until July 31, 1967.

Sihanouk rewarded both North Vietnam and the NLF for their statements by agreeing, in June, to establish diplomatic relations with each of them. North Vietnam was granted full embassy status in Phnom Penh, while the NLF mission was called a "representation," because the Viet Cong still had not declared that their organization was the government of South Vietnam. The establishment of both missions was predicated on an unpublicized understanding, confirmed by diplomatic sources in Phnom Penh after Sihanouk's fall, between Sihanouk and the Vietnamese Communists. The latter could continue to enlarge their bases along the Vietnamese frontier and could even receive shipments of arms, ostensibly consigned to Cambodian troops, through Cambodian ports on the Gulf of Thailand. In return, however, they had to agree not only to avoid roads and populated areas but to withdraw all their troops from Cambodia at the end of the war.

Still, Sihanouk was never so impressed by assurances and propaganda statements as to ignore the immediate threat around him. On September 1, 1967, he abolished all national friendship associations, a move against the Khmer-Chinese Friendship Association, subsidized by Peking and supported by radical leftists. On September 4, in defiance of Sihanouk, the Chinese ministry of culture sent a cable to the outlawed Khmer-Chinese Friendship Association extending best wishes on its third anniversary. The cable congratulated the association for its struggle against "reactionary imperialists"—a phrase that Sihanouk interpreted as a personal insult. The offense was compounded when the country's leading French-language newspaper, *La Nouvelle Dépêche*, edited by the leftist Chau Seng, who was also minister of state for national economy, published the contents of the cable. Sihanouk immediately dismissed Chau Seng and So Nem, minister of health and head of the Khmer-Chinese Friendship Association, from his cabinet. He also suspended all the city's privately owned newspapers, replacing them with a government tabloid published in French, Chinese, Vietnamese, and Cambodian.

The prince was about to withdraw his embassy from Peking when Chou En-lai, horrified at the prospect of the loss of one of China's few remaining friends, renewed the promise of "noninterference" that he and Nehru had enunciated at the Bandung conference. Claiming to have successfully defied a Chinese attempt to subdue his country, Sihanouk promised to remain "very good friends" with China as long as it refrained from challenging his authority. At the same time, Sihanouk cautioned his countrymen against "illusions." The Chinese, he said, had never offered Cambodia military aid against the United States, Thailand, or South Vietnam without expecting "something in return." He knew, he went on, "that compensation would come up later," possibly after Communist victory in Vietnam. "This means," the prince concluded, that, "once the Americans are defeated, China would change its policy toward Cambodia."[22]

Sihanouk's remarks reflected a curious sense of fatalism. Although the prince, his press, and his subordinates often expressed their determination to defeat, or at least repel, Cambodia's traditional enemies, they sometimes qualified their brave words by admitting that the country really was doomed. "We want to push away as long as possible the death of our country and of our people," said Sihanouk at a press conference on November 3, 1967, after accepting Chou's apology. "Sooner or later Asia will be Chinese." Sihanouk's belief in China's long-range future in Southeast Asia was one important reason why he had maintained far better relations with China than with the United States, which he had long been convinced would soon lose interest in the region.

Just as Sihanouk wanted to remain on China's side in view of Peking's regional ambitions, so he was anxious to "befriend the real Vietnam, the Vietnam of the future," which he was certain would not be governed by the Saigon regime. After the Americans had departed, he explained, he hoped that the Vietnamese Communists, on gaining complete control over all Vietnam, would recognize "that Cambodia always supported them." For that reason alone, he went on, it would "not be reasonable" for Cambodia to ally itself with the Americans and "practice aggression against Vietnam or the real Vietnamese."[23] Thus Sihanouk's policies throughout the Vietnam war were motivated by the desire not only to gain diplomatic and military protection against his traditional enemies, the Saigon and Bangkok governments, but to win the favor of the Communist powers, who he feared might turn against Cambodia after accomplishing their aims in South Vietnam.

Again Toward Neutrality

It was ironic that the prince reiterated these views just as he was orchestrating the score for Cambodia's transition toward possibly a more genuinely nonaligned position between the Communist and non-Communist powers. On November 1, 1967, two days before his press conference, the prince received Mrs. Jacqueline Kennedy, the widow of the American President. Although Mrs. Kennedy was in Cambodia ostensibly to tour the ruins of Angkor Wat, the names of some of those accompanying her lent credence to the view that her trip might have been encouraged by the State Department in order to open a dialogue with Sihanouk. They included Lord Harlech, British Ambassador to Washington during the Kennedy Administration; Charles Bartlett, a Washington columnist who had also been close to the late President; and Michael Forrestal, onetime adviser to Kennedy on Far Eastern affairs, whom Harriman had specifically recommended for the trip because of his diplomatic expertise.

Sihanouk was too skillful a host to let politics intrude directly into his conversations with Mrs. Kennedy. "If we have dinner and talk about such things, we might end up with broken plates," he told reporters on November 3. Asked what he thought of the prospects of remarriage for Mrs. Kennedy, whom the gossip columnists were then linking romantically with Lord Harlech, he answered, "Our principle is noninterference in the affairs of others."

The State Department, in fact, had conceived of Mrs. Kennedy's visit as a face-saving substitute for the Harriman mission ever since she had expressed an interest earlier in the year in visiting Cambodia. Harriman himself, according to Western diplomatic sources, had been responsible for the American end of a highly classified series of messages between the State Department and the Australian Embassy in Phnom Penh, which relayed them to and from the prince, who finally extended a formal invitation on September 19, 1967—after the incident of China's telegram to the friendship association. Mrs. Kennedy's visit did not in itself alter the attitude of the prince, but it did mark an important point in U.S.-Cambodian relations. It was not surprising, in light of her visit, that Cambodia received two high-level U.S. officials the next year and was ready to resume diplomatic relations by 1969. The first was the U.S. Ambassador to India, Chester Bowles, who persuaded Sihanouk in January, 1968, of the advantages of reinforcing the International Control Commission, charged with supervising the terms of the 1954 Geneva agreement in all countries of Indochina. Bowles supported his argument by showing Sihanouk photographs of alleged Communist encampments in Cambodia taken from U.S. reconnaissance planes.

The Bowles visit, however, was of little more than symbolic value since the Soviet Union, not wanting to miff the Vietnamese Communists, exercised its power as Geneva conference cochairman to oppose all American moves for strengthening the ICC, made up of Polish, Indian, and Canadian representatives. Sihanouk would not even grant an audience to the next official U.S. visitor, Eugene Black, who arrived in Cambodia in September, 1968. Black's visit was not a failure, though, for he was able to pass along assurances that American troops would not invade Cambodia and to recommend that Cambodia apply for membership in such Western-oriented financial institutions as the International Monetary Fund and the World Bank. Two months after Black's departure, Sihanouk agreed to have his government file the applications. An important figure in arranging Black's visit and improving U.S.-Cambodian relations was the Australian Ambassador, Noel St. Clair Deschamps.

"A few years from now, Americans will find, perhaps to their surprise, that there never was any anti-Americanism in this country," Deschamps told me on November 10, 1968, shortly before he was reassigned after nearly six years in the country. A day later, Sihanouk first enunciated the view, later expressed in his 1970 article in *Pacific Community*, that U.S. forces should stay "in

Southeast Asia in countries that willingly accept" them. He claimed that it would "be in our interests to see external pressures . . . neutralize themselves so that Cambodia remains safe."[24] The magazine *Réalités Cambodgiennes*, controlled by Sihanouk, explained the next month that the prince regarded his old concept of a "neutral belt" around Southeast Asia as "outmoded." The only way for the remaining non-Communist countries to maintain their independence, said the article, was through "the continued existence of a balance of power between China and its rivals."[25]

In early 1969, Sihanouk not only conceded the semipermanent presence of Vietnamese Communist units in Cambodia but, in a backhanded way, invited U.S. forces to attack them. "Though it is easy for them to kill the Vietnamese," said the prince, "the Americans have come only to the areas where they know perfectly well there are no Viet Cong or Viet Minh units."[26] In an effort to induce the Vietnamese Communists to leave, Sihanouk asked an NLF diplomat to accompany a government official on a tour of the scene of an incident in which four Khmer soldiers had been wounded by a Viet Cong shell and one prisoner had been captured. The NLF diplomat acknowledged that "the evidence and testimony of the prisoner were very convincing," said General Nhiek Tioulong in his report.[27]

Such attempts to dissuade the Vietnamese Communists, however, were completely in vain. The Communists may have wanted to placate the prince, but their primary concern was the war in Vietnam. "In return for our support, they have proclaimed recognition and respect for our present frontiers," said Sihanouk, "but what good is respect when they penetrate our frontier armed with modern and automatic weapons?"[28] In the spring of 1969, Sihanouk traveled to all the corners of his country—from Battambang in the west to Labansiek in the northeast—inveighing against the Khmer Rouge, the Viet Cong, the North Vietnamese, the enemies whom he had attempted to ignore for years. The time was indeed propitious for Cambodia to resume relations with the United States. He made increasingly clear in statements and press conferences that he would be glad to do so if Nixon would only send him the same message of "recognition and respect" that he had received from other countries.

Finally, on April 16, 1969, the Australian Embassy, at the request of the State Department, delivered the message. "In conformity with the United Nations Charter," it said, "the United States recognizes and respects the sovereignty, independence, and neutrality of the Kingdom of Cambodia within its present frontiers." Sihanouk described the message as "clear and precise" and expressed the hope that Washington would support Cambodia's claim to the two small off-shore islands that Phnom Penh had always governed but that Saigon persisted in considering part of South Vietnam.[29] In late April, however, the prince took umbrage at the remark of a State Department spokesman that America would not involve itself in border disputes. Sihanouk promptly declared that Cambodia would "never accept renewal of diplomatic relations if the Americans still refuse to recognize that Cambodia has well-defined frontiers."[30] Then, on June 11, Sihanouk, at a news conference, announced that Cambodia had received, on May 27, another message from the State Department, reaffirming its previous declaration of recognition and respect, and that Cambodia and the United States would resume relations.

The diplomatic and political peregrinations of Prince Sihanouk were far from over on June 11, 1969. Three days later, on June 14, he recognized the Viet Cong's new Provisional Revolutionary Government and granted full embassy status to the PRG mission in Phnom Penh. By the end of June, Cambodian troops were already engaged in a series of skirmishes with Vietnamese Communists along the South Vietnamese border, and the prospects for peace were not bright. Sihanouk's reactions might at times have appeared somewhat "mercurial," an adjective correspondents often applied to the prince, but he was always motivated by an intense desire for national self-preservation. "We are caught between the hammer and. the anvil," Sihanouk remarked soon after Mrs. Kennedy's visit. Cambodia's sole aim, he said, is "to remain the last haven of peace in Southeast Asia."[31]

4

Crisis Within

Before Independence

"An oasis of peace" was the term that Prince Norodom Sihanouk liked to use to describe Cambodia, whose populated regions were hardly affected by the war until after his downfall. The population and geographical area of the kingdom are both less than half as large as during the period of Cambodia's greatness from the tenth to the fourteenth centuries, but Sihanouk did not discourage comparisons between his rule and that of Jayavarman VII, best known of the Angkorian monarchs. Sihanouk, before 1970, could well be proud of his country's record of relative peace and his own durability as chief of state. The consummate skill with which he parried the thrusts of domestic rivals was primarily responsible for the length of his rule, just as his final failure to balance his opponents against each other led to his demise.

Sihanouk's fear of competition at home, in fact, went considerably deeper into his own past than did his concern with external aggression. Japan, seizing power from France in all the Indochinese states in March, 1945, attempted to play the young king against Son Ngoc Thanh, who had staged demonstrations in 1942 against the same French authorities who had elevated Sihanouk to the throne in the first place. Sihanouk, under Japanese pressure, declared Cambodia's "independence" from France on March 12, 1945, but carefully maintained liaison with the French, with whom he knew he would have to deal directly again after the final defeat of the Japanese. Sihanouk's doubtful loyalties led the Japanese to install Son Ngoc Thanh as Prime Minister on August 14, 1945, while relegating the king to a purely ceremonial status.

Thanh's power dwindled rapidly, however, after the formal surrender of the Japanese on September 2, 1945, and the subsequent occupation of Phnom Penh by British and French forces. At the instigation of Sihanouk and disloyal members of Thanh's government, French officials arrested Thanh in October, 1945, and deported him to France, where he was held under house arrest for the next six years. In exile, Thanh remained a symbol of Cambodian nationalism. Some of his followers fled to the western provinces of Siemreap and Battambang, still occupied by Thailand as a result of Bangkok's World War II alliance with Japan. Others, including many young intellectuals disillusioned with both royalty and colonialism, gravitated toward the newly formed Democratic Party, which won 50 of 71 seats in the first elections for constituent assembly in September, 1946.

Sihanouk's position, in 1946 as in 1970, was to attempt to play conflicting parties against each other in order to preserve his own power. Although he identified more closely with minor political organizations in favor of maintaining ties with France and retaining the trappings of monarchy, he still hoped to cooperate with the Democrats. The former were led by members of Sihanouk's own Norodom family, while the latter attracted princes from the rival Sisowath family, cousins of the king.

Antagonism between Norodoms and Sisowaths was evident in the drafting of Cambodia's first constitution in late 1946 and early 1947. The leader of the Democratic Party, Prince Sisowath Youtevong, appointed Premier as a result of the election, fought successfully for full constitutional rights and the formation of an elected national assembly, but the Norodom princes succeeded in maintaining the power of the king to dissolve the assembly if recommended by his council of ministers. The Norodoms also insisted upon a bicameral national assembly in hopes that the upper house would negate any intentions that a unicameral body might have entertained of controlling the government.[1]

For all these efforts, however, the Democrats still won 54 of 74 seats in the first National Assembly elections in December, 1947. The Democrats achieved this success without the skillful direction of Prince Youtevong, who had died on July 18, 1947.

The death of Youtevong had a profound effect on modern Cambodian history, for the Democratic Party was increasingly influenced by its left wing, which had become a refuge for former disciples of Son Ngoc Thanh. Although he had opposed Sihanouk's Norodom relatives, Youtevong was still a member of the royal elite whom Sihanouk was bound to treat with respect. After Youtevong's death, the delicate balance on which the Democratic Party had depended for acceptance by a broad range of Phnom Penh officials and politicians went awry. Sihanouk's greatest coup was to induce one of the party's more influential members, Yem Sambaur, to accept appointment as Prime Minister in February, 1949, after the collapse of two short-lived Democratic cabinets.

It was clear in all of Sihanouk's machinations that he was eager for any excuse to throttle the Democratic Party, which strongly opposed his tendency to compromise with the French and demanded proclamation of a Cambodian republic. Exercising his constitutional prerogative, Sihanouk dissolved the National Assembly in September, 1949, and then, on November 8, signed what most Democrats regarded as a humiliating treaty with France. The treaty granted Cambodia sovereignty over only its internal affairs, while France remained solely responsible for foreign policy.

Sihanouk's rationale for conciliation was that Cambodia was still dependent on France, both economically and militarily. He argued that Cambodia would only suffer needlessly if it attempted prematurely—and perhaps unsuccessfully—to expel the French. The Democrats, having grown more radical and outspoken after the death of Youtevong, again increased their opposition after the mysterious assassination, on January 14, 1950, of Youtevong's successor, Ieu Koeus. Democratic politicians charged that Sambaur, secretly supported by Sihanouk, had plotted the killing.

Finally, on May 3, 1950, Sambaur resigned, and Sihanouk appointed himself Prime Minister. This desperate political gesture did nothing to ease tensions. In an effort to appease the Democrats, Sihanouk called elections for a new Assembly on September 9, 1951. Again the results demonstrated the popularity of the opposition. This time, the Democrats won 54 of 78 Assembly seats. One curious aspect of the election was the emergence of the Khmer Renovation Party, a monarchical organization founded by Lon Nol, the national police chief, with the support of large landowners. Lon Nol's first plunge into popular politics was not a success, however,. for only 2 of 71 candidates nominated by his party won seats in the assembly. Lon Nol's involvement in the election indicated his interest, as a conservative potential military leader, in Cambodian politics, but it revealed no sign of future disagreement with the young king.

It was in keeping with Sihanouk's entire approach to internal politics that he should again have attempted to placate the Democrats while still hoping to destroy them. Deeply disturbed by Democratic charges that he was not moving rapidly enough toward independence, he imperiously assumed, in June, 1952, what he called the "royal mandate" to achieve that goal. It was clear, however, that he regarded this mandate more as a pretext to enhance his personal power than as a means for leading his country to freedom. Sihanouk realized, belatedly, that his affection for France had diverted him from the mainstream of Cambodian nationalism. Now he wanted both to emerge as the leader responsible for severing all colonial ties with France and to destroy his truly nationalist opponents in the process.

Sihanouk suppressed overt opposition from the Democrats in Phnom Penh by dissolving the National Assembly on January 13, 1953, after having failed to win its endorsement of his assumption of extraconstitutional powers to carry out his mandate. In the initial contest before independence, there was no question as to who had demonstrated the most strength. The incontestable winner was Sihanouk, who had parlayed his Francophile proclivities, his royal influence and contacts, as well as his political expertise, into a position of unassailable power. Cambodia, after all, had won independence without bloodshed. The Viet Minh had agreed, at conferences with Cambodian officials in Geneva, to withdraw all their forces. Sihanouk's political and diplomatic skill had awed both Cambodian politicians and foreign diplomats, who had not believed that he could possibly be successful against French colonialists, on the one hand, and Communist sympathizers, on the other.

Sihanouk's opposition, although submerged, was active. Son Ngoc Thanh, after returning from exile with Sihanouk's blessing on October 30, 1951, fled to the jungles again, on March 9, 1952, in disagreement with the king on his "soft" policies toward the French. Then, in November, 1954, realizing that Sihanouk would never let him lead a legitimate political party, he fled further west to Thailand, where he began to reorganize his rebel followers into a permanent anti-Sihanouk force. In Phnom Penh, most young nationalists tried to adjust to Sihanouk's policies. Yet, beneath a display of unity, division and opposition still festered, almost unknown to foreign observers. The forces that united against Sihanouk in 1970 were born in the internal political struggles of the period before independence. They merely went underground in the heady years after independence, while Sihanouk, the most cunning of all Cambodian politicians, enlarged his own power and prestige.

The Rise of Sihanoukism

The year 1955 was a period of transition for Cambodia and its leader. If it seemed logical that Sihanouk should want to forge a new, independent foreign policy, it was even more inevitable that he move swiftly to consolidate his internal position. On March 2, 1955, Sihanouk played the boldest stroke so far in his political career. He abdicated as king, retaining the title of prince and relinquishing the throne to his father, Norodom Suramarit. The purpose of this gesture was to enable Sihanouk to gain all the political power he thought he needed, as he indicated in a frank conversation with Malcolm MacDonald, then British commissioner-general for Southeast Asia. "The occupant of the throne shouldn't intervene too much in domestic political questions. He should be above politics," Sihanouk explained. "So my power was limited; I felt restricted; and I decided to abdicate so that I could play my full part in helping my countrymen to progress in modern ways."² Sihanouk averred that he would remain apolitical, but in truth he was planning to dominate Cambodian politics so thoroughly that no opposition group could ever seriously challenge him again. The vehicle fashioned by the prince for his rise to power was the Sangkum Reastr Niyum, or People's Socialist Community, a mass organization into which he attempted to incorporate as many political groupings as possible.

"The creation of the Sangkum was not only in response to the necessity of ending the quarrels and rivalries among parties and political groupings," wrote Sihanouk in the French newspaper Le Monde. "It was necessary finally to educate the people politically, socially, and economically and to make them aware of the possibilities and of the job to be done."³ Sihanouk began the task of informing and inspiring his countrymen by postponing the Assembly elections to September 11, 1955, and then employing all the power of the government—the press, radio, and even police harassment—to ensure that the Sangkum win an overwhelming majority at the polls. The final tally showed 83 per cent of the votes for Sangkum candidates, who won all ninety one Assembly seats.

At the same time, in order to popularize his views, Sihanouk introduced the concept of "direct democracy" by creating the National Congress. At twice-yearly meetings of the Congress, attended by Sangkum representatives from throughout the country, Sihanouk made speeches and listened to the opinions and grievances of the people. In 1957, after the Democrats had protested that the organization was usurping the powers of the National Assembly, the prince had the Assembly adopt a constitutional amendment empowering the Congress to approve the country's basic decisions and policies. The Congress in effect was a propaganda forum at which Sihanouk dominated all "debate" and obtained what he inevitably interpreted as nationwide endorsement for his policies.

More than any other Cambodian leader, however, Sihanouk attempted to meet his countrymen, to communicate with them on all levels, to cut through the barriers separating and alienating the poor from the elite and to imbue in them a sense of participation in the country's future. The success of the prince as a grass-roots politician was due not merely to his intellectual recognition of the need for rapport with his people but to the ease and obvious enthusiasm with which he mingled with the masses. He loved to climb out of his car or helicopter on visits to remote towns and villages and chat with the first peasants he saw. Sihanouk's instinct for this type of politicking both contradicted and reflected his upbringing. As one of Phnom Penh's gilded youth, schooled at the exclusive French-run Lycée Chasseloup-Laubat in Saigon, he played the clarinet, rode horses, and charmed women. Although insulated from any direct relations with the average Khmer peasant, he acquired enough social ease and confidence to shine in any gathering, ranging from elite palace receptions to spontaneous rural encounters.

As if his purely political activities were not enough, moreover, Sihanouk also insisted on controlling most of the country's newspapers, magazines, and news bulletins, virtually all of which were published in Phnom Penh. He personally supervised the editing of three government magazines, including two illustrated monthly reviews designed mainly for foreign consumption, and a Cambodian-language satirical journal aimed mainly at Cambodia's hostile neighbors, Thailand and South Vietnam, and their prime benefactor, the United States. As for the rest of the press, some of it government-owned, some of it private, Sihanouk gained the publicity he wanted by distributing news through the official news agency Agence Khmère de Presse. All of his speeches, supported by appropriate reports and editorials, were broadcast over the only radio and television station, also government-owned.

Sihanouk's efforts, whether political, journalistic, theatrical, or artistic, were intended to strengthen his power position, both internally and internationally, by spreading his philosophy and political views. Among his most intriguing endeavors, in the pursuit of this goal, was his attempt to synthesize Cambodian religious and monarchical traditions with modern political yearnings. In almost all his major speeches, Sihanouk alluded to Khmer civilization at Angkor. A representation of Angkor Wat, the most famous of the temples, dominated the national flag, and nearly all modern Cambodian art and literature, particularly the songs and movies written and produced by the prince, recalled the glories of the ancient era, largely forgotten by later Khmer rulers until French missionaries and scholars in the nineteenth century rediscovered the ruins. Sihanouk deliberately promoted his own image as the "god-king," the successor to those monarchs of old.

In keeping with the traditional upbringing of all young Cambodians, Sihanouk had shaved his head in 1947 and lived briefly as a saffron-robed monk in a monastery. Partly as a result of this experience, he was extremely sensitive to both the strength and weakness of Buddhism as practiced by his people. He realized, for instance, that Buddhism not only helped to unify his country but also that it had a retrogressive, nondynamic influence. Anticipating opposition from devout Buddhist monks as well as young intellectuals, Sihanouk devised the scheme of combining Buddhism with a pliable form of socialism, under the aegis of the Sangkum.

"Khmer socialism is inspired directly by our religious principles," explained a communiqué issued jointly by the government and the executive committee of the Sangkum. "It preaches helpfulness toward one another and social action concerned with the moral improvement of everyone. It implies a great respect for the human self and sets as its goal the well-being and moral expansion of the individual."[4] Thus, Buddhism and socialism formed the framework within which Sihanouk could attempt to construct almost any program he might envision.

It was entirely fitting, after the death of his father on April 3, 1960, that he should have still feared the political limitations of the throne. Rather than reassume the title of king, he had the National Assembly, supported by Sangkum-sponsored demonstrations, amend the constitution to enable him to become "chief of state."[5]

In the course of the 1960's, Sihanouk appeared, superficially, to have emerged as a mythological figure in his own time. "Samdech euv, Samdech euv," was the greeting accorded him on his travels outside the capital. "Father-prince" was the meaning of the words, but it was clear that Sihanouk, so far as his people were concerned, was still the king. Sihanouk's appearance at the dedication of a soda-bottling factory in a town near Phnom Penh on November 12, 1967, produced a typical display of wild adulation. Members of a military band broke out of their ranks and surrounded him, awaiting royal pats on their clasped hands. "Vive le Sihanoukisme," was the slogan I saw emblazoned on banners strung up for the ceremony. Sihanoukism was really the only word to describe the personal ideology expounded by the prince since independence.

The glorification of the prince was even more pronounced the next year, at ceremonies I attended marking the fifteenth anniversary of Cambodian independence. "The Khmer Nation Will Never Perish" was the title of the pageant presented on November 9, 1968, before Prince Sihanouk and Princess Monique, government officials and diplomats, thousands of students, and other "patriotic Khmer" in the modern stadium at the National Sports Complex. The pageant, produced and enacted by the Royal Khmer Socialist Youth, epitomized Sihanouk's attempts to identify with bygone grandeur. Actors and floats depicting Cambodia's achievements rolled onto the stadium grass, and then a single beam of light shone on a bust of the prince. "The light of Cambodia stems from the person of Samdech euv," the announcer declaimed. "It illuminates Cambodia and spreads throughout the world through the medium of the Buddhist principles."[6]

The pageant symbolized the final result of the campaign to link the past with the present, to exploit conservative and progressive forces, and to synthesize them into unprecedented loyalty to the prince. In the final analysis, Sihanoukism formed an entirely new state religion. The question remained, however, whether Sihanouk was a serious ideologue and statesman or merely an intellectual faddist, easily captivated by such postcolonial catchwords as "neutralism" and "socialism." Sometimes he gave the impression that he was basically a show-business impresario to whom nothing was more important than keeping his audience forever entranced by the sound of his voice and the wit of his words and deeds.

Several days later, on November 14, 1968, the prince displayed the full range of his personality and views to correspondents and diplomats on a guided tour of Sihanoukville, the port he had built with French assistance on the Gulf of Thailand. "They used to write that there were two Sihanouks," he remarked while quaffing French champagne in a small, gaily decorated pavilion. "They said there was the Sihanouk before independence and the Sihanouk afterward. Since independence I have had to work. I sleep only five hours a night." Sihanouk scolded the correspondents, to whom he normally denied permission to enter the country, for their sometimes pessimistic predictions on Cambodia's future. "Why have we to surrender to the caprices of some journalists who want me to say, 'After the war in Vietnam, we shall die'?"

The prince, for the rest of the day, never ceased to illustrate and dramatize both his views and his personality. After escorting his guests through a newly constructed brewery, an oil refinery built and partly owned by a French company, and an assembly plant for Czechoslovakian trucks, he led the entire party to a new hotel beside the sea. "It is my Hilton," he said, "and I built it myself." He then donned a navy-blue swimming suit and stepped into the tepid, somewhat dirty waters of a swimming pool in front of the hotel. The diplomats, who had been advised to bring along their bathing suits, followed his example. That night, Sihanouk gave another swimming party, this time in the sea off his villa several miles from the hotel. "There is no politics here. Everything is neutral," he told the gathering.

Sihanouk could not resist delivering a eulogy for another Asian leader known for his glittering parties and "neutral" policies. "Ah, Sukarno, Sukarno," said the prince, fondly recalling the good old days with the former Indonesian "President for life," deposed after connivance with Communists in their abortive putsch against his generals in late 1965. The diplomats, ranging from British and Australian to Russian and Chinese, smiled politely as Sihanouk, who himself had had four wives before settling on Monique, rambled on about Sukarno's appetite for women. "That does not mean I am still for Sukarno politically," he said, laughing, but there was a note of pathos, of sadness for a lost brother, in his tone.[7]

Lon Nol and the Battambang Revolt

Sihanouk may have exuded an appearance of complete confidence, but, over the past few years, his political opposition had risen to almost the same level as before independence. The crux of the problem was that Sihanouk was beset politically, just as he was internationally, by opponents on the left as well as on the right. Sihanouk attempted to survive as a centrist who played his opponents against each other by favoring first one faction, or individual, and then another, but, by the end of 1968, he realized that he was running out of options. The first sign of major political problems in the 1960's was the National Assembly election of September 11, 1966.

Refuting charges that his people lacked genuine freedom to vote as they pleased, the prince for the first time since independence refused to endorse any of the candidates and proclaimed the field open to all politicians. So eager was he to prove his lack of influence on the voting that he forebade the 415 candidates from displaying photographs of themselves with him. Although all candidates were *pro forma* members of the Sangkum, rightist and conservative elements captured nearly three fourths of the 82 seats. The prince, still hewing to his pledge of noninterference, then urged the Assembly to form its own government, unfettered by his recommendations. The Assembly's choice for Prime Minister was General Lon Nol, who had been defense minister in every cabinet since 1955.

Lon Nol had a clear-cut majority over three other candidates, including the outgoing Prime Minister, Prince Norodom Kanthol, one of Sihanouk's cousins. Although Lon Nol claimed his policies were the same as Sihanouk's, he already had a reputation as a conservative, independent thinker who disagreed with the prince on the sensitive topic of U.S.-Cambodian relations. Lon Nol would not have conceived of publicly supporting resumption of relations with the United States, but he was said to have reminded Sihanouk of the material benefits his small army had derived through the old U.S. military assistance and advisory group, with which he had maintained close and cordial ties before its departure in 1963.

Lon Nol's cabinet, chosen by assembly vote, included a number of old conservative allies of his—plus at least two former members of the once powerful Democratic Party. (Sihanouk had outlawed all political parties in 1955, when he organized the Sangkum, but, in the limited milieu of Phnom Penh politics, most officials still were identified with their old organizations.) Perhaps the most significant aspect of Lon Nol's efforts to form his government was that all the leftists refused his invitations to nominate candidates for the cabinet. Then the Assembly, having elected a right-wing government, failed to give it a vote of confidence for two days, largely because of left-wing objections.

Sihanouk soon revealed his own lack of confidence by forming a "countergovernment" made up mainly of leftists, some of whom had failed to win re-election to the Assembly. Sihanouk apparently had staged the open elections—and let a right-wing government into power—in order to offset the threat of a powerful left wing, which might ultimately destroy him. Then, fearful of the right, he seized on the notion of a countergovernment, known as "Her Majesty's Opposition" because his mother still held the title of Queen. The countergovernment, through its own daily news bulletin, began to criticize the Lon Nol cabinet for everything from corruption to inefficiency. Claiming that he could not function against such strident opposition, Lon Nol, on November 6, 1966, offered to resign.

Sihanouk was now so confident of his power that he rejected Lon Nol's resignation and departed in January, 1967, for a two-month medical cure in France. In the meantime the leftists, purportedly supported by the Chinese Embassy, plotted to undermine Lon Nol's government. On March 11, 1967, two days after Sihanouk's return from France, a leftist mob demonstrated outside the offices of the countergovernment bulletin. It did not seem coincidental that the date was also the third anniversary of the first anti-American riots in Phnom Penh. The leftists, anxious to show Sihanouk how much strength they had gained in his absence, demanded the resignation of the Lon Nol cabinet and dissolution of the National Assembly. Against the backdrop of political turmoil in Phnom Penh, Sihanouk also had to cope with open, leftist-supported revolt in the rice-rich western province of Battambang.

The Battambang revolt was in effect a prelude, in a microcosm, of the conflict that would sweep across the country three years later. The implications and issues inherent in the rebellion and the government response encompassed the entire spectrum of Cambodian political, economic, and military problems. Lon Nol, as might have been expected, assumed a firmly conservative, anti-Communist position, urging Sihanouk to authorize the full use of military force to smash the Khmer Rouge rebels, who exploited landlords' attempts to evict small farmers accused of squatting on large estates. Sihanouk, confronted with Lon Nol's recommendations and leftist demonstrations, entirely supported the army's campaign in Battambang. Hundreds of landless peasants were killed, scores of villages burned, and martial law was imposed in the province, before the rebels, estimated at several thousand, retreated to the forests in mid-April, 1967.

Why did Sihanouk, despite his leftist foreign policy, rely so heavily upon Lon Nol's advice and leadership? One obvious answer was that Lon Nol seemed to represent the same forces of "law and order" on which Sihanouk and his predecessors in the royal family had always relied for internal security. Ten years older than Sihanouk, Lon Nol was bred in the same elite French colonial tradition as the prince. He had attended the Lycée Chasseloup-Laubat, as had Sihanouk and many other top members of the Cambodian ruling class, and he had patiently risen through the ranks of the French bureaucracy. Lon Nol's first government position had been that of magistrate at Siemreap, where he had begun his career in 1936. His first military post had been as director of national police, to which he had been appointed after the signing of the controversial 1949 treaty, in which France had yielded a large measure of internal security to Cambodia.

Lon Nol's background was so conservative and traditional that Sihanouk, like the French, was convinced that he could trust him. Polite, quiet, soft-spoken, and unassuming, the general appeared the exact opposite of the flamboyant prince. Yet he had still established his nationalist credentials by dipping, however briefly, into electoral politics in early 1951. Then, undaunted by a total lack of military training, Lon Nol had begun his military career in 1952 as commander of the Battambang subsector. He had distinguished himself in that post by his campaign against both Son Ngoc Thanh's rebels and the Viet Minh. In 1955, after having undergone his only formal military education at the French-advised Royal Khmer Military Academy, he had accepted the appointment as defense minister in Sihanouk's first cabinet.

Accustomed though Sihanouk had grown to Lon Nol's leadership of the armed forces, the prince remained at odds with him for his notable lack of enthusiasm for the Vietnamese Communists and his occasional hints that he would prefer American to Chinese aid. Sihanouk's distaste for Lon Nol's views on foreign policy—and possibly his suspicion that the general might eventually challenge him for power—helped account for the prince's ambiguous course during the Battambang revolt. Basically, Sihanouk attempted to discredit both rightists and leftists in order to preserve his own position. After demanding pledges of fealty to him from all ministers, senior officials, and assemblymen, he accepted the resignation, on March 30, 1967, of one of his severest critics, the secretary of state for plans, Douc Rasy, who was to re-emerge during the campaign to oust Sihanouk nearly three years later.

Then, turning his fire away from Lon Nol, Sihanouk began to blame the leading leftists for their alleged roles in the Battambang revolt. He claimed on April 7, 1967, for instance, that Khmer Rouge prisoners had admitted having received instructions from their superiors in Phnom Penh. Among those named by Sihanouk were five former cabinet members, including Chau Seng, the brightest of the young leftists; Khieu Samphan; Hou Yuon; Hu Nim; and So Nem, head of the Khmer-Chinese Friendship Association. All five, said Sihanouk, would appear before a military tribunal. Having thus attempted to subdue the left, Sihanouk on April 29, 1967, reversed himself again by accepting, on the grounds of "ill health," the resignation of Lon Nol, injured in an automobile accident on March 5 while driving to Battambang. Lon Nol then went to France for medical treatment.

It was typical of Sihanouk's style of splitting political forces that he then favored two of the five, Chau Seng and So Nem, plus three other members of the former "countergovernment," with positions on a new cabinet formed on May 2, 1967. At the same time, he carefully diluted this seeming triumph for the left by ordering the secret executions of Hou Yuon, Khieu Samphan, and Hu Nim, who were reported at the time to have vanished while fleeing to Battambang, allegedly to join the rebels in the field. It was apparently because they still were dissatisfied with Sihanouk's ambivalent strategy that Chau Seng and So Nem made the grave error, as explained in Chapter 3, of publicizing a telegram from China intended as a challenge to Sihanouk's authority. The prince might have had to bow completely to the left had he not been certain that he could still rely on the right. After having dismissed Chau Seng and So Nem, Sihanouk advised Lon Nol that it might be timely for him to return from France. In October, 1967, scarcely a month after the purge of the leftist ministers, Lon Nol quietly reappeared, fully recovered and ready to resume his own bid for power.

Lon Nol's reappearance did not mean that Sihanouk was prepared to restore him immediately to any of his former positions. Rather, Lon Nol was held temporarily in reserve to threaten some of Sihanouk's opponents. Finally, on January 30, 1968, Sihanouk appointed him inspector general of the armed forces with the prerogatives of a minister of state. On May 1, Lon Nol resumed his familiar post of minister of defense. On July 12, 1968, he was appointed Deputy Prime Minister, and, on December 5, he became acting Prime Minister. Lon Nol's rapid renaissance as Cambodia's most powerful leader—after Sihanouk—constituted *prima facie* evidence of Sihanouk's recognition of the dangers posed by leftist rebels and politicians. Sihanouk may still have thought that he could reach a sound understanding with the Communist powers, notably China and North Vietnam, but he needed Lon Nol's conservative anti-Communist military approach for defense against local leftist opposition.

Nor did Lon Nol's re-emergence reflect merely Sihanouk's desire to counterbalance the threat posed by leftist guerrillas and politicians. The Battambang revolt and its political aftermath had dramatized some of the country's economic problems. Lon Nol and other conservatives in Phnom Penh, while reacting swiftly against the Khmer Rouge, tended in retrospect to blame the revolt more on a combination of heavy taxation, poor administration, and corruption than on Communist political influence. Peasants were reluctant to grow rice, by far the greatest source of foreign exchange, for more than local use when they were taxed as much as 40 per cent on all that they sold and also required to pay exorbitant rents to wealthy landowners. Middleman Chinese merchants were equally reluctant to sell rice to the government company responsible for exporting it when they were paid a fixed price regardless of its value on the world market.

The problem of lack of production incentives was reflected in the gross national product. Although precise figures were not available, Western diplomatic analysts in Phnom Penh estimated that the GNP had risen only 10 per cent, from approximately $600 million to $660 million a year, from 1960 through 1969, while the population had increased from roughly 6 to 7 million. For all Sihanouk's claims of economic "progress," the fact was that new industries, ranging from textile mills to cement plants, were of secondary importance compared to rice and rubber, the second largest export product. Cambodia grew enough rice—an average of more than 2 million tons a year*—to obviate any danger of starvation. The question, however, was whether or not the production system would degenerate into an "economy of survival" in which peasant farmers planted only enough for their immediate needs. Since Cambodia derived between 70 and 90 per cent of its foreign exchange from rice and rubber, this question assumed critical proportions. The country, after all, relied upon hard currency for importing virtually all essential raw materials, notably iron and petroleum.

Cambodia's economic predicament was graphically outlined in the official government records of exports and imports since 1963, the year Sihanouk renounced U.S. aid, replaced private import-export firms with government trading societies riddled with corruption and inefficiency, and nationalized banks and major industries. Exports for 1964 were 3,063,209,000 riels, or $55,694,709, comfortably balanced against imports of 2,863,071,000 riels, or $52,055,836. The export figure climbed to a high of 3,690,014,000 riels, or $67,091,182, for 1965 and then plunged steadily until hitting the low of the decade, 2,729,000,000 riels, or $49,618,182, for 1969. It was significant—or at least symbolic—that exports began their decline in 1966, the year before the Battambang revolt. Beginning

* All tons cited are metric (equivalent to 2,200 lbs.).

that year, the trade balance became increasingly unfavorable. Imports for 1969 totaled a record 4,233,000,000 riels, or $76,909,091—more than $27 million above exports—the worst such disparity in Cambodian history.[8]

The primary factor in the decline of foreign exchange earnings was the sharp fall in the export of rice beginning in 1966. Again, the official statistics, while obviously subject to error, illustrate the point. Rice exports totaled 544,748 tons in 1964, 563,770 tons in 1965—and then slipped precipitously to 199,049 tons in 1966. In percentage terms, rice accounted for 59.4 per cent of the country's hard currency earnings in 1964, 60.3 per cent in 1965 and 37.77 per cent in 1966. Rice exports rose slightly, to 222,876 tons in 1967 and 251,782 tons in 1968, but then, for 1969, descended to 102,767 tons, the lowest total since World War II. Rice exports in 1969 accounted for only 24.41 per cent of the country's foreign exchange earnings, also a low since World War II.[9]

Rubber also presented a problem—but of a somewhat different nature than that of rice. First, the price of rubber on the world market fell almost every year from 1960 until 1969. Second, the government reimbursed planters for exports not in foreign exchange but in Cambodian currency at only half its actual dollar value. Plantation owners, most of them Frenchmen, did not decrease their output, but, by similar token, they lacked the financial motivation to expand as much as they might have during this period. In terms of actual tonnage, rubber exports increased from 42,318 in 1964 to a high of 50,781 in 1966 and then declined gradually to 47,485 in 1969. Indicative of the fluctation in the price of rubber on the world market was that it netted Cambodia 879,770,000 riels—$15,994,181—in 1966 as opposed to 671,167,000 riels, or $12,203,036, in 1968 and 1,034,139,000 riels, or $18,802,527, in 1969. Rubber exports, which generally accounted for between one fourth and one third of Cambodia's hard currency earnings, soared in 1969 to 46.9 per cent—nearly twice the amount derived from that year's record low sale of rice.[10]

Cambodia's burgeoning economic crisis was related to the Vietnam conflict in that Chinese merchants had smuggled at least 100,000 tons of rice a year to Vietnamese Communist troops in border base areas since 1966. The effect was to rob the government of both tax money and profits from legitimate international trade. The Vietnamese Communists carefully encouraged Chinese middlemen to ship them rice by offering payment in American dollars at the world price, not at a fixed rate below international standards.

Sihanouk, influenced by his desire for friendly relations with North Vietnam and China and pressured by leftist politicians in Phnom Penh, did little to curb this illicit trade. At stake were both his domestic policy of limited socialism and nationalization as well as his foreign policy built on close ties with his Communist neighbors.

Despite his commitment to these policies, Sihanouk, after Lon Nol's return, was not entirely oblivious to the recommendations of his conservative critics. The conservative element seemed to have triumphed when the National Assembly, on August 24, 1968, adopted a resolution permitting arrest and detention on mere suspicion. The purpose of the resolution, according to political observers in Phnom Penh, was to control the rice trade to the Viet Cong and suppress internal leftist opposition. By the end of the year, Sihanouk in effect accepted some of Lon Nol's recommendations in a major speech in which he said that Cambodia would not "cooperate with any country in particular but with all countries." Cambodia, he said, now welcomed private foreign investment. "Negotiations are taking place with Hong Kong, Singapore, the United States, and even with some socialist countries," he went on. "If they are interested in such cooperation, we will feel very honored, very pleased." Cambodia, as Sihanouk put it, was back on the "international circuit" with a "new political look" that distinctly favored the right wing.[11]

Move to the Right

There was no evidence, as 1969 began, of a serious rift between Sihanouk and Lon Nol. Indeed, relations between the chief of state and his acting Prime Minister steadily improved. Indicative of their rapport was that Sihanouk entrusted the general with the delicate task of meeting Huynh Tan Phat, President of the Viet Cong's newly formed Provisional Revolutionary Government, who arrived in Phnom Penh on June 30, 1969, on a state visit. Lon Nol was personally responsible for addressing Cambodia's first official request to the Vietnamese Communists, as represented by President Phat, to respect Cambodian sovereignty and withdraw their forces. The prince appeared even more prone to cooperate with Lon Nol when he appointed him, on August 12, 1969, Prime Minister of a new Government of Salvation, so named in recognition of its mandate to save the country from economic disaster.

At Lon Nol's insistence, Sihanouk acquiesced in the return to power of the conservative Prince Sisowath Sirik Matak, one of his cousins and a leading member of the Sisowath family, traditional rivals of the Norodoms. Sirik Matak's assignment as Deputy Prime Minister in the new government indicated Sihanouk's desperate realization of the need for economic change. Sihanouk, after having appointed Sirik Matak to key positions in some of his early post-independence cabinets, had exiled him to diplomatic posts, including those of ambassador to Peking from late 1962 to late 1963 and ambassador to the Philippines in 1968.

At first, Sihanouk appeared fully prepared to accept Lon Nol's recommendations for revamping the economy. The prince, in August, 1969, revealed that the government was operating at a deficit of $20 million and was losing revenue at the rate of $4 million a year.[12] Even more disconcerting was the fact that Cambodia was actually importing a relatively small amount of rice—approximately 6,000 tons—from China in 1969, while Chinese merchants in Cambodia were selling many times that amount to the Vietnamese Communists. Sihanouk readily agreed to certain reforms. First, the government, on August 18, 1969, devalued the Cambodian riel from the artificial official ratio of 35 riels to $1 to the actual rate of 55 to 1. Then, on September 25, 1969, Sihanouk concluded a trade agreement with the Viet Cong's Provisional Revolutionary Government, under which Cambodia would sell rice legally to the Vietnamese Communists—and earn money lost to the government by smuggling.

Further evidence of cooperation and coordination among Sihanouk and his ministers was his choice of Lon Nol as Cambodia's representative at ceremonies in Peking on October 1, 1969, marking the twentieth anniversary of the victory of the Chinese Communists. Lon Nol met with both the Chinese Premier, Chou En-lai, and the President of the National Liberation Front, Nguyen Huu Tho, to discuss the possibility of evacuation of Vietnamese Communist troops from Cambodia. Sihanouk himself had already met with Communist leaders, including North Vietnamese Premier Pham Van Dong, when he visited Hanoi from September 8 through September 10 to attend the funeral of the North Vietnamese President and national hero, Ho Chi Minh, who had died on September 3. The fact that the prince and the general were still cooperating so closely in the autumn of 1969 in their policy regarding the Vietnamese Communists lends credence to the view that internal economic problems were primarily responsible for the debacle that followed.

"The nationalization of certain commercial and industrial enterprises should have resulted in handsome returns for the national budget," began an editorial published in August, 1969, by the *Bulletin du Contre-Gouvernement*, still published as a tool of the Sangkum. "As a matter of fact," the editorial went on, "when these activities were carried out by private individuals, the latter realized enormous profits; they were accumulating an astonishing amount of wealth."[13] This editorial precisely reflected the views of the cabinet, and notably of Sirik Matak, who had recommended the reversion to the private sector of at least sixty companies owned by the government.

As a result of his policy of cooperation with Lon Nol, Sihanouk was initially prepared to approve the denationalization program, at least to a limited extent. He was soon dissuaded, however, by the arguments of a limited inner circle allied closely with all the major companies as well as with the Chinese and Vietnamese Communists. At the center of this circle was Sihanouk's half-Italian, half-Cambodian wife, Monique, whom Sihanouk had met while she was a lycée student in Phnom Penh in 1951 and had married the same year. Customs officials, directors of government companies, and so forth channeled funds to Monique under the guise of "contributions" to the Cambodian Red Cross, which she served as president. Monique also wielded her influence with her husband to sell middle-level government positions for fees purportedly as high as $18,000. And she was rumored to have accepted enormous gifts from the Vietnamese and Chinese Communists so that Sihanouk would not act decisively, if at all, against Chinese merchants responsible for the bulk of the illicit rice trade. The skill of the Communists in singling out influential personages in Phnom Penh for bribery was a key factor in the economic confrontation.

Alone, Monique could hardly have exercised great power. She was surrounded, however, by conniving relatives and in-laws who were eager to use their entree into the palace to enlarge their foreign bank accounts, just as Monique was doing. Besides Monique's scheming mother, Mme. Pomme Cheng, there were her half-brother, Colonel Oum Manorine, whom Sihanouk had appointed as secretary of state for surface defense, and her brother-in-law, Khek Vandy, the president and managing director of the Magasin d'État, which marketed imports, including luxury items. Colonel Oum Manorine's position put him in control of the national police, who in turn cooperated with the Chinese merchants and Vietnamese Communists on rice-smuggling. Oum Manorine and Colonel Sosthène Fernandez, secretary of state for national security, also controlled the shipment, through southern Cambodian ports, of arms and ammunition for the Vietnamese Communists. Both of these officers operated independently of Lon Nol, who was familiar with their activities but could do little about them. The new government was equally powerless to suppress Khek Vandy, who was probably the most brazenly corrupt member of the coterie of manipulators in Monique's entourage.

As head of the Magasin d'État, Khek Vandy could ask the state-owned National Export-Import Society, SONEXIM, to import whatever he wanted for private purposes or for resale at inflated rates from which he reaped enormous personal profits. The import items distributed by the Magasin d'État ranged from milk and cheese to textiles to perfume—just the sort of products for which wealthy businessmen and their wives were willing to pay handsome prices. Khek Vandy's activities, moreover, extended far beyond the confines of the Magasin d'État. He controlled the government's new luxury hotel at the port city of Sihanoukville, a royal golf course near Phnom Penh, a government-owned dance hall and a government travel agency. His most colorful—and controversial—enterprise was the state gambling casino in Phnom Penh, opened in February, 1969, in the former Club Nautique, on the Tonle Sap where it flows into the Mekong. The casino theoretically enabled the state treasury to earn money formerly pocketed by illegal Chinese gambling dens, but most of the profits were inevitably diverted. As manager, Khek Vandy retained the lion's share of the earnings, which Cambodian Government sources in Phnom Penh have estimated at the equivalent of $75,000 a day.

"In our system of state socialism, Sihanouk appointed men from his own family," summarized one of his critics, Prom Thos, secretary of state for commerce in the Government of Salvation, in an interview on April 2, 1970, two weeks after Sihanouk's fall. "The government monopolies were monopolies for men close to Sihanouk." Many analysts wondered why Sihanouk permitted himself to come so much under the influence of his wife, in-laws, and relatives. One answer may be that Sihanouk, while pursuing his grandiose aims of state socialism and neutrality in foreign affairs, was blinded to the extent of their corruption. Or perhaps Sihanouk, spoiled by so many years in power, succumbed easily to their flattery, their promises of support against his foes—even, possibly, to the prospect of enlarging his own foreign bank accounts from their earnings.

Whatever may be the precise answer to these questions, the

prince in late 1969 began to shift his policy of cooperation with the Lon Nol government and to resist Sirik Matak's suggestions for economic reforms. On October 6, 1969, addressing a group of Cambodian students returning from abroad, Sihanouk claimed that Sirik Matak was plotting to "strip the power of the palace."[14] On October 30, Lon Nol quietly slipped out of the country to go to France, purportedly for further treatment of the same injuries suffered in his 1967 automobile accident. Two days later, Sihanouk accused Sirik Matak, acting Prime Minister in Lon Nol's absence, of attempting to extend his personal power from domestic to foreign affairs.

Then, while Lon Nol was still in France, Sihanouk convened what turned out to be a pivotal three-day session of the National Congress from December 27 through 29. After berating conservatives who had been closely allied with the Government of Salvation, the prince urged a go-slow policy on denationalization. He did not openly oppose Sirik Matak's proposals, but he railed against "untimely decisions that might do Cambodia more harm than good." Sihanouk was particularly upset about the possibility of foreign—U.S.—banks opening up branches in Phnom Penh. "Cambodia should not put its confidence in foreigners when it comes to serving Khmer national interests," said the prince, playing upon the old anti-American theme. The finance minister, Op Kim Ang, promptly refuted this argument by noting that "banks with foreign investments" would "help Cambodia to acquire more funds for its national construction projects and protect its interests in commercial operations as well."[15]

This byplay might have appeared relatively uninteresting, but it lay at the heart of the entire issue of whether or not to reverse the pattern of state socialism that formed the keystone of Sihanouk's internal policies—and was related to his foreign policy of building ties with socialist countries. Sihanouk, confronted with the destruction of his ideology, if not his career, attempted during the Congress to break up the cabinet by accepting the resignations of four ministers who were still allied with him. Among them was Ung Hong Sath, the leader of the 1966 countergovernment. Ung Hong Sath, appointed second deputy prime minister in the Government of Salvation, had led Sirik Matak's opposition within the cabinet. His resignation suggested that he might form a new countergovernment, which would then replace the Lon Nol cabinet, as had happened in 1967. It seemed particularly appropriate that Lon Nol was still in France during the Congress debate. The impression was that Lon Nol did not really support Sirik Matak and would, as usual, bow to the will of the prince.

On December 28, 1969, Sihanouk was compelled, in what he had anticipated as a final dramatic vindication of his policies, to ask the National Assembly, whose members had attended all sessions of the much larger National Congress, to submit the names of those deputies who favored and those who opposed his policies. "Sihanouk did not reveal the contents of the lists but announced that all deputies who supported him attended today's National Congress session," said Phnom Penh Radio on December 29. "The prince also disclosed that the Royal Government had given him a list naming the cabinet members faithful to him but did not reveal its contents." The ploy of requesting secret lists illustrated Sihanouk's method of dominating the assembly and the cabinet by playing factions against each other. The difficulty, however, was that an overwhelming majority of assemblymen and ministers favored Sirik Matak's economic program more than the prince's policies. Possessed of the lists, Sihanouk must have known that his popularity had declined to a low ebb.

Few understood at the time, however, that Sihanouk had suffered a crucial defeat in what amounted to a vote of confidence that he himself had invited. Sihanouk, who had threatened, rhetorically, to resign during one of the Congress sessions, now decided that he should go to France for treatment of what he described as "obesity, blood disease, and albuminuria." During his trip, he could talk over the situation with Lon Nol, while Sirik Matak struggled with reforms that Sihanouk was still convinced would founder on obstacles raised by his allies both in and out of the government. In the meantime, Sihanouk could ride out the storm—and return just at the proper moment to capitalize on what he anticipated would be a combination of Sirik Matak's weakness and his own popularity. On January 6, 1970, Sihanouk departed Phnom Penh for the last time. Sirik Matak almost immediately began to put some of his hitherto frustrated schemes into action. First, the government, on January 31, closed down the state casino, which had exploited its customers at very little profit to the state. Then he initiated legislation, adopted by the National Assembly on February 12, 1970, to permit private, rather than government, organizations to import and export limited quantities of secondary products.

Such steps toward reform posed little danger in themselves to Sihanouk or to the Vietnamese Communists. They obviously inconvenienced some members of Sihanouk's following, such as Khek Vandy, who could no longer siphon off the earnings from the casino and some of the export-import firms, but they did not alter the basic pattern of the Cambodian economy. SONEXIM still retained an exclusive state monopoly over the export of rice and rubber, by far the largest sources of foreign exchange, as well as maize and semiprecious stones, which ranked next in earnings. Similarly, SONEXIM retained control over a wide range of imports, including alcoholic beverages, air-conditioners and refrigerators, cloth of most types, fertilizers and insecticides, medicines and pharmaceutical products, motors and generators, tractors, raw material for industry and construction—in short, almost everything that any importer was likely to want. The law did provide that importers could purchase some of these goods directly if the national bank did not have the necessary foreign exchange, but, for practical purposes, the long-awaited "liberalization" of the economy had little, if any, effect.

The government still hoped gradually to return most foreign trade to the private sector. Once the basic "liberalization" law was in effect, government officials anticipated that they could then add certain key products to the limited lists of those that the law provided might be imported or exported by private companies. Eventually, it was believed, even rice and rubber might be removed from SONEXIM control. Officials also envisioned improving or selling national industries that continued to operate at financial losses. Before the government could begin to realize any of these ideas, however, events conspired, by a combination of chance and design, to plunge Cambodia into the deep crisis that Sihanouk had anticipated, but that few observers had believed would ever happen.

The trigger for collapse of the structure of power that Sihanouk had carefully erected since his coronation in 1941 was a single state decision that capsulized the whole spectrum of economic, political, and ideological issues over which the elite of Phnom Penh had been wrangling, usually in complete secrecy, for the past five years. The decision, announced on February 24, 1970, was the exchange of new 500-riel banknotes for all the old 500-riel notes, valued at 40 billion riels. The government provided for the needs of most of its citizens by giving them until March 7 to turn in their notes, worth $9.09 at the official rate. There was, however, a very carefully planned proviso in the announcement: In order to change more than 10,000 riels in old 500-riel notes—$182 worth—it would be necessary for an individual or organization to place the excess in a government-controlled account. The money could then not be withdrawn until government officials had checked to discover the real source of the notes and to determine whether or not they were forgeries.

This proviso was a deliberate effort to deprive the Vietnamese Communists of large sums, possibly the equivalent of $70 million, in both real and counterfeit 500-riel notes that they had accumulated for purchasing their rice and shipping war materiel, rice, and other necessities to their sanctuaries near the South Vietnamese frontier. It was highly significant that the government did not announce this drastic economic, military, and political move until six days after Lon Nol had returned from his medical leave in France. The inference was that Lon Nol had fully discussed the proposal with Sihanouk, whom he had seen at the French town of Grasse, and that the plan had the chief of state's tacit, if reluctant, approval. Further evidence of Sihanouk's endorsement was that he had also conferred in France with Touch Kim, the governor of the national bank and an old reliable ally, who apparently had gone to France solely to discuss the move. The idea for undercutting the finances of the Vietnamese Communists had probably been under consideration for more than a year.

The reason for the government's previous reluctance to put the scheme into effect was that Lon Nol and Sirik Matak had not been able to convince Sihanouk that the move was unavoidable. At the same time, Sihanouk feared its possible consequences on the attitude of the Vietnamese Communists, who might, in desperation, turn against Cambodian authorities in their quest for supplies and transport. Lon Nol and Sirik Matak believed that it was imperative, for the sake of national integrity, if not independence itself, to challenge the Vietnamese Communists in precisely this manner. The damage the changeover of 500-riel notes did to the Communists was soon apparent from reports from the border regions. North Vietnamese and Viet Cong cadres forced peasants, in many cases, to accept the old notes, which they said would soon be valid again after Sihanouk's return. For all these problems, however, the Vietnamese Communists still were not disposed to go to war with Cambodia.

As a result of their conversations in France, Sihanouk and Lon Nol decided upon a double-edged policy of intimidation and flattery to assure the Vietnamese Communists that Cambodia did not plan to try to expel them or ally with the Saigon government. Lon Nol was to orchestrate the intimidation, beginning with the recall of the old banknotes, while Sihanouk placed himself in charge of the flattery. Just how enthusiastic the prince was about intimidating the Vietnamese Communists is not known, but one can safely assume that he felt he had no choice but to cooperate. Sihanouk may have hoped that he could soon find a pretext for replacing Lon Nol and Sirik Matak with left-wingers or faithful yes-men, just as he had done after returning from his last "cure" in France in 1967. At any rate, the government signaled the timing of its program by asking foreign embassies, on February 20, 1970, two days after Lon Nol's return from France, to permit inspection, until March 8, of diplomatic pouches, sacrosanct and inviolate by all standards of international law and practice.

This period neatly encompassed the time span for changing the 500-riel notes. The purpose was to prevent the Vietnamese Communists from disposing of their old counterfeit notes by diplomatic pouch or from importing new quantities of $100 bills from Chinese Communist banks in Hong Kong in order to buy new 500-riel notes. Then, on March 8, the last day for inspection of the pouches, Cambodian mobs demonstrated against local Vietnamese residents in five towns in Svay Rieng Province, including the provincial capital of Svay Rieng. The demonstrations were a direct threat against some of the main Communist sanctuaries, only twenty or thirty miles away in the "Parrot's Beak," the part of the province that juts into South Vietnam. In Paris, Sihanouk lived up to his side of the bargain with Lon Nol by announcing that the North Vietnamese Prime Minister, Pham Van Dong, would visit Cambodia in May. Sihanouk also hypocritically thanked Peking for having persuaded the North Vietnamese and Viet Cong to withdraw most of their forces from his country.

So far, both Sihanouk and his government had ably played out their roles. Officials believed that the combination of flattery and intimidation might yet hold the Vietnamese in check. Essentially, both Lon Nol and Sihanouk wanted to persuade the Communists to pull out of Cambodia at the end of the Vietnam war. Neither of them had any desire to plunge Cambodia into its own full-fledged war with the North Vietnamese. By this time, however, economic, military, and political pressures, heightened by the currency changeover, were conspiring to upset all the delicate plans laid by Sihanouk and Lon Nol for holding the country together. The record of cooperation between the chief of state and the Prime Minister was shattered, forever, on March 11, 1970, the sixth anniversary of riots against the American and British embas-

sies and information centers and the third anniversary of leftist
demonstrations against the first Lon Nol government. On that day,
some 10,000 students, Buddhist monks, and soldiers in civilian
clothes, many of them carrying pro-Sihanouk as well as anti-Communist banners and placards, sacked both the North Vietnamese
and Viet Cong embassies.

The demonstrations could not possibly have been held without
government support. Hours after the riots, the cabinet issued a
statement terming them "worthy of praise." The question remained, however, as to whether the government's top leaders had
really wanted them to go as far as they did—or whether extreme
rightists had been responsible for the looting and burning of the
embassy buildings. A corollary question was whether or not Sihanouk had initially favored these demonstrations as part of his
agreement with Lon Nol. It could well have been that he was
ready to go along with peaceful expressions of "popular" sentiment
but was completely opposed to violence. Sihanouk's views were
not entirely clarified by a cable he immediately sent to his mother,
Queen Kossamak, in which he blamed the riots on "persons seeking to destroy irrevocably Cambodia's friendship with the socialist
camp and deliver our country into the hands of an imperialist,
capitalist power."[16]

Sihanouk may have decided that the riots provided just the excuse he had wanted to drive Lon Nol from office and resume
tighter control over wildly careening affairs of state. Certainly he
implied as much in the same cable, in which he said he wished "to
return to the country to speak to the nation and the army and ask
them to make a choice." The implication was that Sihanouk would
stage a popular referendum, which he would be sure to win by an
overwhelming margin, particularly since he was the only Phnom
Penh figure who was widely known among the Cambodian peasantry. Sihanouk, however, had misjudged the forces at work in the
capital. His "oasis of peace" was rapidly running dry. In the next
seven days, a sequence of events, which neither he nor Lon Nol
had conceived, would totally upset the delicate equilibrium on
which Cambodia had hitherto relied for survival.

Seven Days

In the flow of events in Phnom Penh from March 11, 1970, to
March 18, it is safe to assume that almost none of Cambodia's
leaders realized that the country was plunging into war. The climactic struggle for power, unanticipated though it may have been,

still seemed confined to the elite of Phnom Penh, who were not even aware that Sihanouk's position as chief of state was in grave jeopardy. The events of that week were so bizarre—yet subtle and largely unpublicized—that they will probably never be fully known or understood. One reason for the confusion perhaps was the enigmatic nature of Lon Nol, who may have had no deliberate plan for overthrowing the prince. Another major factor was that Sihanouk, for all his previous threats to resign if the "people" no longer wanted him, appeared to have grown overly confident of his ability to manipulate the factions swirling around him in Phnom Penh. He was alarmed by the threat, to be sure, but he was convinced to the last that, one way or another, he would survive.

The prince might have survived, too, had it not been for the strong influence of Sirik Matak, who directly challenged Sihanouk's power, as Lon Nol was unwilling to do, by persuading Lon Nol to draft a letter warning Sihanouk of the seriousness of the situation vis-à-vis the Vietnamese Communists. "We must strengthen our national forces in order to cope with any eventuality," said the letter, transmitted to Sihanouk in Paris on the night of Thursday, March 12, 1970, the day after the riots. "It is absolutely necessary and urgent that we increase our armed forces to about 100,000 units to guard efficaciously our eastern borders. This will oblige our friends [the Vietnamese Communists] to carry out their obligations and behave correctly and sincerely as regards our friendship and not to trample on our policy of reciprocity." The letter, which Sirik Matak, not Lon Nol, made public at a press conference several hours after it was sent, asked Sihanouk to endorse a resolution adopted by the National Assembly demanding urgent measures to defend Cambodia's territory and policy of neutrality.[17]

Lon Nol, as a conservative general, still favored strong measures against the Vietnamese Communists, as was evidenced by the curt one-sentence apology he sent to the North Vietnamese and the Viet Cong for the attacks on their embassies. The same "apology" defended the demonstrations as "an expression of the real sentiments of the Cambodian people exasperated by the persistence of violations, encroachments, and occupation of Cambodian territory."[18] As if this statement were not enough, the government coolly ordered all the Vietnamese Communist troops to leave Cambodia by Sunday, March 15, 1970. Even if they had wanted to oblige the Cambodian Government, it would have been a physical impossibility for the Communist troops, totaling approximately 40,000, to have left so quickly. Indeed, such a retreat, without benefit of transport planes and other modern equipment, might have required months.

In this context, however, Cambodia's demand was meant more as a show of force against Sihanouk than as a serious effort to rid the country of the Communists. Just as Sihanouk was convinced that he could upstage Lon Nol and Sirik Matak by a dramatic, well-timed return, so conservatives, notably Sirik Matak, believed that it was now imperative to put Sihanouk completely on the defensive and compel him to accept their policies on both internal and foreign affairs. Another strong figure in this period was Yem Sambaur, who had served Sihanouk as Prime Minister before independence but then had been relegated to utter obscurity as director of the national library after opposing Sihanouk's decision to ban all political parties and form the Sangkum in 1955. Yem Sambaur, appointed minister of justice in the Government of Salvation, had been elevated to the post of second deputy prime minister in February, 1970. He emerged in the crucial week of March 11 through March 18 as a stubborn anti-Communist negotiator anxious to force the North Vienamese and Viet Cong to respect Cambodia's sovereignty.

It was Yem Sambaur who suggested to the North Vietnamese and Viet Cong embassies that they enter into negotiations on the entire question of Vietnamese Communist activities in Cambodia. The chargés d'affaires of both embassies consented to participate in only one meeting, on March 16, 1970, at which they avoided the military issue and demanded instead full compensation for the damage done their embassies. Yem Sambaur, who was soon to replace Sihanouk's cousin, Norodom Phurissara, as foreign minister, was, as might have been expected, unsuccessful in persuading the Vietnamese Communists to enter into further talks. One reason, perhaps, was that government agents among the demonstrators had stolen millions of dollars in U.S. currency from the embassy buildings, where the money had been stored for conversion into Cambodian riels. This issue was never publicized, but it may have been at the heart of the North Vietnamese and Viet Cong demands for "full compensation." Sihanouk, had he been in Cambodia, might have considered a compromise. Yem Sambaur refused to bargain.*

The government did indeed succeed in its goal of putting Sihanouk on the defensive. The prince, once challenged, reacted by

---

* The currency was found among embassy records and thrown into bonfires before officials recognized what it was. Partially burned $100 bills turned up on the black market in Phnom Penh, at reduced rates, for weeks.

adopting an increasingly hostile, stubborn attitude toward his critics, whom he had accepted as allies only as a matter of political and economic expediency in the past year or so. Sihanouk reflected his obstinacy, his uncustomary lack of realism in the face of harsh reality, by refusing to heed the advice of friends in Paris to hurry back to Cambodia. Instead, he thought he could discredit the cabinet by castigating it in press conferences while maintaining his original return schedule, including stops in Moscow and Peking. "Certain officers of our army and numerous members of parliament and also members of the government desire to be their [the Americans'] allies to obtain dollars for themselves," said the prince on Friday, March 13, 1970, before boarding a special flight from Paris to Moscow. "They are more patriots of the dollar than patriots of Cambodia."[19]

After arriving in Moscow, Sihanouk refused Lon Nol's suggestion, relayed through the Cambodian Embassy, that he receive both his cousin, Norodom Kanthol, head of the palace staff and onetime Prime Minister, and Yem Sambaur, who together would explain to him the situation in Cambodia. "He even announced," Yem Sambaur revealed later, "that, on his return to Cambodia, he would act with the greatest severity in dealing with those deputies, members of the government, and the military who were revealed as opposed to his policy vis-à-vis the Viet Cong and North Vietnamese."[20]

Sihanouk clearly was guilty of overweening pride. Incredibly, although his return would have fomented irreconcilable dissension in Phnom Penh, the government as of March 15 was prepared to welcome him back to Cambodia as chief of state. Flags were flying along the route to the airport. Sihanouk, now scheduled to arrive in Cambodia on March 18, would receive the accustomed noisy, colorful homecoming. Perhaps the fact that Sihanouk was aware of these preparations contributed to his overconfidence. How could he really be in danger, he might well have reasoned, if General Lon Nol and the other ministers were planning to bow before him just as they had always done? In the complicated web of related events in Paris, Moscow, and Phnom Penh, one factor seemed finally to have induced Sihanouk's immediate demise.

That factor was the plot of Colonel Oum Manorine, the secretary of state for surface defense and half-brother of Monique, to intimidate and thoroughly subdue if not overthrow General Lon Nol before Sihanouk's return. Whether Oum Manorine was operating with or without the specific approval of Sihanouk is a matter of conjecture, but, for five days after the March 11 demonstrations, he attempted to undermine the government. His first action, surprisingly but logically, was to spur another three days of rioting after March 11. The riots were directed mainly at local Vietnamese residents and Vietnamese-owned shops. Since 75 per cent of the Vietnamese populace of 200,000 in Phnom Penh was Catholic, it was fitting that the rioters should also have attacked and desecrated two of the largest Catholic churches. The police, controlled by Oum Manorine, did not act to stop the violence. The inference was that the cabinet fully endorsed the continuation of rioting, but the truth was just the opposite. Oum Manorine had instigated the riots in order to discredit the government.

If Oum Manorine's riots appeared to some foreign observers to reflect the will of the cabinet, their true significance was not lost upon the government's allies in the National Assembly. In a letter to Lon Nol, leaders of the National Assembly charged that "dishonest persons have profited from the confusion caused by recent demonstrations to violate the homes of certain people and attack religious establishments in the capital." The letter implored the Prime Minister to prevent "the illicit maneuvers of these men, which threaten to compromise the honor of our country." Indicative of the purpose of the riots after March 11 was that they provided Queen Kossamak with the pretext on March 12 and 13 to write letters to the National Assembly president, Cheng Heng, who was acting chief of state during Sihanouk's absence. She asked the Assembly to retract its resolution, adopted on March 11, supporting the demonstrations against the North Vietnamese and Viet Cong embassies, and then to close its doors to further debate. Queen Kossamak cited specifically the desecration of the churches as examples of the "anarchy" that would besmirch Cambodia's image as a "tolerant, peaceful, and antiracist country."[21]

Summoned to confer with the queen in the palace on March 13, Lon Nol and other cabinet and Assembly leaders patiently explained to her that they were hoping to send representatives—Norodom Kanthol and Yem Sambaur—to meet with her son in Moscow. They evidently succeeded in convincing her of either the gravity of the situation or the futility of further opposition to the National Assembly resolution, for she never again appeared openly to oppose the will of any branch of the government. If the queen was convinced, reluctantly or willingly, by Lon Nol's argument, Colonel Oum Manorine was more desperate than ever to reverse the course of events. The critical day for him was March 16, when National Assembly leaders, eager to destroy his power, called him and Sosthène Fernandez, secretary of state for security, for "interpellation" before a closed meeting of the entire assembly. Although Oum Manorine might have been accused of a wide variety of offenses, ranging from corruption to gun-running for the Communists, he was in reality questioned about only one relatively petty violation.

Why, Oum Manorine was asked, had his name appeared as the addressee on seven crates flown from Hong Kong in January under the label "for personal use" when actually they contained clothing materials valued at $70,000? Oum Manorine hastily passed on the blame to Fernandez, who in turn explained that he had discovered that a Chinese merchant had attempted to smuggle in the material by putting Oum Manorine's name on the crates without Oum Manorine's permission. Fernandez added a touch of sex to the drama by adding that a certain "young lady" had been responsible for recommending this procedure to the Chinese. The hearing on the smuggling of the fabrics, discovered by a customs inspector alerted by the government to prevent illicit shipments through the airport of drugs and other items for the Vietnamese Communists, was merely an excuse for embarrassing Sihanouk's allies. Whether or not Oum Manorine was actually responsible for the smuggling was completely beside the point. The rightists who now dominated the Assembly needed a convenient pretext. One of them, Sim Var, an old-time Democrat and a foe of Sihanouk's for many years, introduced a motion of no-confidence in Oum Manorine immediately after the interpellation.

Sim Var and Douc Rasy, both former cabinet ministers whom Sihanouk in recent years had threatened to bring to trial for their opposition to his policies, were fast mobilizing hesitant or ambivalent deputies to their cause. For all these efforts, however, some deputies still showed a certain reluctance to press for an immediate vote on Sim Var's motion of no-confidence in Oum Manorine. In the confusion of their deliberations, students participating in another anti-Vietnamese demonstration stormed into the Assembly chamber shouting that deputies should "discover who betrayed Cambodia to the Vietnamese." Had Oum Manorine organized this demonstration in order to complicate the proceedings against him? The answer will probably never be known. The result, however, was that Sim Var postponed a vote on the motion until the next day, March 17, 1970. Oum Manorine realized that he was doomed unless he acted immediately. On the night of March 16, he called on several battalions of police to seize key government buildings,

arrest Lon Non, Sirik Matak, and other "collaborators," and restore order. Oum Manorine's attempt at a countercoup—before the
actual coup itself had occurred—was a total failure. Lon Nol's own
battalions, called into Phnom Penh, remained not only loyal but
efficient enough to block Oum Manorine's forces before they had
left their quarters. Indeed, Oum Manorine's countercoup foundered partially on the failure of his own commanders, who were
none too enthusiastic about opposing the army, against which they
felt little, if any, interservice rivalry. During the night, Lon Nol's
tanks and armored cars, most of them old French or American models, rumbled through the city. Virtually no shots were fired. The
countercoup was aborted before it could begin. Oum Manorine was
arrested in his headquarters. The next morning the government
announced his "resignation." Sirik Matak assumed his responsibilities.

Although there is no way to prove the point, it seems more than
likely that Oum Manorine, in his final thrust against Lon Nol, was
acting independently of Sihanouk. The prince may not have been
above approving anti-Vietnamese demonstrations in hopes that
they would rebound against the government, but he had never
engaged in attempts to dislodge his ministers militarily. Rather, he
had founded his power to a large extent on his ability to play off
political factions among the Phnom Penh elite so that none of
them could devour him. Oum Manorine had acquired a reputation,
possibly undeserved, as Sihanouk's "executioner," but, if he had
been responsible for any executions, they were probably of relatively minor Khmer Rouge leftists. One of the difficulties, of which
Sihanouk, still in Moscow, was blissfully unaware was that, after
Oum Manorine and Sosthène Fernandez, there was virtually no
one remaining in Phnom Penh who would effectively support him.
The radical leftist Chau Seng had left for Paris in late 1967, after
Sihanouk had dismissed him from the cabinet. Sihanouk's numerous cousins and uncles might have rallied behind him had he
been in Phnom Penh, but they were basically docile followers not
disposed to fight anyone, much less General Lon Nol and most of
his cabinet.

Some of the men in Sihanouk's entourage in Moscow might
have fought for him had they been in Phnom Penh, but they were
as ignorant as he of the seriousness of the situation at home.
Among them were Penn Nouth, whom Lon Nol had succeeded as
Prime Minister, and Lieutenant General Ngo Hou, Sihanouk's
political adviser. General Nhiek Tioulong, former military com-

mander, might also have aided the prince's cause in Cambodia, but he had retired the previous July and moved to France. Even Khek Vandy, the corrupt business operator who had the most to lose financially, was absent from the capital. He had gone to Japan as Cambodia's representative at the opening of Expo '70 in Osaka. In Moscow, moreover, Sihanouk could not communicate with friends or members of his family by telephone, as he could from Paris. And the Soviet Government had been inaccurately informed by its own Phnom Penh embassy, whose diplomats later acknowledged that they were as surprised by the sequence of events in Cambodia as were most other foreign observers.

The ignorance of both Sihanouk and his Soviet hosts was manifest in the Soviet suggestion that he prolong his stay in Moscow by two more days so as to confer with the Party chairman, Leonid Brezhnev, and other top Party and government officials. Sihanouk, who had planned to leave for Peking on March 16, readily assented —and then decided to extend his stay in Peking from three to five days, in order to spend equal time in each capital. The result was that his arrival in Phnom Penh was rescheduled from March 18 to March 24. The prince, flattered by the attention paid him by Soviet officials, may have assumed that he was succeeding in his scheme of diplomacy with Peking and Moscow. The riots in Phnom Penh could well be cited as reasons why the two Communist giants should try to persuade the Vietnamese Communists to withdraw from Cambodia. At the same time, unaware of what was happening in Phnom Penh, Sihanouk apparently hoped that his conversations in Moscow would convince some of his opponents at home to tone down their activities. Thus, on March 17, 1970, he informed the queen by cable that Soviet officials had warned that "low blows" of "extreme right against our allies" could "inevitably mean war between Cambodia and Vietnam."[22]

The queen was prepared on March 17 to adopt a far more realistic attitude than her errant son. In a last desperate bid to prevent his destruction, she broadcast a message on Phnom Penh radio in which she described the demonstrations, which she had severely criticized only four days previously, as "a clear expression" of "firm nationalism" and "strong indignation over the deliberate aggression committed by our enemy against our territory." She concluded, "in the name of the Throne, the Prince Chief of State, and myself," by conveying "to my beloved children my thanks and felicitations, as well as my full confidence in the attitude of my nationalist children and the intuition and solidarity of the people."

The message was an eleventh-hour *cri de coeur*. It was too late, however, to have any effect.[23]

The final cause of Sihanouk's downfall was the momentum picked up by the investigation of Oum Manorine and Fernandez and then Oum Manorine's arrest and resignation. The Assembly, meeting at 9 A.M. on March 18, voted on Sim Var's motion of confidence—not on the case of Oum Manorine, who was already under arrest and dead politically, but on that of Fernandez. Significantly, the vote was not unanimous. Six of the eighty Assembly deputies deemed it expedient not to attend the session. Thirty-six among the seventy-four who attended decided to abstain from voting. Eight actually voted in favor of the motion. Twenty-five, barely more than one third of those in the chamber, voted against the motion. Five ballots, for reasons unexplained, were ruled invalid. The voting dramatized the divisions within Phnom Penh. Sihanouk's allies—and obviously Sihanouk himself—were not without sympathy and even popularity.* At the beginning of the morning of March 18, Sihanouk's demise as chief of state was far from certain.

Sim Var, Douc Rasy, and their allies then opened the floor to a much broader offensive against Sihanouk's rule. The debate, as announced by the Assembly speaker, In Tam, would focus on "appropriate measures to end violations of national territory by the Viet Cong." In fact, the question of the presence of Vietnamese Communist soldiers on Cambodian soil was not uppermost in the minds of most of the deputies, who spent nearly all of their time in Phnom Penh or large provincial centers and found it difficult to view the Communist forces as an immediate threat. The real issue was Sihanoukism—the cult carefully nurtured by Sihanouk over years in office so that he and his family could enjoy the pleasures and privileges of power at the expense of other lesser members of the Phnom Penh elite. No longer inhibited by Sihanouk's presence or influence, deputy after deputy rose to denounce the prince, his wife, his and her family, and their entire life style. The essence —and inherent priorities—of the debate were summarized the next day by the official Agence Khmère de Presse:

* Fernandez did not remain in disgrace for long. After Sihanouk's fall, he convinced his superiors that he had only acted on orders of the prince. A colonel, he was promoted in June, 1970, to brigadier general and named commander of a military region. Oum Manorine remained under arrest in Phnom Penh.

Sihanouk deceived the people. . . . His activities aimed at only one thing: to serve the members of his family, while his spouse Madame Monique accorded lucrative posts . . . only to functionaries who had the means to pay her. . . . Sihanouk authorized the opening of the casino in order to ruin the people and to serve the interests of his family. . . . Norodom Sihanouk has no concern for the well-being of the people. At a time when the people are hungry, he organizes festivities. . . . A soldier killed on the field of honor receives only 10,000 riels [$182] at the maximum, while to a pretty girl who pleases him he gives 100,000 riels at the least. . . . Norodom Sihanouk pretends that he loves the people and the Khmer country more than anyone, but he caused the transportation of arms for the Viet Cong, who used them then against Khmer.[24]

During the debate, the prince's opponents privately revealed their plans to all members. The talk would end before lunch with a vote of the entire parliament, which included an upper house made up of a dozen members of the Council of the kingdom. This time, it was made quite clear, there would be no opposition. Cabinet ministers, meeting secretly with right-wing deputies for the past two days, had decided that now was the moment for Sihanouk's removal. Just when they finished making up their minds was far from clear, but Oum Manorine's arrest may have led to the final decision on the part of Lon Nol and Sirik Matak. If Sihanouk still had any real allies in parliament (and he must have had some), they were told that it was too late for them to support him as chief of state. At 1:00 P.M. an election committee gathered behind a long table on which were placed three piles of ninety-two small pieces of paper. The papers in one pile were blue, in another white, and in the third white with blue stripes.

It was up to Trinh Hoanh, secretary-general of the Sangkum, to suggest the final motion—a vote of confidence in Sihanouk. Then In Tam invited each member of parliament to file past the table and pick up a piece of paper from one of the piles—white if he favored Sihanouk, blue if he opposed him, white and blue if he wished to abstain. There was not the slightest doubt of the outcome. The whole performance, at this point, was ceremonial. By the time all the deputies had walked by the table, the entire pile of blue pieces of paper had vanished. All the white and the blue and white papers lay untouched. Sihanouk had been voted out of power, 92 to 0, on a motion of confidence. It was up to Cheng Heng, the Assembly chairman who adopted the title, though never the power, of chief of state, to announce the results to the world. "The National Assembly and the Council of the Kingdom, meeting in joint session, have withdrawn on the 18th of March, 1970, at 1:00 P.M.—in conformity with the constitution and by unanimous vote—their confidence in Prince Norodom Sihanouk in the functions of chief of state."[25]

And it was up to the Soviet Premier, Alexei N. Kosygin to break the news to Prince Sihanouk. At an airport press conference before his scheduled departure on the same day for Peking, Sihanouk revealed that he might form a government-in-exile. The internal political feud in Phnom Penh had ended, for the moment. Now the real war for Cambodia, which Sihanouk, in power, had managed to avoid, was about to begin.

5

Plunge into War

Before the Break

The war for Cambodia had begun, in a very real sense, long before Sihanouk's overthrow on March 18, 1970. The essential difference, however, was that, prior to that day, the official government policy was to try to accommodate the Vietnamese Communists, whereas, very soon afterward, the government declared openly that it was willing to fight to force them from Cambodia. The wisdom of Sihanouk's policy in contrast to that of his successors will long be debated. Sihanouk did manage to keep his country out of a war in which he sensed that Cambodia would face overwhelming odds —and could not rely on U.S. or other Western support. If, however, he had cooperated with the Americans and South Vietnamese when the North Vietnamese and Viet Cong first began to exploit potential base areas, then perhaps his country might have been better prepared than it was for the later struggle against Vietnamese Communist influence.

Similar arguments might be adduced in discussing the policy of the government of Prime Minister Lon Nol after March, 1970. If Lon Nol had reached a *modus vivendi* with the Vietnamese Communists, might he too have preserved some semblance of tranquillity for most of his country? Or would he merely have forestalled a still greater conflict than that which had enveloped much of the countryside by early 1971? A corollary question, perhaps more controversial than the others, was whether or not the entry of American and South Vietnamese troops into Cambodia had widened the conflict by compelling the North Vietnamese to range further across the country in search of supplies, base areas, and new routes for the infiltration of men and materiel. Such fundamental military-political issues may never be resolved with any real certainty.

Nevertheless, it may prove useful to describe the build-up of the Vietnamese Communists in Cambodia in the middle and late 1960's—and then contrast and relate events in this period with those in the months following the *coup d'état*.

In assessing Vietnamese Communist activities in Cambodia, one should note that not all Viet Minh had actually left the country as agreed at the Geneva conference in 1954. A small residue of cadres, allied with mountain tribesmen, or montagnards, stayed in the mountainous northeast, much of it rarely if ever visited by Cambodian forces. Still more Viet Minh, in league with local residents of Vietnamese ancestry, remained in villages all along the frontiers, particularly in the mountains extending from Chau Doc Province in South Vietnam across southern Cambodia. The Viet Minh quietly encouraged the Khmer Rouge, but the presence of Vietnamese Communist cadres was not viewed with real seriousness until the early 1960's. Then, in 1962, a year before the assassination of Ngo Dinh Diem in South Vietnam, the National Liberation Front for the first time began obtaining rice and other supplies, except arms and ammunition, from Cambodia. Prince Sihanouk, in view of his hostility toward South Vietnam, did not discourage this relatively small-scale "smuggling," which might have been difficult to prevent under any circumstances, since Cambodian provincial and customs officials, easily bribed by the Communists, were already reaping considerable profits from it.

Nor did Sihanouk discourage the expansion of Communist base areas beginning in 1965, the year the United States sent its first combat forces into South Vietnam. The Vietnamese Communists soon turned what had previously been relatively small encampments into major sanctuaries, sprawling for acres under a dense jungle canopy that rendered them virtually invisible either from the air or from nearby main roads. At the same time, they began to receive their first shipments of arms and ammunition through Cambodian ports. In some cases, the expansion of Communist sanctuaries in Cambodia resulted, at least in part, from the evacuation of similar jungle bases on the South Vietnamese side of the frontier in the face of overwhelming American manpower and firepower.

Perhaps the most famous of the American operations, from the viewpoint of its relationship to the Cambodian sanctuaries, was Junction City, in which some 30,000 American troops between February and May, 1967, drove a much smaller Communist force from War Zone C, a desolate stretch of shell-pocked, defoliated, and virtually unpopulated forest in Tay Ninh Province some 70 miles northwest of Saigon. The significant aspect of Junction City was that it compelled the Vietnamese Communists to withdraw their Central Office for South Vietnam—COSVN—from War Zone C across the border to Cambodia. In the meantime, the North Vietnamese, arriving in ever increasing numbers down the trail system through southern Laos and northeastern Cambodia, were now bearing the brunt of the war in the name of the NLF and the Viet Cong, supposedly South Vietnamese Communist organizations.

The Central Office for South Vietnam controlled all Vietnamese Communist activities in central and southern Cambodia, just as it did in the same regions of South Vietnam. Its leader, Pham Hung, chairman of what was euphemistically known as the "current affairs committee," was also a member of the political bureau of the Lao Dong, or Workers Party, of North Vietnam. The current affairs committee of COSVN was, in effect, an arm of the Lao Dong, the elite Communist Party organization that determined North Vietnamese policy. The current affairs committee at the same time formed the political bureau of the People's Revolutionary Party, a paper organization set up in 1962 ostensibly as the South Vietnamese equivalent of the Lao Dong. Pham Hung, fifth-ranking man in the Lao Dong, viewed Cambodia strictly in terms of its relationship to the Vietnamese conflict.[1]

From Phnom Penh, North Vietnamese and NLF officials, most of them accredited as diplomats, directed local Vietnamese cadres responsible for organizing Cambodia's Vietnamese population, estimated at 600,000. Taxation, generally in the form of "donations," was routine, but many Vietnamese were also compelled to perform other chores. Fishermen, for instance, shipped bags of rice by water, while workers on rubber plantations hauled rice and arms by bicycle to frontier sanctuaries and storage areas. Rubber workers also guided Communist units through the jungles, built roads, relayed messages, carried wounded, and generally fulfilled the role of rear-echelon troops.

Vietnamese Communist leaders, concerned about maintaining cordial relations with Prince Sihanouk, prohibited political agitation by local Vietnamese against the Cambodian Government, which forbade Vietnamese from owning property but compelled them to pay high taxes. Instead, Vietnamese cadres focused almost entirely on winning local Vietnamese sympathy and support for the Communist struggle in South Vietnam. An important element in this campaign was the Liberation Press Agency, the NLF news organization whose Phnom Penh office churned out leaflets and magazines for the Vietnamese community. A sign of the contrast in approach between the Chinese and Vietnamese Communists in Cambodia was that Sihanouk let both the Liberation Press Agency and Hanoi's Vietnam News Agency continue to operate in Phnom Penh after he had expelled the New China News Agency in late 1967.

One curious aspect of the Vietnamese Communist structure in Phnom Penh was that the NLF mission seemed to play a more important role than the North Vietnamese Embassy. The reason apparently was that most of the local Vietnamese were still citizens of South Vietnam and technically fell within the purview of the organization claiming to represent the government of their own country. Since North Vietnam was in over-all charge of both COSVN and the NLF, however, the question of whether North Vietnamese or NLF diplomats exercised primary influence on the Vietnamese community appeared academic. The point was that the Vietnamese Communists, after Sihanouk broke off relations with South Vietnam in 1963 and then recognized Hanoi and the NLF, had the freedom to play upon a vast potential source of support for their bases along the border, which in.turn could sustain forces in South Vietnam itself.

It was essential, from both Sihanouk's point of view and that of the Vietnamese Communists, that the latter conduct operations in Cambodia with as much secrecy as possible. Sihanouk, officially neutral, did not want to appear to have allied militarily with the Communists, while Hanoi and the NLF preferred to avoid accusations of expanding the war, violating the Geneva accords, and so forth. Although the Vietnamese Communists never admitted their presence in Cambodia, even after Sihanouk's fall, the prince himself proved remarkably successful at convincing correspondents, diplomats, and the like that U.S. intelligence officers had erred regarding Communist activities in Cambodia. He often sponsored junkets for correspondents through vast stretches of jungle, where they almost invariably found no traces of elusive Communist forces.

By late 1967, however, the Vietnamese Communist presence in Cambodia had grown too large for the prince to hide. When Sihanouk invited foreign journalists to tour his country for three weeks in November, during and after the visit of Mrs. Jacqueline Kennedy, he was certain that none of them would know where to

find evidence of Communist sanctuaries. His invitation might
have resulted in complete vindication of his claims had it not been
for the enterprise of three Vietnam war correspondents—George
McArthur and Horst Faas, both of the Associated Press, and Ray
Herndon, of United Press International—who had come to Phnom
Penh with information supplied by the U.S. mission in Saigon giving the exact locations of a dozen North Vietnamese and Viet
Cong base camps. Accompanied by skeptical Cambodian soldiers
and officers, McArthur, Faas, and Herndon walked along a trail
running off of Route 7 outside the town of Memot. The trail led
them directly to an empty camp complete with huts of bamboo
and thatch, a concealed truck park, an official paper with Vietnamese writing on it, and tracks leading toward the frontier. The camp
had obviously been abandoned within the last few hours—or minutes.

A week later, on November 22, 1967, as the prince observed the
opening of a new Czechoslovakian truck-assembly plant in Sihanoukville, I asked him to comment on the discovery. "Did they
really find this camp?" he shouted. "If we were accomplices of the
Viet Cong, we should not allow you to check inside the whole territory of Cambodia." It was appropriate that Sihanouk should
have offered these views at Sihanoukville, for it was the main port
of entry for arms bound for Communist troops in Cambodia and
much of South Vietnam. Most of the goods arrived legitimately at
Sihanoukville—or the Cambodian Navy base at Ream, some 20
miles to the east—as Chinese, Soviet or Eastern European military
aid for Cambodian armed forces. From Sihanoukville and Ream,
the supplies were first hauled by the local Chinese-owned Hak Ly
trucking company to Cambodian Army storage depots and, eventually, to transshipment points near the border. A Cambodian
soldier rode with each truckload to ensure its safe passage through
military checkpoints.

Reporters visiting the ports generally found only a freighter or
two, laden perhaps with foodstuffs or hardware, as well as some
fishing vessels. Most of the ships bearing arms offloaded at sea onto
fishing boats, which carried the crated, often unmarked war materiel into the harbor. Despite all Sihanouk's histrionics, the activities of the Vietnamese Communists were gradually publicized in
1968 and 1969 as part of Cambodia's slowly shifting foreign policy.
Among the first indications that Cambodian officials were concerned with the permanent presence of Communist troops was a
three-paragraph item published in October, 1968, in the magazine

Cambodian troops from interfering with the activities of the North Vietnamese. Cambodian officers, returning from patrols in the jungle, said that Sihanouk personally had ordered their commanders to recall them from locales where they might engage Communist troops. Nonetheless, as the North Vietnamese built up their bases in Cambodia, small skirmishes were inevitable. In his conversation with the Vietnamese Communist ambassadors, Lon Nol reported that hostile soldiers had destroyed Cambodian Army road-building equipment in the northeast, had wounded and killed civilian and military officials in the central provinces, and had supplied cadres for local Khmer Rouge forces, who were encouraged to ambush government patrols. Lon Nol's report did not exaggerate the gravity of the threat. Sihanouk had permitted him to make the report and then publish it in a Cambodian magazine only after Lon Nol had convinced Sihanouk of the need for a confrontation with Vietnamese Communist diplomats.

The Communists, like Sihanouk, still hoped to balance their own military interests with those of the Cambodian Government. For this reason both ambassadors informed Lon Nol that they would investigate his charges but claimed that the Americans and South Vietnamese must really be the culprits. This reply provided a face-saving pretext that might have led to a much closer military relationship between the Vietnamese Communists and the Cambodian Government. Sihanouk's aim, once he realized that the Communist presence had become too big to hide, was to reach a definite understanding with Hanoi and the NLF from which Cambodia might profit monetarily, if not militarily.

It was seemingly ironic, in view of this aim, that Sihanouk should have ordered the closing of the ports of Sihanoukville and Ream to the flow of Communist arms in July, 1969, shortly after the visit, from June 30 to July 5, of President Huynh Tan Phat, of the Provisional Revolutionary Government. Sihanouk's decision may have represented a concession to Lon Nol, but it also was a means of inducing the NLF and Hanoi to acquiesce to a written agreement that might not be altogether favorable to them. Sihanouk hoped to put the arms trade on an entirely legal basis, whereby the Cambodian Government profited, rather than the Chinese trucking companies and individual military and civilian officials. Sihanouk's bargaining was partially responsible for the trade agreement signed with the Provisional Revolutionary Government in September, 1969, and might have led to a similar deal on arms had other events not disrupted his plans.

The Vietnamese Communists were not enthusiastic about Sihanouk's desire for a written agreement on arms since they would have had to submit to regularized Cambodian controls and pay considerably more to the Cambodian Government for the use of Cambodian ports, trucks, and storage facilities than they had customarily preferred Cambodian officials and Chinese trucking firms in secret. Sihanouk's order to close the ports was not immediately injurious to the interests of the Communists, who already had all the arms they needed for their fall and winter campaigns stored along the frontier. Cambodian Army supply depots, which served in effect as logistics bases for the Communists, had stockpiles capable of fulfilling their needs for another year or two, provided Cambodia remained willing to transfer these supplies to the Communists.

The Vietnamese Communists might have been well advised at this stage to maintain a "low profile"—a term often used to describe the U.S. diplomatic position vis-à-vis Cambodia—and to attempt to demonstrate their solidarity with the Cambodian forces. In fact, during this period, the Communists began ranging much further from their bases, often wandering at will through villages once entirely off limits to them. Although Cambodian policy toward the North Vietnamese had not changed, Lon Nol decided, in October, 1969, to reveal some statistics that might explain the increase in the number of clashes between Cambodians and Vietnamese Communists. In September alone, he said, the total number of "foreign troops on our soil" had increased from between 32,000 and 35,000 men to between 35,000 and 40,000. Lon Nol estimated that Communist strength along the northern and northeastern borders had risen from 16,000 to well over 17,000 troops and, near the frontiers south and east of Phnom Penh, from 13,800 to 17,000. The remainder were presumably scattered in isolated pockets of strength elsewhere in the country. "In this period nothing indicates that the foreign units will soon leave our soil," his report concluded.[5]

Lon Nol's statistical summary was no doubt realistic, as was his assessment of the prospects for the departure of some of the Communist forces. In the next few months, while Sihanouk was in France, Cambodian troops began to probe more deeply than ever before into regions where they knew they were likely to encounter the enemy. They did not attack, or even threaten, Communist base camps, but they kept Communist weapons whenever they stumbled upon their caches in the forests. The Cambodian command also began to limit the movement of arms for the Communists from Cambodian Army storage depots.

Preliminary Skirmishes

The prospect of war had long hung like an ugly cloud over the lives of most Cambodians, but they had become so inured to it that they were hardly prepared when the cloud finally burst shortly after Sihanouk's overthrow. By the time North Vietnam and the NLF withdrew their diplomats from Phnom Penh on March 27, 1970, it was apparent that the Vietnamese Communists had decided to adopt military rather than diplomatic means to pursue their aims in Cambodia. On a diplomatic level, they had refused to meet with Cambodian officials since March 16, the date on which Yem Sambaur had tried to negotiate the withdrawal of their troops. Instead, Hanoi and the NLF had decided to deal exclusively with Sihanouk, whom the North Vietnamese Premier, Pham Van Dong, had met in Peking on March 21, three days after Sihanouk's ouster as chief of state. On March 23, four days before the final break between the Vietnamese Communists and the government in Phnom Penh, Sihanouk revealed for the first time that he was prepared to ally with the Communists in their war against the men who had deposed him.

Sihanouk, who had already declared that the coup was illegal, claimed in his statement that he was still chief of state and formally "dissolved" the entire Cambodian Government and National Assembly. At the same time, he formed the National United Front of Kampuchea, whose mission, like that of the NLF in South Vietnam, was to liberate the country. Thus, Sihanouk had provided the North Vietnamese and Viet Cong with a popular name—his own—and an organization around which they could rally support for their cause in Cambodia. Despite speculation that Sihanouk was held against his will in Peking, he appeared to have succumbed to a combination of Chinese and North Vietnamese flattery—and the promise that he could have all the facilities he needed for spreading his own propaganda as a prelude to his return to power with North Vietnamese military assistance.

An integral part of Sihanouk's and the North Vietnamese political and military strategy was the encouragement of a mass popular uprising as soon as possible. On March 26, 1970, Vietnamese Communists in rubber plantations near the South Vietnamese border began distributing leaflets and broadcasting propaganda, in-

cluding recordings of Sihanouk's voice on Radio Peking, from
loudspeakers mounted on jeeps and trucks. This phase of the
Communist campaign resulted almost immediately in a series of
minor, short-lived, antigovernment riots, which the Cambodian
Army easily suppressed. On March 27, in the town of Kompong
Cham, 45 miles northeast of Phnom Penh, Khmer soldiers fired
into an angry mob, killing 27 of the demonstrators. The next day,
40 miles south of Phnom Penh, soldiers again fired into crowds of
rioting peasants, killing some 100 of them before they dispersed.

Although Sihanouk was to maintain his "Samdech euv" image
in the countryside long after urban sophisticates were convinced
that he was attempting to sell his country to the enemy, peasant
enthusiasm for defending him soon faded under military force. The
North Vietnamese would doubtless have preferred a genuine pro-
Sihanouk revolt, but, in the absence of one, they decided to send
their own men to battle the Cambodians, who were beginning for
the first time to threaten Communist sanctuaries. The Vietnamese
Communists, by the end of March, 1970, had reversed their posture
on the border. Instead of concentrating on South Vietnam, they
were sending patrols further into Cambodian territory to ambush
and harass Cambodian soldiers approaching their once inviolate
bases.

The new North Vietnamese strategy was apparent to this writer
and a Canadian television team on April 3, 1970, while we were
driving down a dirt road through the Seven Mountains, the range
that straddles the Vietnamese-Cambodian frontier 70 miles south
of Phnom Penh. Our vehicle, chauffeured by a Cambodian Chinese who spoke Vietnamese, French, English, Cambodian, and
several dialects of Chinese, was entering a typical dusty village
when we noticed some men wearing camouflaged pith helmets and
hefting Chinese-made B-40 rocket-launchers standing at regular
intervals, 10 or 20 feet apart, on either side of the road. We drove
by them into the village, where we saw another twenty or thirty
soldiers. Our assumption was that they were Cambodians, but officials at the last town we had visited had told us no government
troops were in the area. They carried no French or U.S. weapons,
had no radios or vehicles, and wore no Cambodian army insignia—
all readily apparent in visits to any Cambodian unit. Their Chinese
weapons, the same as those formerly issued Cambodian soldiers under Sihanouk's aid agreement with Peking, appeared much newer
and in better condition than those I had seen with Cambodian
troops.

Although we were not compelled to stop, the soldiers looked so edgy that we thought we should ask some quesions before driving on into the jungle. "These are soldiers of the Sihanouk army," explained a wiry man in blue pajamas as I got out of the car with the two Canadians, correspondent William Cunningham and cameraman Maurice Embre. "We fight on Sihanouk's orders to return him to power," said the man, who identified himself as chief of the village. "Ninety per cent of the army hates Lon Nol. We are the true representatives of Prince Sihanouk in Cambodia. All the clergy, the students, the farmers support Prince Sihanouk." While the chief was talking, some of the soldiers pointed rifles in our direction. One soldier inspected a map on the back seat of our car, and another gestured menacingly with a pistol. "Are Vietnamese fighting with the Sihanouk army?" I asked. "We are supported by patriotic Vietnamese," the chief replied.

The chief and almost all the soldiers and villagers were clearly Vietnamese. Their finely chiseled features contrasted with the soft, rounded facial structures of Cambodians, who in any case rarely appeared so tense and alert. I asked the chief why these "patriots" were fighting in defense of Sihanouk. He replied by displaying a crudely printed piece of paper reporting Sihanouk's broadcasts from Peking. "Under the multinational front and the Cambodian Liberation Front, I will install another government of the people in Phnom Penh," said a letter in Cambodian signed "Sihanouk." "Then we will prosecute the enemies of the people, the servants of the imperialist Americans, for they have cooperated in the plot against me." It was unlikely, however, that any Cambodian would accept the letter's authenticity, for above the Cambodian script was a sentence written in Vietnamese: "From the great leader Sihanouk to military officers, soldiers, and civilian officials."

The obvious Vietnamese Communist influence, at least in this remote range of mountains, where one entire North Vietnamese Army division had based since mid-1969, substantiated Cambodian charges that the Viet Cong had been responsible for antigovernment demonstrations. I wanted to ask the village chief about some of the riots, but he seemed increasingly nervous. Thus, after listening to a few more words of propaganda, we got up to leave. Some of the soldiers were pointing their rifles at us, but none of them made a move to stop us after Cunningham displayed his Canadian press card. We were, it turned out, the first newsmen to run into Vietnamese Communist troops while driving down seemingly innocent roads near the Vienamese frontier. In the next five days, at least ten other correspondents, most of them magazine photographers or television cameramen, were captured in the Parrot's Beak of Svay Rieng Province, 80 miles northeast of the scene of our encounter. They were the vanguard of a total of some thirty-five journalists who were eventually picked up by the Communists. Fourteen of them were reported killed, although the deaths of only eight had been verified by the end of 1970. Nine were released after periods in captivity ranging from eight hours to nine weeks.

The only reason we were not detained was that Vietnamese Communists in the district were still cooperating with local authorities to the extent of not interfering with normal traffic or commerce. We noticed that a portrait of Prince Sihanouk adorned the glass-topped desk of the police chief in the nearest town, 15 miles to the east of our encounter, and surmised that Phnom Penh authorities had not attempted to assert their authority beyond the provincial capital of Takeo, 30 miles to the north. Hundreds of Cambodian officials would doubtless have preferred to maintain their old relationships vis-à-vis the militarily superior Vietnamese Communist forces. In the first week or two of April, government troops, as well as civilian officials, demonstrated that they were unable to prevent the Communists from widening their border sanctuaries and extending their influence over a 10-to-15-mile-wide swath of Cambodian territory running from the coast to the northeastern provinces, which Cambodian officials were already in the process of abandoning totally to Communist control.

In all their military-political efforts, Vietnamese Communist troops followed the same line indicated in my encounter with them on April 3. Shouting "Long Live Sihanouk" and other slogans, they terrorized defenseless towns near the frontier, set fire to government buildings, hung up portraits of Sihanouk, and forced the populace to attend mass meetings held in Sihanouk's name. The result was confusion in the minds of peasants, who had once revered Sihanouk but who also disliked the Vietnamese—and were generally aware of the shift in power in Phnom Penh if not of the reasons for it. The dilemma confronting Cambodian peasants was etched in terror in the village of Kompong Ampil, which I visited on the afternoon of April 5, 1970, the day after about 100 North Vietnamese troops had chosen it for a demonstration of their power and the government's weakness. "Nobody dares say we support the new government or the old one," said the wife of the chief of the village, in the Parrot's Beak two miles from the frontier. "We dare not say anything at all."

The woman, wearing a Cambodian-style sarong and blouse, was

standing beside her husband beneath the home on stilts where they lived with their eight children. Fifty or so villagers gathered around her as she described, in trembling, almost pleading tones, what had happened. "They burned down the police station and the village office. They were here for three hours. Then they left." The North Vietnamese had fired their rifles in the air but had refrained from harming any of the villagers. Their mission, it seemed, had been only to propagandize the populace. The main question that villagers, as well as government leaders and foreign diplomats in Phnom Penh, were asking was how far into Cambodia the Communists were prepared to go in their effort to overthrow the government and reinstall Sihanouk as their neutral ally.

At the provincial capital of Svay Rieng, 10 miles south of Kompong Ampil, the province chief, Hem Keth Sana, reported that Vietnamese Communists for the first time were attacking key district towns, killing officials, and cutting off roads. Their eventual ambition, Sana went on, was to isolate the province from the rest of Cambodia. Government troops, accustomed for years to garrison duties or road-building, were incapable of counterattacking or pursuing the enemy.

"The Viet Cong want to extend their zone into Cambodia before the Cambodian Army has a chance to bother them," observed a Cambodian battalion commander while his troops waited in buses and trucks before a blown-out bridge several miles north of Kompong Ampil. The battalion would have been powerless if, the Communists had chosen to ambush the convoy, running almost bumper to bumper down the highway. The troops were not protected by any artillery and could not have counted on support from Cambodia's minuscule air force, whose few serviceable Soviet MIG jets and single-engined American-made T-28's already were severely overtaxed and incapable of responding quickly in emergencies.

The impotence of the Cambodian Army, when confronted by Vietnamese Communist hit-and-run tactics, was reflected in the struggle for Route 1, the main road running from Phnom Penh through Svay Rieng Province to Saigon, 40 miles southeast of the Parrot's Beak. Cambodian soldiers in the first week of April were forced to abandon a series of towns along Route 1. By the night of April 9, 1970, five battalions of Cambodian troops were in strictly defensive positions around the town of Prasaut, a typical cluster of Chinese shops, administrative buildings, and Khmer homes on stilts, 21 miles from the frontier. The commander of one of the battalions told me that his troops hoped to drive the Vietnamese Communists from hideouts within 2 or 3 miles of the road. His battalion, he explained, was the forward tip of a defensive triangle anchored in the rear around the town of Svay Rieng, 8 miles further west on Route 1.

That night, attempting to sleep in the government-run guest house in Svay Rieng, I heard the roar of 155mm. cannon firing from their emplacements in the middle of town. Early the next morning, an excited Cambodian Army officer informed Mark Frankland, of the London *Observer*, also staying at the guest house, of a "great battle" at Prasaut. He sent around his Land Rover, which drove Frankland and me behind a relief convoy to the town. The Cambodians had repelled the Viet Cong, said Major Hin Nim, commander of the Cambodian force. Standing before the smoking shells of shops destroyed in the fight, Hin Nim claimed that several hundred Vietnamese Communist troops had attacked, but the actual figure was probably only a fraction of that amount. A few fragments of B-40 rocket-propelled grenades were strewn in the fields surrounding the town. Perhaps only twenty or thirty Vietnamese Communists had been responsible for the entire battle. They had vanished at dawn, leaving behind the bodies of three of their comrades, killed by Cambodian troops.

The most significant aspect of the battle of Prasaut, however, was not the fighting between Cambodian and Communist forces but the killing of some ninety Vietnamese refugees, half of them women and children, sequestered for the previous two days around a farmers' cooperative warehouse on Route 1 at the eastern edge of the town. Interviews with some of those who had survived revealed that Cambodian soldiers had fired directly into them as soon as the battle began. The refugees in Prasaut were among the first of some 200,000 Vietnamese—one third of the country's Vietnamese population—preparing to return to South Vietnam to escape a wave of anti-Vietnamese persecution instigated by the war. Cambodian soldiers had raided their homes and forced them to go to the camp, where they in effect had been held as hostages for slaughter if the Vietnamese Communists attacked. Cambodian officers charged—probably with considerable truth, in view of the pressures exerted on the entire Vietnamese community by Communist cadres—that many of the men had been spies and propagandists for the enemy.

The round-up of Vietnamese in Svay Rieng Province, like the fighting itself, was the precursor of the war that soon spread beyond the frontier region into the heart of the country. By the end of April, 1970, the Communists had overrun Prasaut and were fighting on the outskirts of the town of Svay Rieng. Communist squads were conducting ambushes along Route 1 between Svay Rieng and the Mekong River ferry crossing at Neak Loeung, 35 miles to the west, and were cutting roads leading from the rubber plantations northeast of Phnom Penh. South of the capital, Communist units were advancing north along the Bassac and Mekong rivers and from the Elephant Mountains toward the towns of Takeo and Angtassom. Communist squads were also conducting ambushes on Route 4, the main highway from Phnom Penh to the port of Kompong Som, the original name to which Sihanoukville reverted shortly after the coup.

The total effect of the campaign in the month of April, 1970, gave the impression that Phnom Penh was in danger of attack from the southwest, south, northeast, and east. Impotent against this menace, Cambodian commanders continued to vent their frustrations by rounding up Vietnamese, robbing them of farmland and family possessions, and, in some cases, ordering soldiers to slaughter them. On April 15, 1970, five days after the Prasaut massacre, some 600 bodies floated down the Mekong past the ferry crossing at Neak Loeung. "The stench swept across the broad waters and ferry passengers gagged as the ferry churned through the bodies bobbing in the river," the Associated Press reported on the same day. "A police official at the ferry crossing . . . said he had counted 400 bodies during the morning. Still the bodies could be seen stretching for more than one mile up the river until they disappeared behind a bend."[6] A nineteen-year-old Vietnamese who escaped the massacre said Cambodian soldiers had rounded up the victims from a village near Phnom Penh, transported them in navy boats to an island in the Mekong a mile or two upstream from Neak Loeung, and then ordered them out and shot them.[7]

On April 16, Cambodian soldiers, in an incident almost identical to that at Prasaut, fired into another crowd of Vietnamese huddled in a refugee center at Takeo, killing more than a hundred of them. Again, Cambodian authorities claimed that the victims had been caught in a cross fire, but government sources indicated privately that officials had spread the word among Vietnamese that they would slaughter refugees if the Communists did not call off their campaign. On April 21, sixty Vietnamese men and women, most of them from refugee camps in Phnom Penh, were ordered to walk into the town of Saang, 20 miles south of the capital. The Vietnamese, led by a young seminary student carrying a white flag, stopped every 40 yards while a loudspeaker urged the Vietnamese Communists to abandon the town, which they had occupied for two days. Finally, at a bridge on the outskirts, the Communists opened fire, wounding two of the local Vietnamese and scattering the rest.

The persecution of Vietnamese living in Cambodia appeared at first to have worked solely in favor of Hanoi and the NLF, whose newspapers and radios easily exploited the theme. The reaction of the Saigon government was carefully muted, but the press and politicians demanded official protection and assistance for Vietnamese living in Cambodia. On April 24 and 25, some 200 students stormed the Cambodian Embassy building, vacant since the break in relations in 1963, and hanged Lon Nol in effigy. Saigon, however, was reluctant to criticize Cambodian officials for fear of jeopardizing the possibility of military and political collaboration against the Vietnamese Communists, who were now their common enemy.

South Vietnam's diplomatic stance might have appeared supine and ineffectual, but it was a major factor in preparing for the presence of South Vietnamese troops in Cambodia. President Nguyen Van Thieu, on April 23, 1970, announced the formation of an eight-man repatriation committee to facilitate the movement of Vietnamese refugees from Cambodia to South Vietnam, which many of them had never before even visited. The committee, besides negotiating the transfer of refugees, some 40,000 of whom had been herded into camps in Phnom Penh alone, provided a convenient cover under which Vietnamese officials could discuss and coordinate military operations. At the same time, the publicity surrounding the massacres aroused traditional animosities in Vietnam to the point where the government could be assured of popular and political support for military operations across the frontier.

The question, however, remained how far the Vietnamese Communists would extend their own military activities in Cambodia. The answer, in retrospect, was directly related to U.S. and South Vietnamese plans. The Vietnamese Communists, for instance, did not advance deep into Cambodia until the first major South Vietnamese incursion in mid-April. Even then, their activities were limited to striking at roads leading toward base areas. Although the Communists, fighting in the name of Sihanouk, were clearly interested in weakening, if not toppling, the Phnom Penh government, their fundamental aim was to protect the regions in which their troops had long based for the war in South Vietnam.

Lon Nol, however, was in less of a mood to compromise with the Communists after the initial flurry of fighting than he might have been had they not increased their threat against his own authority. At a press conference on March 30, 1970, he intimated for the first time that Cambodia might request aid from "friendly countries" if the North Vietnamese and Viet Cong did not leave Cambodian soil. He cited as "friendly" those with whom Cambodia maintained diplomatic relations but singled out Indonesia, Australia, New Zealand, and France. He did not specifically name the United States, but no one doubted that Cambodia would request U.S. help if the war escalated much further.

Lon Nol's determination may have been a factor in convincing the Vietnamese Communists of the need for expanding the war even further into Cambodia in order to regain some semblance of their former position in the country. If Lon Nol had not remained adamantly opposed to compromise with the Communists, he could certainly have discouraged the South Vietnamese, as did Sihanouk, from cross-border incursions. Lon Nol did, however, compromise on one important point. After the initial adverse international reaction to the persecution and massacre of Vietnamese refugees, he ordered officials to tone down anti-Vietnamese propaganda. "We hate all Vietnamese," a government official in Phnom Penh told me. "We will fight to the end against the Viet Cong. If South Vietnam helps us, then we do not hate the South Vietnamese—only the VC." This distinction, which obviously was contradictory, assumed increasing importance as South Vietnamese and Cambodian officials negotiated for long-range military and diplomatic cooperation.

While indicating the necessity for foreign aid, Lon Nol also sought to instill a sense of nationalist fervor among Cambodians, to whom the war had previously been irrelevant. Although underequipped and inexperienced, Cambodians began proving almost immediately that they would fight for "the nationalist cause." Lon Nol's army, only 35,000 at the time of Sihanouk's fall, doubled in strength in the first two months after the coup—en route to a total of 180,000, attained by the end of 1970. The government was most successful at winning the support of students, who staged anti-Communist demonstrations, posted signs and banners, and formed their own training regiments. Even in the countryside, where peasants retained varying degrees of loyalty for Sihanouk, government recruiters had no difficulty rounding up as many men as they needed. A steady stream of articles and broadcasts played upon traditional themes in order to destroy the image of Sihanouk. As might have been expected, official propaganda often followed—in style, not substance—the approach perfected by Sihanouk.

Typical of such efforts was a rally attended by Lon Nol and other leaders on April 11, 1970, in the same sports palace where Sihanouk had held his National Day pageants. Just as Sihanouk exploited such occasions to build up popular support for monarchical traditions, so Lon Nol promoted his government's avowed aim of abolishing the monarchy and establishing a republic. Notwithstanding Phnom Penh's interest in forming close relations with the Saigon government, the rally included a pageant portraying Khmer monarchs as traitors who betrayed their land to Vietnamese emperors. The pageant carefully distinguished, however, between Vietnamese Communists and South Vietnamese officials by blaming the former for Cambodia's woes. "These Vietnamese utilize Communist ideology to camouflage their expansionist aims," said an announcer, while girls in Vietnamese dress caressed a pasteboard likeness of Sihanouk.[8]

"Vive la République," shouted the audience of some 40,000 spectators, mostly students, at the end of the pageant. The government also inculcated the concept of a republic by ordering the removal of the term "royal" from the names of government organizations, ranging from Royal Air Cambodge, renamed Air Cambodge, to the Royal Khmer Armed Forces, changed to the National Khmer Armed Forces. In view of Sihanouk's lingering popularity, however, Lon Nol preferred to postpone proclamation of a republic until he was more certain of his government's security and stability—a goal that would require far more time than anticipated at the time of the coup.

Allied Intervention

Well before the American intervention in Cambodia on May 1, 1970, Lon Nol had privately relayed his first tentative requests, through the U.S. chargé d'affaires, Michael Lloyd Rives, for U.S. arms and ammunition to compensate for diminishing supplies of Soviet and Chinese items. The White House and the Pentagon had indicated, through normal State Department channels, that they were seriously studying these requests, but Washington never once intimated that it was contemplating sending American troops across the frontier.

Cambodian officials initially seemed to have had misgivings about the Cambodian operation. Trinh Hoanh, the new information minister, who as an assembly deputy had actively opposed Sihanouk, told reporters on the day of the incursion that Cambodia would indeed "protest" against this "violation of Cambodian territory." At his office at the Présidence du Conseil, however, Lon Nol was reaching a decision that would destroy whatever possibility remained for some form of face-saving compromise with the Vietnamese Communists. On May 5, 1970, five days after the American plunge across the frontier, Lon Nol informed a Chinese diplomat with whom he had been conducting secret talks that he would, under no circumstances, cooperate with Vietnamese Communist troops in Cambodia. Or, as Lon Nol put it in a radio address on May 11, Peking recognized that "these negotiations were fruitless" and broke off diplomatic relations.[9]

Lon Nol implied that he had all along discouraged the Chinese Embassy, but the truth was that he had avoided a definite stand ever since the talks were launched shortly after the departure of the Vietnamese Communist diplomats on March 27. The bargain offered by the Chinese, speaking on behalf of Hanoi and the NLF as well as Peking, was that China would view Sihanouk's overthrow as entirely an internal Cambodian affair, provided Cambodia facilitated the shipment of arms and medical supplies for Communist troops, tolerated North Vietnamese and Viet Cong on Cambodian territory, and offered propaganda support for the Communist cause in Vietnam. Lon Nol's final rejection of the Chinese proposals resulted directly from the U.S. incursion across the Cambodian frontier. If the Americans were willing to send their own troops into Cambodia, so Cambodian leaders reasoned, then surely they would provide all the support the Cambodians needed to drive out the Communists.

A corollary of Lon Nol's decision to reject any suggestion of compromise was that Sihanouk was free to form a government in exile based in Peking. On May 5, 1970, the day of the final rupture between Lon Nol and the Chinese diplomat, Sihanouk proclaimed the "Royal Government of National Union," which Peking immediately recognized as the legitimate regime. China had obviously coordinated its diplomacy in Phnom Penh with Sihanouk, who might have languished as the leader of a mere "front" organization had U.S. intervention not led Lon Nol to clarify his position for Peking's benefit.

One immediate effect of the events of May 5 was to force all countries to choose between the government in office in Phnom Penh and the government-in-exile in Peking. A total of twenty-three governments, including those of China, North Vietnam, the NLF, most of the Arab countries, Cuba, and Yugoslavia, recognized Sihanouk's regime within the next few months. This mass transfer of diplomatic accreditation contributed to the isolation of Lon Nol, who still wanted Cambodia to remain neutral in hopes that North Vietnam and the NLF might eventually change their policies under severe American military pressure. Some thirty governments maintained their embassies in Phnom Penh—with a number of them, such as India and France, not openly expressing any preference for one regime or the other. The latter category included the Soviet Union and four of its Eastern European allies, East Germany, Poland, Czechoslovakia, and Bulgaria.

The Soviet Union's position was particularly delicate, in that it wanted to frustrate Peking's ambitions while retaining its prestige in North Vietnam. The Soviet Premier, Alexei N. Kosygin, possibly armed with information that Sihanouk was about to announce the formation of a government in exile in Peking, may have hoped to undercut this evidence of Chinese influence when he held a press conference in Moscow on May 4, the day before Sihanouk's announcement. Kosygin, sitting beside his foreign minister, Andrei A. Gromyko, called on "the peoples of the world to stop the [U.S.] aggression in Cambodia" but failed to support his words with any suggestion for concrete action.[10]

The ambivalence—possibly confusion—displayed by the Soviet Union aroused speculation that Moscow might attempt to dissuade Hanoi from prosecuting a military "war of liberation" in Cambodia. It was not likely, in fact, that North Vietnam ever contemplated waging such a war entirely on its own. The formation of Sihanouk's government in exile provided a focal point around which the Vietnamese Communists could attempt to rally local Cambodian support for Sihanouk. The prince openly admitted that his front was coordinating "its struggle with that of the fraternal peoples of Vietnam and Laos" but called for creation of his own "National Liberation Army" comprised of "guerrilla units, partisans," and so forth.[11]

The implication was that North Vietnam was still primarily concerned with the struggle for South Vietnam and viewed the fighting in Cambodia as a necessary adjunct to the Vietnam conflict. If a Cambodian "liberation" army could restore a sympathetic government in Phnom Penh, then Hanoi need hardly prosecute its own campaign in Cambodia. Hanoi's interest in promoting local revolt reflected not only diplomatic and political considerations but also its own limited capabilities. North Vietnam by 1970 may have increased its troop strength in Cambodia to 50,000 men, as Western intelligence analysts alleged, but at least half of these served as porters or rear support personnel. Hanoi needed the rest for the war in South Vietnam and could never spare more than 5,000 or 10,000 for fighting a sporadic conflict in Cambodia.

Indicative of North Vietnam's interest in arousing local support was a "summit conference of the Indochinese peoples" held, in late April, 1970, according to a final communiqué released on April 27, "in a locality of the Laos-Vietnam-China border area." Among the participants were Sihanouk and members of his front; Prince Souphanouvong, leader of the Pathet Lao; North Vietnam Premier Pham Van Dong; and Nguyen Huu Tho, president of the NLF central committee. The communiqué reaffirmed such objectives as "peace, neutrality," and prohibition "of all foreign troops or military bases," but it also evinced "special concern for the Cambodian people's struggle."[12] These thoughts, announced publicly three days before U.S. intervention, revealed Hanoi's fear that it would lose its Cambodian sanctuaries, without which it might not win military victory in Vietnam.

Just as North Vietnam's basic concern immediately after the overthrow of Sihanouk had been to defend its sanctuaries, so its ambition after the entry of South Vietnamese and U.S. troops into Cambodia was to open up entire new base areas, sources of food supplies, and routes for the infiltration of men and materiel through Cambodia to South Vietnam. Although Hanoi and the NLF probably had not anticipated U.S. intervention they knew, after the first major South Vietnamese incursions, supported by American air strikes in the middle of April, that none of their bases were immune from attack. Hence, it was not surprising that, when the Americans finally did cross the border on May 1, 1970, they met little initial opposition. The Vietnamese Communists had evacuated most of their sanctuaries, leaving behind mainly snipers and local Viet Cong defenders.

U.S. commanders soon realized that their troops would probably never accomplish President Nixon's avowed goal of smashing "the headquarters for the entire Communist military operation in South Vietnam." U.S. intelligence analysts had not misjudged the general location of the Central Office for South Vietnam (COSVN), but it was far more diffused and mobile than they had anticipated. By May 21, three weeks after the operation had begun, military planners admitted that COSVN had long since vanished from its previous location in the Fishhook, the salient that juts into South Vietnam 80 miles north of Saigon, and had relocated in dense jungle well beyond the 21.7-mile limit set by Nixon for U.S. activities in Cambodia. If they were unable to find COSVN, however, U.S. and South Vietnamese troops were still successful, in narrow, strictly military terms, in discovering enemy arms caches and obliterating sanctuaries spread over miles of jungle.

A visit to a 2-square-mile complex of thatched huts and bunkers 10 miles north of the Fishhook—but only a mile and a half inside the frontier—illustrated the military significance of the allied campaign. The nickname "the city" that Americans had given the complex seemed to underrate rather than exaggerate the value of the sprawling base area, bound together by a network of narrow bamboo walkways and bicycle paths. Not a trace of "the city" was visible from the air, but rickety wooden huts and cavernous log-covered bunkers were hidden around almost every bend in the double- and triple-canopied jungle. "This area is for the people who support the liberation of South Vietnam," said a sign in Vietnamese hanging over one of the bunkers near a helicopter pad hacked out by troops of the U.S. 1st Air Cavalry Division. Beside the sign was a crate of brand new Soviet-made SKS rifles, still coated with a greasy preservative to keep them from rusting in monsoon rains.

U.S. intelligence analysts at first believed that "the city" was the largest base area along the frontier, but they soon discovered that it was only typical of at least half a dozen of approximately the same size. Some 25 miles to the northeast—and 100 miles north of Saigon—1st Air Cavalry Division soldiers uncovered caches in former sanctuaries dubbed by them "Rock Island East" and "Shakey's Hill." At the same time, the 11th Armored Cavalry Regiment roared through the Fishhook, south of "the city," then raced northeast 15 miles up Route 7 from a rubber plantation near Memot to the town of Snoul, 3 miles north of "the city." Half the town, including a row of Chinese-owned shops on the main street, was wiped out in several hours of fighting before the North Vietnamese retreated under cover of darkness. The skirmish demonstrated the inability of the Communists to frustrate the U.S. campaign militarily, but it also illustrated the destruction that might soon engulf much of the country.

The U.S. campaign in Cambodia extended about 30 miles south and west of the Fishhook region to an area on the map known to U.S. officers as the "Dog's Face," which was invaded by soldiers of the 25th Infantry Division. Two brigades of the 4th Division also plunged into the Se San base area, in the highlands of Ratanakiri Province more than 200 miles north of Saigon, but they withdrew after little more than a week. Basically, U.S. operations in Cambodia focused along an 80-mile stretch of frontier from which the North Vietnamese had launched their major offensives in 1968 and 1969 on bases and towns within a 50-mile radius of Saigon. In terms of statistics, with which U.S. commanders measured almost all activities in the war, the Cambodian campaign was by far the most successful of any previous venture. In a "memorandum for correspondents" released on June 30, 1970, the day the last U.S. troops were withdrawn from Cambodia, the U.S. command in Saigon reported that "average daily results" from May 1 through June 23 had been ten times greater than in all American operations inside Vietnam in the previous twelve-month period.[13]

Officers debated whether or not the Americans had found one third or possibly one half of all enemy equipment stored in the "sanctuaries," but most analysts agreed that the campaign had dealt a severe military blow to the Communists. Nor did it seem that the North Vietnamese or Viet Cong could easily regain their old positions once the Americans had left, for South Vietnamese officials planned to keep their troops in Cambodia as long as their presence seemed advantageous in terms of the war in Vietnam. The South Vietnamese, concentrating on a 120-mile arc from the Gulf of Thailand to the Parrot's Beak, disrupted enemy sanctuaries and uncovered caches of weapons, but their primary accomplishment was to relieve Communist pressure on Cambodian towns and cities.

The North Vietnamese and Viet Cong, responding to the first major South Vietnamese incursions across the frontier in the middle of April, had driven Cambodian defenders from the major coastal towns of Kep and Kampot and might have contemplated an attack on Kompong Som. The North Vietnamese also overran a series of towns on main roads northeast of Phnom Penh as allied troops invaded the rubber plantations on or near the border. In all these moves U.S. military analysts believed that the Communists' main objective was still South Vietnam. They had to establish a rear line of defense for their former sanctuaries, to open up new base areas and infiltration routes, and to try to intimidate the government in Phnom Penh into some level of cooperation.

South Vietnamese troops frustrated these plans to some extent by sweeping along the coast almost as far as Kompong Som and north through the Elephant Mountains. The result was that traffic, notably oil trucks, moved regularly, except for temporary interruptions, until late 1970 from Kompong Som to Phnom Penh, although the Communists still retained some of their base areas in the mountains. Equally important, in terms of defending Phnom Penh, was a land-river operation designed to clear the Mekong and open Route 1 all the way to the capital. The need to evacuate some 60,000 Vietnamese refugees, crowded into camps along the river, provided the pretext for a complex series of maneuvers. The operation had already begun, in a sense, with the South Vietnamese thrust down Route 1 from the border on April 29 and April 30.

In the first week of May, South Vietnamese marines and soldiers drove north beside the Bassac River, which splits off from the Mekong at Phnom Penh and parallels it across the delta. On May 8, South Vietnamese officers—and their U.S. advisers—were confident enough of security to send the first of more than 100 boats up the Mekong from the border. By the time the boats arrived at Neak Loeung, a ferry crossing on Route 1 40 miles southeast of Phnom Penh, most of the North Vietnamese troops had fled the town. After driving out the last remaining snipers and rear guards, South Vietnamese soldiers and marines escorted several thousand refugees onto landing craft and barges for the ride downstream. The marines then waited for three days, from May 8 to May 10, for the arrival of a column of Cambodian troops from Phnom Penh. The marines might have pushed their own offensive up Route 1 from Neak Loeung, but diplomacy and politics dictated that Cambodian troops reach the town for the "link-up."

South Vietnamese soldiers and marines then advanced through the jungles beside the road to within 3 miles of Phnom Penh. The boats, arriving in Phnom Penh on May 11, provided some degree of security along the banks. Shifting their threat to the capital's northeastern approaches, the Vietnamese Communists fired at South Vietnamese boats sent to Kompong Cham on May 13. While the boats picked up refugees, the Communists seized the town across the river and threatened to capture Kompong Cham itself. South Vietnamese troops, driving across the French-owned Chup rubber plantation east of Kompong Cham, did not relieve the pressure on the town until late May.

"The North Vietnamese are going to have a hell of a time," remarked Lieutenant General Do Cao Tri, as he led a South Vietnamese task force through the 70-square-mile Chup plantation on May 16. General Tri, discussing the effects of allied operations on the enemy, predicted that Communist troops would "cause the Cambodians trouble" but basically had been "pushed too far back into Cambodia to hurt the lower half of South Vietnam for many days to come."* Most analysts agreed with this view. It seemed highly unlikely that North Vietnam could soon recover either its former sanctuaries or its old infiltration route through Sihanouk-ville, particularly since U.S. and South Vietnamese navy boats had begun patrolling the southern Cambodian coast. If the allied operation had gained time for the governments in Saigon and Phnom Penh, however, it also may have contributed to North Vietnam's determination to capture other towns defended only by Cambodian troops and form an entirely new complex of infiltration routes and base areas from which to launch attacks on Vietnam.

In keeping with this strategy, North Vietnamese troops overran Attopeu, in southern Laos, on April 30, 1970, the day the South Vietnamese Government announced its first cross-border operation "with American combat support." Then, in the month of May, the North Vietnamese attacked every military outpost on the river network between Attopeu and Kompong Cham. The result was that North Vietnam could send men and materiel from road junctions near Attopeu down the Kong River to Stung Treng, at the junction of the Kong and Mekong 30 miles south of the Cambodian-Laos frontier. North Vietnam also controlled the Mekong from the frontier, but the Kong was far preferable, since the Mekong was blocked by waterfalls and rapids in southern Laos. From Stung Treng, the North Vietnamese could ship their goods by sampans as far as Kratie, the next provincial capital, 50 miles to the south. Materiel then had to go by road to new storage sites in the jungle or to the South Vietnamese frontier, 40 miles from Kratie at the nearest point.

Cambodian officials offered hardly a fight for the northeast. In *de facto* concession of the entire territory, the last remaining Cambodian troops—8,000 men in two towns on Route 19—were evacuated by road in the final week of June. Supported by a 5,000-man South Vietnamese task force, they were transported to training camps in South Vietnam. By July 1, only the Communists, in the name of Sihanouk's front, exercised any control at all over the northeastern provinces, one third of the country. The Communists at the same time advanced west of the Mekong, so that

---

* General Tri was killed on February 23, 1971, when his helicopter crashed after takeoff in South Vietnam. Ironically, he was en route to the Chup plantation, where his troops were engaged in a new operation.

Cambodian troops could operate only from beleaguered, isolated enclaves along Route 6 north of the Tonle Sap, or Great Lake. Several thousand Cambodians defended such towns as Kompong Cham, Kompong Thom, and Siemreap, all on Route 6, but the road itself was impassable. Indeed, Cambodian troops could not even venture from Siemreap to drive the Communists from the ruins of the Angkor temple complex, where they encamped in early June.

One question, as the war widened over the entire country, was how—or whether—the Lon Nol government could survive without permanent South Vietnamese and U.S. support. Cambodian officials readily admitted their disappointment over the limitations, in time and distance, set by President Nixon for American operations and were not enthusiastic about entrusting the defense of their country to the South Vietnamese. A signal of lingering suspicions between Phnom Penh and Saigon was the debate over border difficulties between Cambodian Foreign Minister Yem Sambaur and South Vietnamese Foreign Minister Tran Van Lam. The two, meeting in Saigon, temporarily buried their difficulties on May 27, 1970, in a joint communiqué in which they postponed consideration of these problems, which dated from Sihanouk's old quarrel with Diem, and agreed to restore diplomatic relations.

Cambodia hopes for substantial support from a consortium of regional and great powers had already been tempered by the inconclusive results of a two-day conference held at Jakarta on May 16 and 17, 1970, by the foreign ministers of eleven Asian and Pacific nations, including Australia, Indonesia, Japan, South Korea, Laos, Malaysia, New Zealand, the Philippines, Singapore, Thailand, and South Vietnam. Indonesia had convened the conference specifically to discuss the Cambodian crisis, but the most that Yem Sambaur could gain from it was the propaganda value of statements demanding withdrawal of foreign troops from Cambodia. The ministers also called for reactivation of the International Control Commission, disbanded in Cambodia at Sihanouk's request at the end of 1969, but no one imagined that the ICC could possibly extricate Cambodia from its plight. The country's only real hope, as Cambodian leaders were well aware, lay in U.S. aid.

It was partly as a result of Yem Sambaur's lack of success in Saigon and Jakarta that Lon Nol and Sirik Matak decided in June, 1970, to relieve him as foreign minister and leave him the relatively secondary post of minister of justice. His replacement, Koun Wick, Sihanouk's ambassador to Yugoslavia, flew to Saigon on July 6,

1970, in a U.S. Air Force plane to discuss Cambodia's needs with U.S. Secretary of State William Rogers, who had just attended a meeting of foreign ministers of all the nations—the United States, Australia, New Zealand, Thailand, South Korea, and South Vietnam—allied in the Vietnam conflict. Rogers made no promises, but, soon after his return to Washington, the government earmarked $40 million in addition to the $8.9 million in aid that had been proferred Cambodia on an emergency basis before June 30. Most of the aid consisted of small arms, such as carbines and light machine guns, ammunition, trucks and jeeps, and other basic items. South Vietnam supplemented the U.S. program with a series of eight-week training courses for new Cambodian troops, who received carbines, M-79 grenade-launchers, light machine guns, and radios before their return to Cambodia. South Vietnamese C-119 flying boxcars flew in daily shipments of ammunition and other equipment, including some 10,000 Chinese-made AK-47 rifles, captured during allied operations in Cambodia. (The United States refrained from supplying Cambodia with any of its own M-16 rifles as long as the AK-47 remained the basic weapon of the Cambodian Army.)

The U.S. aid program, however, fulfilled only a small fraction—perhaps 20 per cent—of what Lon Nol had hoped the United States would offer in the first year after withdrawal of its troops from Cambodia. Even American air support was a somewhat doubtful quantity. President Nixon, in his June 3 address on Cambodia, had said that U.S. planes would fly missions over the country after June 30 only "to interdict the movement of enemy troops and material, and where I find that [it] is necessary to protect the lives and security of our men in South Vietnam."[14] American planes flew daily missions in direct support of Cambodian troops, but U.S. military analysts conceded that the United States might not offer all the airpower Cambodia needed in a showdown struggle.

The new U.S. Ambassador, Emory C. Swank, reflected Nixon's determination to maintain a "low profile" in Cambodia. The object, said Swank on September 14, shortly after his arrival, was to provide as much aid as Cambodians needed to fight the war on their own—without U.S. troops. Lon Nol gradually came to accept this proposition, but then his government began to press for another $100 or $200 million in economic aid to purchase petroleum, oil, and lubricants, and other vital war materials. Cambodian officials explained that rubber and rice exports had almost ceased since early April. Rubber production had halted on virtually all the major plantations, and rice could no longer be transported from the major rice-producing areas to the port of Kompong Som. The economic tragedy of the war was that Cambodian officials, before Sihanouk's overthrow, had forecast a record rice harvest for 1970 with exports of 450,000 metric tons valued at $44.5 million and an over-all favorable trade balance for the first time since 1965. Rubber was also expected to contribute to the balance with an increase in production of 4,500 metric tons and total exports of 52,000 metric tons worth $20.8 million. Economists had also predicted sizable exports of petroleum products from the Sihanoukville refinery, opened in October, 1968, which previously had limited itself largely to domestic requirements.[15]

After having exported 14,128 metric tons of rubber in the first four months of 1970, Cambodia could only ship stores in stock for the rest of the year, as plantations and processing plants were overrun and destroyed by U.S. and North and South Vietnamese troops. Rubber exports for 1970 finally totaled only 18,426 metric tons, valued at 455,057,000 riels, or $8,273,582.[16] Western diplomats believed, moreover, that Phon Penh might eventually have to import a substantial amount of rice in 1971 to fulfill the dietary needs of the capital, cut off from the main rice-growing regions. Prices in Phnom Penh, not seriously afflicted by inflation before Sihanouk's fall, had doubled on many items by early 1971, while the black market value of the riel had declined from around 60 to 100 riels per $1 during the same period.

In view of these problems, Nixon, on November 18, 1970, asked the U.S. Congress to approve an additional $155 million in aid for Cambodia. The President attempted to put the Cambodian request in the context of the Nixon doctrine by asserting that such expenditures were "essential to the support of our national security goals and our foreign policy interests *as we reduce our direct involvement abroad.*" Congress rapidly approved Nixon's request, which included $70 million for economic and $85 million for military purposes, mainly small arms and ammunition, in addition to $100 million already allocated for military aid.[17]

There seemed little likelihood, however, that such support for Cambodia's unwieldy military establishment would deter the Vietnamese Communists from fighting to regain Cambodia as a safe haven for the movement of men and supplies to South Vietnam. An integral phase of the Communist campaign, in fact, was to further weaken Cambodia's economy by obtaining easy passage to the rice-growing region around Battambang. Hanoi's objective was not to try to starve Phnom Penh but to obtain the food the North Vietnamese troops needed as it had done while Sihanouk was in power. North Vietnamese soldiers continually harassed or cut off Route 4, the link from Phnom Penh to Kompong Som, so the capital would be utterly dependent on the Mekong River channel from South Vietnam for all its imports, including oil.

The Cambodian Army did not appear capable of responding effectively to the North Vietnamese challenge until at least 1973, and the Lon Nol regime might not survive that long. Indicative of Cambodian military impotence was an offensive launched in early September, 1970, to reopen Route 6 as far as Kompong Thom. Some 2,000 North Vietnamese troops, dug in around the village of Taing Kauk, 50 miles north of Phnom Penh, halted the entire offensive, conducted by 6,000 troops, at least 1,000 of them newly trained in South Vietnam.

North Vietnamese resistance to the operation could still be viewed in terms of Hanoi's aims in South Vietnam. Control over Route 6, for instance, provided some degree of defense for infiltration routes to Battambang as well for new routes to southern Cambodia, where troops were based for action in the Mekong delta. Nor had the Communists—and Sihanouk—abandoned their goal of installing a sympathetic regime in Phnom Penh with pro-Sihanouk Cambodian troops. "The rainy season was marked by intensive work training combat units and political and administrative training," said Sihanouk in an interview in Peking as the monsoon ended in September, 1970, and Cambodia braced for a dry season offensive.[18]

There was some question, however, as to whether or not the Communists would welcome Sihanouk's return, even though they continued to fight in his name. Sihanouk, after all, had vigorously pursued and persecuted the Khmer Rouge and had criticized the presence of North Vietnamese troops in Cambodia before his fall. The final irony of Sihanouk's government-in-exile was that its list of members named three, Khieu Samphan, Hou Youn, and Hu Him, who had reportedly been executed on Sihanouk's secret orders in late 1967. Sihanouk—and the Communists—had apparently thought it wise to include their names in order to win back the confidence of the Khmer Rouge and to demonstrate conclusively that he had changed sides in the conflict.

It was largely to counteract Sihanouk's traditional propaganda image as popular king and prince that Lon Nol and Sirik Matak decided finally to change Cambodia from a monarchy to a republic. On October 5, 1970, the National Assembly voted unanimously to declare Cambodia a republic, and, on October 9, In Tam, the president of the National Assembly, issued the required proclamation ending what he said had been "often cruel, capricious rule by the monarchy."[19] Cannon thundered in salute, diplomats and politicians cheered, and Lon Nol unfurled a new flag—a blue field with the white profile of Angkor Wat on a red background in the upper left-hand corner. Previously the Angkor Wat emblem had dominated the middle of the flag, but Cambodian leaders decided to downgrade its importance without ignoring its value as a national symbol. The war was now literally a contest between royalists and republicans, each backed in varying degrees by North or South Vietnamese forces, themselves in turn allied with China or the United States.

Cambodia remained the testing ground for the Nixon doctrine. The question was whether or not the new republic had been stillborn or would survive the next series of military confrontations promised by Sihanouk and the Communists.

III
Thailand: Uncertain Ally

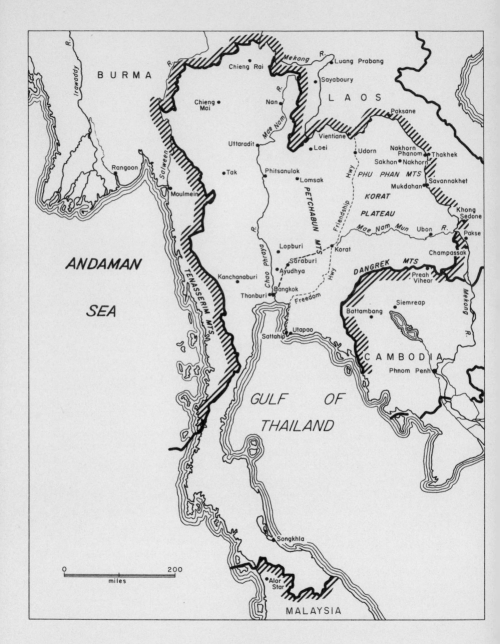

Thailand

6

Foundation of Stability

Renaissance of Military Rule

The extent to which the United States was willing to commit itself on the Indochinese peninsula was studied with fully as much intensity and concern in the Thai capital of Bangkok as it was in Phnom Penh or Saigon. Although Thailand did not face an immediate threat, as did Cambodia and South Vietnam, its leaders had nonetheless gambled a large measure of the nation's security and stability on the strength of the U.S.-Thai alliance. Yet Thailand, unlike all the Indochinese states except North Vietnam, had a record of continuity of rule that seemed to argue against the possibility of sudden shifts in policy. From the failure of the World War II liaison with Japan, there had arisen a military-dominated regime noted for its power over domestic critics as well as its conservative opposition to change.

In a literal sense, the development of military leadership in the post–World War II generation was not a new phenomenon but a rebirth. The Prime Minister from 1939 to 1944 was Field Marshal Phibun Songkhram, an army general whose main rival was the leftist Pridi Panomyong, with whom he had been allied in the 1932 coup against monarchical rule. While Pridi was relegated in 1941 to the secondary role of regent for King Ananda Mahidol, then aged sixteen, Phibun bargained with the Japanese. The same day, December 7, 1941, that Japan attacked the American base at Pearl Harbor, it also demanded Thailand's permission to let its troops cross the country en route to Burma, then controlled by Britain. Phibun agreed. Whatever else happened, he did not want to be on the losing side, and he did not want Thailand to fall under foreign subjugation.

It might be argued that Phibun could at least have offered passive resistance to the Japanese rather than have acceded to all their demands, including the signing of a formal alliance two weeks after Pearl Harbor, but he was also motivated by a revanchist spirit against Britain and France. Japan, in return for Thai cooperation, compelled Vichy France to agree to restore to Thailand the two western Cambodian provinces that Thailand had ceded in 1907. Japan then gave Thailand the four northern Malay provinces ceded to Britain in 1909. In view of Thailand's overriding national interests and its lack of defense against Japanese might, Phibun's diplomatic course was well advised.

It was not, however, Phibun's diplomacy but that of Seni Pramoj, his disloyal ambassador to the United States, that restored Thailand to favor in Washington after the war and ultimately led to the new alliance on which Phibun and his successors thrived. Seni was so convinced of the folly of his government's relationship with Japan that he refused in early 1942 to deliver its declaration of war to the U.S. secretary of state, Cordell Hull. The result of this unauthorized act of diplomacy was that the United States not only did not view Thailand as an enemy but provided Seni with funds and other assistance to operate the "Free Thai" movement from Washington. At the same time, Pridi clandestinely headed the "Free Thai" movement in Thailand itself.

In the critical period after the Japanese defeat, power naturally shifted toward the figures who had opposed Phibun throughout the war. Pridi and Seni seemed ideal for the delicate task of uniting the country, appeasing the Americans and the British, and still maintaining a spirit of Thai nationalism. Pridi forced Phibun's resignation in July, 1944, by which time it was clear that the Japanese were losing, and then supported Seni as Prime Minister shortly after the Japanese surrender the next year. In early 1946, however, Pridi decided that he could best control feuding political factions by serving as Prime Minister himself. Then, in June, 1946, two months after Pridi's appointment, King Ananda Mahidol was found shot to death in the palace.[1]

Who killed the king? The great mystery of modern Thai history has never been solved. The first victim of the investigation, however, was Pridi, the former regent, who resigned two months later in an atmosphere of deep suspicion. His followers remained in power until—irony of ironies—Phibun himself in late 1947 participated in another coup against the government. The renaissance of Phibun, who had gone to Paris after the war, proved that Thailand's military leaders were neither repentant nor particularly unpopular as a result of their alliance with Japan. The country had succeeded, almost, in regaining the respect of the great powers, who had offered to admit Thailand to the United Nations after it had given up the Malay and Cambodian provinces gained during the period of Japanese conquest.

Pridi not only lost all power but had to flee the country, along with some of his followers, whom army officers were also determined to arrest. Although Pridi was probably unjustly accused for political reasons, the death of King Ananda heralded a new era in Thai history. For the next generation, the kingdom was ruled by a close, delicate alliance between military leaders and the new king, Bhumibol Adulyadej, who did not impede the will of the cabinet but was astute enough to build up his own image to the point at which he could carefully make suggestions and check sometimes overweening ambitions of individuals in the government.

Bhumibol, eighteen years old at the time of his brother's death, did not begin to exercise any real influence for another decade. Indeed, he was not even crowned until May, 1950, after he had finished preparing for his unexpected career by studying political science and law in Switzerland. In the meantime, military rulers were gradually solidifying their control. The leaders of the coup at first installed a compromise civilian as Prime Minister but replaced him with Phibun in 1948. The government then had to put down several attempted coups d'état, the most serious of which was a comic-opera incident in June, 1951, in which Phibun was kidnaped from aboard a navy ship during a ceremony to thank U.S. officials for military assistance. After a battle of several days, Phibun escaped as his own forces defeated the navy officers who had perpetrated the coup.

Those responsible for these coups were arrested, imprisoned, and, in some cases, shot and killed without trials. The government turned anti-Communism into a national crusade, an excuse for suppressing all enemies, real and imagined. Pridi indicated his political leanings by exiling himself to China, under Communist rule since late 1949. (He remained in China—possibly against his will for part of the time—until 1970, when he surfaced again with relatives in Paris.) Competition for leadership in the 1950's seemed to revolve around two men, General Phao Siyanon, the deputy director-general of police, and Marshal Sarit Thanarat, the army commander, whom Phibun tried to play off against each other.

Two factors entered into the elections and coups d'état that

finally resulted in the declines of both Phibun and Phao and the
rise of Sarit to a position of almost absolute dictatorship. One was
the belief, common among all Thai leaders since 1932, that Thailand should be governed by constitutional means, and the second
was the country's traditional facility for responding to the influence
of new alliances. Both factors were fused when Phibun journeyed
to the United States and Britain in 1955 and returned to Thailand
imbued with almost a missionary zeal to introduce Western-style
democratic rule. On a more practical level, Phibun may have seen
the restoration of democracy in Thailand as a way to extricate himself from his dependence on the increasing power of Phao, Sarit,
and the officers around them.

For a country ostensibly dedicated to constitutional rule, Thailand experienced remarkable difficulties in arriving at a constitution that struck the proper balance between legitimate political
freedom and necessary central authority. The fourth constitution,
an amended version of the first constitution of 1932, had been in
force for four years when Phibun, on his return from abroad in
1955, not only approved legislation for registering political parties
but also decided to provide a public forum for all views, similar to
London's Hyde Park. In the ensuing political chaos, at least
twenty-five parties competed for varying degrees of power.

The logical sequence to noisy expressions of all manner of public opinion was an election, the fourth since the war. Such an exercise might have seemed of secondary importance in view of the
constitution's provision that candidates could run only for seats in
the lower house, but competing government leaders decided to
demonstrate their political strength. The balloting, in February,
1957, was accompanied by so many charges of corruption and
threats of revenge that the government declared a national emergency. Sarit, who had remained aloof from the campaigning in
which General Phao had enthusiastically immersed himself, led
the armed forces during the emergency and was elevated to minister of defense in March.[2] Thus, Phibun's experiment with democracy led directly to military government and the abnegation of any
pretense of political freedom or constitutional rule for more than
a decade.

For Marshal Sarit, who had risen from command of an infantry
battalion shortly after the war, the emergency provided an excellent opportunity to popularize himself by denouncing all sides in
the elections. In September, 1957, he engineered a coup that resulted in the exiles of both Phibun and Phao. After new elections

in December, 1957, one of Sarit's allies, General Thanom Kittikachorn, was appointed Prime Minister. Sarit himself was confident enough of his power to fly to the United States and Britain for medical treatment. On returning to Thailand in October, 1958, however, he decided that the government still was endangered by leftists who might attempt another coup. This threat, real or not, provided the perfect excuse for a "coup against himself," in which he dissolved the assembly and abolished the constitution.[3]

From 1958 until the 1970's, the Thai Government was dominated by a single clique. The stability of this period was in part a reaction to the era of coups, constitutions, and elections. The cabinet, although it studied the possibilities of a new constitution and eventually put one into effect, did not want to risk opposition from its opponents, who might adopt the techniques of the ruling military officers. Hence, Sarit and his allies resorted to a kind of benevolent dictatorship in which dissidence, particularly from the left, was almost completely suppressed. The government was so powerful without a constitution that Sarit's death in 1963 caused no serious dislocation. Thanom Kittikachorn, his Deputy Premier and heir apparent, succeeded him without controversy.

The confusion of the "prerevolutionary" period prior to Sarit's coup of October, 1958, yielded, then, to an era of bland and ordered uniformity. Just as the generals and their allies had fought for power before the rise of Sarit, so they fought afterward to retain their positions and amass fortunes from private investment and foreign aid. Sarit himself was a case in point. Although he had already begun to acquire his fortune when he was appointed chairman of the government lottery bureau in 1952, he and his family were able to exploit fully their vast holdings during his rule. Sarit's known assets at the time of his death included controlling interest in at least fifteen companies, ranging from a bank with a monopoly on the import of gold, to a construction company with major government contracts, to a brewery, all of which were worth a total of approximately $150 million. The value of Sarit's estate, which included such amenities as fifty-one cars, a helicopter, a fishing boat, diamond jewelry, and twenty houses in Bangkok for his "minor wives" or mistresses, far exceeded that of any of the other national leaders in Bangkok, but the pattern was typical.[4]

Nor was Thailand's prosperity beneficial merely to the wealthy. While the population increased by a third from 1958 to 1970, the gross national product nearly doubled from $2.8 billion to $5.4 billion in 1970—if computed at the 1962 value of the dollar—or

$6.3 billion at 1970 dollar figures. The per capita GNP for the entire country rose in the same period from $90 to $180, at 1970 dollar figures, while per capita GNP for the central plain around Bangkok, where nearly a third of the people lived, was approaching $300 by the 1970's. Agricultural income managed to keep up with population growth for most of this period, but the income from nonagricultural ·sectors—commerce, industry, and services—more than doubled to the equivalent of nearly $4 billion. The result was that agriculture declined as a factor in the GNP from 40 per cent in 1958 to 30 in 1970, while the percentage of those dependent on agriculture for their incomes fell from approximately 85 per cent to 80.[5]

It might be argued, in fact, that the acquisitive business instinct of Sarit and his allies was a healthy phenomenon, for all of them had an immediate personal stake in the country's economic progress. They were not merely bureaucrats, responsible for the money and problems of others, but bank directors, importers and exporters, insurers and landowners dedicated to "free enterprise" as opposed to socialism, with a deep interest in enriching both themselves and their country. As indicated by Sarit's control of a construction company, the building boom was the most spectacular manifestation of Thailand's economic growth. The amount of money invested locally in construction doubled from $175 million for 1964 to $350 million during 1968 and began to level off at approximately $430 million in 1970. In the same period, the output of electrical power and the refining of petroleum, perhaps the two nonfood commodities most needed by the general public, increased by more than 50 per cent.[6]

The Vietnam war—and the U.S.-Thai alliance—provided the framework within which Thailand achieved its greatest economic growth, an average 8 per cent GNP increase each year from 1964 to 1970. The country's leaders and entrepreneurs reaped enormous profits from the construction of U.S. bases and other military spending, while the Thai Government, in the same period, invested the equivalent of $1.5 billion in development of an infrastructure of highways, dams, power projects, and the like.[7]

The country's interest in modernization and Westernization, similar to that expressed during most of its history, was reflected in the first and second plans, inaugurated in 1961 and 1966 respectively. "The First Development Plan focused on rehabilitation and improvement of existing transport and communications facilities, namely highways, rural roads, railways, ports, air transportation and telecommunication services," noted the National Economic Development Board. "By the end of 1966," summarized the board, "Thailand's highway network throughout the country stretched over 9,600 kilometers of which 60 per cent are all-weather roads." By the time of completion of the second five-year plan, the board anticipated, the government would have improved 2,462 kilometers of existing highways and built another 3,734.[8]

The second plan, besides continuing the programs in transport and communications, increased the investment in agriculture from the equivalent of $231.1 million in the first plan to $565 million. "Agriculture will remain as the backbone of the Thai economy for some time to come," said the National Economic Development Board. "The Development Plan therefore lays emphasis on improving agricultural productivity, and large sums are invested in extending irrigation and flood control, as well as transportation." The second plan included a program for building seven new dams and increasing the amount of irrigable area in the country from 4.7 million acres, one fourth of the total land under cultivation, to 6 million acres.

In proposing these plans for national development, the government seemed confident that it had the means to preserve its power and raise living standards as well. Army officers, government officials, and Sino-Thai businessmen unquestionably profited, but it was impossible at the end of the 1960's to quarrel with the assessment of Pote Sarasin, minister of national development since 1963 and a member of the board of a dozen major companies. "Thailand has successfully attained two of its priority policy goals simultaneously: to keep the currency stable and to achieve a high rate of growth. It has, therefore, become a centre of stability in South East Asia."[9]

Constitutional Politics

As the immediate threat of revolution or *coup d'état* subsided, government leaders, pressured by intellectuals, politicians, students, and dormant political parties, began to lobby for a constitution and elections. One of the strongest voices for a new constitution—the country's fifth since 1932—was King Bhumibol, who quietly prodded members of Thanom's cabinet to consider the advantages of new elections and at least an appearance of real democracy.

King Bhumibol thought that a constitution might provide a legal basis for controlling the whims of the military rulers—and perhaps for checking any attempts to reduce his role to that of a figurehead. Although Thanom and his Deputy Premier and minister of interior, General Praphass Charasutien, recognized the symbolic value of the monarchy, they were not inclined to heed the king's advice and forgo their own programs. And yet Bhumibol, more than many Western monarchs, already exercised considerable subtle influence through his vast family connections, wealth, contacts, and his realism about how far he could press his power before yielding to the will of his ministers.

The king, moreover, had some convincing arguments. One of them was that Thailand, by balking on the issue of constitution and elections, was behind its Western-oriented neighbors, including Laos, South Vietnam, and Malaysia, all of which had held parliamentary elections in some form during the 1960's. Another reason for a constitution and elections was the feeling among some officials that the entire process might help close the gap between the government and the people, particularly in the north and northeast. At the same time, the government opposed the kind of electoral system that might result in a repetition of earlier periods of political chaos.

Thus, Thailand warily approached a new era of constitutional democracy. The government, anxious to appease criticism and perhaps genuinely interested in sampling the will and feelings of the people, sought a compromise. In a statement on his administration in March, 1967, Thanom charged that critics of the government wanted parliament "to have much more power than the executive branch" in order to overthrow his regime. "Since these principles were used in all of the previous Thai constitutions, and since they caused countless difficulties in political quarters," he cautioned, "you can decide for yourselves . . . whether it is advisable for us to replace them with new principles, particularly the principle of cutting down the legislative branch's power in order to maintain a balance with that of the executive branch for the purpose of creating stability."[10]

These considerations led to the drafting in 1968 of a constitution that required the appointment by the king (advised by his cabinet) of the Senate and the popular election of members of the lower house. The constitution, formally signed and presented by the king on June 20, fulfilled all of Thanom's requirements for ensuring the continuity of his government. It provided, for instance, for the resignation of cabinet members only after a vote of no confidence by a majority of both houses meeting together. Since the cabinet in effect controlled almost all 164 members of the Senate, it would need only a handful of votes from the 219-member lower house. The constitution, moreover, did not require the government to submit its programs to a vote of confidence at all—and it exempted ministers from answering directly to the electorate by forbidding members of parliament from sitting in the cabinet. Indeed, the Prime Minister and other cabinet members did not even have to belong to the political party controlling the largest bloc of votes in either the Senate or the lower house. Should any obstreperous lower-house members attempt to ram through a bill displeasing to the government, they would face two obstacles: The constitution required "joint sittings" of both houses for adoption of some measures and gave the upper house the right to delay voting for a month on budgetary bills and a year on all other legislation. The constitution did guarantee freedom of speech, religion, and assembly but also provided for special laws to curtail these freedoms in case of national emergency.

In view of these restrictions, it was surprising that the first national elections, required within 240 days of promulgation of the constitution, attracted real interest among serious politicians. Yet the period from June 20, 1968, to February 10, 1969, the day of the elections, was one of political ferment, in the form of public criticism, party organization, and so forth, unprecedented since the rise of Sarit and his allies. The campaign not only compelled government leaders, notably Thanom and Praphass, to argue for their programs as they had never done before but also opened up national debate on such issues as corruption and inefficiency.

The Senate did not actually pass an electoral law, formally legalizing political parties for the first time since 1958, until late in 1968, but the two major groupings had already formed and were proselytizing for votes. They were the government's own political organization, the Saha Pracha Thai, or United Thai People's Party (UTPP), and the Prachathipat, or Democratic Party, led by Seni Pramoj, who remained as opposed to military rule in 1968 as he had been during World War II. Besides these two parties, nine others registered as required by law, including two with some following in the northeast. They were the Prachachon, or People's Party, led by Liang Chaiyakarnn, whom the voters in the town of Ubon had sent to parliament in every election since 1933, and the Naew Sethakorn, or Economist-United Front, headed by Tep Chotinuchit, a long-time leftist who had been released in 1966 after eight years in prison.

The government party might have preferred not to campaign at all, but it was apparent from the outset that the Democrats, royalist and conservative but still liberal compared to the military regime, were determined to turn the elections into a test of political strength. In cosmopolitan Bangkok, where the citizenry was often able to glimpse its ministers in person and frequently heard stories of their excesses, the Democrats proved the most powerful political force. The government, caught somewhat unprepared after a decade of unquestioned power, attempted to win popular favor by permitting public assemblies and lowering bus fares—but was basically no match for its main opposition in the metropolitan area.

One reason for the Democrats' relative strength in Bangkok was that government officials had underestimated them. Indicative of this tactical error was the government's failure to support a slate in the Bangkok municipal elections on September 1, 1968, partly because officials thought that candidates sympathetic to their policies would win on their own. The Democrats, crusading against the rising price of pork and other meat products, stunned the government by winning 22 of 24 seats on the municipal council. Seni and other Democratic candidates appealed not only to idealistic youth but to disaffected workers, clerks, teachers, intellectuals, and even some government officials with their repeated attacks on corruption in high places. Corruption, in fact, was by far the most important single issue in a campaign that never quite threatened the government's position but still proved a serious embarrassment.

"The government has all the means to win this election," Seni told me in an interview on February 8, 1969, two days before the voting. "The way they put themselves on radio and TV costs them nothing, but we have to pay 20,000 Baht [$1,000] per hour. Every hour in the morning, the government radio has attacked me." Democrats charged that cabinet ministers, their wives, and children were directors and stockholders of more than 300 corporations engaged in business with the government. "General Praphass himself controls the pig and livestock business," said Seni. "At Chieng Rai [the northernmost provincial capital], they've set up a quarantine system so the peasants can't sell their pigs outside the province. They have to sell to one big firm at half price." At a Democratic rally the day before the election, some 50,000 persons cheered Seni as he held up a cartoon depicting Praphass as a pig and then read off the numbers of twenty-seven phones in the general's nine private residences.

The Democrats linked the problems of corruption and conflict of interest directly to the government's efforts to win over the peasantry and fight Communism in the north and northeast. "We want complete support of the peasant economy," said Seni. "Nowadays the farming is left to the people. Nothing is done about fertilizer or insecticides." Seni's remark was not altogether correct, since the government, coordinating with American officials, had for years doled out aid and advice to farmers. The Democrats' basic point, however, was that personal greed had blunted the government's efforts in this and other programs. "We call for more effective, wholehearted defense against the Communists," said Seni, whose party, if anything, was more opposed to Communism than the UTPP.

The government, once its UTPP had begun functioning after the municipal election in September, based its campaign on the theme of peace and prosperity. "You never had it so good" was, in essence, the rallying cry. "In the administration, we are concentrating on national development to make our economy progressive in order to make the people contented and happy," said Thanom in June, before the king presented the constitution. "What would happen," Praphass asked, "if we allowed the establishment of a weak government or a government that is unaware of the facts concerning national defense, or that is less experienced than the present government?"[11]

For all these arguments, the difference in the attitudes of Bangkok citizens toward the UTPP and the Democrats was evident in comparing reactions to their rallies. On the day before the election, while Seni was enthralling a mob outside the palace, only several hundred persons turned out to listen to government candidates in the city's largest public park. Antigovernment antipathy ran so deep in Bangkok and Thonburi, a teeming industrial community across the Chao Phraya River, that Democratic candidates swept all 21 seats in the lower house—15 from the former and 6 from the latter. The turn-out of voters, to be sure, was only 35 per cent, but the results at least proved the success of the Democrats in publicizing their charges.

The government, however, compensated for this humiliation by running strong in the northern and northeastern provinces and in the central plain around Bangkok. The government's success in the rural areas was due in part to the peasant's traditional acquiescence to authority. Another factor was the government's control over local administrative machinery, which was able to publicize favored candidates more forcefully in rural communities than in Bangkok.

The final returns showed that the government party had won 75 of 219 seats in the lower house as opposed to 57 for the Democrats and 15 for ten minor parties. The government had determined the outcome of many of the elections outside of Bangkok and Thonburi by vote-buying and intimidation. The fact that officials did not succeed in these techniques in Bangkok reflected not so much the honesty of the nation's leaders as their fear of the consequences of repression of the popular Democrats, who were supported by student poll-watchers.

Even if the UTPP had not won a plurality of seats, however, the government was still certain to control a majority in the lower house. A total of 805 of the 1,644 candidates were "independents," most of whom, if elected, could be bribed to support the government. Many of the independents were members of the Free People's League of Thailand, organized by General Praphass, who counted on the name to evoke memories of the "Free Thai" movement of World War II. The "independents," who won the remaining 72 seats, were said to have been offered the equivalent of $10,000 each to join the UTPP. By 1970, the UTPP had 110 loyal followers in the lower house, a majority of one vote over all opposition members combined.

In the first year or so after the election, the parliament appeared to have fulfilled the government's view that it should serve as a safety valve for releasing pent-up emotions and frustrations. Although the Democrats frequently criticized the government, they rarely disagreed on matters of foreign or economic policy. Seni himself, aging and ailing, seemed reluctant to provide the leadership needed to turn the party into an effective opposition. Perhaps the Democrats' greatest achievement, reminiscent of their campaign, was to introduce an anticorruption bill, finally voted down after a debate that resurrected the charges made during the election campaign.

In the months following the elections, many parliamentarians thought it better to work with the system than to alienate the military sector of the leadership, particularly since the military, in the final analysis, had the power to suppress any real opposition. It was, then, somewhat surprising that the lower house in 1970 provided the forum for the first serious challenge to the existing regime in twelve years. Maneuvering revolved, superficially at any rate, around the issues of taxes and government spending, but it symbolized incipient discontent with the entrenched leadership and also indicated General Praphass's own desire for greater power.

The immediate issue was the government's worsening monetary problems. While the country had profited from U.S. military spending, its export trade, on which it would rely in the long run, declined drastically in relation to imports. Exports from Thailand were valued at $585 million in 1964 as opposed to $679 million in imports in the same year. By 1969, the value of exports had increased to only $711 million while that for imports was $1,262 million— a trade deficit of $551 million. The irony of this situation, however, was that Thailand's foreign reserves still rose from a total of $483 million in 1962 to a peak of $898 million by the end of 1968.[12]

"Foreigners have bought more goods and services, invested, or lent more money to Thailand than Thai have bought from foreign countries," explained the *Standard Bangkok Magazine* in November, 1969.[13] Indicative of Thailand's dependence on foreign investment was that foreign exchange reserves had decreased by $48 million to $850 million by the end of 1969 and fallen to $817 million in June, 1970. Thailand had not prepared itself for the combination of decreased American military spending and a marked decline in the export of rice, the leading local product. Earnings from the sale of rice abroad reached a peak of $224 million for the export of 1,482,000 metric tons in 1967 and then fell to a low of $141 million for 1,023,000 metric tons in 1969.[14] This decline was due in part to improvements in rice-growing in some of Thailand's foreign markets, but Thailand's trade imbalance might have been narrowed had government leaders placed higher priority on the over-all economic situation than on their own investments.

The state of the Thai economy became a political issue as a result of the government's growing budget deficit and its consequent efforts to raise taxes. Despite a deficit of 20 per cent for the fiscal year from October 1, 1969, through September 30, 1970, the government in May, 1970, drafted a budget for the next fiscal year for the equivalent of $1.465 billion, an increase of 7 per cent over the previous year. Then, in July, it asked parliament to adopt a bill calling for increased tariffs, higher taxes on private gross business earnings and personal income, excise taxes on liquor and soft drinks, and, perhaps most galling, rises in excise taxes on gasoline and cement—items that immediately affected individual consumers. The government, in the ensuing uproar, canceled the increases in gas and cement taxes but rammed through the rest of the bill by a vote of 102 to 101. The government then persuaded the lower house, by a somewhat wider margin, to authorize a budget for the equivalent of $1.43 billion—2 per cent below that originally proposed.

Thanom in effect acknowledged the threat posed in parliament by announcing a military alert in Bangkok and Thonburi beginning at midnight, July 7, 1970, the day before the start of debate on the tax bill. Even if the bill had been defeated, political analysts were certain that enough lower-house members would have been intimidated into passing a somewhat amended version. The worst that could have happened, if parliament passed neither the tax nor budget bills, would have been a cabinet reshuffle in which perhaps two or three ministers might have offered their resignations. Opposition in parliament, however, was not without meaning, for it also revealed Praphass's own cunning drive for power.

Much of the debate, in fact, had not transpired in parliament but in weekly meetings of the UTPP, at which a number of members of the Free People's League, who had run as independents and then joined the UTPP, had expressed their opposition to the government's budgetary proposals. UTPP members voted as a bloc with the government on the floor, but the party was partly responsible for the establishment of a twenty-three-member "budget committee" which included only six of its own members. The committee suggested revisions and criticisms, many of them embarrassing to those members of the government who were directly responsible for fiscal policies. Because Praphass still controlled the Free People's League, some observers believed that he had personally manipulated the opposition within the UTPP—and then the formation of the budget committee—to undermine Thanom.

Praphass's ambitions may have been partly responsible for Thanom's remark at an informal dinner at his residence on August 10, 1970, that he would not seek reappointment as Prime Minister after the next lower-house elections in 1972. At the same time, there was also the possibility that Thanom approved of Praphass's efforts at forming an independent base that might permit the two men and their allies to suppress more easily any real opposition from the Democrats or leftists. Nor were these fears completely unjustified. The immediate political questions surrounding the assembly debate had highlighted still deeper issues regarding Thailand's alliance with the United States, on which it had depended in large measure for both security and stability.

Thanom, Praphass, and other government officials shared some of the doubts of the opposition regarding the United States, particularly in view of the U.S. policy of withdrawal from Vietnam, but they feared that open criticism of the alliance might encourage political revolt against their authority. "This government considers that national stability is of the greatest importance in helping to increase economic prosperity, to create social justice, and to achieve success," said Thanom in a statement of policy shortly after the 1969 elections. "Therefore, this government will do everything possible for Thailand to remain stable."[15]

Another factor, not directly related to the politics of the capital, also influenced the government. Amid the debates in parliament, Communist-led rebels persisted in low-level warfare, notably in the northern and northeastern provinces. If the government did not curb criticism in Bangkok, its leaders feared an alliance of extreme left-wing politicians and guerrilla bands, led perhaps by figures who had been jailed or silenced for many years. Some analysts tended to minimize the importance of guerrilla revolt, but the fighting was always a major consideration in any evaluation of Thailand's political, military, or diplomatic outlook.

7

Simmering Revolt

Seeds of Insurrection

"Good News," scrawled in Thai, headed the handwritten leaflet tacked to a tree in the spring of 1969 near the U.S. air base outside Nakhorn Phanom, a bustling market town in northeastern Thailand across the mile-wide Mekong River from Laos.

"The people already have their own Liberation Force," the leaflet began. "The establishment of this force, with its own headquarters, was announced on January 1, 1969." The leaflet, typical of Communist propaganda in the poverty-stricken, politically sensitive northeastern provinces, claimed "the people," in the three-year period before the "force" was formed, had "endured and overcome the cannon, aircraft, and napalm of the bandit American-Thanom clique."

"Dear countrymen," the leaflet went on, "the Liberation Force of Thailand is under control of the Communist Party of Thailand. It is a true revolutionary force. It heartily serves the people. It never steals property. It never destroys their plantings. It never violates their girls. It never coerces its members or tortures its prisoners."[1]

Much the same message was posted in villages throughout the northeast. The mere fact that Communist propagandists operated so boldly in a region dominated by government police and army soldiers illustrated their determination to revive the long-simmering revolt. The formation of the Liberation Force of Thailand did not alter the basic structure of the Communist guerrilla organization, estimated at roughly 1,500 men in the northeastern provinces alone, but it was a significant attempt to give a popular impression of strength and legitimacy. The Communist rebels, driven into remote mountain bases after three years of government campaigns against them, had now re-emerged with a new front, a new program—and, for the first time in their struggle, some uniforms and insignia.

The ten-point program of the Communist Party of Thailand was first announced on January 11, 1969, in broadcasts by Radio Peking and the Voice of the People of Thailand, beamed from Yunnan Province in southwestern China. The program, similar to resolutions issued by the NLF in South Vietnam, indicated the basic appeal of Communism in outlying provinces where farmers averaged only a third the income of their countrymen in the central plain around Bangkok. Besides calling for expulsion of "U.S. imperialism," overthrow of "the Thanom clique," and establishment of a "people's government," the program outlined appealing plans for land reform, equal rights, and the like.[2]

The launching of what was formally known as "the Supreme Command of the Thai People's Liberation Armed Forces" was the latest, and perhaps most important, in a series of efforts by the Communists to turn their guerrilla struggle into an effective "war of liberation" against the government. The "war," flaring sporadically for nearly a decade in the northern and northeastern provinces, was born in the resistance to Japan in World War II. The Communist Party of Thailand emerged as a legal organization in October, 1946, with the repeal of the anti-Communist act of 1933.

One reason for the repeal of this law was that Thailand wanted the Soviet Union to support its application for membership in the United Nations, but the decision also reflected an atmosphere of intellectual and political liberalism in Bangkok after the military rule of World War II. The Party at first appeared relatively contented with its position as a legitimate, and loyal, opposition group, but in 1949 its complexion began to change. Its Bangkok-based Chinese leaders were deeply impressed by the victory of Communism in mainland China and sought to emulate that success in Thailand. Peking's new Communist regime, in turn, began to focus on the possibilities of spreading propaganda and revolt throughout Southeast Asia.

It is still a moot point whether or not the Communist Party of Thailand at this stage posed a serious threat to the government— or whether high-ranking officials described it as such in order to ban it. The party may have concluded that it had no chance of realizing any of its aims by following a legal, nonrevolutionary course. The budding alliance between Thailand and the United States, indicated by the signing of military and economic agreements in 1950, also affected the approach of the Party, which decided to view the United States as Thailand's worst enemy. The promulgation of this outlook was accompanied by an increase in subversive activity. The government, probably exaggerating the danger in order to smash the Party before its strength increased, arrested several hundred local Chinese in late 1952 in a series of raids on Sino-Thai companies and associations. At the same time, parliament passed a law outlawing Communist activities.

The raids, the first of a number in recent Thai history, were focused primarily on the Chinese community, partly because certain Chinese provided the money and political skill without which the Party might not have functioned at all. Another factor was that Thai officials hoped to use the threat of anti-Communist reprisals as a means of exerting pressure on the entire Chinese community, approximately 10 per cent of the country's 35 million population. After seizing power in 1957 and 1958, Marshal Sarit Thanarat drove leftists and Communists out of positions on university faculties, newspapers, and trade unions and banned commerce with China.

Sarit's outlook differed from that of his predecessors, however, in that it was not so much anti-Chinese as anti-Communist. Indeed, Sarit seemed to encourage the assimilation of non-Communist Chinese by cooperating with their organizations, notably the Chinese Chamber of Commerce, which reciprocated by offering complete support of his policies. Sarit appeared to have adopted the strategy, for both himself personally and the country in general, of profiting from the Chinese while forcefully discouraging any dissidence among them. This formula made sense in that many of Thailand's leaders were of partly Chinese ancestry and owed considerable fortunes to the skill of Chinese managers and partners. Sarit convinced most of the Chinese community of the wisdom of opposing Communism but still failed in eliminating a small Sino-Thai minority as the main source of the Communists' support.[3]

The Communists, after their Party was outlawed, set up a floating headquarters in Thonburi, the crowded, canal-laced city across the Chao Phraya River from Bangkok. The headquarters, although protected by substantial bribes paid to police and others in government, had to move from one "safe house" to another to escape detection. The Party's orientation was almost entirely toward Peking rather than Moscow, but the Sino-Soviet dispute, which became public in 1956, did not yet require all Communists to indicate their allegiance to one side or the other. Chinese Premier Chou En-lai, far from pursuing an overtly militant line, attempted to allay the suspicions of Southeast Asian leaders by espousing the "principles of peaceful coexistence" at the Bandung conference in 1955. The outline of China's possible aims, however, was clearly etched on the Thai political conscience. For all Chou's peaceful promises, Pridi Panomyong presence in China aroused speculation that the Chinese would support an attempt to have him installed as the ruler of a leftist, "neutralist" government. Besides occasionally lending his name to propaganda emanating from Peking, Pridi conferred with Thai visitors on political tasks they might carry out at home. Among those whom Pridi advised was Tep Chotinuchit, a leftist national assemblyman who was jailed after returning to Thailand but released in time to lead a socialist front in the 1957 election. The political program of Tep's front, calling for neutralism and repeal of the anti-Communist act, fit in with the aims of the Communist Party of Thailand.

Tep was jailed again in 1958, this time for eight years, as Peking began shipping weapons and ammunition to small guerrilla bands forming in the northern and northeastern provinces. In the late 1950's and early 1960's, according to intelligence reports reaching Bangkok, young Sino-Thai trained in Peking were organizing propaganda and subversion in those regions. In March, 1962, the "Voice of the People of Thailand" initiated regular broadcasts, while Radio Peking tripled the number of hours devoted to Thai-language programs.

China's ambition of fomenting revolution in Thailand was matched only by that of North Vietnam, which had begun in 1960 to send its own troops into Laos and opposed any government that supported anti-Communist leaders in the Laotian capital of Vientiane. In 1962, North Vietnam opened a school at Hoa Binh, 40 miles southwest of Hanoi, at which it gave regular courses for Thai who were not of Chinese origin, as well as Pathet Lao cadres. Chinese and North Vietnamese also collaborated in training Thai and hill tribesmen from the north in small camps in the Laotian jungles. Besides offering courses, North Vietnam occasionally sent its cadres into Thailand to advise and lead guerrilla units or infiltrate the Vietnamese refugee community, comprised of some 50,000 persons who had settled in the northeast.

While the level of revolt, supported by Peking and Hanoi, was rising in Thailand's northern and northeastern provinces, the Communist Party of Thailand was enlarging its organization in Bangkok. Operating from safe houses in Thonburi, Sino-Thai Communist leaders attempted to coordinate guerrilla operations with covert propaganda and fund-raising campaigns among leftist urban intellectuals, politicians, officials, and businessmen.

Government agents, however, uncovered some of these activities. The army and police in February and August, 1967, raided the homes and headquarters of Communist officials in Bangkok and Thonburi and arrested more than thirty Party leaders, including at least six members of the central committee. Among the latter was the secretary-general of the Party, a Sino-Thai with the adopted Thai name of Thong Chaemsri. Trained for several years in Peking, Thong stubbornly resisted all efforts to interrogate him, refusing even to reveal his real name. Several times, when asked to sign confessions or other statements, he replied by picking up a pen and scratching "Long Live the Communist Party of Thailand" on the wall of his cell.

The raids of 1967, followed by another series of arrests of lesser Party figures in October and November, 1968, were believed to have snuffed out the last vestiges of organized Communist Party power in Thailand. The Party, as a result of the government's reprisals in both the capital and the northeast, was unquestionably at a low ebb. At the same time, as indicated by the formation of a "supreme command" of the Liberation Forces in early 1969, the Communists were still determined to prosecute their "war of liberation" for Thailand. "We must do propaganda work among the masses, organize the masses, arm them, and help them to establish revolutionary state power," said the supreme command in its first communiqué.[4]

The struggle, at the beginning of the 1970's, still focused on the northern and northeastern provinces. These two regions, separated by rugged mountains, formed, in effect, different fronts of the same conflict, which was, in turn, an integral facet of the much larger war for control of the Indochinese peninsula. The two fronts differed widely from each other in terrain, climate, lines of communication, and even the ethnic background of their inhabitants. The same Thai Army and police bore the brunt of the fighting, however, and the same Sino-Thai cadres financed and led operations for the Communists.

Stalemate in the Northeast

The Korat plateau rises 1,500 to 2,000 feet from the Bangkok central plain 100 miles north of Bangkok and extends across the country's sixteen northeastern provinces to the Mekong River border between Thailand and Laos. The Petchabun mountain range, slicing down the center of Thailand to the central plain, divides the northeast from the north. The range turns east at Saraburi, the last town on the plain before the mountains, and then joins the Dangrek Mountains along the Thai-Cambodian border. The total effect of the mountains is to separate the northeastern provinces from the rest of Thailand almost as if they were another country—a buffer between the peaceful central plain and the war-racked former Indochinese nations. The northeastern provinces for most of the year are arid and barren of the lush green vegetation that covers both the central plain and the valleys of the north. The output of the region's 11 million inhabitants, who subsist on one crop of rice a year at best, averaged the equivalent of $60 per person as compared with $180 for the entire population of 35 million in 1970. The gap between the northeast and the other provinces, according to a report by the National Economic Development Board, is widening rather than narrowing, despite an array of road-building and other assistance programs. The average per capita income in the northeast has hardly changed since 1961, while that for the entire country increased by more than 6 per cent per year from 1961 through 1970.[5]

Exacerbating these differences is the fact that many Thai, particularly officials and intellectuals in Bangkok, tend to look down on northeasterners as social, cultural, and even ethnic inferiors. The ethnic factor reflects the Lao origin of most northeastern natives. "Thai-Lao" is the common designation for northeasterners who identify more closely with the pure-blooded Lao across the Mekong than with the Thai to the south. In a sense, the onset of the Communist revolt in the northeast was a blessing for the Thai-Lao, for it awakened the government to the urgent need to invest men and money in the region. Thai officials in Bangkok still regard assignments in the northeast as a form of exile, but persistent guerrilla activities forced the government in 1964 to launch the Accelerated Rural Development (ARD) program, focused primarily on that region.

"We are facing a situation in which the national security is at stake," said Prime Minister Thanom in February, 1965, outlining the rationale for the new emphasis on the northeast. Noting the fighting in Laos and Vietnam, Thanom remarked that Thailand "could easily be thrown into such an undesirable state of affairs if no protective and remedial measures were promptly taken to rectify the situation in certain areas of the country."[6] The government by 1968 was investing one fifth of its national budget of $1 billion in the northeast.

"We still have done hardly enough to meet necessary requirements," Prasong Sukhum, secretary-general of the ARD program, told me in a conversation in Bangkok on April 15, 1969, "but at least we are getting to the people through our road-building programs. We've built 1,800 kilometers of roads, 70 per cent of it in the northeast, and we are moving at the rate of 1,000 kilometers a year." Prasong estimated that new ARD roads had directly reached 580,000 persons and indirectly bound a total of 5 million to highways and trading centers. "We mean to eliminate the middleman for these people," he said, so that "they can move and trade freely and identify more closely with their own country."

An integral phase of the northeastern strategy was the emphasis on police and military programs, which rely on road-building to transport arms and men to flash points of rebellion. Besides sending several thousand army soldiers and national policemen to the northeast, the government in December, 1965, attempted to coordinate all activities by setting up the Communist Suppression Operations Command under General Praphass Charasutien. The CSOC in turn controlled joint headquarters, in seven critical provinces, for civilian, police, and military operations. Formed after a tough administrative fight, CSOC was always secondary to separate army commands, which exercised real military power in the north and the northeast. The main CSOC main contribution in its first five years of operations was not over-all authority but coordination of individual projects aimed at specific target areas of Communist activity.

The formation of CSOC was almost a reflex reaction to the first major "incident" of guerrilla war in the northeast. "Since November, 1965, when the heroic Thai people founded their first unit of the people's forces, like a prairie fire, the single spark of people's war has rapidly spread across the length and breadth of Thailand," said the *Peking Review* in early 1969.[7] Lieutenant General Saiyud Kerdphol, director of the operations and coordination center of CSOC, agreed as to the date of the start of the armed phase of the struggle. "Some of you may recall that Communist-inspired and directed armed insurgency in Thailand became a shocking reality in November, 1965," General Saiyud told reporters and editors on February 29, 1968. "A group of police officers . . . were ambushed and killed on the road leading from District Mukdahan, Nakhorn Phanom Province."[8]

The ambush on the road from Mukdahan, a sleepy Mekong River town 40 miles south of the provincial capital at Nakhorn Phanom, dramatized the extent to which the government had neglected the northeast in the preceding years. The main base area for the Communists was—and still is—the Phu Pan Mountains, a low-lying range of jungle-covered ridges and valleys extending 100 miles west from near Mukdahan to Sakhon Nakhorn, the capital of the province bearing the same name. One of the first North Vietnamese cadres to infiltrate this region was Nguyen Ai Quoc, who went there in 1928 to proselytize among the small community of Vietnamese living in northeastern villages. Quoc, later known as Ho Chi Minh, left the next year, but officials in Sakhon Nakhorn and Nakhorn Phanom still refer with awe to his fleeting presence.

Despite Ho Chi Minh's early activities, Hanoi did not begin seriously to work with the Vietnamese refugees until the early 1960's. Thai authorities by 1970 were in the awkward position of wanting to expel the entire refugee community but of having nowhere to send them. North Vietnam in 1964 refused to admit Vietnamese from Thailand after having accepted some 40,000 of them in the previous five years, and South Vietnam banned them on the grounds that they were pro-Communist. Thai officials spoke occasionally of resettling all the remaining refugees in a camp, possibly on an offshore island, but no leader in Bangkok was eager to accept the responsibility, or the blame, for a program that would inevitably result in widespread suffering and possibly death and disease. Besides, as Thai officials realized, most refugees preferred to live quietly, performing minor jobs as restaurateurs, tailors, small merchants, and rice farmers. Communist cadres attempted to fortify often flagging ideological support among them by offering special classes and lectures in private homes away from the careless eyes of Thai police.

The Communist program to subvert the Vietnamese refugee community might not in itself have greatly disturbed Thai authorities if its purpose had been only to gain money and manpower for the war in Vietnam. Young Vietnamese from the northeast, however, were often sent to North Vietnam for six months to two years of training. Some of them, on returning to Thailand, helped enlarge already existing base areas in the Phu Pan Mountains and expand the number of Communist guerrillas from perhaps 500 or 600 in 1965 to a steady level of 1,500 after 1967. They formed the second level of leadership under the Sino-Thai, most of whom had been born and raised in Bangkok and trained in China.

After the arrest in 1967 of Thong Chaemsri, then the secretary-general of the Communist Party of Thailand, the most important party name probably was Wirat, the Thai alias for a Sino-Thai who succeeded Thong as secretary-general and hid in a mountain camp about 30 miles southwest of Sakhon Nakhorn. Wirat, regarded as an intellectual theoretician after two or three years' study in Peking, surrounded himself with about fifty deputies and staff members, carefully trained to hide or flee on a few minutes' notice. Intelligence analysts in Bangkok estimated in 1970 that between 300 and 500 Sino-Thai, supported by 400 or 500 Vietnamese, dominated the movement in the northeast. Beneath them was a basic army of perhaps 1,000 more soldiers, many trained at centers near the Communist-controlled town of Muong Sai in northern Laos. The rest had either been trained locally or been recruited several years before to fight with the Pathet Lao in Laos and had later joined the "liberation force" in Thailand. Besides this small army of full-time soldiers, at least 10,000 villagers, many of them Vietnamese refugees, worked part-time as recruiters, fundraisers, propagandists, food-buyers, or intelligence sources. The force depended on these sympathizers, as it did on wealthy Chinese in Bangkok, for survival.

The guerrilla army in the northeast by the late 1960's was ebbing in terms of actual power or potential. American and Thai statistics, while never final proof of weakness or strength, indicated that the Communist movement had reached a peak in 1966—in terms of activity, though not size—and then begun to decline. Communist terrorists assassinated forty-four government officials in 1966, thirty-nine in 1967, and four in 1968. Reports of armed propaganda meetings, according to American and Thai officials, fell to one a month from April to November, 1967, after having averaged approximately ten a month for the previous year. "These later meetings were held mainly to conscript food supplies and not as a show of force or to propagandize as before," said General Saiyud, indicating the problem of hunger besetting the Communists, as peasants sent most of their crops to government-controlled towns and markets.[9]

CSOC, toward the end of 1966, designated 11 critical regions of guerrilla operations in the northeast, including 173 villages, as target areas but the next year added three more and expanded the program to sensitive regions in the north and in the south along the Thai-Malaysian frontier. The northeastern regions were dominated by mountainous jungle where Communist terrorists retreated between forays to surrounding villages on which they depended for food and recruits. "We encouraged the people to move out so we could identify who were the terrorists," Saiyud explained to me in an interview in August, 1968, in the CSOC operations center in Bangkok. In villages particularly subject to terrorism, CSOC assigned joint-security teams, supported by "strike forces" made up of army or border patrol police platoons. One control team—three or four men equipped with radios—coordinated activities in each target area.

One advantage of this program, according to Saiyud, was that the government kept its troops in the vicinity and did not abandon it to terrorists in a few months or years. The program also frustrated Communist plans to connect individual base areas into a single prolonged front. The CSOC strategy, in short, endangered the Communist "liberation struggle" by denying it freedom of movement and village support. The over-all effect was almost to starve out the terrorists, whose local guerrillas tended to defect or return to their homes within weeks or months after they were recruited. Hard-core terrorists, in 1967 and 1968, had to abandon temporarily their plans for conquering the countryside, from which they hoped to spring on the towns and the city heartland of Bangkok, in accordance with the guerrilla strategy of Mao Tse-tung. The terrorists in this period were forced to retreat from base area to base area, pursued and harassed periodically by government forces transported by U.S.-supplied trucks and helicopters.

A clash between guerrillas and police near Sakhon Nakhorn in August, 1968, illustrated the nature of the struggle for the region. Officials told me that a police patrol had ambushed a small band in the mountains near a village 30 miles south of Sakhon Nakhorn. The terrorists had run at first shot, and all but two of them had escaped, although some others may have been wounded. The incident was the first in weeks in which these district police had been able to surprise the terrorists. It was also one of the few times that police had captured weapons and notebooks—the latter, in this case, filled with slogans and songs.

The incident indicated that government forces, as a result of their presence in the region, not only had the confidence of a significant portion of villagers, who were willing to supply them with information on enemy movements, but also were alert and well enough equipped to respond to intelligence reports. The manner in which the police and soldiers exploited the ambush for propaganda purposes demonstrated an awareness of the mentality of the villagers, who in the final analysis had to ally with whomever appeared the strongest. On the negative side, however, the ambush illustrated the weakness of government forces, who were so poorly trained as to let most of the terrorists escape their carefully prepared ambush. Also illustrative of government weakness was the failure to assign at least a squad of men to attempt to pursue guerrillas through the jungle. Police and army soldiers rarely remained outside their compounds overnight. Terrorists generally had all the time they needed to flee to base areas in the mountains.

The failure of the government to achieve a higher level of military preparedness and expertise was in part responsible for the Communists' slow recovery by 1971, after having receded in strength in the later 1960's. Guerrillas in 1970 were inciting at least 100 incidents a month, almost as many as in 1966 and 1967, according to American counterinsurgency experts. Most of these incidents were armed propaganda meetings, but terrorists also continued to assassinate officials and impress peasant youth into service. One favorite technique was to attack a defense post on one side of a village while sending agents to the other side to collect food.

Without massive foreign support, however, the chances of still greater success for the Communists in the northeast appeared dim. The frustration of the Communists was evident from their reaction to the ARD program, which was building dams and roads and was also involved in public health and information projects. Terrorists occasionally burned bridges and fired at workmen, according to officials in the northeast, but more often they attempted to claim the credit for government projects. Few officials, however, were convinced that the Communists' lack of success meant that the struggle for northeastern Thailand was reaching a quiet conclusion. "They have a timetable," remarked a senior U.S. official in a conversation in Sakhon Nakhorn in April, 1969. "They can wait, but we never can. We're too impatient. They're regrouping in the mountains, but they'll come back to the villages when they think we're too tired—or lax and overconfident."

Failure in the North

In his speech to the Foreign Correspondents Club of Thailand on February 29, 1968, General Saiyud devoted only two sentences to the incipient revolt in the northern provinces, a region of untracked hills and cultivated valleys separated from the northeast by the Petchabun Mountains. "In the northern part of Nan and

Chieng Rai [the two northernmost provinces], where Communist subversive operations have only recently been exposed and forced into the open," said Saiyud, "there are an estimated 150 Communist terrorists organized into 6 or more groups. Most of them are believed to be hill tribesmen who have been trained by the Communists in Peking, Laos, and/or Hanoi and reinfiltrated back into Thailand."[10]

By late 1970, the judgment of analysts in the U.S. Embassy in Bangkok was that the number of terrorists in all three northern provinces had increased to 3,000, twice as many as were fighting in the northeast. Some officials believed that the Communists might have delayed their campaign in the north if the government in 1967 had not sent some 3,000 troops into the hills—to hunt not for terrorists but for 1,400 former soldiers of the Chinese Nationalist Army, who had profited from the region's opium trade since the Communist victory on the Chinese mainland in 1949. Government officials finally agreed not to harass the Chinese Nationalists if they in turn cooperated by providing information on the activities of Communist guerrillas who had ambushed Thai soldiers and police.

"After the terrorists tried to kill one of our district chiefs in 1967, we organized village protection teams and the Volunteer Defense Corps," the governor of Chieng Rai Province, Chusanga Chaiyabandu, told me on August 10, 1968. "We put Volunteer Defense posts into areas infested by terrorists to protect the villages." The governor, pointing to a map in his office, said the terrorists could walk in "only a few minutes" from bases across the border from Laos, which is dominated in the north by the same range of rough, largely untracked mountainous jungle. "We are only 70 miles from Yunnan," he went on. "The Communists get all their supplies from China."

Officials had picked up the first report of the use of Chinese weapons in the province in February, 1968. "A group of terrorists entered one of our villages and held an armed propaganda meeting," said Governor Chusanga. "They forced villagers to attend." The governor then read a propaganda leaflet illustrating the approach of the terrorists in the other northern provinces. "The mobile groups [propaganda teams] welcome the people and beg to solve their problems by cooperating with the chief of the village and other teachers and volunteers," it said. "Your government will only oppress all the people until you lose your country to the United States." After the "people have risen up to save their country," the pamphlet promised, "you will get free tractors and electricity and fertilizer. Please, all mothers, fathers, and loved ones, wait for us who will get rid of the traitors as soon as possible and return the country to you."

The Communists made their deepest impression on the "white Meo," a minority branch of the Meo tribe, who were easily impressed by the Communists' pledge to oppose the government's campaign against opium-growing, their main source of income. An unofficial Thai Government report in 1968 expanded on the problems in dealing with the tribesmen. "These hill tribes are generally illiterate, have ill health, are isolated and economically deprived," said the report, alleging that two thirds of the best forests in some northern provinces had been destroyed or damaged by nomadic tribesmen who cut down the trees, burned what they wanted, and farmed the land for several years before moving on. The only solution, the report went on, was to introduce stabilized farming from which tribesmen could earn as much money as they customarily derived from haphazard opium-growing.[11]

The government, in the midst of a brief military campaign in 1968 of shelling, bombing, and burning suspected enemy positions in some of the northern hills, moved 20,000 tribesmen from their homes and resettled them in lowland camps away from the fighting. This program was hardly successful, however, in persuading tribesmen to change their traditional living habits. "Hill tribes do not like to be sent to settlements where there is a management to operate it and they have to conform to rules and regulations," observed General Praphass, noting that government work units could not assist tribesmen with new agricultural and welfare programs if they were scattered in tiny isolated communities.[12]

Another reason for merging small villages into camps, said Praphass, was to organize tribesmen to fight the Communists. "The Communist terrorists are trying to cause misunderstanding between hill tribes and government authorities," he explained. "When authorities are no longer there, the Communists come in to persuade hill tribes to side with the Communists." But Praphass promised that the government would "train the hill tribes to govern and defend themselves, with the government giving them support in the form of weapons and ammunition and in the promotion of their means of living."

Despite such reassuring words, Thai authorities faced unexpected problems at every turn. Praphass himself cited a case in which tribesmen quit rifle training after guerrilla propagandists told them that the government would "lead them to their death in fighting." He also conceded that a combination of petty official corruption— and tribal ignorance bordering on superstition—was slowing down the government programs. As a case in point, a tribal representative claimed officials demanded money for government identification cards supposedly given to tribesmen for nothing. And tribes- men, it turned out, were extremely reluctant to pose for photo- graphs needed to put on the cards. "At first, they refused to be photographed," said Praphass. "Then they demanded money each time." Most of the women still would not pose under any circum- stances. Hill people in one area made a modest living by hiring themselves out as models for those who could never get over their fear of the camera.[13]

The failure of the government to persuade tribesmen of the value of its efforts was reflected at a Yao refugee camp in Chieng Rai near the Laotian border. The chief of the camp, an entire tribal village of some 1,000 people, stood before the district officer and a couple of his assistants, who had accompanied me on a visit in August, 1968. "The soil is not good enough," complained the chief, a gnarled old man named Hae. "We know how to grow rice in the mountains but not in the rice paddies of the lowlands." The chief's remark reflected the despair of the tribesmen, herded from many hill villages around the valley into even rows of stilted huts, built over muddied lanes bulldozed by government soldiers.

"I never feared the Communists. I just moved here on the gov- ernment's orders," the chief went on, adding that he was now afraid that terrorists would "come down here at night and make us give them more food." Hae's most serious complaint, however, was that his people could no longer grow opium poppies, the source of almost all their previous income. "Our program is to try to keep them from opium-growing and teach them something else," said a welfare official assigned to the district.

The frustrations of coping with tribesmen led the government in 1969 to alter its outlook. Reversing the policy of forcing entire villages to relocate into refugee camps, officials opened new centers in the valleys where tribesmen could go voluntarily. The hope was that tribesmen, availing themselves of medical, educational, and other services offered at the centers, would return to the hills with some sense of loyalty or identification with the Thai Government. At the same time, a new Thai commander for the northern prov- inces, Lieutenant General Samran Patayakol, eliminated virtually all the "free fire zones"—areas of suspected Communist activity in the mountains into which Thai forces could fire without checking to see if civilians still lived there. The government's position was that soldiers and police should protect the populated valleys and not dissipate their energies in the hills.

This change in policy was, in a real sense, an admission of the inability of soldiers and police to eliminate the Communist threat. Communist cadres, entering the country in increasing numbers, soon contested government control in the valleys as well as the mountains. The Communist strategy was to establish unassailable base areas in the hills and then extend them into lowlands inhabited largely by Thai rather than mountain people. Sino-Thai and Thai cadres formed an elite officers' corps, supported by bands of mountain people, mainly from the Meo tribe. These bands, by 1971, were bold enough to roam in groups of up to 100 men each as opposed to only ten or twenty only two years before. The long-range Communist strategy was to mold the north into a powerful hammer, which could then threaten to smash the heartland of the country.

The Communists in 1970 could legitimately claim to control several villages along the Laotian border in Chieng Rai and Nan provinces. The Communist Party of Thailand, at about the time the Voice of the People of Thailand was announcing this success on its broadcasts, transferred some of its more experienced leaders from base areas in the northeast to the north. An integral phase of this organizational drive in the north in 1970 was the construction of a road from the town of Muong Sai in Laos to the Mekong River. Chinese workmen, following the path of an old French logging trail, hacked out the road for trucks to transport AK-47 rifles, ammunition, and other materiel. The road, approximately 80 miles long, paralleled infiltration routes from Communist training centers near Muong Sai, headquarters for Communist activities in Thailand.

The result of Communist efforts in the north was that nearly all the guerrillas, by 1970, were armed with AK-47 rifles instead of old carbines, Springfields, and even muzzle-loading muskets with which most of them had fought only one or two years before. Guerrillas staged a series of ambushes in June and July, 1970, to keep government soldiers and engineers from building a new road near one of the Communists' "liberated areas" in Nan Province. "The government does not plan to yield part of the country to terrorists," a U.S. counterinsurgency official told me in Bangkok on September 3, 1970, but it was clear that Thai authorities could do little to prevent a partial takeover. The mountain people, pawns in the conflict, would ally with whomever appeared most capable either of controlling and coercing them or of offering the greatest freedom from control and coercion by the other side.

Problems in Counterinsurgency

"Should the primary military effort be directed to search-and-destroy operations, the usual military strategy, or to the more passive secure-and-hold tactics?" Two highly experienced students of guerrilla warfare in Southeast Asia posed the question in an article that appeared in October, 1969. The authors were George K. Tanham, the minister-counselor for counterinsurgency with the U.S. Embassy in Bangkok from 1968 to 1970, and Dennis J. Duncanson, former counselor to the British Embassy in Saigon and former adviser to the late Ngo Dinh Diem. If a government focused on search-and-destroy operations in combating guerrillas, warned Tanham and Duncanson, "the elusive enemy may lead the pursuing force a long chase without itself being destroyed, while no permanent friendly base can be established because adequate forces will not be available to protect it." But, "if too many forces are allocated to secure-and-hold operations," the authors continued, "the enemy may also secure and hold his area, and this may result in the *de facto* loss of part of the country—an outcome the counterinsurgent government is trying to prevent."[14]

The article analyzed the general problem of counterinsurgency rather than its application to a specific country, but, in view of Tanham's official post, it had immediate relevance for the conflict in Thailand. One of Tanham's main concerns, in fact, was to induce Thai forces to strike an effective balance between "search-and-destroy" and "clear-and-hold" operations. U.S. officials had been shocked by indiscriminate bombing and shelling of Communist-infested regions in the north, just as they were alarmed by the reluctance of Thai officials to send patrols off the main roads and into Communist base areas.

The problem was complicated, moreover, by the sensitivities of Thai leaders, often hostile to what they regarded as foreign "pressure." U.S. advisers, anxious to maintain friendly relations with the Thai, atempted to dispense their views without appearing to tell the Thai how to handle their own problems. Similarly, U.S. officials were afraid of offending the government by divulging critical or controversial material to correspondents. The problems in the north and the northeast were so acute, however, that advisers sometimes revealed what they knew in hopes that limited, nonsensationalized publicity might induce Thai officials to listen to them.

A vivid example of the web of problems raised by the guerrillas was a long-simmering campaign in the Petchabun Mountains along the military-administrative line between the northern and northeastern provinces. Communist strategists selected this area in order to exploit the rivalries between the Thai 3d and 2d Army commands, responsible for the north and northeast respectively. The terrorists focused specifically on a region of high—5,000-foot—mountains that also straddled the line between the 4th and 6th police regions and the "triborder" juncture of Petchabun, Phitsanulok, and Loei provinces. Communist leaders, on the basis of long experience, knew that Thai units would prefer to stop at the borders of their area of jurisdiction rather than cross a boundary even in the midst of a running battle.

The terrorists initiated their offensive in the zone, 15 miles in diameter, with an attack on November 22, 1968, on a government-trained unit of mountain tribesmen in the village of Hui Sai Tai in Phitsanulok Province. Nine Meo tribesmen were killed in the attack, an attempt to demonstrate the risks of allying with the government. Reports indicated that only 200 guerrillas, all of them Meo tribesmen, were in the vicinity, but they always had the advantage of surprise. They could surround isolated outposts without firing more than a few shots. They could assassinate lone officials, draft young men into service, spread propaganda—and then flee across the next boundary before soldiers and police had organized their search.

Such activities dramatized the question regarding the wisdom of search-and-destroy as opposed to clear-and-hold operations. The government attempted to reach an ideal solution by following both approaches in establishing a combined headquarters for military, civilian, and police operations in the town of Lomsok near the triborder juncture of Petchabun, Phitsanulok, and Loei provinces. Some 2,000 troops, most of them from the 2d Army in the northeast, were marshaled for a drive that U.S. advisers had hoped would set a precedent for future efforts at eliminating the enemy presence.

The results of the experiment in the region hardly lived up to initial expectations. "The members of the joint command are not cooperating well and not doing much," was the estimate offered me by a U.S. official in September, 1970. "The troops are not well trained, and the leadership is not very good." Thai commanders, he noted, were divided at this stage on whether their troops should "go out and bash the terrorists" or remain in the villages and towns. Neither alternative offered much hope of success. The Thai in the mountains, despite modern equipment, were unable to find the Meo, who had lived there all their lives and could run and hide with skill and agility.

The problem of impressing Thai authority on the region was no doubt deepened by the contempt with which the Thai traditionally looked on the hill people. Leaders were so disdainful of appealing to them on their own terms that they opposed suggestions for broadcasting propaganda in tribal languages until 1969, five years after the Voice of the People of Thailand had begun to beam programs in Meo and Yao dialects. The importance of broadcast propaganda might appear surprising, in view of the hill people's lack of sophistication, but nearly every village had at least one inexpensive transistor radio around which the citizenry eagerly clustered in the early morning or evening.

The inability of Thai authorities to empathize with the mountain people was thoroughly predictable, but Thai police and army officers sometimes seemed almost as inept in their relations with lowlanders. An American correspondent, Kim Willenson, illustrated these problems in two articles written in January, 1969, after he and his interpreter had visited ethnic Thai villages in Phitsanulok Province. In one village, a fifty-man patrol was setting up a base camp to protect the lowlands from terrorists in the nearby hills, Willenson reported. The police deliberately selected a plot, surrounded by two streams and a grove of trees, that afforded maximum protection to themselves and minimum defense for the village. To an old man who protested against the loss of his land for this purpose, a police lieutenant replied, "If you speak like that, I will go away and leave you here. Then the bad men will come and kill you." The police ordered villagers to dig trenches and surrender some of their chickens with no compensation. The police lieutenant admitted his men did not patrol at night. The post, in case of serious attack, would have been almost useless. It would not have been effective for even "clear-and-hold," much less "search-and-destroy," purposes.[15]

It was not difficult for the Communists to exploit these inequities in propaganda broadcasts, leaflets, and personal contacts. The ten-point program of the Communist Party of Thailand, promulgated on January 11, 1969, was designed to answer complaints of the populace, ranging from hill people in the north to Thai-Lao in the northeast to pure-blooded Thai in the valleys and even in the heartland around Bangkok. Point two, for instance, appealed to leftists in the capital by calling for "the rights of freedom of speech, writing, publication, holding meetings, organizing associations, holding demonstrations," but it also was aimed at the hill people who had no interest in the right to do anything but roam the mountains and grow opium. The people, it said, were entitled to "security of employment, maintaining religious belief, and preserving their customs and habits and livelihood."[16]

Point five of the resolution was written still more specifically for tribesmen. "The various nationalities," it began, "shall enjoy the right of autonomy within the big family of Thailand." The Communists, in other words, said that tribesmen could govern themselves free from interference by hated Thai officials. The promise was pure propaganda, of course, because Sino-Thai, Thai, and Vietnamese were already leading and controlling those tribesmen who had joined the terrorists. The same point attempted to reinforce this promise by declaring that the "nationalities" would "enjoy equal rights, respect each other, support and help each other, and oppose national oppression and racial discrimination."

The program appealed, in different terms, to northeastern peasants by calling for abolition of "the feudal system of exploitation," reduction of "rents and interests," abolition of "unjust debts"—all issues of interest to Thai-Lao, who had been trampled on for generations by arrogant landlords and officials. Communist leaflets, posted on trees in northeastern villages, emphasized this point while ignoring the issue of "nationalities"—of interest to northern tribesmen but not to Thai-Lao in the northeast. Communist organizers were extremely skillful at appealing broadly to all regions and levels of society—and then at gearing propaganda campaigns to the needs of different audiences.

The principal problem afflicting the government's effort to combat Communist propaganda was the same combination of arrogance and inertia that hampered military operations. The government in the north only rarely introduced defectors at village meetings or broadcast their remarks on the radio. Government airplanes dropped propaganda leaflets from time to time, but they were hardly effective in mountain villages infiltrated by armed Communist agents. The government was more successful at propaganda in the northeast. A radio station in Sakhon Nakhorn gained broad popularity for its combination of music and news—interspersed with anti-Communist slogans. The station, in fact, was so influential that terrorists periodically answered its appeals to surrender by handing themselves over directly to the station manager rather than entrusting their lives to local police or army officers.

The government in the northeast had the additional advantage, as a result of road-building programs and military operations, of "mobile information teams." These teams, originally advised by young U.S. information officials stationed in the main northeastern towns, traveled from village to village dispensing music, news, official information, and propaganda. Americans were far from confident, though, that the Thai would operate these units with much enthusiasm and efficiency after the U.S. Information Agency decided to relinquish its role in the program in 1970. U.S. officials in Bangkok regarded Washington's decision as "premature." They believed that Thailand would lose one of its few proven propaganda methods of fighting the Communists.

The American presence, however, was not always desirable, as both U.S. and Thai officials fully agreed, in propaganda terms. Neon-lit nightclubs and restaurants lined the streets of the major northeastern towns, Korat, Udorn, Nakhorn Phanom, and Ubon, near U.S. air bases. Airmen and soldiers, most of the latter engaged in building highways to the bases, brawled with Thai over girls and money. Some Americans, such as Special Forces advisers, were carefully stationed away from towns to avoid conflicts, but enough of them were visible in population centers to create an adverse impression. The Communists, naturally, exploited the issue. "Weed out the reactionary and corrosive U.S. imperialist and feudalist culture which poisons the spirit of the people," said the last of the ten points in the new Party program.[17]

The sensitivities aroused by Americans in Thailand sometimes compromised the efforts of military and civilian advisers. All U.S. officers, for instance, were forbidden to visit Thai units on combat operations. U.S. Army helicopters in the first couple of years of revolt in the northeast sometimes ferried Thai troops to trouble spots, but Thai helicopters, supplied by the United States, replaced them in January, 1967. Special Forces advisers, permitted to accompany Thai troops on training missions, could arm themselves only with pistols. There were some exceptions to these rules. At the "green beret" bar in Sakhon Nakhorn, a bistro run by U.S. soldiers, one often heard stories of isolated incidents in which Americans had carried and fired automatic rifles while "training."

The official rationale for de-emphasizing the U.S. role was the desire to encourage Thai troops to "do the job for themselves." U.S. Ambassador Leonard Unger stressed the necessity of preventing any relationships similar to those in Vietnam, where American advisers inevitably accompanied their Vietnamese counterparts on field operations. "In the northeast, we stepped in with some aid and advice when counterinsurgency began. There was something of an emergency," said Unger in an interview on April 12, 1969. Unger insisted, however, that the rules against direct U.S. participation were well defined. "My philosophy is that this sort of thing is basically a Thai problem and not the kind of thing in which a foreign country should directly involve itself," he explained. "There were times when the Thai would have welcomed more helicopter support, but the conscious decision was to minimize involvement in this way."

The ambassador, who had been deputy assistant secretary of state for East Asian and Pacific affairs before his posting to Bangkok, extended this reasoning to the defense of the Royal Thai air bases, constructed and used largely by the Americans. Noting the attack in July, 1968, in which terrorists had damaged several U.S. planes at Udorn, Unger said the "immediate question" was "how much we should become involved in the protection of the bases." Unger believed that "these bases were a Thai responsibility, and the Thai saw it the same way; the idea was that such attacks were part of the insurgency problem." Unger did not deny America's "supporting role" in providing arms, equipment, and advice, but he claimed he was confident that "in anything like an insurgency situation, the Thai will be able to handle it themselves."

The problems the Thai experienced in combating Communism, although most acute in the extreme northern and northeastern provinces, recurred wherever the terrorists chose to surface. Intelligence reports indicated that guerrillas were gathering in "larger groups"—as many as fifty men each—in Tak Province along the mountainous central frontier with Burma. They also were reported increasing in strength and numbers near Ubon, 150 miles south of Nakhorn Phanom, and in the hills between Ubon and Korat, the "gateway to the northeast," on the main highway running north from Bangkok. Officials tended to view the terrorists in these areas as considerably weaker than their comrades in the north and northeast, but there was always the danger that they would attempt to mount a major campaign.

Communist terrorists also posed a grave, but somewhat different, kind of a threat in the jungles of the southernmost tip of Thailand north of the Malaysian border. The difference between the threat here and elsewhere was that it was aimed almost entirely against the government of Malaysia. The leader of the insurgency in the south was Chin Peng, who had fled to the frontier jungles after the failure of the Communist insurrection in Malaya from 1948 to 1960. Despite occasional rumors of his death, his followers, totaling approximately 1,000 men mainly of Chinese extraction, have been able to cross the frontier, ambush Malaysian policemen, distribute propaganda—and then retreat before the Malaysians could capture them. At the Malaysian command center in Alor Star, officials in November, 1968, noted a lack of cooperation from the Thai, who were not overly concerned about Chin so long as his men focused mainly on Malaysia.

Authorities in Bangkok, alarmed by terrorist recruiting campaigns among Thai in the south, agreed in 1968 to set up a combined Thai-Malaysian headquarters in the town of Songkhla, 20 miles north of the border, to send troops on joint patrols with Malaysian forces, and to cooperate on intelligence reports. Still, Malaysian officers complained that the Thai were lax, often sent information too late to be of any help, and balked at letting Malaysian patrols pursue guerrillas fleeing north across the 361-mile frontier. Thailand had already declared martial law in the nine southern provinces, but Malaysian officials viewed this sign of Thai concern as more symbolic than real.

Perhaps more significant was Thailand's refusal to yield to Malaysian suggestions to clear all villages immediately north of the border—a move that would have enabled patrolling troops to presume any unidentified figures seen at night were guerrillas. The Malaysians, who had cleared their own border villages several years before, charged that terrorists on the Thai side regularly held night meetings at which they collected taxes, recruited troops, and spread propaganda. Thai officials attempted to mollify Malaysian leaders by promising to evacuate border villages when necessary, but they obviously were in no hurry to initiate such drastic action.

It was a moot point whether or not this type of move would have the desired effect. Political analysts speculated that intensified Thai interest in the south might turn the terrorists there against Thailand as well as Malaysia. Some officials, both U.S. and Thai, believed that the Thai were so burdened by their own administrative problems and inefficiency as to be unable to prosecute a guerrilla campaign with any more success in the south than in the north.

These factors formed the greatest obstacle to Thai efforts to combat Communist revolt wherever it arose. "The Thai Army just isn't very aggressive," summarized an experienced U.S. official in Bangkok in March, 1970. "You can train them and equip them, but if the bosses still don't want to fight, then the troops aren't going to do much." The primary concern of most Thai officials, both military and civilian, was their set of relationships with superiors and subordinates. "Each guy has to worry about his own place in the pecking order."

There was, however, another approach that might help relieve military pressure exerted by Communist guerrillas and their cadres. If Thailand moved toward compromise or rapprochement with some of the Communist powers, perhaps North Vietnam and China might not be so inclined to encourage a "war of liberation." The question lay at the heart of the entire structure of Thai diplomatic relations—and Thai efforts at combating local revolt with U.S. aid and advice.

8

Shifting Alliances

Bases of Cooperation

The leaders of Thailand had often said that they did not believe in the "domino theory"—the idea that Communist victories in South Vietnam, Cambodia, and Laos would inevitably induce the downfall of other non-Communist governments of Southeast Asia. The fighting in the northern and northeastern provinces, however, inevitably reminded them of the regional rivalry that might result from the renaissance of a powerful, united Vietnamese state. "To us, the Vietnam war is not a war against an ideology," said Prime Minister Thanom Kittikachorn, "but a necessary resistance to forces which attempt to take over South Vietnam."[1]

It was, then, partly in order to resist such forces that Thailand, after the defeat of the French in Indochina, entered into an extremely durable alliance with the United States. Thai military leaders were convinced, after having witnessed the success of the Americans against the Japanese in World War II, that the United States offered the greatest security in traditional Thai conflicts, particularly with the Vietnamese. U.S. officials, for their part, viewed Thailand as an ideal base area and bulwark in the "containment" of Communist "aggression." Thailand indicated changes in its diplomatic position, however, as soon as the United States began to reduce its commitment to Indochina—and, implicitly, Thailand.

That Thailand's declaration of war was never delivered to the United States during World War II unquestionably smoothed the path to alliance, but the victory of Communist forces on the Chinese mainland in 1949 probably helped convince both Thai and U.S. officials of the strategic advantages of cooperation. Although the United States had loaned Thailand some $10 million to build up its transportation system after World War II, the real turning point was the signing of economic and military aid agreements in 1950 and the admission of Thailand to the World Bank and the International Monetary Fund. Such assistance was meant to raise living standards and strengthen the armed forces against external aggression, but Field Marshal Phibun Songkhram also welcomed it for the power it offered over internal opponents.

In view of the latter motivation, the best Thai units, equipped by the United States, were permanently stationed in or near Bangkok. Washington, even if it had wished, could not have prevented the use of U.S. materiel for purposes other than national self-defense. The first article of the military agreement, signed on October 17, 1950, stated that Thailand would "retain title to and possession and control of any equipment, material or services received" unless the United States should "otherwise consent." If it did not want its arms to serve as instruments of domestic politics, Washington would have to exercise its right of "consent" in advance, not after Thailand already had the "title" to equipment transferred under the program.[2]

The military and economic agreements together comprised the framework within which Thailand and the United States would cooperate on building up Thailand and combating the common Communist enemy. The alliance was strengthened by the Manila treaty of 1954 forming the Southeast Asia Treaty Organization, which followed the French defeat in Vietnam earlier in the year. Whether or not Thailand would have approved of membership in SEATO without the combination of U.S. aid, the French defeat, and the resurgence of military rule in Thailand is highly problematical. Certainly the deep divergence between Phibun and the leftists—and the triumph of Phibun—coincided with plans for long-range Western, mainly U.S., support.

Thailand's enthusiasm for SEATO was also heightened by the hostile attitude of China, which interpreted Thailand's burgeoning relationship with the United States as a threat to its own ambitions in the region. China at this time was emphasizing the necessity of peaceful coexistence, but it was clear that this concept was contingent on the "neutrality" of the countries to which it might apply. Chinese Premier Chou En-lai, after the conclusion of the 1954 Geneva agreement on Indochina, did his utmost to discourage participation in the Manila pact. The cause of peace "would be endangered," and the Geneva agreement "might be disrupted," he warned, if any nation, such as Thailand, "should join the United States aggressive circles in these divisive activities."[3]

China's position might have seemed reasonable to a more centrist government, but the fears of military rulers were inevitably increased by the emergence of Pridi Panomyong, the leftist who had fled the country in 1947, as an instrument of Peking propaganda—and, by inference, of political subversion as well. Pridi, in an article published on July 29, 1954, in *People's Daily*, the leading Chinese newspaper, accused the "U.S. imperialists and the Thai reactionary government" of "lording it over Thailand" in order to turn the country into "a base for aggression to menace peace and create international tension."[4]

For this reason alone, it was fitting that Thailand should not only join SEATO but provide the ground for its headquarters in Bangkok and emerge as its most loyal member after the United States. Thailand, in fact, was the only Asian country to demonstrate much enthusiasm for the alliance. Pakistan eventually relinquished an active role in the organization, while moving closer diplomatically to Peking, and Philippine support declined amid commercial and economic differences with Washington. Australia and New Zealand followed the U.S. lead diplomatically, but their military facilities were limited. Britain and France, the remaining two members, steadily reduced their activities in SEATO, and France finally stopped participating altogether.

In view of its interest in promoting SEATO and bilateral U.S.-Thai relations, the United States assiduously cultivated the Phibun government until the upheavals of 1957. Washington may have preferred Phibun over other Thai leaders because his government had cracked down on any real opposition to the special U.S.-Thai relationship, easily the most successful American diplomatic venture in Southeast Asia. U.S. officials were somewhat nervous about the political leanings of Phibun's successor, Field Marshal Sarit Thanarat, who had gained popularity by criticizing the strongly anti-Communist General Phao Siyanon, but Sarit proved as interested as Phibun had been in maintaining the alliance.

Ironically, Thailand under Phibun and Sarit became more anti-Communist than the United States. Thailand's outlook was affected in part by the opposite drift in Cambodia, which recognized Communist China in 1958, and the deterioration of the political and military situation in Laos, always viewed by Thai nationalists as an essential if inferior ally against a combined Chinese and Vietnamese threat. Encouraged by the Manila pact, Sarit expected the United States to fight for a right-wing anti-Communist regime in the Laotian capital of Vientiane. His government urged the United States and its allies to invoke the SEATO agreement, although members differed strongly on the extent of Communist "aggression" in Laos after Pathet Lao units, supported by North Vietnam troops, renewed their sporadic war for the country in 1959.

The greatest disappointment, after the failure of SEATO to intervene in Laos in 1960, was the refusal of the new administration of President John F. Kennedy to send in U.S. troops in 1961 without SEATO support. Donald C. Nuechterlein, a senior U.S. official in Bangkok at the time, has observed that Thai leaders "were astonished and even angry because they could not believe that the United States would adopt such a course in Southeast Asia," particularly after Kennedy had already asked the Soviet Union "to help stop the fighting."[5] Thailand, in view of its commitment to the United States, had no other major ally to which it could turn and had to accept, reluctantly, the U.S. decision to participate in the second Geneva conference, which lasted from May, 1961, until the middle of 1962.

During this period of frustration and disappointment on Laos, Thanat Khoman emerged as the architect of Thai foreign policy. Thanat, a polished graduate of the University of Paris who had been ambassador to the United States before his appointment as foreign minister in 1959, carefully supported and publicized Thai policies in delicate diplomatic conversations and often acerbic speeches and interviews with foreign journalists. Sarit and Deputy Premier Thanom Kittikachorn still formulated Thai foreign policy, but they relied on Thanat's advice on such questions as how to try to manipulate the Americans, how to react to trends in the United States, and how to cope with other Communist and non-Communist Asian states.

On Thanat's recommendation, Thailand began before the second Geneva conference to try to reduce its dependence on the United States by improving relations with the Soviet Union, with which it had signed an agreement for commercial, cultural, and technological exchanges in 1960. Thanat also applauded gestures toward regional unity outside the SEATO framework, but he did not actually go beyond the verbal level and begin to remove Thailand from the U.S. orbit. Thanat's diplomacy, however, was a major factor in inducing the United States to renew and increase its assurances. Finally, in March, 1962, Thanat and U.S. Secretary of State Dean Rusk issued a joint communiqué defining the special relationship between their respective governments.

"The United States regards its commitments to Thailand under the Southeast Asia Collective Defense Treaty and under its Bilateral Economic and Military Assistance Agreements as providing an important basis for United States actions to help Thailand meet indirect aggression," said the communiqué. It added, with a prescience little noted at the time, that Rusk and Thanat had also reviewed "the actions being taken by the United States to assist the Republic of Vietnam to meet the threat of indirect aggression."[6] Thai confidence in the United States was further bolstered by Kennedy's decision, after talks with Thai officials, to land 1,800 marines in Bangkok in May, 1962, and then to send in another 8,000 ground and air force personnel. The deployment not only symbolized America's commitment to defend Thailand but also indirectly influenced the Communists to sign the second Geneva agreement in July, 1962, and halt or postpone some of their activities in Laos.

Thai officials were again upset by U.S. efforts to woo Cambodia with military and economic assistance, particularly in view of the loss of the Preah Vihear temple to Phnom Penh as a result of the International Court of Justice ruling in June, 1962. On the basis of the meeting between Rusk and Thanat, however, the United States convinced the Thai Government that it would never neglect Thailand provided the Thai reciprocated by supporting U.S. aims. The combination of the build-up of U.S. strength in Vietnam and Communist insurgency in Thailand's northern and northeastern provinces seemed to demonstrate the wisdom of Thai reliance on America's commitment to the regional anti-Communist struggle. Indeed, in a direct and practical sense, U.S. and Thai military priorities coincided in much of the highway construction of the 1960's.

Thailand needed roads to transport soldiers and police and bind the outer provinces to the central plain, while the United States valued them for shipping spare parts, bombs, and bullets from the port of Sattahip to half a dozen new air bases. U.S. engineers in 1966 completed construction of the Friendship Highway, running from the central plain to the Laotian border, and three years later finished building the Freedom Highway from Sattahip on the Gulf of Thailand to the Friendship Highway at Korat. The purpose of the later road was to bypass the Bangkok area in moving military materiel from the coast to bases in the northeast.

Aside from common military interests, however, the special U.S.-

Thai relationship was posited to a large extent on American money. The United States, between 1949 and the end of 1970, had poured some $2.3 billion into Thailand, in the form of economic and military assistance and military expenditures. The rate of U.S. spending in Thailand seems to have increased in proportion to the closeness of U.S. Thai relations. American military aid, for instance, spurted from $49 million in 1961 to $88 million in 1962, the year Thanat and Rusk signed their communiqué. Military aid by the end of the 1970 fiscal year had totaled $874.4 million, including $522.9 million for the previous eight years.[7]

The year 1962 was equally significant as a turning point in U.S. military expenditures beyond military assistance. The United States estimated expenditures from 1963 through 1969 at $855 million, including $369.7 million for military construction and an average of $22 million a year spent since 1964 by soldiers on leave from Vietnam.[8] The total cost of American construction from 1963 through 1969 was $607.4 million, including $113.4 million for a vast communications network. Significantly, the United States in all the years prior to 1962 had spent only $97.5 million on construction, $2.4 million of it in economic aid programs and most of the rest in military assistance for Thai forces. The most expensive single aspect of the U.S. build-up was construction of the Sattahip-Utapao complex. The deep-water port for unloading U.S. munitions at Sattahip cost $63.2 million. The price of the adjacent air base at Utapao, from which giant B-52 bombers flew missions beginning in 1967, was $105.9 million.[9]

The wealth that accrued to Thailand as a result of the U.S. presence during this period far overshadowed any direct assistance benefits. Economic assistance totaled only $622.2 million from 1949 through 1970, including $339.1 million for the last eight years. It did not increase sharply until the middle 1960's, when it rose from $19 million for the 1965 fiscal year to record levels of $58.3 million for 1966 and $56.7 million in 1967 as a result of efforts to combat insurgency in the north and northeast.[10] Even these figures, however, seem to have paralleled increased expenditures for the bases, on which U.S. spending crested in 1966. The total cost of U.S. construction in Thailand rose from $76.9 million from January 1, 1963, through December 31, 1965, to a high of $200 million in the 1966 calendar year, fell to $135.8 million in 1967, and began tapering off to $24.3 million in 1968 and $54.3 million in 1969.[11]

These statistics suggest the price of the privilege of flying bombing missions over Vietnam and Laos from air bases in Thailand. Although Thailand wanted the United States to prosecute the Vietnam war for reasons of national security, it was highly unlikely that Thai leaders would have permitted Washington to use the country as a base area for Indochina had it not been financially worthwhile to them. The United States, for its part, would certainly not have become so deeply involved in Thailand merely for Thailand's sake. Evidence of Washington's priorities, beyond the distribution of funds, lay in the disposition of troops. The number reached an authorized peak in August, 1969, of 48,000, including 34,000 airmen and 12,000 army soldiers, most of them in logistics, engineering, and communications units, all needed to support the air war in Vietnam and Laos. No more than 3,000 U.S. servicemen were ever engaged at one time in advising or assisting Thai forces.

The monetary relationship between Bangkok and Washington was, if anything, defined still more clearly in the agreement of November 9, 1967, under which Thailand sent a full combat division to Vietnam. The United States not only paid all expenses for training, equipping, transporting, and supporting the division but also provided overseas allowances, mustering-out bonuses, and death and disability benefits. The total cost of maintaining an 11,000-man division on these terms averaged $50 million a year, with the first Thai troops arriving in 1966.[12]

The real price was much higher, moreover, than just the expense of maintaining a Thai division in Vietnam. An explicit provision of the 1967 agreement was that the United States would also increase military aid to Thailand from $59 million in the 1967 fiscal year to $76.5 million for 1968 and $73.5 million for 1969. The rationale was that more aid would help compensate for the loss of troops who were needed to combat counterinsurgency at home.[13] The United States had already embarked in 1966 on a long-range program for modernizing and fully equipping Thai armed forces. The 1967 agreement promised to enlarge on this program without changing its basic pattern.

The single most expensive budgetary item in military assistance was the Thai Air Force, for which the United States supplied 120 fixed-wing planes, 40 helicopters, and spare parts and maintenance. The Americans, at a cost of $18,778,000, also built a training academy for the air force between 1966 and 1968.[14] At the same time, the United States introduced the latest machine guns, rifles, radios, and other standard equipment for the entire Thai Army. This phase of the program focused initially on the 3d Thai Infantry

Division in the northeast, the scene of the greatest threat in the middle and late 1960's. Then, as guerrilla warfare increased in the north, the Americans began modernizing the 4th Thai Division, assigned to that region.

Besides providing materiel, the United States emphasized the training of Thai cadres, who in turn would train rank-and-file troops. A 300-man Special Forces company, headquartered at Lopburi, north of Bangkok, was responsible for the country-wide program, which included several training centers. Supplementing the U.S. Special Forces company was a 1,000-man Thai Special Forces group, which the Americans had initially formed and advised. Special Forces soldiers, both U.S. and Thai, trained all Thai bound for Vietnam at Camp Kanchanaburi on the River Kwai west of Bangkok at a cost to the United States of $4,395,000. Theoretically, Thai troops, after having served in Vietnam for a year, could offer combat experience for units fighting insurgency in Thailand.

Symbolic of the monetary basis of the U.S.-Thai alliance, however, was that almost all Thai soldiers who volunteered for Vietnam were lured by the American-paid overseas allowance, which more than doubled basic Thai military salaries. On returning home, most of them were glad to accept the $400 mustering-out bonus, also paid by the United States, and leave the service.[15] On a broader scale, Thai officials often lost interest in military or economic programs if the United States was not willing to finance them. The quest for U.S. funds tended to obscure the importance of these efforts in terms of their basic purpose of providing security against insurgency or attack. The overwhelming U.S. presence was an embarrassment that could only be justified by its financial rather than military advantages. A sign of Thai discomfort was the government's refusal until March 9, 1967, to admit that U.S. planes based in Thailand were bombing North Vietnam. Even then, Thai officials in most cases denied permission to correspondents to visit the bases, which remained under Thai command. The government did not want publicity about how extensively it had collaborated with a foreign military power and would probably never have conceded the real purpose of the bases, had it not been for widespread reports about them in the American press.

Thailand's disillusionment with the United States was indicated initially at the highest levels of government rather than by intellectuals and leftists, who were unable to express their views publicly. Significantly, Prime Minister Thanom reflected his country's traditional suspicion of foreign influence at approximately the same time that Thailand was admitting its supporting role in the bombing of North Vietnam. Thanom may have wanted to counterbalance the adverse propaganda effect of this admission by appearing to agree with skeptics and critics who had already expressed doubts privately about U.S. activities.

"Foreign culture based on materialism has flowed swiftly into Thailand, being brought into the country directly by tourists or indirectly by mass media," said Thanom in a statement released in March, 1967. "These changes are rapid and have in a short time shockingly damaged the good morale and culture of certain groups of people." The result, he went on, was that "pretty girls turn to the business of being mistresses, bar hostesses, masseuses, or prostitutes," while their brothers "rob and extort honest persons." Thanom admitted, moreover, that "government officials who are unable to resist materialistic charms resort to corrupt practices in order to gain income sufficient for a luxurious life, the same as others."[16]

The Thai press, carefully taking its cue from the country's leaders, then began to interject indirect criticism of the U.S. presence into articles and editorials. A notable example of this incipient anti-Americanism was an angry commentary prompted by the publication of a brief book on Thailand by Louis Lomax, who had upset Thai officials by his scathing observations on corruption, inefficiency, and dictatorial rule.[17]

Kukrit Pramoj, editor of the newspaper *Siam Rath*, or *Free Thai*, regarded as a serious voice in national affairs, accused Lomax of "deliberately distorting facts and the truth in every way in order to use them as confirmation for his views and reasoning that in the end Thailand would not remain in existence." Then Kukrit, the brother of Seni Pramoj, leader of the Democratic Party, criticized Americans in general. "They look down on us with contempt for playing up conflicting interests of world powers in the past," wrote Kukrit, noting that Thailand's seemingly ambivalent policies had been "the reason why we survive."[18]

Any substantial shift in Thai policy, however, could only arise from grave doubts as to America's strength and aims in the region and the long-range practicality of alliance with the United States. In short, was the United States, like Japan in World War II, destined to leave Thailand to the mercy of its enemies? The analogy between the Thai-Japanese and Thai-American alliances was imperfect in that Thailand had not profited economically off the former—and was not in immediate danger of attack by major powers as a result of the latter. Nor was the United States confronted in Indochina with the total defeat that Japan had suffered at the end of World War II. Still, the example of World War II, limned against the background of Thailand's diplomatic maneuverings vis-à-vis the colonial powers, had certainly impressed on Thai leaders the wisdom of diplomatic flexibility.

Signs of Strain

This issue might not have emerged so clearly at the end of the 1960's if the United States had not, in the same period, begun the protracted process of disengagement without victory from Vietnam. Until then, the Thai could justify their alliance with Washington, just as they had their relationship with Japan, as the most attractive available alternative. But, if the United States were determined to retreat and abandon its allies, then the government might encounter insurmountable political and military difficulties. To offset this possibility, Thanat began in 1968 to emphasize the themes he had broached at the beginning of the decade, in the period of U.S. weakness and indecision on Laos. Thailand might have done well to have applied the lessons of Laos much earlier and improved its relations with nonaligned and Communist countries, but Thanat hoped that his government could still follow this course if the United States insisted on withdrawing from Vietnam.

Thanat at first may have thought that the mere suggestion that Thailand might have to "look elsewhere for friends" could induce the United States to maintain its commitments in Indochina. On March 31, 1968, the day on which President Johnson halted the bombing of North Vietnam above the 19th parallel, Thanat said that he was "cautioning my people not to put all their eggs in one basket."[19] In a conversation six weeks later in Washington with Prime Minister Thanom, Johnson attempted to assuage Thai fears and doubts. Seeking Thailand's continued cooperation in the war, Johnson assured Thanom of America's commitment to his country's economic development and military security and then "paid tribute to the contribution Thailand is making to our common defense interests by making base facilities available for use by the United States."[20]

Thanat, however, was even more alarmed about U.S. policy on August 23, 1968, when I interviewed him in Bangkok, than he had been the previous spring. This time he was hoping to convince the United States of the folly of ending the bombing of the "panhandle" of North Vietnam below the 19th parallel. "If the bombing is stopped without valid assurance and if that measure were to lead to greater losses of lives of men fighting the Communists," he said, "then I do not think it would be very popular." He did not believe, he went on, that the United States, alone and without the approval of other Southeast Asian countries, had a moral or legal right to abandon its commitment to Vietnam or SEATO, much less negotiate a Vietnam compromise displeasing to Saigon or to Bangkok.

As the war dragged on, however, it seemed that the denouement feared by Thanat and his government might actually come to pass. Thus, Thanat directed foreign policy along two different lines. First, he emphasized the importance of a nonmilitary Asian alliance, such as the Association of Southeast Asian Nations or the Asian and Pacific Council, both of them anti-Communist but not allied directly with the United States or European powers. Second, and perhaps more significantly, he tried to improve communications with leaders of Communist countries.

"We realize that problems in Asia stem mostly if not in all cases from certain activities on the part of Communist regimes in Asia," remarked Thanat on March 29, 1969, nearly five months after President Johnson, on October 31, 1968, had ordered the cessation of all bombing of North Vietnam. "Realizing that such problems exist, we also feel that it is our duty to talk with the instigators of many difficulties arising in Asia and try to find out their views, motivations, and principles which have guided these Marxist regimes in Asia to act in the way they do."[21] At the same time, Thanat asserted that American planes would not base in Thailand after the Indochinese conflict. Clearly, his aim was to arrive at a *modus vivendi* between Thailand and some of the Communist powers once U.S. troops had withdrawn from the region.

Again, however, Thanat's remarks seemed somewhat rhetorical. Certainly no Communist government, at that stage of the war, was prepared to enter into serious talks with Thailand, still the most pro-American country in Asia except for those states—South Korea, Taiwan, and South Vietnam—that relied on U.S. aid for their very existence. Hence, it seemed expedient for Thailand to try to form close relations with the administration of President Nixon after his inauguration in 1969. Nixon, after all, had not only visited Thailand on a number of occasions as Vice President between 1952 and 1960 and then as a private citizen but had always seemed sympathetic with Thailand's aims as an American ally.

Thai leaders were indeed heartened—and superficially convinced

—by Nixon's apparent sincerity when he saw them in Bangkok in July, 1969, after having enunciated the Nixon doctrine at Guam. "Our determination to honor our commitments," said Nixon, "is fully consistent with our conviction that the nations of Asia can and must increasingly shoulder the responsibility for achieving peace and progress in the area."[22] Nixon was clearly evincing his desire to maintain the U.S.-Thai alliance—and still to persuade Thailand to improve its own defenses, supported by American materiel and advice, in accordance with the Nixon doctrine.

Thai leaders appeared at first to want to rationalize Nixon's policy with their vision of Thailand's relationship with the United States. "The Americans approve and support Thailand's policy of self-reliance," said Thanat after a two-and-a-half hour conversation between Nixon and Prime Minister Thanom. The United States, Thanat went on, had "expressed readiness to give aid and support to the Thai Government and to the Thai people in order to help them safeguard their freedom and independence."[23] Thanat still feared, however, that sentiment in the United States against U.S. activities in Indochina might directly affect White House strategy toward the Vietnam war and the Thai alliance despite official assurance to the contrary.

American criticism of involvement in Thailand in particular fell into two basic categories. First, there was the issue of the extent of U.S. commitment to defend the country. Would the United States send in combat troops in case of invasion by North Vietnamese and Chinese armies? What if guerrilla forces in the north and northeast, supported only by Chinese and North Vietnamese cadres, increased to a point at which the Thai were not able to prevent them from threatening the heartland of the country? The second issue was an immediate corollary of the first. How much money should the United States invest in Thailand? Was the Thai alliance worth hundreds of millions of dollars? Did the United States have to buy Thailand's friendship? Were Thai leaders mere opportunists who would ally themselves with the highest bidder?

No questions upset Thai sensitivities more than these, yet all of them were asked, in both Bangkok and Washington, with increasing frequency in this period. The issue of U.S. commitment arose when Senator J. William Fulbright, chairman of the Senate Committee on Foreign Relations, declared in August, 1969, shortly after Nixon's visit, that the United States had entered into a "secret treaty" to defend Thailand.

The "treaty," in reality, was a 400-page military "contingency plan," negotiated and signed in 1964 by Thanom and Major General Richard G. Stillwell, then the U.S. commander in Thailand. The details of the plan were never officially released, but military sources in Bangkok said that it called for coordination between U.S. and Thai troops in any of a number of detailed patterns in case of overt attack by land, sea, or air. The plan not only specified which U.S. units would fly to Thailand to support Thai forces but also stipulated where ammunition, arms, and other equipment would be stored during fighting on various fronts. Finally, it provided for a permanent stockpile near Korat, where the United States had built an army camp for logistical and engineering units.

These facets of the agreement might not have seemed unusual as advance military planning, but one other provision was extraordinary: All combat troops introduced into Thailand would fight under Thai authority. "I as commander-in-chief of the Thai armed forces would also be the commander of the U.S. Army in this country in the event of open aggression," said Thanom in a statement first addressed to Thai students on August 15 and then released by the foreign ministry on August 18, 1969. "Under the SEATO treaty, I am entitled to direct the operations of both U.S. and Thai soldiers fighting for this country during an open aggression," he explained. Thanom had insisted on this provision to counter any criticism that he would relinquish Thai sovereignty in case of national emergency.

There was no doubt, so far as Americans were concerned, that the Thai would have exercised only nominal control over U.S. troops, just as Thai commanders of Royal Thai Air Force bases were essentially figureheads who gave no direct orders to American airmen. Critics in the U.S. Congress immediately charged, however, that Washington had agreed on the unprecedented step of submitting Americans to foreign control. While the face-saving nature of this provision, in terms of Thai pride, may have been clear enough, the fact that the United States had entered into any agreement at all angered congressmen who were already upset over the extent to which Washington had committed itself to Thailand without congressional consent.

It was both to counter public reaction in the United States and to reassure the Thai that Robert J. McCloskey, deputy assistant secretary of state, attempted, on August 15, 1969, to explain the contingency plan as a purely technical ramification of the long-established, publicly acknowledged U.S.-Thai relationship. The agreement, he said, had "not expanded our defense commitment

to Thailand beyond that already contained in the SEATO treaty."
Nor did the plan constitute a firm pledge even within the SEATO
context, McCloskey went on, for it stated that it could not "be
carried into effect without the specific agreement of both the U.S.
and Thai governments."[24]

Such explanations, however, failed to persuade Thanat not to
begin to provide evidence that Thailand was prepared to loosen
some of its ties with America. "If the people in the United States
feel they should not overcommit themselves to Thailand, they
should begin withdrawing the American troops that are now in
Thailand," he said.[25] That August, while the first U.S. troops were
leaving Vietnam, Thanat and Unger began negotiations on the reduction of forces in Thailand. Thanat had considerable bargaining
power, since the United States still wanted full use of the air bases
for the war in Laos, slowly building in intensity as North Vietnamese troops prepared for another major offensive.

Thai authorities were also concerned about Laos, as they had
been for more than a decade, but the political advantage of
announcing even a token withdrawal of U.S. forces seemed to out-
weigh any possible loss in military security. Both sides were convinced, moreover, that Washington could meet the aerial requirements of that conflict with a somewhat smaller force than it had
in Thailand at the time. The talks between Unger and Thanat
culminated on September 30, 1969, in a joint announcement by
Nixon and Thanom of the withdrawal of 6,000 troops "as expedi-
tiously as possible consistent with operational requirements related to the Vietnam conflict."[26] The implication, politically desirable in both Bangkok and Washington, was that the United
States would pull out all its forces as soon as they were no longer
needed for the security of the area—a deadline that was purpose-
fully unpredictable and flexible.

Another reason, besides national pride, for Bangkok to favor
reduction of American activities was to relieve U.S. domestic pressure on Washington that might lead to abrogation of the contingency plan. Thai leaders were concerned about the tenor of an
investigation of American involvement conducted in November,
1969, by the U.S. Senate Subcommittee on United States Security
Agreements and Commitments Abroad of the Senate's Committee
on Foreign Relations. Senator Fulbright, the committee chairman,
devoted much of the hearings to challenging the administration's
right to have entered into any agreement without the consent of
Congress. "It would appear," Fulbright told Unger, "that the gov-

ernment can agree simply by the Prime Minister of Thailand and a U.S. General sitting down and agreeing, and that is considered a binding agreement on this country."[27]

The hearings also produced facts and figures documenting for the first time the economic *quid pro quo* of the U.S.-Thai relationship, particularly during the Vietnam war. The State Department persuaded the Committee on Foreign Relations to postpone releasing a transcript of the hearings, which diplomats believed might embarrass Thai officials and possibly strain the alliance. Then, the *New York Times*, on December 1, 1969, published a wildly inaccurate article citing "informed Congressional sources" as having said that the United States had pledged about $1 billion in military and economic aid to Thailand in return for Thailand's promise to send a division of its own troops to Vietnam.

The State Department, in view of the *Times* article, should not have objected to release of the transcript, which later would reveal that the troop deal cost less than one third of that amount, when computed at $50 million a year for the division for five years, plus increases in military aid of $15 million a year for part of that period. The article not only created a furor in Bangkok but fueled the U.S. Senate's campaign to keep the administration from involving the country in a wider war in Southeast Asia. During December, 1969, the Senate debated and then approved, by a 73 to 17 majority, an amendment to the defense appropriations bill forbidding the use of American combat troops in Laos and Thailand.

Immediately after the vote, the United States again went through the elaborate exercise of reassuring Thailand of America's commitment. Vice President Spiro Agnew, in Bangkok in early January, reiterated Nixon's promises of five months earlier. Agnew and Thanom also discussed the debate on the U.S.-Thai alliance "in American Congressional circles, as well as by mass media," said Thanat after the conversation. "It was asserted [presumably by Agnew] that the statements made by those persons do not represent the view of the American Government, that they are personal views with the objective to create disunity between Thailand and the United States."[28] Agnew could offer no guarantee, however, that the United States, constricted by the vote in the Senate, could send its own troops into Thailand in case of national emergency.

Thailand, then, had to go on downgrading a foreign presence that would only be resented by other countries, such as the Soviet Union or even China, to which it might eventually have to appeal.

Symbolic of the desire among Thai officials to reduce U.S. influence was a requirement, effective on January 1, 1970, barring most private American citizens from extending their fifteen-day visas without leaving the country and then re-entering—on another fifteen-day permit. This regulation was a deliberate effort at harassing American companies, which had increased their investments in Thailand from $20 million in 1960 to more than $200 million by 1970. The inconvenience was a reminder that pressure might eventually be applied to the entire U.S. establishment in Thailand.

In assessing the motives of Thai leaders, however, it was sometimes difficult to distinguish between Thailand's desire for military, as opposed to economic, security. Officials were as easily upset by publicity on the economic aspect, laden with overtones of "bribery," as they were by criticism of the alliance from the viewpoint of commitment of U.S. troops. The publication in April, 1970, of the Senate hearings on Thailand only deepened the humiliation of a regime that already knew that it depended far more on American money and materiel for stability than it did on the promise of American troops for defense.

While Thai officials publicly emphasized national self-reliance, they appeared extremely pessimistic in conversing privately with U.S. officials who might be able to persuade Washington to provide more aid. To relieve some of the anxieties among the Thai elite, the economic counselor of the U.S. Embassy in Bangkok, Konrad Bekker, led a panel discussion in October, 1969, on the "impact of U.S. military spending." Bekker's basic thesis was that Thailand might compensate for a decline in American funds by such "alternative factors" as "government spending, tourism, exports, foreign lending, improved agricultural technology, or foreign or domestic investment."[29]

Despite these encouraging words, Bekker conceded that "net military spending in the Thai economy" had totaled $759 million from the beginning of 1965 through 1969. This figure included $450 million invested locally in material and labor for construction of the air bases but excluded the cost of products purchased abroad for the bases and also did not include sums expended in military and economic aid programs. The annual spending on what Bekker regarded as "the Thai economy" reached a high of $215 million in 1968, then slipped to $170 million in 1969, largely as a result of the gradual de-escalation of the Vietnam war, the consequent decrease in the number of soldiers on leave in Thailand, and the decline in military construction.

Bekker added that some of the results of U.S. spending would have long-range economic benefit. At least $80 million had been invested in military and port construction "of a civilian infrastructure type," such as the harbor complex at Sattahip. Also, some 16,000 Thai employed on the air bases had acquired training and skills that might help in Thai military and industrial projects after the Americans departed. He forecast real difficulties only in those base towns, notably Ubon and Udorn, that had thrived on business provided by the airmen but had little local industry or commerce.

Bekker's argument, however, tended to overlook the effect of U.S. spending and construction on the entire economy. This stimulus was artificial—a reflection not of true growth and prosperity but of a phenomenon that might soon vanish. The boom atmosphere in Thailand would evaporate as U.S. investment steadily diminished. The Thai Government, already confronted by financial difficulties, would be that much more dependent on U.S. military assistance to maintain and equip its armed forces, totaling 170,000 men. Disappointed though Thai leaders may have been by America's policy of disengagement, they had to cooperate with the United States for the sake of its aid programs, which Nixon had indicated would continue under any circumstances.

From the interlocking viewpoints of both economics and security, Thailand at the beginning of the 1970's had few other alternatives. Thanat might urge that regional organizations replace the American alliance, but no such grouping was willing or strong enough to unite militarily against Communist attack on one of its members. Thailand maintained cordial if cool relations with the Soviet Union, but the Russians, although they did not openly support Communist revolt as did the Chinese, appeared in no mood to oppose a war of liberation, particularly in view of Bangkok's record vis-à-vis the United States and Vietnam.

Beneath all the words and symbolic gestures, then, Thailand's best strategy lay in attempting to adapt to power realities without reacting too sharply one way or another. The need for flexibility, rather than sudden change, was evident as North Vietnamese troops overran the Plain of Jars in Laos. The offensive impressed on Bangkok its reliance on whatever assistance America could offer, in the form of arms, materiel, and air support, if not troops, in case Thailand's traditional enemy approached the Mekong boundary. Yet, even a renewed threat from Laos could no longer force Thailand into an unequivocally anti-Communist position. After the fall of Prince Sihanouk as chief of state of Cambodia on March 18, 1970, Bangkok balked at offering more than token military support to the anti-Communist regime in Phnom Penh.

In the uncertain period of U.S. withdrawal, Thailand could not afford to overcommit or overextend itself in the widening war across the Indochinese peninsula. In the end, as Thai leaders were the first to recognize, the diplomacy of shifting alliances might provide the final defense against the military threat from across the Mekong.

IV

Laos: Neutrality Challenged

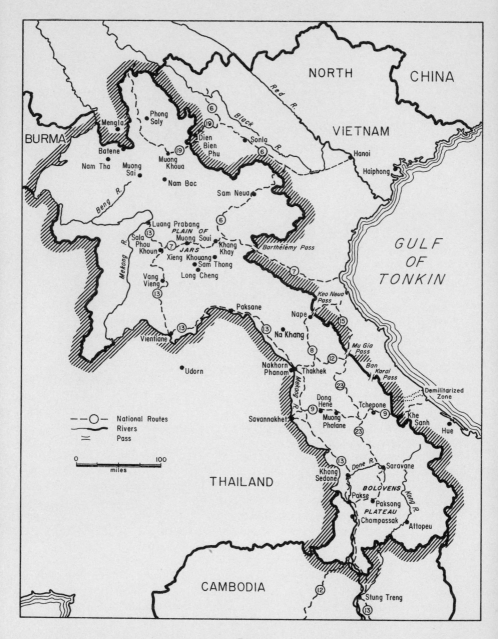

Laos

9

Reconciliation and Failure

Origins of Conflict

The struggle for Laos before 1970 had settled into what many U.S. officials had come to regard as almost a humdrum routine. Communist forces, including both North Vietnamese and Pathet Lao soldiers, advanced regularly during the winter dry season and then retreated in the monsoon rains of summer. The logic behind this pattern was simple. The Communists, moving on foot, could easily drive back the Royal Lao troops when it was possible to walk through the jungles. Government units, however, were able to stem the Communist advances when the jungles were drenched, the rivers and streams at flood level, and the lowland rice paddies shoulder-deep in water. The government always had the advantage of transportation on U.S. supplied—and usually U.S. operated and owned—helicopters and aircraft, which could move them on a year-round basis, in almost any kind of weather.

The pattern of the Laotian conflict was set long before the 1962 Geneva agreement guaranteeing the country's "sovereignty, independence, neutrality, unity, and territorial integrity." Before 1954, in the first Indochinese war, the Viet Minh regarded the kingdom across the mountains as a vital rear area. Viet Minh soldiers not only were based in the Annamite range dividing Laos from Vietnam but sometimes ventured into the lowlands of Laos and northeastern Thailand in search of food, recruits, and political support.

The contemporary history of Laos, while traceable to the precolonial era of conflict between Thai and Vietnamese, begins during the first Indochinese war with the proclamation, by King Sisavang Vong, of independence from France. The king, who had ruled since 1904 and had maintained good relations with the French during most of his reign, signed the proclamation on April

8, 1945, under Japanese pressure. The close of World War II marked the opening of another, much longer struggle for the Indochinese region. The French effort to recolonize Laos, Cambodia, and Vietnam was the first phase of this struggle. The second—by far the costliest and bloodiest—was the American-led drive to support anti-Communist regimes in both Laos and South Vietnam.

The hope of Lao nationalists in 1945 was to capitalize on¹ the departure of the French and the weakening of the Japanese. The leading architect of this plan was Prince Phetsarath, viceroy of King Sisavang Vong since 1941, elder brother of Prince Souvanna Phouma, and half-brother of Prince Souphanouvong. The divisions that have racked all Laotian history were evident in Phetsarath's decision to support Japanese pressure on the king to proclaim independence from France. Phetsarath, descendant of a rival for the throne in Luang Prabang, resented the king's power. Although Phetsarath never schemed to overthrow the king, he was anxious not only to prove his own influence but also to rid the country of the French, whose presence he saw as an immediate deterrent to his hopes.

Thus, Phetsarath, after the surrender of the Japanese, reaffirmed, on September 1, 1945, the royal proclamation. Then, without the king's approval, Phetsarath issued another proclamation, on September 15, reunifying the kingdom of Luang Prabang and southern Laos into one independent country. Two days later, the king attempted to negate all of Phetsarath's efforts by sending him a telegram declaring that the treaty of protectorate with France was still in effect.[1]

The conflict between King Sisavang Vong and Prince Phetsarath set a postwar precedent for dissidence and national disintegration. On October 12, 1945, Phetsarath and his allies formed the Lao Issara or Free Lao government, which the king tried to destroy by withdrawing Phetsarath's titles of viceroy and Prime Minister. The newly formed Provisional People's Assembly on October 20, 1945, then voted to depose the king, who was recrowned the following April only after he had agreed to accept the constitution and to attempt to win French recognition of an independent Laotian state. The recoronation of the king appeared expedient in view of the fledgling government's inability to stave off advancing French reoccupation forces. Indeed, French troops recaptured Vientiane on April 24, 1946, the day after Sisavang Vong was restored to the throne in Luang Prabang.

The combined machinations of the king and the French resulted in complete loss of confidence on the part of the Lao Issara government, whose members fled from Vientiane to Thailand immediately before the return of the French. Indicative of the king's real attitude was a *modus vivendi* signed by the French and his son, Crown Prince and later King Savang Vatthana, which formalized French economic, military, and political power while confirming the "sovereignty" of the king of Luang Prabang over a unified Laos.

The Lao Issara leaders, in the meantime, set up a government-in-exile in Bangkok. Phetsarath retained the post of Prime Minister while Souvanna, who had been minister of public works in the government in Vientiane, was also appointed Deputy Prime Minister. Souphanouvong, who remained Lao Issara commander-in-chief, arrived in Bangkok in late 1946 after having led his forces in league with the Viet Minh against the French in southern Laos in 1945 and early 1946 and then having visited Hanoi in July, 1946. Although the Lao Issara superficially appeared united, its leaders soon fell to arguing over whether to compromise with the French or the Viet Minh, which had been formed in September, 1941, as a means toward achieving national independence. Phetsarath was probably the most "neutral" of the three. He seemed to have opposed either alternative while Souvanna and Souphanouvong veered toward opposite poles. The conflict among the brothers, then, was superimposed on the brothers'—mainly Phetsarath's—quarrel with the king.

The issue of collaboration with the French or the Viet Minh soon crested over Souphanouvong's propensity for accepting Viet Minh arms and advice. Souphanouvong, married to an anti-French Vietnamese whom he had met while serving as an engineer for French authorities in central Vietnam, had decided well before the return of the French that the Viet Minh were the stronger force. His rebellious outlook was attributed in part to the fact that he was the youngest of the viceroy's twenty children—the offspring not of a legal princess but of a concubine—and was anxious to rival his half-brothers. During studies in Paris, in which he compiled a brilliant academic record in civil engineering in the 1930's, Souphanouvong was first subjected to the intellectual influence of the Vietnamese Communists.

The question of where the real power lay seemed to dominate Souphanouvong's attitude toward the Vietnamese Communists throughout his career. Souphanouvong, like his half-brothers, was essentially a nationalist, not an ideologue, but he was impressed

from the outset of the post–World War II struggle by the dyna-
mism of the Viet Minh and refused to yield to his half-brothers'
suggestions to disband his forces and cooperate, temporarily, with
the French. Finally, in May, 1949, the Lao Issara, meeting in
Bangkok, expelled Souphanouvong, who had frequently absented
himself to lead his men on anti-French raids with Viet Minh support.

Anxious to deepen the split among Lao Issara leaders and retain
the good-will of the king and some of his followers, the French
bargained to admit the Kingdom of Laos into the French Union.
A Franco-Lao convention, signed on July 19, 1949, formally
recognized Laos as an independent power within the union, in return for which Laos agreed to adhere to the union as an associated
state. Souvanna Phouma, more tractable but less brilliant than his
younger half-brother, then argued for the dissolution of the Lao
Issara on the grounds that the convention met most of its demands. The Lao Issara government, over Phetsarath's objections,
voted on October 24, 1949, to dissolve itself—a month before Souvanna and his followers returned to Vientiane. Phetsarath probably would have gone back if the king had graciously restored to
him the title of viceroy, withdrawn in 1945, but the wounds were
too deep. Souphanouvong, for his part, had already begun to trek
overland to northern Vietnam.

From the seeds of inner dissension planted after World War II
grew a full-blown Communist revolt, ostensibly led by Souphanouvong but always encouraged and equipped by Hanoi. The cycle
of reconciliation and warfare between Souvanna and Souphanouvong emerged clearly in the decade between the break-up of the
Lao Issara and the death of the king in late 1959.

In another one of those parallels that seemed to apply in all
phases of the Indochinese conflict, the policy of the Viet Minh in
the early 1950's was the antecedent of Hanoi's later strategy of controlling the provinces of northeastern Laos for the sake of its multi-
fronted war against the Americans, the American-supported Lao
and South Vietnamese, and, much later, the American-supported
Khmer. The Vietnamese Communists demonstrated their strategic
need for these provinces to secure their position in Vietnam. In
April, 1953, more than a year before the fall of Dien Bien Phu and
the convening of the first Geneva conference, four divisions of
Viet Minh soldiers, calling themselves a Lao "liberation army," invaded northern Laos. One division overran Sam Neua, the capital
of the extreme northeastern province, and then advanced toward

the royal capital of Luang Prabang. The French turned back the invasion during the monsoon, but the Viet Minh still clung to their positions in Sam Neua.

Almost as important as Sam Neua, only a few hours from Hanoi by car was Phong Saly, the capital of the northernmost province. In between Sam Neua and Phong Saly, on the Vietnamese side of the frontier but on a main route linking the two, was Dien Bien Phu, a stronghold surrounded by high hills. Some 60 miles south of Sam Neua is Route 7, the main east-west road between Laos and Vietnam over the Barthélémy Pass.

The key to control of Route 7, in turn, is the Plain of Jars, a flatland 15 to 20 miles across, set in the mountains some 80 to 100 miles northeast of Vientiane. A small road network crisscrosses the plain, named for its clusters of enormous jars left there by some prehistoric civilization. Route 7, after crossing the plain, continues some 30 miles west to Sala Phou Khoun, where it joins Route 13, leading north to Luang Prabang and south to Vientiane. Another road turns south to Xieng Khouang.

French officials thought the Plain of Jars was so important as to make the difference, possibly, between control or loss of all Indochina. It was not difficult, in fact, to imagine that enemy troops, after having overrun the plain, would advance toward the lowlands, menace northeastern Thailand, and penetrate Cambodia and South Vietnam. From the viewpoint of the Viet Minh, it was equally easy to conclude that French soldiers, moving from the security of the plain, would ruin the Communists' hope of victory over the French at Dien Bien Phu in 1954. Viet Minh strategy in 1953 was to pin down the French in their enclaves on the plain as an adjunct to the much more important campaign in Vietnam itself.

The Viet Minh, however, had not achieved all their aims in northern Laos when the summer monsoon totally stymied them. They failed to capture Luang Prabang and had to retreat from most of the towns they had occupied to the west of Phong Saly and Sam Neua as French troops returned in tanks, armored cars, and airplanes. The wet weather hindered the French as well, but it was still possible to move down some of the main roads in tracked vehicles. And airplanes, although they could not land in heavy monsoons, could sometimes nose through the cloud covers and put down on short landing strips between showers.

As soon as the rains abated in December, 1953, the Communist forces not only regained temporarily lost ground but fought their way to the Mekong River port of Thakhek 130 miles southeast of Vientiane, across from the northeasternmost Thai town of Nakhorn Phanom. This bold tactic cut Laos in half by blocking traffic down the Mekong and also down Route 13, which turns east after reaching Vientiane and then follows the Mekong River valley southeast through Paksane, Thakhek, Savannakhet, and Pakse before crossing into Cambodia and eventually South Vietnam. Viet Minh troops occupied Thakhek from December 25 until early January, 1954, then melted before a French drive, and renewed the northern phase of their Laotian campaign.

French officials were sure that the enemy would again attempt to overrun the royal capital at Luang Prabang, but the Viet Minh, like the North Vietnamese Communists a generation later, had no intention of tying down significant numbers of their troops so far from Vietnamese soil. Viet Minh commanders decided that their troops had done enough merely to keep the French forces off balance and on guard. The Viet Minh withdrew from Laos in the middle of winter shortly before the battle of Dien Bien Phu began in earnest in March, 1954.

The historical parallel between Communist strategy in this and later periods also applied to the political side of the conflict. Souphanouvong, after reaching northern Vietnam in 1949, met General Vo Nguyen Giap and cemented the basic military-political relationship between the Viet Minh and the Lao Communists. Then, on August 13, 1950, Souphanouvong summoned the "First Resistance Congress" somewhere in the mountains of northeastern Laos or northern Vietnam. The congress attempted to legitimize its bid for power by forming a "resistance government" administered by Souphanouvong as Prime Minister and foreign minister.

The delegates' most significant long-range achievement, however, was the formation of a Pathet Lao, or Land of the Lao, army, behind which the Viet Minh could hide politically in order to carry out their military aims. Significantly, two of the Pathet Lao's highest leaders, Nouhak Phoumsavan and Kaysone Phomvihan, finance and defense ministers respectively in Souphanouvong's cabinet, had begun by serving the Viet Minh rather than the Lao Issara. Nouhak, a peasant's son, had shipped arms for the Viet Minh as a truck driver along Route 13 in southern Laos, while Kaysone, the son of a Vietnamese father and Lao mother, had joined the Viet Minh after having studied in Paris. The Pathet Lao, recognizing the need for support in the jungles, also courted mountain or tribal leaders. Among the most useful from the outset were Sithone Kommadane, the son of a southern tribal chieftain executed by the French, and Phay Dang, leader of a faction of Meo tribesmen. Both were named ministers without portfolio.[2]

Although Souphanouvong gladly allied with these men, he was more closely identified with three other delegates to the congress, Phoumi Vongvichit, appointed Deputy Prime Minister of the "resistance government," Prince Souk Vongsak, minister of education, and Singkapo Chounlamany, who emerged as the Pathet Lao military commander. Significantly, all three, like Souphanouvong, were products of elite Lao families. Phoumi's father had served as an official for the French colonial government, Souk was a member of a branch of the royal family in Luang Prabang, and Singkapo was from a leading family in Thakhek. The Pathet Lao from the outset, then, was an amalgam of dissatisfied but prominent Lao nationalists and Viet Minh–oriented leftists, allied wherever possible with leaders of local minority groups.

The organization of the Pathet Lao represented, in a sense, a marriage of convenience. Souphanouvong, although not a Communist, realized the necessity for Viet Minh political, military, and logistical support. The Viet Minh, while theoretically opposed to the elitist tradition, clearly viewed Souphanouvong's prestige, as well as his dedication and intelligence, as attributes that might advance their own aims in Laos. In March, 1951, Souphanouvong and the Viet Minh conclusively demonstrated their mutual loyalties at a meeting of the Lien-Viet, or United Front, sponsored by the Viet Minh. The Lien-Viet promoted the Vietnamese Communists' rather grandiose aim of replacing the French as the rulers of all Indochina by establishing an alliance of patriotic Vietnamese, Cambodian, and Lao fronts. The bond between Souphanouvong and the Viet Minh was solidified on April 19, 1953, immediately after the Viet Minh had conquered Sam Neua, when Souphanouvong installed his headquarters there and proclaimed his government the country's only legal authority.

While the Communists were forming long-range strategy, Souphanouvong's opponents, notably Souvanna Phouma, were hardening their positions. Souvanna, appointed Prime Minister on November 21, 1951, also wanted independence for Laos, but he preferred to rely on diplomacy rather than force. He insisted first that France relinquish military and economic controls exercised under the 1949 Franco-Lao convention. French Premier Joseph Laniel agreed on July 3, 1953, that it was time to "perfect the independence and sovereignty of the Associated States of Indochina."

The French National Assembly, in a debate in October, adopted a motion that the armed forces of Cambodia, Vietnam, and Laos should replace French troops, that all factions in the struggle should seek peace by negotiations, and that the French Union, including the Indochinese states, should be responsible for defending the independence of all its members. The treaty, signed on October 22, 1953, by King Sisavang Vong and the French Premier, granted independence to Laos—as a member of the Union.

The pattern of the future of Laos had emerged in the eight previous years of fighting and talking. The sides had been chosen and the issues clarified by the time the Geneva conference was convened on May 8, 1954, the day after the defeat of French forces at Dien Bien Phu. The Viet Minh, although most of their troops had withdrawn from Laos, had left enough advisers and support personnel behind to ensure Prince Souphanouvong's security in the northeastern provinces of Phong Saly and Sam Neua. The royal government seemed in control of the lowlands as well as the Plain of Jars. In between these two basic spheres of influence were vast stretches of jungle, a virtual no man's land, over which troops from all sides would fight for many years.

The First Coalition

From the outset, coalition was an illusory goal. The 1954 Geneva agreement specifically provided that Pathet Lao forces, totaling probably no more than 2,000 men, most of them mountain tribesmen, could remain in the northeastern provinces pending "a political settlement." In view of the extent to which the Viet Minh forces had penetrated Sam Neua and Phong Saly, it seemed inconceivable that they would abandon their gains for the sake of Lao national reconciliation.

The government and the Pathet Lao might never have reached an understanding, however short-lived, had it not been for the persistent belief among Chinese, Russian, and Vietnamese Communist leaders that somehow they could persuade Souphanouvong's opponents to remain "neutral" but anti-Western. Communist officials apparently hoped that the royal government, like that of Prince Norodom Sihanouk of Cambodia, would sympathize enough with their strategic aims as to obviate the necessity of protracted guerrilla warfare by the Pathet Lao.

The Communists, in fact, were pursuing a dual policy, as was evident in two statements issued on January 7, 1956. First, the International Control Commission, set up under the Geneva agreement to guarantee adherence to its provisions, demanded that the Pathet Lao yield control of Phong Saly and Sam Neua. The ICC, composed of delegates from Poland, neutral India, and Canada, would not have made its unanimous demand had not the Communist countries thought it advisable. Then, a congress of the Pathet Lao's United Front declared it had restructured and renamed itself the Neo Lao Hak Sat (NLHS), or Lao Patriotic Front. The Pathet Lao, on the other hand, would not have formed the NLHS had Hanoi not wanted to improve its mechanism for increasing its political influence over Laos.

At the same time, the Communists organized the clandestine Phak Pasason Lao, or Lao People's Party, the unit by which the Lao Dong, or Workers' Party of North Vietnam, would control the Pathet Lao. It was through the Phak Pasason Lao that the Lao Dong channeled views, policies, and orders. Significantly, Hanoi relied not on Souphanouvong, who might ultimately place national over Party interests, but on Nouhak Phoumsavan and Kaysone Phomvihan to lead the Party. Nouhak, as chairman, and Kaysone, as secretary-general, may each have exercised more power over the Pathet Lao than Souphanouvong.[3]

Nevertheless, Souphanouvong played a key role in applying the tactic of compromise in order to extend the influence of the Pathet Lao. As chairman of the NLHS, he publicly represented the Pathet Lao—and may have confused this appearance of power with the real substance of authority wielded by the Vietnamese Communists through the Phak Pasason Lao. In order to gain entree into the central government by negotiations, the Pathet Lao proposed talks on March 30, 1956. Souphanouvong then conferred with Souvanna in August, 1956.

As a result of the talks, Souvanna agreed to guarantee the neutrality of his government, the rights of the NLHS as a legitimate political party, and representation of the NLHS in Vientiane, in return for the surrender of Pathet Lao control over Phong Saly and Sam Neua and the integration of Pathet Lao units in the royal armed forces. After having reached this understanding with his half-brother, Souvanna and other high-ranking officials flew to China and then to North Vietnam. They met Mao Tse-tung, Ho Chi Minh, and a host of other Communist leaders, who only a year before had seemed to oppose them. The theme of neutrality dominated statements by both sides.

The process of reconciliation in Laos continued throughout 1957, beginning with an agreement in February on elections, also required by the Geneva conference. A sign of the depth of the difficulties, however, was that all through the talks Souvanna had to contend with the suspicions of right-wing politicians, who were no more prone to long-range compromise than the Communists. The National Assembly on May 29, 1957, adopted a motion criticizing Souvanna's relationship with Souphanouvong and decrying further delays in reintegrating the Pathet Lao with government forces. Souvanna promptly resigned, only to return to office on a vote of confidence on August 9, 1957, after the failure of his opponents in Vientiane to unite around a common policy.

Souvanna's skill as a compromiser led finally to the formation on November 19, 1957, of the first government of national union, including cabinet posts for Souphanouvong and his most trusted lieutenant, Phoumi Vongvichit. The spirit of compromise, however, did not last beyond special elections for the National Assembly, held on May 4, 1958, as the last step in fulfillment of the Geneva agreement. Exploiting rivalries among their opponents, NLHS candidates won nine of twenty-one contested seats—and a neutralist "peace" party allied with them picked up another four.

Government officials, as well as U.S. diplomats, were appalled by the results. Rightists alleged that the NLHS cheated and coerced many voters, but the weakness of anti-Communist candidates suggested that the leftists had deserved whatever they had won. The outcome, however, was tolerable neither to the Americans, already enmeshed in military and economic aid programs to halt the spread of Communism, nor to right-wing generals and politicians, long since antagonistic toward compromise.

After the elections, the United States suspended aid on the grounds that it had been misused. The charge was no doubt true, but the purpose of the move was to pressure Souvanna into abandoning his seemingly pro-Communist neutrality. The U.S. Central Intelligence Agency, allied with military officers opposed to Souvanna, encouraged the machinations of the anti-Communist Committee for the Defense of National Interests, made up of youthful officers and civilian officials. The CDNI, in turn, led the assembly first to a vote of no-confidence in Souvanna, who resigned on July 22, 1958, and then to a two-thirds majority for Phoui Sananikone, appointed Prime Minister on August 18.

The glue that had bound opposing elements of the government came unstuck when Phoui excluded the Pathet Lao ministers, Souphanouvong and Phoumi Vongvichit, from a new cabinet dominated by CDNI members and sympathizers. Then, in January,

1959, Phoui pressured the National Assembly into granting him special powers after a fresh series of North Vietnamese attacks and frontier violations.

The purpose of the Communist violations may have been only to force Phoui to restore the 1957 coalition, but Phoui hoped instead to destroy any possibility of a Pathet Lao resurgence. His next step was to try to undercut the Pathet Lao military base, consisting of two battalions awaiting merger with government forces in accordance with the Geneva agreement. Royal troops in April, 1959, surrounded the Pathet Lao camps, one near Luang Prabang, the other on the Plain of Jars, after their leader, Colonel Singkapo Chounlamany, refused to bow to Phoui's terms for reintegration. Most of the men in the camp near Luang Prabang surrendered, but the battalion on the plain slipped away on the night of May 18, 1959, eluded a government force ten times its size, and escaped to sanctuary along the Vietnamese frontier.

Far from blunting the drive of the rightists and the CIA, this demonstration of the government's military incompetence only enhanced the position of General Phoumi Nosavan, the secretary of state for defense, who advocated a much tougher anti-Communist policy than did Phoui. Supported by CDNI military officers and politicians, Phoumi not only forced Phoui to resign by the end of the year but then, in April, 1960, sponsored the crookedest elections for National Assembly in the country's history. Dispensing CIA funds as bribes, the army ensured that government candidates won the vast majority of seats. The NLHS boycotted the entire procedure, partly because Souphanouvong and fourteen other Pathet Lao leaders had been languishing in jail since the May escape of the Pathet Lao battalion. One month after the elections, however, Souphanouvong and his allies bribed their guards and escaped from Vientiane.

Still more humiliating to the government was the derring-do of a thirty-year-old army captain named Kong Le, the five-foot-tall son of a southern tribesman. On the night of August 8, 1960, Kong Le's battalion of paratroopers seized all government offices and military installations in the capital. The next morning, Kong Le declared over the radio the rise of a new regime dedicated to ceasing the war against the Pathet Lao and pursuing a policy of genuine neutrality.

Kong Le nursed no illusions about his ability to head a government. Instead, he called upon Prince Souvanna Phouma. The coup d'état was cloaked in legality when the National Assembly unanimously adopted a motion of no-confidence in the ousted government and King Savang Vatthana asked Souvanna to form a new cabinet. It was typical of Souvanna's political strategy of compromise and reconciliation that he attempted, albeit unsuccessfully, to persuade Phoumi to serve as Vice Premier and minister of interior.

A significant factor in the atmosphere of disunity in Vientiane throughout this period was endemic distrust among families, military officers, and politicians. Leaders from the three major regions —Luang Prabang in the north, Vientiane in the center, and Pakse and Savannakhet in the south—had quarreled with each other for centuries. The tradition of competition among a relatively small elite of perhaps fifty families helped to explain why General Phoumi's forces could retreat to the south, where Prince Boun Oum na Champassak, the region's elder statesman and most powerful figure, welcomed their presence.

While Phoumi and Boun Oum were plotting in Savannakhet, headquarters for their "revolutionary committee," Souvanna began making overtures to the Soviet Union, with which he established diplomatic relations in October, 1960. The Americans viewed Souvanna's position as proof that he was really pro-Communist despite his protestations of neutrality, but Souvanna's primary concern was to ensure the preservation of his neutral government against all opposition. When fighting between rightists and Kong Le's men engulfed the capital on December 9, 1960, however, Souvanna was compelled to flee Vientiane. The king then appointed Boun Oum as Prime Minister and General Phoumi as defense minister on December 12, and several days later, Kong Le's followers fled to new positions on Route 13 north of Vientiane. The real beneficiaries of the internal crisis in Vientiane were the Pathet Lao, who responded by recapturing Sam Neua, advancing beyond the northeast, and allying with Kong Le, whose forces encamped on the Plain of Jars in early 1961.

Souvanna himself appeared to have allied with the NLHS when he flew in late February to the plain and re-established the nucleus of a coalition government at the town of Khang Khay, where both Kong Le and the Pathet Lao had their headquarters. With the Communist powers still recognizing him as Prime Minister, Souvanna then departed on a world tour to win support for his position. Moscow went on shipping arms, ammunition, and fuel for Kong Le and the Pathet Lao on the plain, just as Washington supplied Phoumi in Vientiane.

Boun Oum's regime might have survived if Phoumi's army had not been exposed as incredibly weak and poorly disciplined. Government forces lost the critical junction of Routes 7 and 13 at Sala Phou Khoun on March 9, 1961, and retreated south toward Vientiane and north toward Luang Prabang. The United States in this period had to decide whether to enter Laos in force or to attempt a negotiated compromise. "We strongly and unreservedly support the goal of a neutral and independent Laos," said President Kennedy on March 24, 1961, scarcely two months after his inauguration. These words provided the framework within which the United States could rationalize a shift in allegiance to another government acceptable to both east and west.

The Second Coalition

Souvanna's close relationship with the Communist powers was a major factor in the Soviet Union's decision, as cochairman with Britain of the 1954 accords, to join in April, 1961, in calling for a new conference, which opened at Geneva in May. The Communists, including leaders in both Hanoi and Peking, believed that they could now gain by talking what they had not achieved by fighting. Moreover, the Soviet Union, although the major source of supplies for the Pathet Lao and the neutralists, did not want to risk direct confrontation with the United States. Kennedy's meeting with the Soviet Premier, Nikita S. Khrushchev, in Vienna on June 4, 1961, demonstrated the desire of both countries to work out a compromise. In a joint statement, the two leaders said Laos should remain "neutral and independent" and recognized the "importance of an effective ceasefire."

By this time, the United States had already indicated that Souvanna, the Soviet favorite, might be acceptable as the leader of a new government. W. Averell Harriman, at Kennedy's request, had talked with Souvanna in March, 1961, in Delhi and Paris. Souvanna, Souphanouvong, and Boun Oum, meeting in Zurich in June, 1961, agreed on the principle of coalition rule. Then, in February, 1962, after the rightists had gone on raising obstacles, the United States withdrew most of its aid from the Vientiane government, thus completely reversing the previous administration's policy.

The rightist regime might still not have relented if the Pathet Lao had not won an important victory. Pathet Lao gunners, supported by North Vietnamese, dug into the hills around the northwestern town of Nam Tha and began shelling its airstrip in March,

1962. Finally, on May 7, 1962, the Pathet Lao overran the town and its several thousand defenders, who were short on supplies as a result of the cut-off of U.S. aid and the loss of another nearby airstrip to the enemy.

The Pathet Lao might have advanced much further but for the intimidating effect of President Kennedy's decision to land troops in Thailand in May and June, 1962. As it was, Boun Oum had to agree in June to a new coalition in which Souvanna returned to power in Vientiane. With no real army at all, Souvanna not only won the posts of Prime Minister and defense minister but obtained portfolios for nine other neutralists on the nineteen-man cabinet. The rightists and leftists were balanced against each other with four seats for each side. Boun Oum decided to retire, but Phoumi and Souphanouvong were appointed Deputy Prime Ministers.

Superficially, the future of Laos appeared more secure than five years before, particularly after fourteen Communist, neutral, and Western powers had signed the Geneva agreement on July 23, 1962, pledging to support the country's sovereignty and neutrality. In reality, however, the new coalition government was stillborn. The root cause of its failure was North Vietnam's historic and long-range interest in extending hegemony over Laos. This drive, immediately after the signing of the Geneva agreement, was translated specifically into a carefully calculated effort to turn Kong Le's forces on the plain into de facto extensions of its own authority.

Hanoi and Moscow believed initially that the key to Communist power over the neutralists would be the airlift supply operation. North Vietnamese strategists, inheriting control over the shipment of supplies on Soviet planes after the signing of the Geneva accords, may have assumed that Kong Le would recognize Hanoi as the ultimate source of his power and ally with them. Communist hopes were doubtless fortified by Souvanna's rapport with Moscow, which had recommended him as the coalition's compromise choice for Prime Minister. Kong Le's record of conflict with the rightists also suggested pro-Communist proclivities.

Both Kong Le and Souvanna soon proved, however, that they were no more inclined to compromise with the Communists than with the rightists. A Communist embargo on Kong Le's supplies, beginning in late 1962, marked the beginning of the inevitable failure of the 1962 coalition. Souvanna seemed to have completely reversed his deceptively leftist stance when he arranged in October,

1962, for the shipment of supplies to Kong Le aboard Air America planes, contracted by the U.S. Government. By this time, the NLHS had decided to adhere technically to the terms of an agreement for merging all forces, neutralist, government, and Pathet Lao, by recognizing as neutralist only those units that were loyal to them.

The Communists' neutralist ally, in place of the obstinate Kong Le, was Colonel Deuan Sunnalath, who had been with Kong Le since the *coup d'état* of August 9, 1960. Colonel Deuan did not formally establish what he called the "true neutralist forces" until April, 1963, but an artillery unit he commanded was credited, on November 27, 1962, with having shot down a transport plane owned and operated by Air America, contracted by the U.S. Government to fly men and supplies in Southeast Asian countries. Then, Pathet Lao sappers, possibly disguised as neutralist soldiers, assassinated Kong Le's deputy commander, Colonel Ketsana Vongsouvan, on February 12, 1963. In March, 1963, the "Deuanists" began attacking Kong Le's men on the plain. In perhaps spontaneous retaliation, the pro-Communist—but nominally neutral—foreign minister, Quinim Pholsena, was assassinated in Vientiane on April 1, 1963, by a guard loyal to Kong Le.

The following month marked the final destruction of the coalition. Pathet Lao and Deuanist forces drove Kong Le's men almost entirely off the plain and might have annihilated his army had he not allied with his former rightist enemies. The Pathet Lao, who had swept across the plain in 1961 with Kong Le's help, were again in control of strategic positions through which supplies could roll from North Vietnam to units threatening main roads to Luang Prabang and Vientiane. During the fighting, Souphanouvong and his ally, Phoumi Vongvichit, minister of information in the 1962 coalition, fled from Vientiane. Souphanouvong re-established his headquarters in Khang Khay, where he and Souvanna had agreed only two years before to form a new coalition.

The flight of Souphanouvong and Phoumi Vongvichit was not immediately recognized as the end of the coalition. Later in 1963, Great Britain and the Soviet Union, as cochairmen of the conference, and the International Control Commission, disbanded in Laos in 1958 but reorganized under the 1962 Geneva agreement, urged talks to reunite the factions. While Kong Le and Colonel Singkapo discussed a possible military rapprochement on the plain, Souvanna met twice with Souphanouvong in 1964, first at Sam Neua in January and again at Khang Khay in April. These negotiations appeared only to deepen political and military divisions, for rightist officers in Vientiane staged a brief *coup d'état* on April 19, in which they arrested Souvanna, who had threatened the day before to resign.

Souvanna, then, was confronted by serious pressures from right and left. He quickly convinced the rightists to respect his rule, but the pretense of coalition evaporated with his announcement on May 1 of an agreement under which he would lead both rightists and neutralists. The two remaining Pathet Lao cabinet members, Prince Souk Vongsak, secretary of state for public works and transport, and Kampheuane Tounalom, secretary of state for planning, left Vientiane in June. Two left-leaning neutralist cabinet members, Khamsouk Keola, minister of public health, and General Heuan Monkonvilay, another secretary of state, had already fled to the Plain of Jars, forming the political nucleus of the "true neutralists," led militarily by Colonel Deuan. The only remaining NLHS representation in Vientiane was a military mission of some 100 soldiers who lived in two spacious houses owned by Souphanouvong opposite the central market.

Souvanna attempted valiantly to maintain the appearance of coalition by not filling the four Pathet Lao seats in his cabinet reorganization of April 23, 1964, in which he formally discharged the two dissident neutralists. The absence of Souphanouvong and his allies, however, underlined the fact that Laos was again divided into two principal factions—those who agreed with and those who refused to participate in the Vientiane government. The political split reflected the military division of the country between regions under Communist and government control. Diplomats sometimes referred to a "cease-fire line" separating the "two halves" of the country at the time of the signing of the 1962 agreement, but there never was any formal demarcation.

Rather, the Pathet Lao after 1962 seemed determined not only to maintain their own traditional strongholds but to regain areas which they had shared with Kong Le's troops. The failure of the talks in early 1964 between Souvanna and Souphanouvong provided ample pretext for new Pathet Lao attacks beginning on May 16, 1964, on Kong Le's remaining positions on the Plain of Jars. Within a week, Pathet Lao troops had driven Kong Le's forces to the western fringes of the plain, where they remained for two-and-a-half years.

Behind the Pathet Lao's political and military maneuvers were the North Vietnamese, who continued to exercise final authority through Party and army channels. After 1960, Hanoi strongly encouraged Pathet Lao recruiting and training. The result was that intelligence specialists in Vientiane estimated that the Pathet Lao had grown from perhaps 2,000 men in 1960 to some 20,000 by 1963. In addition, Hanoi supplemented the Pathet Lao with its own forces, as was evidenced by the fact that only forty North Vietnamese formally left Laos in accordance with the provision of the agreement calling for withdrawal of all foreign troops. Some 6,000 remained, most of them in Sam Neua and Xieng Khouang provinces in northeastern Laos.*

Officials in Vientiane were inclined to ascribe to North Vietnam a primary role in Kong Le's defeat on the Plain of Jars in 1964. "If the Pathet Lao have not disappeared from the scene, it is because of the support they have received from their North Vietnamese ally, who has maintained, armed, trained, and officered the Pathet Lao forces in their guerrilla activities," said a late-1964 government white paper entitled "North Vietnamese Interference in Laos." The paper cited as evidence letters found on slain North Vietnamese soldiers. "I am actually fighting in Laos; I have already been in battle," said one letter. "The only hat I have here is a Pathet Lao hat," said another. Interviews with three North Vietnamese prisoners, the paper went on, provided proof that "North Vietnamese have helped the Pathet Lao not only with war materials and food, but by sending units of their regular army."[4]

Some of the Lao Government's claims were no doubt exaggerated, but the pattern of the North Vietnamese build-up in Laos was revealed in the firsthand account of Captain Mai Dai Hap, a North Vietnamese military adviser from 1964 until his defection to government forces in December, 1966. North Vietnamese strategy in 1964 still emphasized the build-up of the Pathet Lao as the cutting edge for eventual Communist victory. An organization known as Doan—or Group—959, four kilometers from Hanoi, directed "political guidance and administrative support to the Pathet Lao," according to this defector's account.[5]

"Group 959 receives its instructions from the Central Committee of the Lao Dong Party and from the Commander-in-Chief of the North Vietnamese military forces," the report went on. "It maintains a forward command post in Sam Neua Province, where the Pathet Lao have their central headquarters," and was believed to perform "an advisory mission with the Central Committee" of the Phak Pasason Lao. At the same time, strictly military guidance emanated from North Vietnam's Northwest Military Region Head-

* All figures on Pathet Lao and North Vietnamese strength in Laos are necessarily estimates by Lao and Western diplomats and intelligence analysts.

quarters at the town of Sonla, 50 miles east of Dien Bien Phu. Military advisers, answering to that headquarters, pervaded—and in effect controlled—the entire Pathet Lao military structure.[6]

Although the North Vietnamese were reluctant to entrust the Pathet Lao with more than a secondary military role, the Phak Pasason Lao and the NLHS were responsible for low-level political organization. Since Lao, like Cambodians, traditionally feared and disliked the Vietnamese, Lao cadres could be more effective than Vietnamese in daily personal contacts. Besides, from the point of view of international diplomacy and propaganda, it was far more expedient for North Vietnam to shield its aims behind the facade of an indigenous front than to appear at all interested in extending political control. While driving Kong Le's forces off the Plain of Jars in 1963 and 1964, Pathet Lao cadres began installing their own officials in newly "liberated areas." The Pathet Lao on the plain quickly established a local administrative complex capable of recruiting soldiers, collecting rice, and supplying porters for the military effort.[7]

The Pathet Lao organization on the plain was probably representative of the system that Hanoi would have liked to establish in all Communist-controlled areas, covering roughly 20 per cent of the population scattered over half the country. In many cases, however, the Communists had to settle for sporadic taxation and recruiting among a populace already milked dry of young men suitable for combat. Moreover, more than half the inhabitants of Pathet Lao regions were mountain or tribal folk who defied attempts at organizing them by traversing wide stretches of land in search of food and living space. Pathet Lao leaders knew from experience that the best way to win over tribesmen was to side with their chiefs in local feuds.

That the Pathet Lao seemed to play the leading role in these activities increased their importance in terms of North Vietnam's aims. Just as the Communists were determined to seize military control over clearly defined regions beyond the lowlands, so they had corollary plans for establishing their own government. Perhaps the best indication of Communist aims, however, was the departure of NLHS leaders from the coalition in Vientiane as soon as they saw that Souvanna would not let them use it to extend their power beyond areas already held by their troops. The lines were drawn, in 1963 and 1964, for another five years of political, diplomatic, and military sparring before the Communists would again attempt seriously to upset the balance in Vientiane.

IO

Military Escalation

North Vietnamese Interests

During the fragmentation of the second coalition, the nature of the struggle changed partly as a result of Hanoi's increased interest in Laos as another front in the Vietnam war. The pressures of the conflict in Vietnam did not account for North Vietnam's long-range aims in Laos, but they helped to explain why Hanoi, beginning in 1964, escalated its own direct involvement there and eventually encouraged the Neo Lao Hak Sat (NLHS), the Lao Patriotic Front, to adopt a much tougher political line than was envisioned at the time of the signing of the 1962 agreement.

North Vietnam's hope throughout the second Indochinese war was that the government in Vientiane, whether led by Souvanna or a more malleable replacement, would sympathize with its use of southern Laos as a corridor for the movement of men and materiel to South Vietnam. As long as the government attempted to discourage this type of activity, either by its own haphazard offensives or by permitting U.S. air strikes, Hanoi was bound to try to protect its interests. North Vietnam's aim was to wear down and overextend the government's army of some 60,000 men—and eventually to force Souvanna to grant policy-making authority to NLHS leaders in perhaps a new coalition in Vientiane.

In fighting for this goal, Hanoi would have preferred, for political and diplomatic if not military reasons, that Pathet Lao rather than North Vietnamese troops spearhead operations in the north. In July, 1964, however, royal Lao forces launched a monsoon counter-offensive that undid many earlier Pathet Lao gains. The government not only opened Route 13 between Vientiane and Luang Prabang but also set up new positions in Phong Saly and Sam Neua provinces, long regarded as Pathet Lao terrain. Most important among the towns abandoned by the Pathet Lao on Route 13 were Vang Vieng, 50 miles north of Vientiane, and Sala Phou Khoun, another 50 miles north at the junction of Routes 7 and 13.

The success of the government offensives against the Pathet Lao resulted in the first sharp increase in North Vietnamese troop strength since the flurry of fighting during the Geneva conference. Analysts in Vientiane, ranging from members of the International Control Commission to foreign military attachés and diplomats, estimated that the number of North Vietnamese troops in Laos more than doubled from 15,000 at the beginning of 1964 to well over 30,000 a year later. North Vietnam divided its troops almost equally between the northern provinces and the southern corridor, known as the Ho Chi Minh trail, to South Vietnam and northeastern Cambodia. The expenditure of troops in northern Laos during the Vietnam war may have seemed wasteful, but they protected the corridor indirectly by dispersing and tying down opponents, who might otherwise have harassed it.

In view of the importance of the trail system in the Vietnam conflict, North Vietnam escalated its activities in Laos as fighting intensified in South Vietnam. Traffic on the trail remained at a fairly low level in the early 1960's, when the Viet Cong seemed capable of defeating the Saigon government without the aid of North Vietnamese troops. As the fighting flared after the assassination of President Ngo Dinh Diem on November 1, 1963, North Vietnam sent larger shipments of arms and materiel to the South and encouraged Pathet Lao political and military maneuvers.

Then, on February 7, 1965, President Lyndon Johnson ordered the bombing of North Vietnamese military installations, which, according to a joint South Vietnamese–American statement, "had been employed in the direction and support of those engaged in aggression in South Vietnam." The bombing of the North, as well as the corridor through southern Laos, comprised the first phase of massive U.S. escalation aimed at relieving the immediate threat to the Saigon government. In the next few months, President Johnson ordered more than 200,000 soldiers to South Vietnam, the vanguard of a force that reached 547,000 men before President Richard Nixon began the gradual withdrawal of U.S. troops in the summer of 1969.

The North Vietnamese, after the entry of U.S. troops, responded by a massive escalation of their own. They not only increased the quantity and quality of materiel consigned to the South but also, for the first time in the war, began sending their own combat soldiers to fight alongside the Viet Cong. North Vietnamese engaged government forces in southern Laos in early 1965, as the first North Vietnamese units began to appear in the northern provinces of South Vietnam. The number of North Vietnamese in Laos leveled off at 40,000 in 1965, as North Vietnamese engineers, often aided by local tribesmen, began to double the size and capacity of the trail system.

On March 9, 1965, the Communists opened up that year's offensive in Laos by attacking a reserve officers' school at Dong Hene, 30 miles east of Savannakhet on Route 9, the main highway from southern Laos to Quang Tri, the northernmost province of South Vietnam. The motives of the North Vietnamese, who led the attack, were clarified in a report by the International Control Commission, whose Canadian and Indian representatives conducted an investigation after the Polish member refused to participate. Nine prisoners, according to the report, said that they were en route to South Vietnam before the battle. One prisoner said that his particular group of twenty-six soldiers had been "ordered to help Pathet Lao so that they could find a new route to South Vietnam."[1]

Superficially, the North Vietnamese were not successful in their initial forays in southern Laos. In the Dong Hene attack, for instance, some 100 North Vietnamese and Pathet Lao soldiers were killed by Lao officers' candidates and instructors, who easily held their ground with the help of Lao Air Force T-28's, highly maneuverable single-engine planes of World War II vintage. Then, in November, 1965, at the beginning of the next dry season, Lao soldiers repelled several mixed North Vietnamese and Pathet Lao battalions 2 miles outside of Thakhek. The Lao again captured North Vietnamese prisoners who informed Indian and Canadian ICC representatives of their identity and purpose.

Despite such tactical defeats, however, North Vietnam succeeded in diverting government troops from the Ho Chi Minh trail system. Only 60 miles east of Thakhek, on Route 12 in the Annamite Mountains, was the Mu Gia Pass through which Viet Minh soldiers had marched to fight the French in 1953. North Vietnamese engineers in the latter 1960's built alternate routes in the pass to compensate for U.S. bombing. They also constructed a series of split-offs turning south from Route 12 before it reached the lowlands.

Without the convenience of an old French colonial highway to follow, the North Vietnamese carved an entirely new road system through another pass, 30 miles south of the Mu Gia, at Ban Karai, which, in turn, was 30 miles north of the Demilitarized Zone (DMZ) created by the 1954 Geneva agreement between North and South Vietnam. The Mu Gia and Ban Karai passes bore most of the traffic to South Vietnam, but North Vietnamese troops could also traverse the Keo Neua Pass, which entered Laos at the town of Nape, some 60 miles northwest of the Mu Gia. The North Vietnamese rebuilt Route 8 over the Keo Neua or Nape Pass as the war in the south and heavy American bombing of the trail network compelled them to search for still more routes. The North Vietnamese could conceivably have sent materiel for the South through the Barthélémy Pass, another 100 miles northwest of Nape, but the distance was prohibitive for normal purposes. The Barthélémy's main value was for transporting supplies along Route 7 to positions surrounding the Plain of Jars.

Road-builders surfaced almost the entire network totaling 1,550 miles with crushed rock—and occasionally laterite—capable of supporting heavy truckloads except during the monsoon season. The system, crisscrossed by alternate emergency routes, also included repair facilities, bomb shelters, and truck parks, sometimes in caves, as well as drums, dropped off at regular intervals, containing gasoline and engine oil pumped across the. mountains through hidden pipelines. The 559th Transportation Group, made up of several thousand engineering troops, was responsible for upkeep and repair.

At first, the main road south through the system was Route 23, a barely passable track before North Vietnamese engineers began working on it in the mid-1960's. Originating in a complex of roads south of Route 12, Route 23, running down the center of southern Laos through Saravane and the Bolovens Plateau, formed the western border of the network. The North Vietnamese did not literally follow the old roads. When necessary they bypassed towns, such as Saravane, or built parallel tracks of their own. American military maps gave special numbers to some of these new routes between Route 23 and the Vietnamese frontier. The route across the Ban Karai Pass, for instance, was 137, which led into Route 911, another main artery to the south. Route 1036 cut from North to South Vietnam around the western end of the DMZ. Route 92 was one of several North Vietnamese roads leading to the southern extremities of Laos. From these north-south roads, branches fed into the South Vietnamese highlands. Several roads led to north-eastern and northern Cambodia, through which the North Vietnamese also sent men and materiel to points still lower on the map.

While the North Vietnamese were improving their road system, a deceptive sense of calm and progress descended over much of the lowlands. Since North Vietnamese troops appeared incapable at first of holding any territory beyond the trail region, diplomats and officials believed that Lao forces were gaining strength and might eventually range over the entire country. Intelligence analysts tended to interpret minor North Vietnamese and Pathet Lao attacks in 1965 and 1966 as "rice raids," in which the enemy's main purpose was to gather food for the next monsoon.

"These people, the enemy, don't make contact," observed a U.S. military attaché in an interview in November, 1966. "It's a brush in the night, and then they're gone." American officials said that government forces, advancing from the lowlands, had formed a buffer zone between areas of government and Communist control. Perhaps most encouraging to them was the success in the northeast of a clandestine army of Meo soldiers financed and advised by the U.S. Central Intelligence Agency and led by a former French army sergeant, General Vang Pao, also a Meo. "Vang Pao's army," as it was known, led three monsoon counteroffensives from 1964 through 1966, in which the government recovered small outposts in Sam Neua and Xieng Khouang provinces. Even in the south, where North Vietnamese troops had to defend the trail system, the government reopened the Done River from the Bolovens Plateau to the town of Pakse and launched a program, with U.S. aid, for exploiting the area's rich farmland.

This picture of apparent stability and peace in the lowlands was reflected in Vientiane after Phoumi Nosavan's last effort at overthrowing Souvanna Phouma. Troops loyal to Phoumi attacked Vientiane on January 31, 1965, but were repelled by the forces of General Kouprasith Abhay, Vientiane military commander, who had allied with Phoumi in 1960. Phoumi and General Siho Lamphouthakoul, the military police commander, fled to Thailand. Souvanna then appointed another rightist, Leuam Insisiengmay, head of a prominent southern family, as Deputy Prime Minister in place of Phoumi, but basically Souvanna was now the sole leader of a Vientiane regime more united than ever before.

Two other events illustrated Souvanna's increasing political security. First, the government in 1966 placed Kong Le's forces under its over-all command but left them in their previous positions at Muong Soui, on the western edge of the Plain of Jars, at Vang Vieng, and elsewhere. Kong Le, who had refused to bow to the will of the Pathet Lao, proved equally unwilling to accept subordination to military leaders in Vientiane. He left his headquarters at Muong Soui on October 17, 1966, and went into self-imposed exile several weeks later in Thailand and eventually Paris. After his departure, the government encountered little opposition in fitting the "Forces Armées Neutralistes" into its defense establishment.

The second indication of Souvanne's strength among officers and politicians opposed to the Pathet Lao was the utter failure of a *coup d'état* by air force commander General Thao Ma, who led ten of his T-28's on a strafing and bombing run over Vientiane on October 21, 1966. Was General Ma attempting to overthrow Souvanna and reinstall Phoumi? This hypothesis seemed possible, but he and his fellow conspirators flew to asylum in Thailand without landing when they saw they had no support in Vientiane. The gain in government prestige seemed to outbalance the temporary furor and damage—not to mention the loss of planes and pilots—caused by the attack.

For all the hopeful signs, there were also many indications that the North Vietnamese and the Pathet Lao had not abandoned their military or political goals. The NLHS, presumably at Hanoi's urging, had, on October 3, 1965, signaled the Communists' long-range determination by renaming its depleted forces the Laotian People's Liberation Army and calling for "an unflinching struggle aimed at defeating the intervention and aggression in any forms of the U.S. imperialists. . . ."[2] This statement reflected Hanoi's concern that the United States, directly or indirectly, would try to prevent it from sending men down the Ho Chi Minh trail system. By the middle of 1967, however, Hanoi had 100,000 of its own troops in South Vietnam and had to infiltrate replacements at the rate of 10,000 men a month. This requirement alone seemed to negate the possibility for any lasting stability in Laos so long as the war continued in South Vietnam.

Soviet Versus Chinese Aims

If the North Vietnamese would only agree to maintain the *status quo*, if the Soviet Union, as cochairman of the Geneva conference, would exert subtle pressure to discourage new Communist offensives, then U.S. officials thought that Laos might begin to realize the dream of permanent stability. The U.S. Ambassador, William Sullivan, who had helped to negotiate the 1962 Geneva agreement and was responsible for executing the shift in American policy from loyalty to the Phoumi rightists to support of a neutral coalition, summarized his thinking in a conversation at the U.S. Embassy on November 12, 1966. "We'd be happy to see an arrangement in which there's a mutual understanding flowing largely from a tacit understanding by the Soviets and ourselves," he said, "that neither we nor they see any great possibilities for exploitation."

Ideally, Sullivan explained, Laos should form a buffer between the Communist and capitalist powers—and the Soviet Union and America should agree not to disturb the arrangement. U.S. strategy was not to establish a "cordon sanitaire," he went on, but to permit the country to "find its own balance." Underlying Sullivan's view was his perception that Hanoi regarded Laos as "second priority" after Vietnam. Although this estimate was no doubt valid, it failed, retrospectively, to consider the full importance of Laos for Vietnam.

It was always conceivable that the Soviet Union, as Sullivan suggested, might view Laos from the same strategic perspective as the United States, but two factors weighed against this hope. First, the Russians, for reasons of prestige within the Communist movement, did not want to appear to frustrate the aims of North Vietnam, or, if North Vietnamese interests were not publicly acknowledged, then those of the leftist Pathet Lao or NLHS, which were dominated by a clandestine Communist Party. Second, in Southeast Asia, the Soviet Union was competing for prestige and influence with China, which was providing full propaganda and material support to the Communist campaign in Laos. Since China borders on Laos and North Vietnam, it also afforded rail and road facilities for shipping men and materiel from North Vietnam to northern Laos. The main route led around the tip of Phong Saly, the northernmost Laotian province, to the junction town of Meng La, whence it branched east into Phong Saly and south toward Nam Tha.

In view of China's proximity to Laos and North Vietnam, the Soviet Union's most effective channel for exercising diplomatic influence was through its role as cochairman of the Geneva conference. This position gave Moscow an ideal opportunity not only for countering some of China's aims but also for appearing to support those of the Pathet Lao and the North Vietnamese. Thus, the Soviet Union in mid-1964 suggested that Britain, as the other cochairman, sign a joint declaration condemning U.S. reconnaissance flights, first disclosed by the U.S. State Department on May 11 of that year. Moscow drafted another note in early 1965, after the United States had revealed that two of its jet reconnaissance planes had been shot down over central Laos.

The British cochairman refused to join in circulating these messages, just as the Soviet Union in late 1965 rejected Britain's request to circulate an ICC report on North Vietnamese troops in Laos. Moscow and London for the next five years exchanged a series of draft notes, almost none of them acceptable to the other side. Under no circumstances would the Soviet Union consider opposing or even acknowledging the activities of the Communists, whereas Britain worded notes to indicate that all belligerents should share the blame and responsibility. "I feel bound to tell you," said British Foreign Secretary George Brown, in a note to the Soviet foreign ministry in April, 1967, that the "cause of the present instability in Laos lies in the occupation by North Vietnamese troops of Laotian territory from which they support North Vietnamese intervention in South Vietnam and help the Pathet Lao forces in attacks against the lawful Government of Laos."[3]

The diplomatic byplay between the British and Soviet cochairmen was of secondary importance, but it indicated that Moscow would not live up to Ambassador Sullivan's hopes. The only comfort in the Soviet Union's position was that it did seem considerably milder than that of Peking, which had begun in 1964 to regard Souvanna as the leader "of a government controlled by the rightist group" rather than a true neutralist. "U.S. imperialism is the sworn enemy of the peoples of Laos and other Indochinese States," said a typical Peking statement, a letter, dated August 20, 1966, from Chinese Foreign Minister Ch'en Yi to Phoumi Vongvichit, general secretary of the NLHS. "The Chinese people remain forever the reliable and powerful backing of the Laotian people in their struggle against U.S. imperialism."[4]

Although Soviet statements on Vietnam and Cambodia appeared considerably more restrained than those from China, Moscow still competed with Peking for the role of major arms-supplier. China provided nearly all the rifles and light machine guns, but Russia gave heavy rockets, cannon, trucks, and other sophisticated equipment. The Communists in Laos, as in Vietnam, wanted friendly relations with both, partly to ensure that China would not assume too strong a position. The Chinese presence was, if anything, more apparent in Laos than in North Vietnam. China, like North Vietnam, the Soviet Union, and other signatories of the 1962 agreement, maintained an embassy in Vientiane, but it also had an economic and cultural mission at the town of Khang Khay, the former neutralist capital on the Plain of Jars, and a consulate-general at Phong Saly.

The presence of the cultural center and the consulate constituted open defiance of the authority of Vientiane, which not only did not recognize these missions but could not possibly send its own emissaries to visit them.[5] The mission at Khang Khay, besides disseminating Chinese propaganda, monitored the flow of Chinese-made military supplies, transported from Hanoi by North Vietnamese trucks and Pathet Lao porters, and advised units in the region on tactics and training. The center, commanded by a Chinese general, also advised the Pathet Lao on the operation of a clandestine radio station, which broadcast a stream of invective against the Vientiane government. The Chinese consulate at Phong Saly was the power base of the province, ruled directly by General Khammouane Boupa, a "neutralist" who had defected to the Pathet Lao in 1964..

By the 1970's, China appeared to view Phong Saly Province as almost a vassal state controlled by a sycophantic warlord. In their possessive attitude toward Phong Saly, the Chinese seemed to have reached a clear understanding with the North Vietnamese, who adopted the same view toward Sam Neua, the seat of Souphanouvong's Pathet Lao government after his flight from Vientiane in 1962. Chinese control over Phong Saly provided a powerful hammer with which Peking could threaten not only Laos but Thailand and even Burma. This threat was underlined by the enlargement, in the middle and late 1960's, of the road network that the Chinese had begun to build in 1962 from the town of Meng La. The pretext for building these roads was that they were part of an aid program, offered free of charge, for the people of Laos. China and Laos had indeed entered into an agreement in January, 1962, on construction of the first leg from Meng La to Phong Saly, which was completed in April, 1963.

The next phase of the project appeared to represent a deliberate deviation from an understanding reached between rightist Deputy Prime Minister General Phoumi Nosavan and Chinese officials, in Peking in late 1962 in the brief period in which the second coalition was actually functioning. The New China News Agency reported that Phoumi had asked Chinese authorities if they could extend the road from Phong Saly to Nam Tha.[6] This conversation apparently provided China with the rationale for building the road in 1963 and 1964 from Meng La to Nam Tha—although not via Phong Saly. At this point, intelligence analysts began to foresee

the grand Chinese design for a network that would effectively cut
off northern Laos and provide a bridge from North Vietnam to
Thailand. Chinese engineers, between September, 1968, and January, 1969, built a road from the border village of Batene to the
town of Muong Sai, 50 miles to the southeast and 50 miles north
of Luang Prabang. Muong Sai, the forward command headquarters
for all Communist operations in northern Laos, was also a supply
and training center for the Pathet Lao and Meo tribesmen recruited in Laos and Thailand.

From Muong Sai, the Chinese road-builders could veer southwest toward Thailand, following an old logging trail down the
Beng River valley, or northeast toward Route 19, leading across
the North Vietnamese frontier to Dien Bien Phu. Turning northeast in November, 1968, the road-builders had completed the road
as far as Muong Khoua on Route 19 by 1969. North Vietnamese,
in turn, improved Route 19 from Dien Bien Phu to Muong Khoua.
By mid-1970, trucks could drive the entire 70 miles from Muong
Sai to Dien Bien Phu. The Chinese in 1969 began building the
spur from Muong Sai toward the Thai border. Within a year, they
had constructed a two-lane track paralleling the Beng River almost
as far as the conflux with the Mekong 70 miles southwest of
Muong Sai. A well-traveled trail covered the remaining 18 miles
south to the Thai frontier.

Estimates of the number of road-builders varied considerably,
but intelligence analysts in Vientiane believed that 6,000 of them
were in Laos at the height of the program. Major General Tiao
Sayavong, commander of the northern military region and a
brother of the king, said in an interview in February, 1970, that
some 2,000 Chinese had built the last extension of the road along
the Beng River with the aid of ten bulldozers and 150 trucks. Most
of them were not armed and were not escorted by combat units.
The main Chinese defense, besides North Vietnamese and Pathet
Lao, was a series of 37mm. antiaircraft guns mounted on hilltops
overlooking the Beng River valley. These guns were said to fire at
any planes that seemed to threaten the road, but they were seldom
used.

The Chinese were able to build a military road network through
Laos with impunity because Lao officials were afraid of upsetting
the delicate balance on which their government depended for
survival. If Lao forces supplemented by U.S. jets attacked the
roads, the North Vietnamese could escalate their own attacks.
Also, the United States, for reasons not entirely related to the

struggle for Laos, wanted to avoid open conflict with the Chinese. U.S. policy-makers knew that China would regard attacks on Chinese road-builders as almost tantamount to a declaration of war and might seize upon this excuse to send its ground troops into the region or, on a different level, end any possibility of talks between U.S. and Chinese diplomats.

In view of the complex diplomatic and military restraints placed upon U.S. and Lao officials, it was somewhat ironic that a series of battles in a valley only 15 miles east of Muong Sai marked one of the high points of the decade in terms of Lao Government power and authority. Lao troops drove into the Nam Bac valley in August, 1966, when the strength of the North Vietnamese and Pathet Lao was at its seasonal low ebb as a result of monsoon rains. For a year and a half, the Lao forces loosely held the valley, through which ran an old trail leading east to Sam Neua. The valley might have formed a base from which aggressive troops could extend Lao rule in all directions, toward Phong Saly, Muong Sai, and Sam Neua. The government erred, however, in believing that its forces were strong enough to retain permanent control of the valley, much less pursue the enemy through surrounding mountains. Chinese and North Vietnamese strategists could only view Lao troops in the Nam Bac valley as a threat to both the road network, much of it then still in the planning stage, and their nearby bases.

Chinese and North Vietnamese concerns coincided in the desire to reassert Communist control over the Nam Bac valley. If China's aims in northern Laos ever conflicted with those of North Vietnam, neither of them indicated it in their propaganda. Hanoi's only protection against China was the influence of the Soviet Union, which never criticized Peking specifically for its activities in Laos. North Vietnam was too preoccupied with other interests, notably the trail system and Vietnam, to want to risk confrontation with China, which, in turn, viewed its alliance with Hanoi as a means to achieve some of its aims in the region.

Laos and the Tet Offensive

The Communists' dry-season offensive in the winter of 1967 was planned mainly to replenish rice supplies, capture a few weapons, and spread propaganda. The country was basking in such relative security that year that the U.S. Information Service in Vientiane began handing out mimeographed copies of a release stating that "more than half of Laos" was under "firm government control" and another 20 per cent "under marginal RLG [Royal Lao Government] control."[7] The briefing sheet was probably not exaggerating the extent of Lao Government influence, if not exactly "firm control," but the Communists in July and August began reinforcing positions near Nam Bac, the main town in the valley. At approximately the same time, they sent reinforcements east of the Ho Chi Minh trail network in the vicinity of the towns of Saravane and Attopeu, north and south of the Bolovens Plateau. In retrospect, these movements signaled the opening the following January of the Lao phase of the Communists' winter-spring Tet offensive.

The term Tet offensive was never applied to the 1968 campaign in Laos, partly because Lao Theravada Buddhists do not celebrate the same Tet or lunar new year holidays as do the Mahayana Buddhists of China and Vietnam. Also, few observers at first realized any connection between the fighting in Laos and attacks launched by North Vietnamese and Viet Cong troops on every major city and town in South Vietnam on January 30 and 31, 1968. The campaign in Laos, unlike the Tet offensive in South Vietnam, was not one sudden thrust but a series of isolated jabs at a few carefully selected, strategically important positions. The purpose was not to win a sudden victory or foment a popular uprising, as in South Vietnam, but to defend the trail system and divert and disperse Lao forces in the north.

North Vietnam opened its campaign in Laos with an attack on Lao positions in the Nam Bac valley on January 13, 1968. The attack was so far from Vietnam—even from the nearest supply routes capable of transporting men and materiel to the South— that any connection between it and the Vietnam war seemed illusory. A year later, however, intelligence analysts in Vientiane cited Nam Bac as the first battle of the Tet offensive. In two days, North Vietnamese troops, supported by artillery in the mountains, dispersed some 2,000 government soldiers, most of whom surrendered or fled rather than face what they assumed was a far superior force. The ministry of foreign affairs published a *White Book* alleging that four North Vietnamese regiments, one North Vietnamese battalion, and five Pathet Lao battalions had participated in the attack.[8]

A year later, as Lao Army stragglers still were returning from surrounding hills and jungles, military analysts questioned whether or not the Communists had really deployed as many troops as indicated in the *White Book*. The real problem was that ill-disciplined Lao were no match for Vietnamese, whose total strength in the battle may have been no more than 1,000 men. No one doubted, however, the two main motives offered by the government for the attack. The first was to drive away the "menace on the west flank" of the North Vietnamese, who occupied most of the territory to the east of Nam Bac town, and the second was to draw as many Lao troops as possible into the region to facilitate the passage of North Vietnamese regiments along the Ho Chi Minh trail.[9]

The battle of Nam Bac was the most important in northern Laos that year, but North Vietnamese and Pathet Lao troops also drove Lao defenders from a series of lesser outposts. On January 13, 1968, the day the battle began, two Russian-made Antonov-2 biplanes were shot down in a raid on a U.S. radar and navigational aid site atop Phou Pha Thi, a 5,860-foot mountain 17 miles from the North Vietnamese frontier. The planes were among four, all piloted by North Vietnamese, that were sent across the border to attack the site, opened in 1966 to guide American bombers on missions over North Vietnam. On March 11, 1968, North Vietnamese ground troops overran the site, killing a dozen U.S. airmen, forcing it to close, and possibly influencing President Johnson's decision of March 31 to cease bombing North Vietnam above the 20th parallel (and later the 19th parallel).

Hanoi was equally determined to prosecute the offensive in southern Laos. In February, at the height of the fighting in Vietnam, the Communists began their prolonged siege of the key panhandle towns of Saravane and Attopeu, near or on some of the main infiltration routes. Both towns, isolated from the surrounding countryside, soon had to rely almost entirely on airplanes for military and civilian supplies. The defending Lao troops were almost powerless to go beyond their defensive perimeters. In the same period, the Communists drove government forces out of the Done River valley, reopened only two or three years before, and rampaged at will over much of the Bolovens Plateau.

It would be unfair to conclude that Lao soldiers were incapable of fighting. At Lao Ngam, a town about 25 miles southwest of Saravane on the Bolovens Plateau, a Lao battalion fended off an enemy force twice its size on the night of February 22, 1968. The next morning, Lao soldiers found the bodies of some eighty regular North Vietnamese troops in the tangled barbed wire defenses. The Lao captured six prisoners and assorted equipment ranging from two 82mm. cannon to twenty-five AK-47 rifles, the basic Communist infantry weapon. Despite these losses, however, the North Vietnamese posed enough of a threat to convince the Lao to withdraw from Lao Ngam rather than face similar attacks in the near future. The aim of the North Vietnamese was complete control of the Bolovens Plateau, covered by potential supply routes.

Equally important was Route 9, running north of the plateau from Savannakhet, over the Annamite Mountains to South Vietnam and ending at the base town of Dong Ha, where it joined Route 1, Vietnam's main north-south highway, 10 miles below the DMZ and 8 miles west of the coast. The North Vietnamese overran a series of outposts on Route 9 in Laos in early 1968 while three North Vietnamese divisions laid siege to the U.S. marine combat base at Khe Sanh, on the same road only 6 miles inside the South Vietnamese frontier. Some analysts believed that the Vietnamese, by surrounding Khe Sanh from late January until early March, hoped to open a corridor along Route 9 through which they could ship supplies to the Vietnamese coastal lowlands. At the town of Tchepone, 25 miles west of the border on Route 9, was a central base area from which the Communists directed movement on the trails leading into the South Vietnamese highlands. A secondary purpose of the Khe Sanh siege may have been to tie down U.S. troops while the Communists sent men and materiel along still other routes from around Tchepone to Vietnam.

Only in central Laos did the Communist offensive of 1968 appear not to exceed the routine dry-season level. North Vietnamese and Phathet Lao troops, moving from the hills that rim the Plain of Jars, overran outposts in Xieng Khouang Province held by General Vang Pao's army of Meo tribesmen. Then, driving south toward the Mekong, the Communists threatened to cut Laos in half, as they could have done at almost any time. Their purpose, however, was only to spread Pathet Lao influence through the hills beyond the river and to heighten the impression of a nationwide offensive without seriously upsetting the balance.

It was still possible, by the end of 1968, for U.S. and Lao officials to rationalize that year's fighting in terms of the annual seasonal pattern of the conflict. The Lao, as analysts in Vientiane had predicted, mounted their offensive during the rainy season beginning in May. Government commando units reopened Route 9 as far as Muong Phalane, a bombed-out town 50 miles east of Savannakhet, and ventured over some of the roads on the Bolovens Plateau. In the northeast, Vang Pao's Meo guerrillas recovered dozens of tiny positions abandoned during the dry season. By the end of the monsoon in November, 1968, the Meo had occupied an outpost within 12 miles of the Pathet Lao headquarters at Sam Neua.

These gains seemed to substantiate the view that the government gets back in the rainy season what it loses in the dry season, but Lao forces failed to recover all their losses. The Tet offensive marked another major step in escalation of the war in Vietnam and Laos. The parallel also extended to the conceptual framework with which the Communists rationalized their activities. The NLHS convened a congress in Sam Neua in November, 1968, at which it proclaimed a twelve-point political program modeled after that of the Alliance of Nationalist, Democratic, and Peace Forces, a Communist front formed in South Vietnam among non-Communist intellectuals and professional men shortly after the Tet offensive.

It was questionable, in fact, whether the NLHS program had really been written by Pathet Lao leaders or had only been presented to them by Hanoi for their rubber-stamp approval. The program defined why North Vietnam had escalated the war in early 1968 and why it would continue to fight. Hanoi's first priority was to rid the country of the U.S. presence, which it accurately viewed as the prime deterrent to its aims in every country in the region.

Conveying the urgency of North Vietnam's anti-American drive, the first paragraph of point one of the program called for mobilization of "all the forces of the country in order to defeat the U.S. imperialist aggression and overthrow the traitors." If North Vietnam was not yet prepared militarily to overrun the lowlands and install a Pathet Lao regime, the Communists would try to force the Vientiane government to agree to a coalition dominated by NLHS leaders. While this aim was already known, the NLHS indicated the political means for achieving it by promising "to respect and protect the throne and unite broadly with all organizations, social strata, nationalists, religions, and political parties . . . opposed to the U.S. and their lackeys."[10]

The vow to "respect and protect the throne" was at once an appeal to ancient Lao traditions and an effort at further dividing Lao leadership. King Savang Vatthana, it was widely believed, would ultimately cooperate with whatever group seemed most likely to gain power. At the same time, the wording of the program suggested that the NLHS would welcome any neutralist who was prepared to side with the leftists against the government. The NLHS, in other words, was entirely in favor of dividing a new coalition among neutralists, leftists, and rightists—so long as the neutralists were Pathet Lao allies and the rightists were left-leaning remnants of Souvanna Phouma's following, once regarded as neutral.

Beginning of the End?

Five weeks after the NLHS had released its program, Souvanna Phouma described it as "an attempt to mislead the gullible" and accused the Pathet Lao of conspiring "to overthrow our system of democratic government and set up in its place a system of dictatorship based on North Vietnamese Communism."[11] It was because of Souvanna's adamant refusal to compromise that the Communists, on January 14, 1969, warned Vientiane by blowing up an ammunition dump only 21 miles north of town. "It was such a professional job that we think the North Vietnamese were involved," said a U.S. official in an interview the following April. "Explosive charges were planted throughout the area. There were explosions for two-and-a-half hours beginning shortly after midnight."

The destruction of the ammunition dump, however, was only a propaganda display compared with a fresh series of attacks on outposts and roads from the northeast to the south. "The difference between this year and other years was that the North Vietnamese dry-season offensive of 1968 never really stopped," explained the same official. "They let up in the rainy season, but they kept on shelling and cutting off roads wherever they could."

The situation was perhaps most serious in the south, where the North Vietnamese were turning the Bolovens Plateau into a no man's land over which they could roam at will, free from any harassment except sporadic American bombing. The fighting on the Bolovens Plateau had focused since November, 1968, around the town of Thateng, 15 miles below Saravane on Route 23. "For the past two months, three mixed North Vietnamese–Pathet Lao battalions have surrounded Thateng," said the deputy commander of Laotian forces in the region, Brigadier General Kane Insisiengmay, interviewed in Pakse in April, 1969. "We have only 50 men there. We have lost 150 men wounded and 30 men killed since September."

Laotian officers estimated that 30,000 enemy troops—25,000 North Vietnamese regulars and 5,000 Pathet Lao—were in the southern provinces by mid-1968. Sapper squads in April knocked out thirteen bridges on an 80-mile stretch of Route 13 and attacked a series of outposts north and south of Pakse with new 106mm. cannon, never before used in southern Laos. About 55 miles to the east, six North Vietnamese battalions were surrounding Attopeu, whose commander told me that the town's 1,500 defenders and 3,000 inhabitants could hardly venture into vegetable plots along the perimeter without risking enemy fire. The town relied on parachuted airdrops for virtually all of its supplies. Helicopters ferried troops in and out when absolutely necessary, but even this form of transportation was risky.

"Last year we could go everywhere, but not this year," said General Kane. "Now they outnumber us. We have only 15,000 troops around here, and we are armed with old American carbines and M-1 rifles. They have AK-47's, rockets, and cannon." The Laotians tended to exaggerate the imbalance to cover up their own ineptitude, but no one questioned the enemy's success. "Eighteen months ago, the whole Done [River] valley was opened for agricultural projects," said the chief U.S. aid adviser for the region, Earl Diffenderfer, whom I interviewed on the same trip. "This land is no longer available. What had been perimeter posts, defending the valley and Route 23 through the Bolovens Plateau, are now simply enclaves—Saravene, Thateng, Attopeu."

It was still possible in April, 1969, to hire an old French taxi in Pakse and drive to Paksong, some 30 miles east on the western rim of the plateau. The taxi followed Route 13 several miles south of Pakse, past a cement slab noting "Saigon 608 kilometers," and then, turning east onto Route 23, it began the slow ascent to the plateau, some 4,000 feet above sea level.

At Paksong, a two-street market town of Chinese shops and Lao homes on stilts, I talked to the Reverend Michel Louis, a grey-haired veteran of a generation of missionary work in Asia, in the darkened attic of a cement house converted into a Catholic church. "Only one year ago we could drive from here to Saravane," said Father Louis, wearing baggy white pants and a blue shirt with a small red cross sewn over the heart. "Now it is impossible to go anywhere except Pakse. Small groups of Pathet Lao are only 3 or 4 kilometers away." Two companies of government troops were stationed on knolls overlooking the town, he said, but they rarely sent men on patrols.

The only American living in Paksong, John Kiechle, a twenty-five-year-old agricultural adviser, described government troops and officials as "too scared" to challenge the Communists outside the town. "A village will go the way the power goes," said Kiechle.

"When government officials or soldiers visit the village, they collect taxes and rice the same as the Pathet Lao." U.S. AID engineers had hardly finished building a laterite road to Houei Kong, a town 12 miles to the east in the middle of the plateau, before the Pathet Lao and North Vietnamese began harassing traffic. "The last four vehicles were ambushed," said Kiechle. "Since then, no one's dared drive the road except in military convoy."

Even the convoys had not moved, said Kiechle, since the Communists two or three months ago had blown up a bridge. "I don't know if the Pathet Lao want Paksong," Kiechle went on. "What they're doing is keeping the government officials in town while they run over the countryside." At a hospital sponsored by the AID program, a team of Filipino doctors told me that all forty beds were often filled by patients suffering from burns and wounds incurred in isolated ambushes and firefights. "We know that some of our patients are Pathet Lao," said Dr. Pedro Joaquin, the hospital director, "but we don't ask who they are or how they were hurt. We just take them and ask what are their complaints and treat them. That's all."

It was out of the question to try to get to Thateng, 15 miles north on Route 23, but refugees from the town were more than willing to describe the conditions that had forced them to leave. "The Vietnamese wanted me to be a soldier," said a farmer named Yo, who had walked by night to a refugee center near Pakse. "They asked for my pig for food. There are so many Vietnamese, it is impossible for us to work." Refugees also complained about U.S. air strikes. "The bombs fell on some houses and killed my brother," said one of them. "We fear the planes as much as the Vietnamese." Whether U.S. bombing or Communist harassment was more to blame for forcing some 20,000 farmers to flee the plateau was a moot point. Either way, much of the area was uninhabitable.

As was the case with the fighting on the Bolovens Plateau, proof of the seriousness of the situation in the northeast in 1969 lay in the number of refugees it had generated. Some 40,000 mountain people were slowly walking across the rugged northeastern hills in April, 1969, to escape the fighting. The refugees, almost all of them Meo, were looking for any of a number of camps where U.S. officials were providing minimal food, shelter, and medicine. Dr. Charles Weldon, in charge of public health for the U.S. mission, described the scene as "pretty goddam grim" after a visit that month to the small overcrowded hospital at Sam Thong, General

Vang Pao's headquarters 80 miles north of Vientiane. "The North Vietnamese have put a lot more resources into their program this year than last," said Dr. Weldon, who had arrived in Laos in 1964. "A lot more people have been displaced as a result." Some of the refugees had left their villages before the fighting began, but many more had filtered through the forests and mountains after Vang Pao's troops had retreated. Dr. Weldon estimated that a third of the 220 patients in the 140-bed hospital at Sam Thong had been wounded, either by ground fire or by shrapnel from American bombs.

Most of the wounded never made it to the hospital. They either received first aid, often from kits carried by American-trained medical workers at refugee sites, or died before they could be treated. Still more of them—no one knew how many—died from diseases such as malaria or dysentery contracted during their treks through the jungle. The plight of the refugees was the most visible sign of the underlying failure of the Laotian Government, supported by U.S. funds and airplanes, to hold back the enemy. "I think we have to reconcile ourselves to the idea that we don't have the capabilities," said one official. "The best we can do is help the refugees and concede most of the northeast to the North Vietnamese." As an indication of the enemy's determination, the official noted that the Communists had launched their dry-season offensive in November, 1969, a month before the December harvest. Usually the enemy waited until after the harvest, in hopes of reaping some of the crops as well as territory.

In the spring of 1969, the government was attempting to establish a rough line of control along a river 20 miles south of Na Khang, a key position on Route 6 overrun by North Vietnamese troops on March 1 and 2. Then, after the rainy season had begun, perhaps Vang Pao's troops could recover some of their lost territory. There was, however, the chilling realization that the 1969 offensive was different from the others, that the enemy, in hundreds of small, rarely publicized battles had revealed its desire to drive all government influence from the northeast. The real question was how many more positions Vang Pao's men would have to abandon before the dry season ended and the situation began to stabilize.

Despite the virulence of the 1969 offensive, however, both Laotian and American officials doubted if the North Vietnamese would totally upset the delicate equilibrium of forces that still prevailed from the fragmentation of the second coalition. Souvanna persisted in the view, expressed in an interview with me at the height of the offensive in April, 1969, that the North Vietnamese would eventually reach a settlement of their larger war in South Vietnam and no longer need to fight in Laos. "If peace ever comes to Vietnam, then Hanoi would apply less pressure," said Souvanna. "The enemy does not want to create a second front," he reasoned, despite "the temptation of annexation of Laos into Vietnam."

Souvanna thus recognized the importance of Laos in terms of Hanoi's interest in South Vietnam, but he seemed overly optimistic about the prospects for a settlement that would lead to de-escalation of the Laotian conflict. Whatever solution emanated from the Vietnam war, it still was not likely that Hanoi would cease to regard Laos as a vital adjunct to its power position. The unlikelihood of a solution in Laos was evident in May, 1969, when the North Vietnamese Ambassador to Vientiane, Le Van Hien, called on Souvanna for the first time in nearly five years. Hien's purpose, according to diplomatic sources in Vientiane, was to persuade Souvanna to demand that the United States "cease bombing neutral Laotian territory." The quid quo pro would have been a Communist promise not to extend the war beyond the areas they controlled.

Souvanna, on the basis of previous experience, believed that the Communists would only use a bombing halt to increase their harassment of Lao troops, who would be completely helpless without U.S. air support. He tried, unsuccessfully, to convince Hien that North Vietnamese and Americans were free to do as they wished on the Ho Chi Minh trail—as they had been doing for the past five years—since he was powerless to prevent them.

After Hien's meeting with Souvanna, the NLHS made explicitly clear what its twelve-point program implied—that the existing regime in Vientiane had "absolutely nothing to do with the national-union government" set up in 1962 and would have to suffer the consequences of continued warfare until it bowed to the will of the Communists. The NLHS ranked a bombing halt "first and foremost" as a prerequisite for ending the conflict.[12]

The Communists, then, demanded both a cessation of the bombing and the installation of a new government amenable to their wishes. Souvanna at one time might have been acceptable to Hanoi as a sympathetic neutral leader, but he had committed himself irrevocably to the other side by accepting U.S. assistance and not objecting to American air strikes over the Ho Chi Minh trail. The fighting had escalated beyond the point at which genuine neutrality and lasting peace were serious alternatives.

I I

Laos and the United States

Aid and Air Strikes

Lao Government officials pointed out that the Geneva agreement of 1962 had authorized them to seek foreign aid for national defense purposes. Since the North Vietnamese had sent at least 40,000 men in Laos by 1965, the government contended that it had no choice but to accept arms and ammunition from the United States to protect its neutrality and sovereignty, as guaranteed by the agreement. In actuality, however, the United States and Laos, like North Vietnam and the Pathet Lao, every day violated provisions of the agreement banning the introduction of foreign troops or war materiel in more than limited conventional quantities. Perhaps the most flagrant violations were constant U.S. air strikes, carried out with Souvanna's permission, on North Vietnamese and Pathet Lao forces in Laos.

Thus the neutral government in Vientiane, for all of Souvanna's protestations, was hardly neutral in any respect but name. The Laotian armed forces, theoretically totaling some 70,000 men, including 60,000 in the royal army and 10,000 in the neutral army, had been equipped by the United States since 1963 with everything from helmets to boots, from rifles to jeeps, from maps to airplanes. U.S. troops were not directly involved, except on a highly limited advisory and technical level, but the United States spent some $80 million a year from 1963 through 1970 to support the Laotian military establishment. U.S. planes, most of them owned by Air America and Continental Air Services, two private companies under contract to the U.S. Government, flew arms, supplies, and troops. Former members of the U.S. Special Forces, the "green berets," highly experienced in jungle warfare in Vietnam, Thailand, Latin America, and elsewhere, were hired by the Central

Intelligence Agency to lead Lao guerrillas deep into enemy-held areas.

The United States proffered advice to Laotian forces through military attachés assigned to its embassy. U.S. and Lao officials did not deny the attachés' presence, but they were as reluctant as the Prime Minister to divulge the extent of American involvement. The United States in 1962 had carefully lived up to the letter of the Geneva agreement by withdrawing its entire 666-man Military Assistance and Advisory Group by October 7, the final deadline set by the agreement for the departure of all foreign troops, except for the French training mission. Both the Lao and U.S. governments, understandably, preferred to emphasize Hanoi's blatant violations of the Geneva agreement and gloss over, if not totally deny, any American violations.

As the level of conflict escalated, however, it became impossible for officials to conceal the extent of U.S. military involvement. Correspondents and other interested observers were generally denied permission to board Air America and Continental planes leaving Vientiane for remote bases, but they still heard and reported enough stories and rumors to penetrate the official secrecy. If correspondents had been able to tour the entire country, as they could in South Vietnam, they would have seen Air America and Continental planes loading and unloading arms and ammunition, ferrying troops into the field, delivering wounded men to hospitals— all in violation of the Geneva agreement. The U.S. mission ordered officials to cancel these activities during scheduled press junkets, but reporters still saw American planes flying missions from bases in Thailand.

The busiest U.S. base in Laos undoubtedly was Long Cheng, built in 1962 and 1963 to support military activities in the northeast. About 6 miles south of Sam Thong by straight line but 15 miles by mountain road, Long Cheng provided logistics and communications facilities for Vang Pao's army.

A rare journalistic visitor to Long Cheng was writer Don Schanche, who spent several weeks with Vang Pao's legendary U.S. adviser, Edgar "Pop" Buell, a fifty-five-year-old Indianan who had come to Laos in 1960 as a low-paid worker with the International Voluntary Service and later joined the U.S. Agency for International Development. "When I first visited Long Chien [sic] eight years ago," Schanche wrote in 1970, "it was an abandoned opium poppy field in a bowl-like declivity high in the mountains. When I saw the Meo stronghold last year, it was the second largest city in Laos, bigger than the royal capital of Luang Prabang and almost as large as the political capital of Vientiane."[1] Long Cheng was not marked on any civilian maps, but its population, according to the best estimates available in Vientiane, had soared to some 40,000, including perhaps twenty U.S. Air Force helicopter and reconnaissance plane pilots, crewmen, and technicians and another fifty former Special Forces soldiers now in the CIA. The vast majority of the town's—or base's—inhabitants were Meo soldiers and their families and relatives, who had fled the war-torn northeastern mountains for the relative security of a military encampment.

The rise of Long Cheng—and Vang Pao and "Pop" Buell—was part of the process of U.S. escalation in Laos after 1962. Although U.S. officials avoided public references to this mysterious base, they were compelled, at hearings conducted by a subcommittee of the U.S. Senate in October, 1969, to reveal some of the events that led to its construction and development. The original basis for U.S. involvement in Laos after the Geneva conference was a formal request by Souvanna, dated September 10, 1962, for supplies, spare parts, petroleum, oils and lubricants, and other commodities to support the Lao armed forces, then recoiling under the first signs of pressure by the Pathet Lao and North Vietnamese on the Plain of Jars. The U.S. Ambassador to Laos, Leonard Unger, later ambassador to Thailand, set up an office in the U.S. AID mission in Vientiane to handle the Lao Government's requirements. On November 8, 1962, Ambassador Unger notified Souvanna of formal approval of his request.[2]

Compliance with Souvanna's wishes did not at first constitute violation of the Geneva agreement.[3] In order to transport armaments to the Plain of Jars, where Kong Le's forces were engaged, it was deemed necessary in the 1962–63 period to build the Long Cheng base in what was then a relatively secure, defensible area within only a few minutes' flight of the airstrips nearest the fighting. It was also at this time, in a move directly related to consignment of American war materiel, that the CIA began to finance and build up Vang Pao's army, which the U.S. Special Forces had begun to train as a small guerrilla force before the signing of the Geneva agreement requiring withdrawal of U.S. advisers. The clandestine reintroduction of military advisers, under the aegis of the CIA, was the first serious U.S. violation of article four of the agreement forbidding the entry of "foreign regular and irregular troops, foreign paramilitary formations, and foreign military personnel. . . ."

From this beginning, U.S. efforts to buttress the Vientiane government proliferated as a result of the administrative requirements of distributing the aid. Former Ambassador William Sullivan, promoted in 1969 to the post of deputy assistant secretary of state for East Asian and Pacific affairs, admitted at the October, 1969, Senate hearings that 558 Americans were employed by the U.S. Government in Vientiane. This number included 338 Americans on "direct hire" with AID and another 127 serving as military attachés. These figures covered most of the Americans who were in Laos on duties not necessarily implied by their job titles.[4]

The U.S. AID mission was providing covert support to the military operations in two different ways. The first, and less serious, was through the AID Requirements Office, set up in late 1962 to process and administer Souvanna's request for military aid. This function would normally have been served by a military advisory group, which also would have had much greater freedom than the Requirements Office in checking to make certain that materiel arrived safely at its destination and was used correctly. The Requirements Office staff of twenty-six persons, mostly retired military officers, reported technically to the director of AID but actually worked on a daily basis with military attachés and officers based in Thailand. The second out-of-the-ordinary function served by AID was that of providing a cover for CIA personnel, notably those former Special Forces officers advising Vang Pao's army and several other guerrilla units in the jungles. CIA "AID advisers" also relayed intelligence information on enemy movements and, on occasion, acted as forward observers for air strikes in the northeast where they could pose as "refugee workers" aiding Meo tribesmen fleeing the scenes of battle.

While these activities were carefully concealed from public scrutiny, officials made no attempt at hiding the fact that the number of military attachés far exceeded that normally needed for diplomatic duties. Officials did not admit publicly that these attachés actually played military roles, but no one ever attempted seriously to deny the reason for their presence. Besides working with Lao officers in Vientiane, attachés served in all five regional headquarters, from Luang Prabang in the north to Pakse in the south, and often visited units in the field. They not only advised the Lao on tactics and equipment but sent lengthy evaluation reports to the chief of the attaché section in the U.S. Embassy. The only surprise in Sullivan's testimony regarding the attachés was that the number he gave was at least fifty higher than any number ever announced in Vientiane or Washington.

The vehicle for increasing the number of attachés without announcing their presence was Project 404, a program introduced in 1966 as the need for a full-scale military assistance group became urgent. Project 404 personnel were under the direct command of DEPCHIEF, or Deputy Chief, Joint United States Military Assistance Group, Thailand, headquartered in Bangkok to expedite supplies through Thailand to Laos. Project 404 personnel in Laos did not have diplomatic status but still were called attachés and performed the same functions as their military colleagues in the U.S. Embassy.[5] The American mission did not even bother to maintain the pretense of attaché in the case of some ninety other officers and enlisted men rotated in and out of Laos for "temporary duty" of two weeks to six months. These men were mainly air force and communications technicians, needed to cope with the escalating air war and the expansion of the military communications network linking Laos with Thailand and South Vietnam.

So the total number of Americans in military or paramilitary advisory and assistance roles in Laos—regardless of whether or not some of them were physically in Thailand—had gradually risen to well over 500, as opposed to 666 before the departure in 1962 of the Military Assistance and Advisory Group. This number, which may actually have been much higher than was ever revealed, included some but not nearly all of those engaged in an entirely new and different dimension of the war, the bombing of the Ho Chi Minh trail through southern Laos and of Communist supply routes and base areas in the northeastern provinces. Air attachés assigned to a top-secret command operations center in Vientiane performed intelligence and targeting functions, but the heart of the air war over Laos was the vast base at Udorn, 40 miles south of Vientiane in Thailand. At the Udorn headquarters, air force officers, acting with the approval of the U.S. Ambassador in Vientiane, coordinated with the air attachés in Vientiane on missions from all six bases in northeastern Thailand.

The mystery of the air war, at least initially, was deepened by the official U.S. policy of denying that American planes were bombing Laos at all. "At the request of the Royal Lao Government, the U.S. has since 1964 been conducting reconnaissance flights over Laos escorted by armed aircraft," said an official military handout published by the U.S. Embassy. (The Lao "request" for armed reconnaissance flights and bombing was a mere formality. Souvanna Phouma often stated that his government had no control over the trail region and could not prevent American or North Vietnamese activities there.) "These reconnaissance flights are frequently fired upon by Communist forces on the ground," the summary went on. "By agreement with the [Royal Lao Government], the escort fighter aircraft may return fire. These flights have been announced publicly since they began."[6] Despite this standard disclaimer, it was common knowledge among officials and journalists that U.S. planes every day were pounding the Laotian jungles from north to south, though never within sight or sound of the still inviolate Mekong River valley.

The gradual escalation of the air war over Laos, beginning with the first reconnaissance flight on May 19, 1964, above the Ho Chi Minh trail region, seemed to parallel North Vietnam's rising activities. The focal point was the Ho Chi Minh trail, an extension of the routes the U.S. planes were hitting in North Vietnam, but the bombing also escalated in northern Laos. Senator Stuart Symington, former secretary of the air force and chairman of the subcommittee investigating U.S. activities in Laos, revealed during the October, 1969, hearings that strikes had increased by "a hundred times" in northern Laos from 1964 to 1965. Then, in 1966, according to Sullivan's testimony, the number of strikes in the north was doubled. The implication was that U.S. planes flew several hundred strikes over northern Laos in 1965 and nearly 1,000 in 1966;[7] the air war over the Ho Chi Minh trail in the south was much greater—several hundred strikes a day in the dry season.

Strikes over both regions increased immensely after President Johnson's decision to stop bombing North Vietnam in 1968. That decision had no effect at all on the number of missions flown by American planes over Indochina. The only difference was that bombs that might have fallen on North Vietnam were dropped instead on similar targets in the jungles of Laos. U.S. military officers were not altogether happy with this redeployment of air power. They reasoned that it was easier to slow down the movement of supplies from North Vietnam by ranging over the entire supply line than by hitting relatively short bottlenecks in Laos— or, worse, waiting until North Vietnamese troops had surfaced in battle against Lao forces.

The shift in air activities to Laos did not, in short, entirely compensate for the halt in the bombing of North Vietnam. Still, Lao leaders and U.S. officials welcomed any increase in American air power as the best, and perhaps the only, substitute for lack of infantry troops capable of defeating the North Vietnamese on the ground. U.S. diplomats and military attachés easily convinced Lao officials, in late 1964, of the advantages of sending Lao T-28's on raids on the Ho Chi Minh trail. The logic here was that some of the Communist troops pouring over the passes from North Vietnam might attack Lao positions rather than join their comrades in the long march to the south.

The passes and the trail system, except where the latter neared towns such as Saravane and Attopeu, constituted in effect "free-fire zones," where strikes were almost automatically approved. The question of where and when to strike assumed more subtle overtones, however, in the air war in northern Laos. American officials did not want to upset completely the delicate balance wherein all signatories still paid at least cursory obeisance to the stipulations of the Geneva agreement. Hence, the U.S. Ambassador and the chief air attaché carefully discussed strike plans for that region before offering their approval or disapproval to officers in Udorn, Thailand. Sullivan, while he was ambassador from 1964 through early 1969, established the precedent of not authorizing strikes without at least *pro forma* approval of the Lao government. For this reason, a Lao Air Force colonel was assigned, as a matter of diplomatic formality rather than military necessity, to the embassy's command operations center, which was responsible for the technical details of coordinating missions with Udorn.

The bombing, by 1970, was by far the largest and costliest phase of the U.S. effort to maintain Laos as a non-Communist buffer, but most of the manpower and money expended on it was included in allocations for the air force and navy rather than in military or civilian assistance programs. The only reflection of the air war in the U.S. mission in Vientiane was the outsized number of air force attachés and personnel on temporary duty. All the jet fighters and bombers flew from bases in Thailand or carriers on the South China Sea. After the cessation of all bombing of North Vietnam on October 31, 1968, however, the air war over Laos alone included more than 600 strikes a day, supported by thousands of military personnel and hundreds of millions of dollars.

Success and Defeat

Was such U.S. activity in Laos really working? The bombing of the Ho Chi Minh trail was doubtless effective in slowing down and hindering the movement of supplies, but the North Vietnamese were highly skilled at building alternate routes and camouflaged storage points and truck parks. Military intelligence analysts admitted that most Communist supplies—perhaps more than 90 per cent—reached South Vietnam despite delays caused by the bombing. The North Vietnamese were equally successful at infiltrating men and materiel into northern Laos, although military observers credited the strikes with keeping the Communists from totally annihilating Vang Pao's dwindling Meo army in the 1968 and 1969 offensives. U.S. air power, in fact, was the main deterrent, aside from political and diplomatic factors, capable of preventing the North Vietnamese from cutting off Route 13 between Vientiane and Luang Prabang and overrunning the lowlands.

This conclusion, shared by most Western military observers in Vientiane, raised obvious questions about the value of conventional military aid, totaling $90 million a year for 1968 and 1969 and surpassing $100 million in 1970. U.S. attachés complained that, unlike their predecessors in the Military Assistance and Advisory Group, they could not accompany troops on operations in the field for more than brief periods and were unable to inspect and advise them on that basic level. Attachés also pointed out that most of the Laotian Army was still equipped with M-1 rifles and M-2 carbines, used by Americans in World War II and the Korean conflict, while the North Vietnamese all carried modern Chinese-made AK-47 rifles and AK-50 light machine guns. The Americans began supplying M-16 rifles, the equivalent of the AK-47, by the late 1960's but were reluctant to give them to the entire Laotian military establishment. They feared that corrupt Lao officers and soldiers would sell them or that Lao troops would merely abandon them while running away from ambushes and battles.

Another problem was that Lao officers in the lowlands tended to disdain General Vang Pao, whom they regarded as a social and ethnic inferior, even though his army constituted the last real defense for northern and central Laos. Vang Pao's troops, once totaling nearly 40,000 men, dwindled steadily before the North Vietnamese onslaught in the 1968 and 1969 offensives. Armed with an assortment of muzzle-loading muskets, old French rifles, carbines, and a few M-16's, the once proud Meo army, by 1970, was a horde of teenagers and middle-aged men. Some of the new draftees, seized from refugee bands, were twelve- and thirteen-year-olds scarcely taller than the outdated rifles they were forced to carry into combat.

While the bombing saved the remnants of Vang Pao's army from destruction, officials erred in believing that North Vietnamese troops would retreat with the onset of monsoon rains in June, 1969. For the first time in the jungles north of the Plain of Jars, the North Vietnamese prosecuted their dry-season offensive well into the wet season, finally forcing government troops, on June 28, 1969, to evacuate the town of Muong Soui on Route 7, 30 miles east of the junction of 7 and 13. Muong Soui and Vang Vieng, 50 miles southwest on Route 13, were the two main neutralist strongholds abandoned by the Pathet Lao after the summer, 1964, government counteroffensive. The "neutral" battalions left in charge of them had been integrated into the government command structure and had performed effectively against local Pathet Lao troops. Like most of the government forces, however, they were no match for the North Vietnamese.

After the government's ignominious defeat at Muong Soui, Vang Pao was the only Lao general who seemed at all eager to try to recapture it. In August, 1969, his forces launched a six-week campaign that proved one of the greatest surprises of the war. After a month of harassing Pathet Lao positions around the Plain of Jars, Vang Pao's army in the first two-and-a-half weeks of September reoccupied Muong Soui and drove the last Communist troops from the plain, including the town of Khang Khay, which the government had not held since the defeat of Kong Le's forces in 1963 and 1964.

The victory of Vang Pao's army appeared incredible at the time, but later analysis revealed that it depended on factors quite unrelated to the questionable strength of the Meo troops. One of these was that the United States, in August, 1969, again increased the air war over the north, this time by approximately 75 per cent over the level reached in June before the fall of Muong Soui. The rationale for steady U.S. escalation of the bombing of northern Laos in the spring and summer of 1969 was that the Communists, particularly the North Vietnamese, had escalated their offensives in 1968 and 1969. The number of air strikes was never disclosed, but it probably exceeded 200 a day at the height of the fighting in the north.

Another factor in Vang Pao's success was the retreat of North Vietnamese troops before his army had begun to counterattack on the Plain of Jars. Military analysts much later surmised that the North Vietnamese, by fighting for more than six weeks into the rainy season, were unable to maintain their supplies of ammunition, weapons, and food throughout the monsoon. Vang Pao's troops met little opposition on the plain and almost none in Khang

Khay, near which U.S. planes had been bombing steadily. Despite explicit American policies against striking populated centers, these and other towns were largely destroyed. North Vietnamese, Chinese, and Pathet Lao officials had left Khang Khay well before the arrival of Vang Pao's troops and their CIA advisers. The combination of U.S. air power and Vang Pao's courage, if not really the strength of his forces, had resulted in a military reversal unprecedented in the history of the war in Laos.

"I control almost all the Plain of Jars," Vang Pao boasted to reporters who interviewed him at Sam Thong in October, 1969. "They now have only 7,000 men—before they had 25,000." Vang Pao put the enemy's losses, in terms of materiel captured or destroyed, at 6,000 rifles, 20 tanks, 50 antiaircraft guns, 200 trucks, and 6,000 tons of ammunition. U.S. officials insisted that Vang Pao was not exaggerating. The North Vietnamese and Pathet Lao had deserted some of their largest stockpiles, not expecting that Vang Pao's army would soon invade the plain and capture them. "They thought I had no more troops," he said. "They went further and took Muong Soui, but then they advanced too far. They were too far from their supply points, and I was able to cut their supply lines." In keeping with official policy, Vang Pao lied when asked how much of his victory was due to U.S. air power. "We use only our own T-28's," he remarked as a couple of American jets from Thailand whizzed overhead toward still more targets on the plain. "The U.S. planes fly over sometimes but only on reconnaissance missions. I have never seen a B-52. I would like to."

Few knowledgeable observers believed that Vang Pao could hold the plain for long after the North Vietnamese and Pathet Lao launched their 1970 dry-season offensive. "It ain't gonna last," said Vang Pao's closest adviser and confidante, Edgar "Pop" Buell, who was a bona fide U.S. AID official and not a CIA man. "Vang Pao's soldiers are mostly little kids and old men. They just ain't got the strength to keep going. They'll get pushed out soon, and I'll have another 70,000 refugees to take care of. It's like starting all over again."[8] The Pathet Lao leader, Prince Souphanouvong, left no doubt of the Communists' intentions. "The Lao Patriotic Army and people," said Souphanouvong in December, 1969, were "launching intensive counterattacks against their enemy" after having "bogged down more than forty [enemy] battalions in Xieng Khouang and the Plain of Jars."[9]

In January, 1970, as soon as intelligence analysts perceived the extent of the fresh Communist build-up, U.S. and Lao officials laid plans for an "orderly retreat." In the first two weeks of February, some 20,000 refugees were airlifted from villages on and around the plain and resettled in camps in the lowlands. The Americans completed the evacuation on February 10, 1970, two days before North Vietnam's 144th Regiment attacked the airstrip at Xieng Khouang village, which Vang Pao's troops had captured in a diversionary attack the previous April.

U.S. advisers immediately closed the airstrip, which had been available for reconnaissance and cargo planes in the few months in which government forces had controlled the town, formerly a key Communist headquarters and supply base. For the next ten days, some 6,000 North Vietnamese troops attacked secondary positions on Route 7 and the plain while preparing for the climactic battle at Xieng Khouang, just southwest of the plain. The United States, for the first time, attempted to retaliate by sending eight-engined B-52 "stratofortresses," the most feared instrument of war in South Vietnam, on bombing missions over the plain. The B-52's, based at Guam, Okinawa, and the southern Thai base of Utapao, had been pounding the Ho Chi Minh trail for two years but had not previously been assigned further north lest the Communists interpret their use in direct support of government troops as another major "escalation."

The North Vietnamese, however, had two factors in their favor. First, the plain and surrounding mountains were shrouded in haze from the burning-off of trees and tall grass by mountain people accustomed for centuries to clearing plots for planting during the dry season. U.S. air power was most effective in the weeks between the monsoons and the dry-season burning but of limited value at the height of the rains or the drought, when pilots could not see their targets. Second, the North Vietnamese had vastly increased their supplies between seasons and also introduced an entirely fresh division, the 312th, which supplemented the 316th, worn down from several years of constant warfare. The arrival of the 312th, some 10,000 men supported by more trucks, tanks, and other heavy equipment than any other Communist or non-Communist division in Laos, all but eliminated the need for assistance from local Pathet Lao troops, whom Hanoi was convinced were almost useless militarily.

The North Vietnamese encountered virtually no opposition on the ground. In the final battle at Xieng Khouang, rather than hold out to the end, a reinforced garrison of 1,500 Meos staged a carefully controlled retreat on February 20 and 21, 1970, as some 3,000 North Vietnamese recaptured the town amid heavy bombing that prevented them from remaining there for more than a few hours.

Most of the Meo defenders disappeared into the nearby hills and later rejoined Vang Pao's forces around Sam Thong and Long Cheng.

The North Vietnamese on February 25, 1970, entered Muong Soui, defended by only 200 men, and advanced in the next ten days half way to the junction of routes 13 and 7, which they had menaced in the middle of the 1969 monsoon. Rather than fight for the junction, however, they decided to concentrate their drive on the bases at Sam Thong and Long Cheng, the nerve center southeast of the plain for all operations in northeastern Laos.

By March 17, 1970, some 3,000 North Vietnamese troops from the 316th Division had advanced to within 5 miles of Sam Thong after occupying several secondary Meo outposts in the hills and at least one more airstrip. Air America planes on the same day evacuated some 200 patients from the refugee hospital at Sam Thong, along with 20 U.S. attachés, CIA advisers, and refugee workers. Among the last to leave was "Pop" Buell, who had lived in a three-room home at Sam Thong for nine years but remarked that he had had to "run before the enemy" on nineteen previous occasions in northern Laos. Buell and three other Americans were flown out by helicopter at dusk—eight hours before two elite North Vietnamese companies seized the airstrip and set fire to the wood-frame hospital and other buildings.

The normal chaos of evacuation and attack was compounded by the inefficiency of the Lao command, which lost radio contact with the last defenders at noon on the day of the battle. For more than a day, U.S. and Lao officials in Vientiane were not certain who controlled how much of Sam Thong, but, on March 20, 1970, an American attaché told reporters that the Meo had prudently fled into the surrounding mountains. He said that no more than a few North Vietnamese troops had actually entered Sam Thong, where they knew they would be easy targets for U.S. jets.

Sam Thong, like Xieng Khouang and Muong Soui, was not converted into a North Vietnamese base after the North Vietnamese victory. Rather, it was a no-man's-land, which no one could enter without risking heavy ground fire or bombing. "The enemy hit Sam Thong to solidify his position on the plain," explained Lieutenant Colonel Edgar Duskin, the U.S. Army attaché, noting that the battle represented "the first significant enemy push south of the plain since the signing of the Geneva accords in 1962." Duskin rated the Meo defeat as a "psychological factor" that might further demoralize Lao Government forces. Militarily, however, the Communists still needed to take Long Cheng, the American-built stronghold 5 miles to the south, before they could regard their campaign for the region as really complete. The Communists signaled their intention of attacking Long Cheng by firing six rockets into the base on the same day they entered Sam Thong.

After capturing Sam Thong, however, the North Vietnamese were unable to build up enough strength for a full-scale assault on Long Cheng. One factor was the introduction, in secret, of two battalions of Thai troops, who manned the Long Cheng perimeter, freeing several companies of Meo to battle the North Vietnamese in the hills. The Meo, almost without a fight, re-entered the deserted ruins of Sam Thong at the end of March, 1970. The North Vietnamese were apparently held back by increasing difficulties of infiltrating men and supplies under U.S. bombing, which had become more effective as the haze and smoke began to lift from the mountains near the end of the dry season.

The Communists' 1970 dry-season offensive, then, fell short of its primary goal of destroying Vang Pao's army and threatening the lowlands. The fighting had further weakened the Meo, but Souvanna Phouma still seemed in control of often conflicting factions in Vientiane. At the same time, he betrayed a certain lack of understanding of military realities. "Our aim is to contain the offensive until the rainy season," he had said on February 20, as the Meo were abandoning Xieng Khouang. "We will maintain our position on the Plain of Jars." Less than a month later, as the battle of Sam Thong revealed the futility of these hopes, almost the entire official Lao community was gathered at Souvanna's residence—not to map strategy against disaster but to attend the lavish ceremony at which the Prime Minister's son, Prince Panya, was married to a top fashion model from Bangkok.

Internal Weakness

The spectacle of an imported Filipino band fiddling at a wedding reception while Sam Thong burned seemed to symbolize the government's lackadaisical attitude toward the war. Officials in Vientiane, at the urging of the U.S. Embassy, arranged a series of trips in March, 1970, for correspondents reporting on preparations for what some of them predicted might be a final series of North Vietnamese attacks. The embassy hoped to win favorable publicity for American policy in Laos, which was under severe criticism in the U.S. Senate and press, but most of the trips only exposed the weakness of the Lao Government.

At a battalion-sized outpost in a valley 6 miles north of Luang Prabang, for instance, a Lao Army captain predicted in March that enemy forces would attack "several more times" in the next month or so. His men were responsible for patrolling within a radius of 5 miles but could not call in artillery fire if they found enemy troop concentrations. The big artillery pieces, said the captain, were in Luang Prabang, thirty minutes away by truck. In any case, his troops rarely patrolled further than was necessary for the immediate defense of their perimeter.

Luang Prabang, for political reasons, was still virtually immune from attack, but officials were always concerned about the security of Sala Phou Khoun at the junction of Routes 7 and 13. "I am sure we can hold out for a long time, if we have enough supplies and air support," said General Kouprasith Abhay, the Vientiane regional commander, standing on a sandbagged bunker at an artillery base on the top of a mountain 2 miles south of the junction. "It's like hitting the head on the rock."

Although Kouprasith may not have exaggerated the difficulties of dislodging his troops, the Communists could still cut the road to the south or north, safely out of range of stationary artillery positions. The AID mission attempted to increase mobility by enlarging the airstrip at Muong Kassy, 20 miles south of the junction on Route 13, but a company of North Vietnamese could probably have taken the town, which was protected only by a few sandbags and almost no barbed wire or mines, before reinforcements arrived. "Their plan is to begin by destruction of our back," summarized General Kouprasith. "They introduce big units into our rear area and then begin in the lowlands by hitting sensitive points, roads, and bridges."

As destructive as the enemy's tactics, however, was the weakness of the Lao leadership, as capsulized in a prepared statement by Robert H. Nooter, AID's deputy assistant administrator for East Asia, before the Senate subcommittee investigating U.S. activities in Laos. "The Lao Government operates at relatively low effectiveness at both the national and local levels," said Nooter, citing "a complex variety of factors," including tax evasion, "the use of governmental positions" for personal gain, "regional and family factionalism," "a paucity of trained, capable officials," lack of funds, and "the deleterious effect of prolonged warfare on the social fabric of the country."[10]

Stories corroborating this general statement were rife in Laos. The top generals often were more interested in smuggling opium on Lao Air Force planes than in focusing on immediate military dangers, much less long-range development. The opium, grown by tribesmen in the mountains, was shipped by former Chinese Nationalist soldiers living along the borders of Burma, Laos, and Thailand. The town of Houei Sai, on the Thai frontier, only 40 miles from one of the roads built by Chinese Communist engineers, was the main center for the trade. Lao officials also reaped fortunes in thousands of lesser ways, ranging from diversion of government funds to secret business arrangements with local Chinese and Vietnamese merchants.

On a somewhat lower level, army officers customarily overstated the number of men in their units and pocketed the extra pay. Officials and their families conducted private business in American-supplied jeeps and other vehicles. "See that ambulance," said an AID official in Paksane in April, 1969, pointing to a military truck with a large red cross on it parked outside a home reverberating with the sounds of a party. "Whenever we need it to take sick refugees to the hospital, it's not available." Our jeep, driving on the main street of Paksane, overlooking the Mekong 60 miles east of Vientiane, passed by a long frame structure. "U.S. AID built that as a town hall," remarked the AID man, "but the governor wanted to turn it into a beer hall and make some money off it. Now they're going to make it into a public recreation hall."

Americans insisted that outright misappropriation and misuse of AID funds, a rampant problem in the 1950's, had been conquered by the introduction of a tight control system, but they admitted that it was impossible to persuade Lao officials to put all the equipment and material they received to effective use. At the same time, U.S. aid created an attitude among Lao officials of complete dependence. The United States, from 1954 through 1970, had poured in nearly $700 million in nonmilitary assistance—enough to buttress the Lao economy and bring about limited improvements, in the lowlands, in agriculture, transportation, and education.

The most significant aspect of U.S. economic aid was the Foreign Exchange Operations Fund, set up in 1963 to provide a convertible money to stabilize the value of the Lao kip at 500 to $1 (U.S.). The United States, Japan, Britain, Australia, and France all participated in FEOF, but the U.S. contribution was 75 per cent of the annual pool of $25 million. This pool sufficed to balance the Lao budget of approximately $34 million, which also included $9 million from customs and other taxes. Approximately 40 per cent of the taxes was derived from the legal import of gold, which Lao merchants then shipped to other Asian countries.

The fragility of the Lao economy was dramatized in 1968 when gold exports decreased sharply as a result of the decline in value of gold on the world market. Lao generals and other officials involved in the trade suffered somewhat, but the biggest loser was the United States, which had to increase its dole to FEOF from $13.8 million in 1967 to $18.6 million in 1968 to help compensate for the loss in government tax revenues. In this environment of artificial economic stability, Lao living in or near lowland towns were able to market their crops, open small-scale factories and shops, buy and sell what they needed, and generally live in prosperity and tranquillity. The gross national product in the second half of the 1960's rose from roughly $100 million to $200 million a year, and the average annual income in the towns went up from $80 to $120 a year.

These figures, however, reflected the gains of a small sector accustomed to dealing in currency. The annual income of the subsistence sector—that is, 90 per cent of the country's 3 million inhabitants—increased only slightly. AID officials in Vientiane put the average income of the farmer at perhaps $60 a year in 1970, only $10 more than it had been in 1965. For most farmers, who traded in goods rather than currency, the annual income had not increased at all. In a very real sense, then, foreign aid in Laos merely served the interests of the elite. The dependence of the Lao ruling class on the United States was even more sharply delineated by the figures for military spending. Approximately $17 million—half the national budget—was allocated to the armed forces, which spent the money on payrolls. The United States, on the other hand, spent $100 million on equipment, arms, and ammunition for Lao forces in 1970.

While fortifying their own positions with U.S. aid, Lao leaders made virtually no attempt at assisting 700,000 persons displaced by the war. Sole responsibility for the refugees, in effect, rested again with the U.S. mission, which said that there were more than 250,-000 of them by the middle of 1970. "In general, the current refugee situation in Laos is far from being either satisfactory or stable," said a U.S. Senate staff report on refugees in Indochina. "Serious shortages of food are evident, and grossly inadequate public health and housing facilities are reported throughout Laos," the report observed. "It is apparent that neither the [Royal Lao Government] nor U.S. AID has the resources or capability to meet the humanitarian needs of most refugees."[11]

If the government did not have the money to care for refugees, it might at least have tried to proselytize politically among them and among villagers and farmers outside the main towns. Non-Communist political activity, however, seemed to exist mainly in the form of almost meaningless movements, reflecting varying degrees of anti-Communist zeal, among politicians in Vientiane.

Souvanna himself, in an effort to retain the image of political neutrality, sponsored the formation in 1970 of the National Neutralist Party, theoretically designed to unite conflicting factions behind a strong anti-Communist front, in case the Pathet Lao agreed to participate in elections for a new Assembly. A select Groupement des Jeunes, made up of young officials and other members of the elite, met at Souvanna's house to draw up statutes for the party. They soon fell to debating, however, with members of another elitist group, the Mittasone, or Students Returned from Abroad. Young Mittasone members, charging that the purpose of Souvanna's party was to suppress the rightists, gravitated toward the Saha Phoumine, a patriotic group whose name, translated literally, means United Country.

Such fermentation attracted no more than a handful of well-bred Lao, who never seemed to consider the possibility of popularizing their views outside their own narrow milieu. Even those privileged or wealthy enough to participate in Vientiane politics did so with notable lack of enthusiasm. For all its corruption and inefficiency, the government seemed stable enough to withstand non-Communist opposition as long as the Americans continued to support Souvanna. U.S. officials might complain about the shortcomings of the Lao regime, but none of them could suggest an alternative. For better or worse, Souvanna appeared to most diplomats as Washington's last hope for any kind of stability, much less progress, in Laos.

Worsening Confrontation

President Nixon on March 6, 1970, enunciated the U.S. outlook on Laos in a written statement released at his weekend retreat at Key Biscayne, Florida. Nixon, outlining both North Vietnamese and U.S. activities in Laos, declared that U.S. assistance had "always been at the request of the legitimate government of Prime Minister Souvanna Phouma."[12] Nixon's reaffirmation of U.S. support for Souvanna amounted to a commitment that might have been seriously compromised by overt signs of revolt on the part of right-wing politicians and generals discontented with Souvanna's continuing efforts at reaching a new compromise with the Pathet Lao. Nixon wanted to maintain, if not increase, U.S. support of the Vientiane government, but he realized that his entire policy might founder on criticism in the United States if Souvanna were overthrown.

Indeed, Nixon's statement was aimed primarily at stifling demands on the part of senators and newspapers for full disclosure of U.S. involvement in Laos as a possible prelude to a major shift in policy. Nixon acknowledged what was already widely known and reported—that the United States was bombing northern Laos as well as the Ho Chi Minh trail—but rationalized this activity on the basis of the presence of what he said were 67,000 North Vietnamese troops in Laos. Officials explained that this figure, which was considerably higher than most estimates available in Vientiane, included some 15,000 North Vietnamese en route to South Vietnam, as well as more than 50,000 permanently stationed by then in the jungles of Laos.

One purpose of Nixon's statement may have been to dramatize U.S. firmness on Laos for the benefit of the Communist powers and particularly the Soviet Union, which U.S. officials still believed might eventually persuade North Vietnam to abandon some of its aims and cooperate with the Vientiane government. It was partly for this reason that Nixon, in his statement, revealed that he had "written letters today to British Prime Minister Wilson and Soviet Premier Kosygin asking their help in restoring the 1962 Geneva agreements for that country." His letters, he said, "support the Laotian prime minister's own current appeal to the co-chairmen for consultations; urge the co-chairmen to work with other signatories of the Geneva accords; and pledge full United States cooperation."

Prospects for Soviet cooperation in a solution to Laos did not appear bright, particularly since Soviet propaganda for several years had excoriated the United States for the bombing. The Soviet Ambassador to Vientiane, Victor Minin, in early 1969 had flown to Hanoi and then driven to the Pathet Lao headquarters in Sam Neua with a message from Souvanna to Souphanouvong, but the Soviet foreign ministry at the same time had issued a statement condemning American "aggression." Kosygin's reply to Nixon in mid-March, 1970, seemed totally negative, for the Soviet Premier said "consultations between the signatories of the Geneva agreements . . . would be unrealistic . . . when the United States is continuing the war in Vietnam, expanding armed interference in Laos, and when the coalition government . . . has been paralyzed as a result of the actions of the right-wing forces."

Kosygin's message repeated, almost word for word, a five-point program for peace presented by the Neo Lao Hak Sat on March 6, 1970, the same day President Nixon released his statement on Laos. The main point of Kosygin's message, like the Pathet Lao statement, was that "first of all" it was "essential for the United States to stop in the nearest future the escalation of the war and to end completely and unconditionally the bombing of Laotian territory."[13]

It seemed significant that the Pathet Lao statement emanated from Hanoi, not Sam Neua or some other "liberated zone." Although formally released by one Phau Phimphachan, identified as director of the Hanoi information bureau of the NLHS, it was probably written by North Vietnamese propagandists. Point one demanded an end to U.S. "intervention and aggression in Laos," and point two called for "a foreign policy of peace and neutrality." Point three proposed general elections and the establishment of a government of national union "truly representative of the Lao people." Point four suggested, as an interim step before elections, a "consultative political conference composed of representatives of all Lao parties concerned in order to deal with all the affairs of Laos and set up a provisional coalition government." Point four also called for "unification of Laos" after withdrawal of "pro-American forces" from "areas they have illegally occupied. . . ."[14]

The Communists, by issuing the statement at the height of the North Vietnamese offensive in northeastern Laos, hoped to put Vientiane in a position in which it would have to make concessions, beginning with a demand for a U.S. bombing halt. The drama of the Communist strategy was heightened by Souphanouvong's "urgent message" to Souvanna on March 8 in which he told his half-brother that he wanted "to send to Vientiane at the earliest possible date a messenger carrying a letter to you on my part."[15] Souvanna promptly replied that he would be "happy to accept Prince Souphanouvong's message, the sooner the better." While officials awaited the arrival of the "messenger," presumably coming in on the weekly ICC flight from Hanoi, the North Vietnamese were attacking Sam Thong and threatening Long Cheng. The purpose of Souphanouvong's message, which arrived several days after the fall of Sam Thong, was to present the government with an alternative to slow, agonizing defeat.

The message, borne by a Pathet Lao colonel, restated the five points and concluded with the hope that "your highness, as a sign of sincerity, will confirm the immediate and unconditional

cessation of the American bombing. . . ."[16] Souvanna instead
called for a "cease-fire" and "retreat of foreign troops illegally introduced into Laos in all zones without any exception"—a suggestion that would have meant capitulation by the Pathet Lao and
North Vietnamese, who had no intention of withdrawing any
troops until a new regime was safely installed in Vientiane.[17]

Thus, after three increasingly virulent Communist offensives,
after vast escalations in U.S. bombing, after innumerable statements and recriminations on both sides, the Vientiane government
and the Pathet Lao reiterated the same inflexible positions that had
characterized their attitudes toward each other for some twenty
years. The situation itself might have changed, but the issues
seemed to have remained the same. There was no apparent way
in which either side could compromise without yielding its essential base of power—or without countering the basic drives of the
other major countries in the Indochinese region, including both
Vietnams and Thailand, as well as the interests of their major
Western and Communist benefactors. In the tug-of-war for Laos,
however, the Vietnamese Communists were in a stronger position
than before. For all the U.S. bombing and military aid, the North
Vietnamese and the Pathet Lao had captured, by 1970, almost all
the regions controlled by the Pathet Lao·and neutralist forces in
mid-1962.

Many diplomatic observers in Vientiane believed that the North
Vietnamese would attempt to negotiate after advancing to the so-
called 1962 cease-fire line—the rough division, never formally
agreed on by any of the warring factions, between the government-
controlled lowlands and the Pathet Lao or neutralist northeastern
and southeastern provinces. By capturing the plain in 1970, according to this argument, the Communists were merely retrieving
what they had lost in Vang Pao's summer offensive in 1969—and
what they had controlled as a result of their alliance with Kong
Le's "neutralists" in 1962. The Pathet Lao, by this logic, would
have been entitled to most of the towns between Vientiane and
Luang Prabang on Route 13.

Instead of advancing further north, however, the Communists
seized two towns in southern Laos that they had surrounded for
three years and had shelled sporadically but still had not directly
attacked on the ground. Attopeu fell on April 30, 1970, as South
Vietnam and the United States launched operations in Cambodia.
Six weeks later, on June 10, some 300 North Vietnamese troops
overran Saravane in a predawn attack before U.S. jets or Lao T-28's

had even been alerted. Neither of these towns had been under Pathet Lao control in 1962. The North Vietnamese decided to strike them—and other outposts in the region—as part of an effort to expand their infiltration routes into northern Cambodia and compensate for the loss of routes from Cambodian ports on the Gulf of Thailand to jungle sanctuaries bordering South Vietnam.

The Lao Government in effect conceded Attopeu to the enemy but launched a disastrous counteroffensive to retake Saravane several days after it fell. Patrols of Lao troops re-entered Saravane under cover of air strikes, then fell back as the North Vietnamese cut them off from their supplies and ambushed their reinforcements. The question now was whether or not the Lao could defend some of the lowland centers, such as Champassak, south of Pakse, or Khong Sedone, to the north. The North Vietnamese seemed determined to annex the southernmost provinces of Laos and combine them with the three northeastern Cambodian provinces, already under their control. The result would be a vast Communist-controlled base region from which North Vietnamese troops could menace central Cambodia, South Vietnam, the rest of southern Laos, and northeastern Thailand. No amount of U.S. aid and air strikes was capable of buttressing Laotian Government troops, whose commanders were still mired in their own world of petty corruption, factionalism, and politicking in Vientiane.

It was indicative of the lack of realism of Lao right-wing politicians that they should, at this stage of impending disaster, have suggested the overthrow of Souvanna. And yet, in mid-May, some of them relayed word to U.S. Ambassador G. McMurtrie Godley that they were considering a *coup d'état* to install a government unfettered by Souvanna's desires to return to the 1962 coalition and eventually enter into talks with the Pathet Lao. Godley, following the policy established by Sullivan, advised the rightists that the United States might have to withdraw its military aid program and cease flying air strikes in support of Lao troops if such a government were installed. Souvanna, the artful compromiser, gave up his own position as defense minister and appointed the rightist Sisouk Na Champassak, who already was finance minister, in his place.

Another crisis had been averted, but the future of Laos remained as indefinite as ever. How much longer could the country remain a buffer—a remote battlefield between Communist and non-Communist forces—before the government and army finally crumbled under Communist pressure? The only other alternative, it seemed, was a still wider war among Thai, North, and South Vietnamese troops in their traditional contest for control of the Mekong River valley.

The question was answered, at least in part, in early 1971 when U.S. and South Vietnamese officials decided to launch a massive operation from northern South Vietnam across the Annamese Mountains into southern Laos. On February 8, 1971, South Vietnamese combat forces entered Laos for the first time in more than small-unit strength. "This limited operation is not an enlargement of the war," said a statement issued that day by the State Department several hours after President Nguyen Van Thieu had formally announced the incursion. "The principal new factor," the State Department claimed, "is that South Vietnam forces will move against the enemy on the ground to deny him the sanctuaries and disrupt the main artery of supplies which he has been able to use so effectively against American and South Vietnamese forces in the past."[18]

Despite this disclaimer, it was obvious that the war, perhaps inevitably, had widened again, just as it had in April, 1970, when South Vietnamese troops had first entered Cambodia after Sihanouk's fall. Within four days, some 10,000 South Vietnamese, supported by American jets and helicopters, had advanced into the region of Tchepone, the bombed-out center of a sprawling North Vietnamese base area on Route 9 some 25 miles west of the South Vietnamese frontier. There were reports that several thousand ethnic Lao from northeastern Thailand had been recruited to supplement depleted Laotian forces approaching from the east. The North Vietnamese judiciously dispersed, as they had done before American and South Vietnamese intervention in Cambodia, while awaiting an opportunity to counterattack. No part of Laos was immune from the threat of a wider war.

Superficially, Lao leaders appeared to approve of the incursions. Souvanna Phouma remarked, on January 31, 1971, as the South Vietnamese were moving toward the Laotian frontier, that he believed the North Vietnamese planned another offensive against Laotian positions.[19] The implication was that Souvanna had endorsed any action that might diminish enemy strength. He apparently reasoned that he could no longer hope to deter the Communists by further efforts at reconciliation or compromise. No matter how Souvanna chose to fend off opposing forces, however, the future of the Lao, who basically wanted only to be left alone, appeared bleak and desolate, if not unbearably tragic and cruel.

V

Conclusion—or Continuation?

I 2

Prospects for Peace

Hanoi's Strength and Aims

Despite the threat posed by Vietnamese Communist cadres and troops in Cambodia, Thailand, and Laos, in early 1971, there was considerable doubt as to Hanoi's real military aims in these countries. One vital factor in the equation was North Vietnam's internal problems, as revealed in an ordeal of self-criticism virtually unprecedented in the history of the Communist movement. Then, hanging over the future of the entire Indochinese peninsula was the question of to what extent the United States, the Soviet Union, and China would support opposing governments, fronts, and parties in the region.

The key to the equation, in terms of North Vietnam's immediate capabilities, may well have been the capacity of its depressed economy and the attitude of the populace. Certainly a spate of utterances from Hanoi in 1969 and 1970 indicated the government's preoccupation with such considerations. "Our people's low living standards have become even lower as a result of the protracted war," wrote Nguyen Van Tran, secretary of the Hanoi branch of the Lao Dong, or Workers' Party. Tran was not criticizing the theory of protracted war, expounded in late 1969 by General Giap and early 1970 by Party Secretary Le Duan, but commenting on the debilitating effects of a long struggle on industry, agriculture, and morale.[1]

Analysts viewed the remarks of Nguyen Van Tran and others within the framework of Le Duan's statement of February, 1970, stressing the need for long-range planning and economic and technical improvements. Since February, however, the criticism had reached such proportions in North Vietnam that Western intelligence specialists wondered whether Hanoi would have to cut back its military activities—and possibly consider a peace settlement on less than entirely favorable terms. North Vietnamese propaganda did not specify the dimensions of the country's difficulties, but some optimistic Western observers inferred, as they had throughout the war, that Hanoi might not be able to pose a military threat in all the countries of Indochina for much longer. The hope was that North Vietnam might settle for a compromise in order to buy time to recover at home—and then not send more troops beyond its own borders for another two or three years. The fact that Hanoi emphasized the economy implied that some of its leaders placed higher priority on rebuilding the home front than on fighting an expanded war from northern Laos to the Mekong River delta.

The nature of these statements from Hanoi, particularly by such little-known figures as Nguyen Van Tran, may have signaled a serious dispute within North Vietnam's ruling hierarchy. Had certain younger officials allied with top rulers, such as Le Duan, against other members of the political bureau of the central committee? Or was there really, as some Hanoi-watchers believed, unanimity among North Vietnamese Party and Government leaders? Many analysts had predicted a power struggle within North Vietnam's ruling clique after the death of Ho Chi Minh on September 3, 1969, but there was no solid evidence of a split. The record showed only that Hanoi was acting, quite pragmatically, to recover from the ravages of a generation of war.

Although North Vietnamese propaganda was constantly calling for improvements at home, it never alluded to North Vietnam's military role in Cambodia, Thailand, and Laos—or even in South Vietnam, except indirectly, by stating that Vietnamese had the right to defend their fatherland. In order to reach conclusions about North Vietnam's power and potential in these countries, it was necessary to examine diplomatic, military, and political maneuvers as well as notebooks, orders, and other papers captured in battle. Indirectly, these indices substantiated the impression, gleaned from Hanoi's propaganda, of North Vietnam's desire to scale down the level of conflict. Economic, and possibly political, turmoil within North Vietnam seemed to have been reflected in its changing posture in the region.

The Communists could and did open new base areas in northeastern Cambodia, but they lacked the manpower to maintain the same level of pressure as before on strategic points in northern Laos and the Mekong Delta. Evidence of this decline in strength was that North Vietnam, during the 1970 summer monsoon, withdrew the bulk of the 312th Division from northern Laos. This division, sent into the region to spearhead the 1970 dry-season offensive across the Plain of Jars in February and March, was needed to support Hanoi's efforts in the fall at enlarging infiltration routes through southern Laos and northern Cambodia. Elements of the 312th returned to the Plain of Jars, but it was questionable how much farther North Vietnam would want to advance in that region while focusing on the trail system to the south.

Despite the failure of the first exchanges between Souvanna and Souphanouvong in March and April, 1970, the Pathet Lao unexpectedly evinced a desire to go on with the talks. After a series of public and secret messages, on July 28, Prince Souphanouvong dispatched one of his most trusted associates, Prince Souk Vongsak, to Vientiane. At the same time, the Pathet Lao accepted a proposal by Souvanna for further negotiations between plenipotentiary representatives of Souvanna and Souphanouvong at Khang Khay on the Plain of Jars. In his initial conferences in Vientiane, Prince Souk, who had been a secretary of state in the 1962 coalition, raised certain long-standing objections, without altogether excluding the possibility of compromise.

There was, in fact, a difference between the Pathet Lao's position in the summer and fall as opposed to the spring of 1970, as was indicated in an interview Souvanna granted on August 7. "Has the Pathet Lao retracted its demand for suspension of U.S. bombing?" asked the correspondent for Tokyo's *Sankei Shimbun*, one of the largest Japanese newspapers. "Are both sides going to begin talks unconditionally?" "That is not yet clear," replied the Prime Minister. "However, I am satisfied that special envoy Vongsak has not yet made such a demand."[2] The Pathet Lao, to be sure, would continue to require an end to all "acts of aggression," including the bombing, but the Communists might not insist that Souvanna order the United States to cease such activities over all of Laos. The North Vietnamese, on whom the Pathet Lao relied for policy guidance and materiel and manpower support, may have wanted a separate settlement in northern Laos that would permit the withdrawal of the 312th Division, comprised of 10,000 men, or half their troops in the region.

It was possible that the Pathet Lao would bargain only on cessation of bombing of northern Laos, under the guise of a cease-fire, and accept Souvanna's *pro forma* position that he was not responsible for activities along the Ho Chi Minh trail, the bombing of which he had previously "requested." Under this kind of temporary settlement, North Vietnam could consolidate its gains in northern Laos, at far lower cost in men and materiel. This arrangement would have seemed particularly fortuitous from Vientiane's viewpoint, since General Vang Pao's depleted forces, during the 1970 monsoon season, had failed to recover territory lost to the Communists during the 1970 Plain of Jars offensive.

By early 1971, however, hopes for such a temporary solution had foundered on two basic considerations. First, Souvanna refused to support a cessation of bombing over even part of Laos without sufficient guarantees that North Vietnam would also observe a cease-fire. Second, the North Vietnamese still believed that application of military pressure would ultimately force Souvanna to yield— and on this premise again attacked Lao positions near the Plain of Jars in northern Laos and the Bolovens Plateau in southern Laos in a sequel to the virulent 1968, 1969, and 1970 dry-season offensives.

The refusal of both sides to compromise had an immediate escalatory effect. American and South Vietnamese officials had no difficulty obtaining Souvanna's tacit endorsement of intervention against the Ho Chi Minh trail system, while North Vietnam threatened to widen the war by expressing the determination of "our Vietnamese people" to "support the fraternal Laotian people in their national salvation struggle, and to fulfill their international duty toward the nations on the Indochinese peninsula."[3] At the same time, the Pathet Lao broke off the preliminary talks in Vientiane.

The reason for Hanoi's almost desperate response becomes clear if one views southern and northeastern Cambodia as a special war zone or separate entity on the map of Indochina. The North Vietnamese, after Sihanouk's overthrow and the entry of U.S. and South Vietnamese troops into Cambodia, had attempted to unite the entire territory from Route 7 in Cambodia to the Keo Neua Pass in Laos into one area of operations. In the months before the South Vietnamese incursion, North Vietnam faced what may have amounted to the war's greatest concentration of U.S. airpower on one region. Anticipating increased traffic along infiltration routes at the start of the 1970–71 dry season, the United States had shifted almost all B-52 bombers based on Guam and Okinawa to the southern Thailand base of Sattahip. These planes, the most powerful weapon ever used in the war, flew nearly 1,000 sorties a month over southern Laos and northern Cambodia in late 1970 and early 1971. B-52 sorties over South Vietnam dwindled to almost none, except during occasional battles along the demilitarized zone or around outposts besieged by North Vietnamese troops. Air strikes alone, however, could not eliminate Communist base areas in mountainous, often uncharted jungle where roads and bunkers were hidden under dense layers of trees and brush. This consideration finally impelled President Nixon to heed the pleas of his military advisers and Saigon government officials and sanction South Vietnamese intervention in force in southern Laos. There was, however, an obvious irony in the fact that previous allied intervention in Cambodia had only half succeeded in Nixon's aim of preventing the Communists from turning that country into "a vast enemy staging area and springboard for attacks on South Vietnam along 600 miles of frontier—and a refuge where enemy troops could return from combat without fear of retaliation." Most of Cambodia north of the Fishhook, 80 miles above Saigon, fit the description that Nixon, in his address on April 30, had warned might apply to the entire country.

Hanoi could not afford, however, to invest between 40,000 and 60,000 men in Cambodia. It was partly for this reason—as well as for diplomatic and political prestige—that North Vietnam attempted to organize an indigenous Communist front, just as it had done in Laos and South Vietnam. "Occupied areas must be held until they are transferred to friendly [Khmer Rouge] troops," said an extract from a notebook of an unidentified North Vietnamese soldier. "Attacks should be conducted in close coordination with the establishment of the governmental infrastructure."[4]

Communist officials, however, could barely staff local "liberation" governments with qualified Cambodians, much less form entire military units capable of defending roads and towns. The organization of a Communist infrastructure in Cambodia was an emergency drive of doubtful permanent value. The North Vietnamese were attempting in a matter of months to accomplish what the Pathet Lao and Viet Cong had still not achieved in a quarter of a century. By the end of 1970, three fourths of Cambodia was an administrative no man's land. The North Vietnamese did not have the manpower or material resources to rule the regions that they controlled militarily. Many Cambodians who did not flee to Phnom Penh or other towns under government control did not recognize Communist authority, except under military pressure.

North Vietnam could rationalize its activities in Cambodia and Laos in terms of its interests in South Vietnam, but the guerrilla conflict in northern and northeastern Thailand could not pass this elementary test except possibly after South Vietnam's incursion into southern Laos. In view of the need for economy of strength, North Vietnam in 1970 turned over to Peking some of the responsibility for training guerrilla cadres for the conflict in Thailand. A major center at Hoa Binh, southwest of Hanoi, canceled its entire program for Thai insurgency, while at least a dozen new camps were opened in Yunnan Province in southwestern China and in northern Laos. If North Vietnam did not regard Thailand as another front in the Vietnam war, however, it still was fearful of Thailand's possible entry as a full-fledged participant in the struggle. North Vietnamese activities in Thailand may have been designed to divert Thai attentions from Laos and Cambodia.

Certainly the leaders of Thailand indicated that Communist insurgency was having precisely that effect when they refused to send combat troops to Cambodia. "We have said the commitment of Thai forces is dictated by the requirements of Thailand," Foreign Minister Thanat Khoman told me in an interview on September 4, 1970. For this reason, Thanat went on, his government planned to pull its troops from Vietnam. Thailand's foreign policy, in keeping with the pragmatic tradition of modern Thai history, was governed by a desire to reach an understanding with some of the Communist countries in order to compensate for the prospect of a massive decrease in U.S. military and economic aid, defense commitments, and private investment and spending.

Thailand continued to view China as its worst enemy, particularly as Peking increased its aid to Meo guerrillas, but it was still possible that Bangkok would reach a *modus vivendi* with Hanoi. The government hinted at such an understanding through an article in the *Bangkok Post* by the paper's executive editor, Theh Chongkhadikij, regarded as a mouthpiece for the foreign ministry. "In this way, it looks as if an unwritten agreement has come into existence," wrote Theh. "The North Vietnamese and Viet Cong forces do not come within any point of the Thai territory which Thailand would consider of direct bearing on its security, while Thai forces are being held back until this point is reached."[5]

Although Cambodia and Thailand had restored diplomatic relations on May 13 and seemed to have reached some understanding on future cooperation during General Lon Nol's visit to Bangkok in July, Thailand had no intention of upsetting its delicate equilibrium with North Vietnam. Thailand's involvement in Cambodia appeared roughly equivalent to North Vietnam's aid for the guerrilla effort in northeastern Thailand: Just as North Vietnamese cadres trained local Thai-Lao soldiers, Thailand agreed to help train some 5,000 Thai citizens of Khmer ancestry to combat the North Vietnamese in Cambodia. While Thailand turned over to Cambodia five U.S.-built T-28 planes, along with surplus weapons and uniforms, North Vietnam continued to ship old-fashioned weapons, ammunition, and other supplies to northeastern Thailand.

There was, however, no evidence that regular Thai troops would go to Cambodia's rescue. Such "intervention," wrote Theh, would "depend on the sort of threat the North Vietnamese and Viet Cong are ready or willing to pose against Thailand."[6] Thailand's leaders sensed that North Vietnam had already overextended its forces and would not want to risk another major escalation so long as U.S. troops were still in the region. The Mekong River valley through Laos and the Dangrek mountain range along the Thai-Cambodian frontier still seemed to demarcate their spheres of immediate interest.

In the long run, however, rivalry between Thailand and North Vietnam for the Mekong—and the buffer states of Laos and Cambodia—still threatened to devolve into a regional struggle reminiscent of those between Thai and Vietnamese armies before the French colonial period. In such a war, it was conceivable that Hanoi might fight for the agricultural riches of the valley for sheer national survival. Certainly this consideration dominated Hanoi's drive to unite the industrial but underfed North with the rice-rich South, the major source of food for all of Vietnam during the colonial era.

And yet, just as European colonialism had stifled purely indigenous wars, it appeared that great-power interests might again prevent local armies from fighting to the finish for nationalist goals. The prospect of continued U.S. military and air support for Laos, Thailand, Cambodia, and South Vietnam might prolong the conflict beyond the limits of North Vietnam's endurance. Even if Communist troops could outlast their demoralized enemies, however, the conflict between the Soviet Union and China might force Hanoi to consider a compromise rather than lose the favor of its two principal benefactors.

North Vietnam and the Sino-Soviet Dispute

North Vietnam's policy was to balance the competing ambitions of the Soviet Union and China. North Vietnamese leaders, always mindful of China's ancient history as the ruler of Vietnam, wanted Soviet aid both to prosecute the war and to demonstrate to Peking that they were not solely dependent on Chinese largesse for national survival. At the same time, Hanoi could not ally entirely with the Soviet Union lest China should cut off overland supply routes and commerce, threaten military outposts, and possibly even send its troops across the frontier.

North Vietnam's leaders also had ideological and theoretical reasons for wanting to maintain warm relations with both countries. Although Ho Chi Minh had avoided one side or the other in the Sino-Soviet dispute, other members of the Political Bureau were often described as leaning toward Moscow or Peking. Le Duan, Party secretary and most powerful man in Hanoi after Ho's death, seemed to some analysts to favor the Soviet Union, while Truong Chinh, chairman of the standing committee of the National Assembly, was regarded as pro-Chinese. Such assessments were rather risky, since none of the members of the hierarchy ever publicly stated his preference for one Communist power as opposed to another.

Truong Chinh, however, had been responsible in 1956 for North Vietnam's disastrous land reform program, influenced by China's collectivized farm system. Truong Chinh had admitted "serious mistakes," but he indicated little change in his thinking in a speech on "weaknesses, shortcomings, and mistakes" in agricultural cooperatives, published on January 29 and 30, 1969, in the Party newspaper, *Nhan Dan*. If Truong Chinh could never reconcile the theory of complete collectivization with the practice of limited private enterprise in agriculture, he still revealed considerable flexibility. "We must . . . grasp the motto of 'long-drawn out fight and relying mainly on one's self,'" he said on September 16, 1968, possibly reflecting the reality of heavy North Vietnamese and Viet Cong losses in the Tet, May, and September, 1968, offensives.[7]

Truong Chinh may also have been criticizing Le Duan, probably the prime mover behind these sudden thrusts toward decisive victory. If Le Duan objected to such criticism, however, he had obviously adjusted his thinking by the time his famous essay on the necessity for pragmatism and flexibility appeared in *Nhan Dan* on February 14, 1970. Yet, Le Duan seemed to differ with Truong Chinh in his application of socialist theories to daily realities. He stressed improvements in production and management without dwelling on the theoretical issues involved in cooperatives versus collectivization.

These internal discussions were extremely important in terms of Soviet versus Chinese influence because each country looked upon North Vietnam as a manifestation of its power and ideology in Indochina. If Chinese influence were paramount in Hanoi, China might extend its influence through the rest of Indochina and parts of Thailand. And if all Indochina were tacitly recognized as a Chinese sphere of influence, surely Peking, aided by sizable overseas Chinese mercantile communities in every city and town in Southeast Asia, might dominate the rest of the region. Unfortunately for this variation on the domino theory, the Soviet Union, much less the United States or Japan, by far the strongest trader in Southeast Asia, had no intention of granting China such an opportunity. Soviet policy in Indochina was often contradictory, but Moscow was at least as interested in frustrating Peking's ambitions as in curbing Washington's.

Perhaps the most noteworthy contradiction in Soviet policy was that Moscow emerged in the late 1960's as the largest donor of arms for Hanoi while still presenting at least an appearance of genuine interest in negotiations to end the war. U.S. intelligence analysts estimated that the Soviet Union by 1969 and 1970 was providing approximately 80 per cent of North Vietnam's war materiel. Russia throughout the war had supplied heavy equipment, ranging from trucks to surface-to-air missiles to artillery pieces, while China had contributed such basic infantry weapons as AK-47 rifles, AK-50 machine guns, B-40 rockets, and so forth, with which North Vietnamese and Viet Cong soldiers actually did most of the fighting. After the extremes of its 1966–68 Cultural Revolution, China focused on domestic economic difficulties and Party reorganization. Meanwhile, the Soviet Union supplemented Chinese shipments with its own small arms, including SKS semi-automatic rifles, the equivalent of American M-2 carbines, and weapons from the AK series. Moscow and Peking also supplied North Vietnam with rice and wheat, which North Vietnam needed as much as military materiel.

Although the Soviet Union was Hanoi's most generous source of aid, Russian leaders were still anxious to maintain friendly relations with non-Communist governments. In contrast to China, which had opposed North Vietnam's entry in 1968 into peace negotiations on the Vietnam conflict, the Soviet Union not only encouraged these talks but also seemed disposed toward diplomatic and political rather than military solutions for Cambodia and Laos. Moscow did not seem willing to exert pressure on Hanoi to abandon any of its goals in South Vietnam, but the Soviet Union, unlike China, did not necessarily favor the installation of pro-Communist front governments in Laos and Cambodia. Indeed, in the summer of 1970, Western diplomats in Vientiane and Saigon reported privately that Moscow was urging Hanoi to pressure the Pathet Lao to enter negotiations leading to a political settlement of the Laotian sphere of the Indochinese conflict.

The Soviet position was directly related to China's gradual escalation of military activities in northern Laos and Thailand. If the Pathet Lao and the Vientiane government reached a new understanding acceptable to North Vietnam, China could not rationalize its encroachment on Laotian territory as part of the Lao struggle for "liberation" from the "lackeys of U.S. imperialism." Hence China, anxious to frustrate a political solution contrary to its immediate aims, withheld any support for the talks. The attitudes of the Soviet Union and China were predicated to a large extent on their policy toward Thailand. The Soviet Union wanted to befriend the Thai Government, to encourage the development of trade and cultural contacts. One way to win Thailand's confidence was to oppose China, whose activities in northern Laos were an integral part of the "liberation" struggle in northern Thailand.

The Soviet Union, in contrast to China, may have wanted to maintain the government of Laos as a neutral buffer between North Vietnam and Thailand if the latter would also revert to a policy of neutrality. Soviet policy toward Thailand was a two-edged sword, which had the potential to undercut America's position while utterly destroying China's political and military campaign. Foreign Minister Thanat, in his interview with me on September 4, revealed that Moscow had said it would sign a commercial treaty with Bangkok. "The Soviet Union has said it does not want Southeast Asia dominated by a major Asian power," said Thanat, referring to China. The inference was that Russia might eventually guarantee Thailand's security against Chinese attack, just as the United States had done since the formation of the Southeast Asia Treaty Organization in 1954.

Thanat's hopes were largely based on the so-called Brezhnev doctrine, which Leonid Brezhnev, general secretary of the Soviet Communist Party, had pronounced in a speech on June 7, 1969, before the International Conference of Communist Parties in Moscow. "We are of the opinion," said Brezhnev, "that the course of events is putting on the agenda the task of creating a system of collective security in Asia."[8] It was far from clear what kind of system

Brezhnev envisioned, but Russian officials had convinced Thanat that it could only help—and never hinder—Thailand's interests. "The Soviet Union does not have to come to Thailand," said Thanat in reply to my question as to whether or not Russian troops might base on Thai soil, as the Americans had done. "Its ships are in the Indian Ocean." Thanat's words were a warning to both Thailand's worst enemy, China, and its closest ally, the United States, which Thailand feared would continue to reduce its military and economic interests in the region.

It was partly because of its desire to placate Thailand—and oppose China—that the Soviet Union pursued a rather puzzling course in Cambodia. Moscow would have liked to appear sympathetic toward the government-in-exile of Prince Sihanouk while not opposing the government in Phnom Penh. It was doubtful, however, that this position would please Hanoi, particularly in view of U.S. and South Vietnamese intervention in Cambodia. Again, however, Moscow was preoccupied by its dispute with China, which harbored Sihanouk and his entourage. In a curious reversal of China's customary argument of U.S.-Soviet collusion against China, Moscow tried to rationalize its ambivalent policy by charging that Peking had indirectly encouraged the United States to send troops into Cambodia.

"Ever since the Lon Nol–Sirik Matak clique engineered a coup in Cambodia on March 18, the Maoist leadership has been raising noisy clamors against U.S. imperialism," said a Radio Moscow commentary. "Meanwhile, Peking has also repeatedly pledged its full support for the Cambodian Government headed by Sihanouk by saying that the Chinese people are a dependable pillar of support for the people of the Indochina state and that the vast Chinese territory is their reliable rear." As evidence to the contrary, however, Moscow charged that "Mao Tse-tung and his followers are unfurling an anti-Soviet vilification campaign on an unprecedented scale" just "when all the peace-loving nations are faced with the solemn and pressing question of how to adopt united action to counter the aggressors. . . ." By escalating "anti-Soviet hysteria," the commentary went on, Mao "in his explicit and simple fashion told the Washington politicians that Peking's hands were tied" along China's northern frontier with Russia. "In turn," the commentary reasoned, "Washington immediately took advantage of the opportunity and expanded its aggression against Southeast Asia without the slightest risk."[9]

As these remarks indicated, diplomatic speculation that U.S.

intervention in Cambodia might unite Moscow and Peking was unfounded. If anything, the total Cambodian episode, beginning with the fall of Sihanouk and then U.S. and South Vietnamese incursions across the frontier with General Lon Nol's blessing, deepened rather than resolved Sino-Soviet differences. Soviet and Chinese attitudes on Cambodia paralleled those on Thailand and Laos in that China again was supporting the "liberation" forces, while Russia appeared willing to compròmise with the anti-Communist government in the capital. There was even talk among Western diplomats that their Soviet counterparts had advised Hanoi that Moscow could supply enough weapons for North Vietnamese troops to prosecute the struggle in South Vietnam but was not interested in financing a new war across Cambodia.

Some diplomatic observers, after perceiving that Moscow and Peking were not reconciling their quarrel on Cambodia, then speculated that the former was writhing in an agony of indecision and embarrassment while the latter was winning power and respect for its revolutionary aims. Certainly Peking appeared delighted with the opportunity to castigate the United States and the Soviet Union, while unequivocally supporting a revolution that might extend Chinese influence to the Gulf of Thailand. "U.S. imperialism, which looks like a huge monster, is in essence a paper tiger, now in the throes of its death-bed struggle," said Chairman Mao, in a rare public statement on May 20, 1970. "It is not the Vietnamese people, the Lao people, the Cambodian people, the Palestinian people, the Arab people, or the people of other countries who fear U.S. imperialism; it is U.S. imperialism which fears the people of the world." Encouraging its Indochinese allies to keep fighting, Mao noted that the "people of a small country can certainly defeat aggression by a big country."[10]

For all China's speed and decisiveness in exploiting U.S. intervention in Cambodia, however, it was far from certain to what extent Peking would really profit from expansion of the war. By remaining sympathetic with all sides except the United States, the Soviet Union may have played a more subtle game than its Chinese rival. There was even some possibility that the Kremlin might extend its policy of compromise to South Vietnam, particularly if the government of President Nguyen Van Thieu was replaced by a "third-force" regime more palatable to the NLF and North Vietnam. Moscow signaled these thoughts by occasional references to peace negotiations among all the warring countries. Such references increased Soviet prestige in every anti-Communist capital in

Southeast Asia—but especially in Phnom Penh, Vientiane, and perhaps even Saigon, where non-Communist but antigovernment politicians and intellectuals were eagerly seeking a compromise way out of the war.

Prospects for Peace

From the Soviet Union's hints about expanded peace talks emerged the thought that Moscow might urge Hanoi to compromise in all of Indochina, just as it had apparently cautioned against expanding the war across Laos and Cambodia. The future of the region, then, depended on the nature of the compromise. Optimists in Washington erred in concluding that Russia would approve of a *status quo* of pervasive U.S. economic and military influence on the governments in Saigon, Phnom Penh, Vientiane, and Bangkok. Soviet statements, especially during U.S. intervention in Cambodia, indicated that Moscow would no more encourage American than Chinese hegemony over a region that it ultimately wanted to disengage from any military alliance with the United States.

"The spread of U.S. military actions to Cambodia is the direct continuation of U.S. aggression in Vietnam and of the armed intervention in Laos," said a Russian statement of July 15, 1970, two weeks after the last U.S. ground forces had left Cambodia. The statement proclaimed that the Soviet people were "on the side of the peoples of Vietnam, Laos, and Cambodia," but it failed to specify whom it meant by "peoples."[11] While China left no doubt that its support went to Communist-front movements throughout Indochina, Moscow did not rule out a favorable attitude toward non-Communist political organizations and governments that showed some propensity for reconciliation with Hanoi. The Soviet Union gave the impression that it might officially endorse an expanded peace conference just when—but not before—it saw a clear prospect of an Indochinese settlement posited upon this kind of compromise.

"The real situation appears to be that only a new Geneva conference could bring about a fresh solution and relax tensions in the Indochina peninsula," Soviet Ambassador to the United Nations Jacob Malik told a news conference on April 17, 1970, two weeks before the entry of U.S. troops into Cambodia.[12] Two days later, Malik described the possibility of reconvening the Geneva conference as "unrealistic," but the feeling persisted among diplomats that he had meant to test international reaction. The Soviet

Union, as cochairman with Great Britain of the 1954 and 1962 Geneva conferences, could have opened fresh negotiations in Geneva by accepting repeated British suggestions that they jointly reconvene the signatories of the two Geneva agreements. Instead, Russian officials preferred to await the opportune moment—perhaps a withdrawal of all U.S. combat troops before the 1972 U.S. Presidential election, perhaps a political upheaval in Saigon, perhaps another series of North Vietnamese military offensives designed to weaken the will of Saigon, Phnom Penh, and Vientiane.

In the meantime, the United States seemed to move closer to Moscow's view of a possible solution to the conflict by launching a peace initiative that was quite contrary to the wishes of its Indochinese allies. On October 7, 1970, four weeks before U.S. congressional elections, President Nixon proposed a "cease-fire-in-place" of all armed forces in Indochina, along with an Indochina peace conference encompassing Cambodia and Laos as well as Vietnam. Nixon declared that the United States was "ready to negotiate an agreed timetable for complete withdrawals as part of an overall settlement" and asked "the other side to join in a search for a political settlement that truly meets the aspirations of all South Vietnamese." Finally, he proposed "the immediate and unconditional release of all prisoners of war held by both sides."[13]

Despite its timing for domestic political purposes, Nixon's "peace initiative" was a counterproposal to an eight-point package presented at the Paris peace talks by Madame Nguyen Thi Binh, head of the NLF delegation. The Viet Cong plan demanded withdrawal of all allied—U.S., Korean, Thai, Australian, and New Zealand—troops from South Vietnam by June 30, 1971, and called for a coalition in which all but the three highest leaders of the present Saigon government might be eligible to serve. It also pledged to enter into discussions on the exchange of prisoners of war after the United States had agreed to meet the deadline on troop withdrawals.[14]

In the light of the Viet Cong plan, Madame Binh, predictably enough, rejected Nixon's suggestions. "Regarding the military problem," she said, Nixon "did nothing but recall in a very general manner the principle of an agreement on the timetable for troops withdrawal without saying whether or not the U.S. accepts [withdrawal of] all its troops and troops of the other foreign countries in the American camp from South Vietnam before June 30, 1971." As for Nixon's plea for a political settlement that met "the aspirations of all South Vietnamese," she claimed he wanted only to maintain "the tyrannical, fascist, and bellicose" administration of President Nguyen Van Thieu, Vice President Nguyen Cao Ky, and Prime Minister Tran Thien Khiem, the three whom she had said would not be acceptable in a coalition. By proposing a cease-fire, she continued, "the U.S. only aims at legalizing its aggression and depriving the peoples of Vietnam, Laos, and Cambodia of their right to legitimate self-defense against aggression."[15]

The gulf between the U.S. and Vietnamese Communist positions may not have been so wide as these statements implied, however, as American officials considered which politicians might be acceptable to Hanoi in a new South Vietnamese Government. Although there would still be 284,000 American troops in South Vietnam by May, 1971, it seemed inconceivable, in view of the antiwar pressure in the United States, that most allied forces would not have been withdrawn by mid-1972. This goal would still not conflict with endorsement by Washington of continued South Vietnamese operations, supported by U.S. air power, in both Cambodia and Laos, in a final effort to induce the Communists to compromise. In the meantime, South Vietnam would hold its elections for the lower house of the National Assembly in late August and for president on October 3, 1971. Even if Thieu were re-elected, it was quite possible that his grip on his government would have weakened. This process might lead Nixon to move closer to Madame Binh's position—all within the framework of his own peace initiative.

Both Hanoi and Saigon were deeply sensitive to the possibility of political change in South Vietnam, Cambodia, Laos, and perhaps even Thailand. While the Communists' current disagreement with Nixon did not exclude possible agreement at a later date, South Vietnam's official endorsement of Nixon's proposal was phrased to indicate a difference of views. On the day of Nixon's broadcast, Thieu's office released a statement—not attributed to Thieu personally—reiterating Nixon's points in a manner that indicated the government's objections. "The cease-fire should not be used by either side to build up its strength by an increase in outside combat forces," said the statement. "It should include all kinds of warfare, encompass all of Indochina, and should lead promptly to the restoration of peace." Since there was no possibility that North Vietnam would honor such an agreement, even if its representatives signed it, there was no chance of South Vietnam's acquiescence to a cease-fire while Thieu was in office.[16]

Thieu swept away any lingering doubts regarding his own feelings in his state of the nation address on October 31, 1970, the eve of the seventh anniversary of the overthrow of President Ngo Dinh Diem. "I will never enter into coalition with the Communists," Thieu told a cheering joint session of the South Vietnamese National Assembly. He did not specifically allude to Nixon's proposal, but he emphasized his rejection of all plans for peace short of total victory by vowing that he was "determined not to pay attention to any spectacular display of appearances," such as a new suggestion for ending the war on unfavorable terms. Significantly, Thieu's sentiments were not shared by his primary rival, General Duong Van Minh, leader of the anti-Diem coup, who declared at a reception the next day that peace was his "priority objective" and that "to achieve that goal we have to accept those who do not share with us a common policy. . . ." General Minh's remarks constituted open defiance of Thieu's refusal to deal with the Communists except as defeated enemies.

The political struggle in Saigon directly affected the entire Indochinese peninsula in that both Vietnams would continue to involve Laos and Cambodia in the war until settling their own conflict—which might eventually spill over into northeastern Thailand. The central question for Laos and Cambodia was whether or not the Saigon government could fight long enough to weaken Hanoi's threat. If Thieu were replaced by a government more likely to consider a compromise, Vientiane and Phnom Penh would have to enter into compromise arrangements with the North Vietnamese as part of an international settlement of the Indochinese issue. The Vientiane government, since it was already a coalition, might survive within the context of the 1962 Geneva agreement on Laos —but with far greater representation than before for the Pathet Lao. Non-Communist ministers might have to endorse a statement demanding that the United States and South Vietnam cease all military activities in Laos, including both air strikes and ground operations.

The United States, if it still wanted to reach a formal agreement or understanding with the Communists before 1972, might not be averse to such a request, which it had totally opposed through 1970. The alternative might be increased North Vietnamese attacks on Laotian towns in the Mekong River lowlands, especially if the North Vietnamese, through the Viet Cong, gained a secure foothold in a coalition in Saigon and no longer needed so many troops in South Vietnam. Although President Nixon, in early 1971, had approved the commitment of ground troops, supported by American air power, to southern Laos, his enthusiasm for this type of venture might rapidly decrease following heavy South Vietnamese losses. The Nixon doctrine, calling for Asian self-reliance, was artfully designed to rationalize expansion of the war by South Vietnamese forces—or eleventh-hour compromise and reconciliation.

Diplomatically and politically, the Cambodian Government had considerably more to fear from reconciliation and compromise in Vietnam than did Laos. At least North Vietnam and China maintained diplomatic relations with Vientiane, but they were both pledged to the destruction of the Lon Nol regime. Nor was America's position particularly encouraging. Vice President Agnew, visiting Phnom Penh on August 28, 1970, nine days after the signing of a U.S. military aid agreement for $40 million for that fiscal year, told reporters on the plane to Bangkok that the United States was interested in "a continued nonaligned status for Cambodia" and would "continue to be a help in the military assistance program" but was not "going to become militarily involved in Cambodia."[17]

These words offered scant comfort to the leaders of a country whose army had clearly demonstrated its inability to defeat the North Vietnamese. Even though the United States, by the end of 1970, had indicated its willingness to offer still more aid, the Cambodian Government needed allied ground forces in addition to massive infusions of equipment. Phnom Penh could not even count on assistance from South Vietnam, whose leaders, in the first flush of the Cambodian campaign in May, had suggested an alliance but then quarreled over who would bear the costs. South Vietnamese troops also antagonized Cambodians by a series of incidents in which they looted towns, killed civilians, and, in some cases, aided Vietnamese living in Cambodia. South Vietnam promised to defend the Mekong and pursue the Communists near the frontier, but Cambodian forces had to bear the brunt of much of the war in the heart of the country.

At the same time, South Vietnam still promised to send troops deep into Cambodia on what amounted to "emergency" missions, as evidenced by an operation, supported by American jets and helicopters, in which South Vietnamese and Cambodians, in January, 1971, temporarily reopened Route 4 from Phnom Penh to Kompong Som on the Gulf of Thailand. South Vietnam also sent some 20,000 troops across the Cambodian frontier in early 1971 to drive the North Vietnamese from rubber plantations and rice paddies northeast and east of Phnom Penh—and possibly to deflect Hanoi's attention from the almost simultaneous intervention in southern Laos. Phnom Penh's overwhelming inability to defend itself was illustrated by a Communist sapper attack on the capital's military and civilian airport on January 22, in which some thirty planes, including nine tenths of Cambodia's air force, were destroyed. Military authorities in Phnom Penh promptly ordered Cambodian troops from outlying towns to positions closer to the city—giving the North Vietnamese still greater flexibility in surrounding regions not defended by South Vietnamese forces.

Among nations affected by widening conflict across the Indochinese peninsula, only Thailand, confronted by a different kind of military threat, seemed at all secure. Bangkok preferred to remain as remote and aloof as possible in a military showdown. Laos and Cambodia might fall under indirect North Vietnamese rule in the event of a compromise in Vietnam, but Thailand would survive, as it had for centuries, by its extraordinary diplomatic skill and favorable geographical position between big-power spheres of influence.

In the final analysis, Thai leaders could count on diplomatic support from the Russians, who had endorsed the Viet Cong's peace proposals while Peking remained silent. Moscow might not dissuade North Vietnam from fighting in Laos and Cambodia, but it could almost certainly keep the war from spreading further—provided that Bangkok loosened its ties with Washington, which, in any case, was decreasing its commitments to Bangkok, just as it was to South Vietnam. Only 32,500 U.S. troops, mainly air force, would remain in Thailand by July 1, 1971, as opposed to a peak of 48,000 in 1969. If Thailand gradually assumed a neutral position and if North Vietnam reached a compromise with a new government in Saigon and limited its Indochinese aims to supporting sympathetic regimes in Phnom Penh and Vientiane, there was still reason to hope for an end to a struggle that had ebbed and flowed across the Indochinese peninsula, including parts of Thailand, for more than a generation.

Other non-Communist countries of Southeast Asia, such as the Philippines, Malaysia, Singapore, and Indonesia, might not welcome the rise of pro-Communist regimes on the Indochinese peninsula, but they could live with this solution if Thailand did not also succumb to Communist expansion. Southeast Asian governments had already demonstrated their inability to persuade the Communists to scale down their activities. Such organizations as the Association of Southeast Asian Nations provided anti-Communist propaganda forums but failed to produce any real semblance of military or diplomatic unity. The conference on Cambodia, convened in Djakarta in May, 1970, proved the unwillingness of non-Communist Asian leaders to provide any significant force in support of verbal pleas to end hostilities.

There was always the possibility that the fighting might eventually slow down in a contortion of human agony and suffering. Without reaching any formal settlement, perhaps the principal protagonists would tire of war, fail to replace troops in the field, and agree on *de facto* cease-fire lines and local understandings. Even this kind of solution, however, might not soon halt the continuing bloody conflict, which Communist sources indicated had already cost the lives of 600,000 of their soldiers in South Vietnam, Cambodia, and Laos by the end of 1970. North Vietnam might not have the manpower or resources to keep on replacing its losses, but it could almost certainly keep up a sporadic and protracted war for some years.

Nor was there much likelihood that all those soldiers and politicians sympathetic with President Thieu or Vice President Ky would peacefully lay down their arms and pledge allegiance to new leaders amenable to a policy of reconciliation with an enemy whom they had been fighting for years. There was every prospect of a war—perhaps several wars—for control of non-Communist forces in Saigon, just as there had been a "war within a war" during the student uprisings in Hue and Danang during the spring of 1966. This possibility would increase with the departure of U.S. troops, who would no longer block lines of communications, as they had very deliberately done since the introduction of American combat units in 1965 after a succession of military coups in Saigon.

The chances for reconciliation were even more remote in Cambodia than in South Vietnam. Hanoi, after reaching an understanding with a coalition in Saigon, might not encourage the bloodbath in Vietnam that many analysts had predicted would accompany or follow the departure of U.S. troops, but there were no forces in Phnom Penh with whom the Communists could reach some face-saving compromise. Certainly Sihanouk—or the North Vietnamese —could bargain with lesser politicians and army officers or perhaps with members of Sihanouk's family, but the only way in which Sihanouk's front could enforce the bargain would be by arresting and executing hundreds of Khmer officials who had dedicated themselves and their country to fighting both Sihanoukism and the Vietnamese Communists.

The possibility of bloodshed and upheaval was less obvious in Vientiane, where the Russians would probably discourage reprisals against members of the 1962 coalition. Yet, a purge might result if the government bowed to Communist pressure for a new government and rightists refused to cooperate. It seemed altogether unlikely that Lao Army officers would agree to merge with the Pathet Lao military establishment unless North Vietnam was able to inflict a crippling defeat on government forces. North Vietnam had repeatedly driven Lao soldiers from outposts and towns, but the army, losing perhaps 4,000 men a year and suffering severe morale problems, had survived with the help of U.S. materiel and bombing.

The likelihood of bitter conflict during and after withdrawal of U.S. troops from the Indochinese peninsula seemed a convincing argument against the Nixon doctrine of decreasing U.S. involvement. The other alternative—endless war between the United States and the Vietnamese Communists—also offered little hope. The only result would be greater destruction of cities, towns, and countryside, still more killing of soldiers and civilians—and probably greater suffering than the region would face if left to fight on without U.S. troops. Between these alternatives, the only room for reconciliation lay in further debate on the proposals presented by Madame Binh and President Nixon. No matter what might be said, however, there was no solution that could settle the struggle either peacefully or happily. In the end, even if the United States were no longer involved, there would be winners and losers, survivors and victims. The region would have to endure the horrors of wider war, whether Nixon had wanted one or not. Then, perhaps, there would be peace.

Notes

(Translations of foreign-language materials, with the exception of those written in French, were made available to the author through the Joint U.S. Public Affairs Office, Saigon; the U.S. embassies in Bangkok, Vientiane, and Phnom Penh; and the U.S. Consulate General in Hong Kong. French-language materials, unless otherwise specified, were translated by the author.)

Chapter 1

1. D. G. E. Hall, A History of South-East Asia, 3d ed. (New York, 1968), pp. 686–700.
2. Joseph Buttinger, The Smaller Dragon: A Political History of Vietnam (New York, 1958), pp. 160–65.
3. Hugh Toye, Laos: Buffer State or Battleground? (London, 1968), pp. 9–22.
4. Virginia Thompson, Thailand: The New Siam, 2d ed. (New York, 1967), pp. 181–82.
5. See H. R. Trevor-Roper, Introduction to Lords of Life: A History of the Kings of Thailand, by H.R.H. Prince Chula Chakrabongse, 2d ed. (London, 1967).

Chapter 2

1. Richard M. Nixon, "Asia After Vietnam," Foreign Affairs 46, no. 1 (Oct., 1967), p. 113.
2. Ibid., p. 124.
3. Richard M. Nixon, "Peace in Vietnam," text of an address broadcast by radio and television from the White House, May 14, 1969.
4. Official transcript of the President's Guam briefing, 6:30 P.M., July 25, 1969.
5. Richard M. Nixon, "Vietnam Address," delivered to a nationwide television audience, Nov. 3, 1969.
6. Le Duan, "Under the Glorious Party Banner, for Independence, Freedom and Socialism, Let Us Advance and Achieve New Victories," published on February 14, 1970, in Nhan Dan (The People), daily newspaper of the Lao Dong (Workers' Party) of North Vietnam.
7. Vo Nguyen Giap, "The Party's Military Line Is the Ever-Victorious Banner of People's War in Our Country," serialized in Nhan Dan and Quan Doi Nhan Dan, Dec. 14–17, 1969.
8. Vietnam Guardian, Nov. 13, 1969.
9. Interview with the author at General Truong's headquarters in Hue, Sept., 1969.

10. Abrams revealed some of his thoughts on Cambodian operations at an informal dinner with correspondents on May 26, 1970.
11. Richard M. Nixon, "Address on Southeast Asia Situation," broadcast by radio and television, April 30, 1970.

Chapter 3

1. Richard M. Nixon, "Report on Cambodia." The statement, released in written form, was not read by the President on radio or television.
2. Norodom Sihanouk, "How Cambodia Fares in the Changing Indochina Peninsula," *Pacific Community* 1, no. 3 (April, 1970), Tokyo, p. 346.
3. *Ibid.*, p. 348.
4. *Ibid.*, p. 350.
5. *Ibid.*, pp. 350–53.
6. Sihanouk made these remarks on November 14, 1968, during a tour of the port of Sihanoukville. The author was among the correspondents on the tour.
7. Norodom Sihanouk, *La Monarchie Cambodgienne et la Croisade Royale pour l'Indépendence* (Phnom Penh, 1961), pp. 102–3.
8. *Ibid.*, pp. 103–7.
9. See Roger M. Smith, *Cambodia's Foreign Policy* (Ithaca, N.Y., 1965), p. 69.
10. *Ibid.*, pp. 63–64.
11. *Ibid.*, pp. 163–65.
12. Norodom Sihanouk, "Le Rejet de l'Aide Américaine" (Phnom Penh, 1963), p. 25. Despite lapses, Cambodia appeared to most observers, at least in retrospect, to have used its U.S. aid and assistance fairly honestly.
13. New China News Agency, Dec. 4, 1963.
14. Sihanouk, "Le Rejet," *op. cit.*, pp. 19–21.
15. See Michael Leifer, *Cambodia: The Search for Security* (New York, 1967), pp. 146–50.
16. *The New York Times*, Nov. 9, 1964.
17. New China News Agency, Feb. 24, 1965.
18. *Newsweek*, April 5, 1965. Krisher's report was largely accurate. The queen indeed profited directly from brothels on land owned by the royal family. She did not run them herself, but sources in Phnom Penh told this writer in November, 1967, that she kept close watch over the balance sheets.
19. *The New York Times*, Oct. 13, 1965. Topping's article was the first of a three-part series on Cambodia. Subsequent articles appeared on October 14 and 15.
20. *Études Cambodgiennes*, no. 7 (July–Sept., 1966), pp. 6–7.
21. Robert Shaplen, "Letter from Cambodia," *The New Yorker*, Sept. 17, 1966, p. 188. In his "Letter," Shaplen did not mention his role as courier in arranging for the visit.
22. Phnom Penh Radio, Sept. 18, 1967.
23. *Ibid.*
24. Agence Khmère de Presse, Nov. 12, 1968.
25. *Réalités Cambodgiennes*, Dec. 6, 1968, pp. 3–5.
26. Phnom Penh Radio, March 29, 1969.
27. *Le Nationaliste*, March 24–30, 1969, p. 61. Although *Le Nationaliste* is a

Cambodian-language magazine, the report was published in French—presumably to attract international attention.
28. Phnom Penh Radio, March 28, 1969.
29. *Ibid.*, April 21, 1969.
30. *Ibid.*, April 28, 1969.
31. *The Washington Post*, Dec. 29, 1967.

Chapter 4

1. See Roger M. Smith, "Cambodia," in *Government and Politics of Southeast Asia*, ed., George McTurnin Kahin, 2d ed. (Ithaca, N.Y., 1964), p. 611.
2. Malcolm MacDonald, *Angkor*, 2d ed. (London, 1965), pp. 147–48.
3. Norodom Sihanouk, "Dix Années d'Indépendence," *Le Monde*, Oct. 8, 1963. Article reprinted in *Cambodge: Terre de Travail et Oasis de Paix*, ed., Ministry of Information, Phnom Penh, Oct., 1963, p. 5.
4. Quoted in A. Dauphin-Meunier, *Le Cambodge de Sihanouk* (Paris, 1965), p. 160.
5. See Constitution du Royaume de Cambodge (Phnom Penh, 1966), Article 122, p. 26.
6. Official program, "Pageant Presented by 'The Royal Khmer Socialist Youth' in honour of Samdech Norodom Sihanouk on the fifteenth anniversary of national independence." Program was published in French, English, and Khmer.
7. Sihanouk escorted correspondents and diplomats on the tour of Sihanoukville, which included the party at his villa, on November 14, 1968.
8. Institut National de la Statistique et des Recherches Économiques, *Annuaire Statistique, 1969*, p. 125. For 1969 figures, see Banque Nationale du Cambodge, *Bulletin Mensuel*, no. 8 (Aug., 1970), p. 11. All rates computed at current official value of 55 riels to $1 (U.S.).
9. *Le Cambodge Économique*, a biweekly review, ed., Chamber of Commerce, Industry, and Agriculture of Phnom Penh, no. 46 (June 19, 1970), pp. 1–2.
10. *Ibid.*
11. Phnom Penh Radio, Dec. 29, 1968.
12. Bernard K. Gordon with Kathryn Young, "Cambodia: Following the Leader?", *Asian Survey* X, no. 2 (Feb. 1970), p. 171.
13. *Le Bulletin du Contre-Gouvernement*, Aug. 25, 1969.
14. Phnom Penh Radio, Oct. 6, 1969.
15. *Ibid.*, Dec. 29, 1969.
16. *Ibid.*, March 12, 1970.
17. *Ibid.* It was indicative of the confusion during this period that Phnom Penh Radio broadcast statements from officials on all sides, ranging from Sihanouk to his enemy Sirik Matak.
18. Agence Khmère de Presse, March 13, 1970.
19. United Press International, March 13, 1970.
20. Yem Sambaur, speech delivered at the Djakarta Conference, May 16–17, 1970.
21. *Le Bulletin du Contre-Gouvernement*, March 13, 1970.
22. Agence France Presse, March 18, 1970.
23. Phnom Penh Radio, March 17, 1970.
24. Agence Khmère de Presse, March 19, 1970. Entire summation republished

in *Cabinets Ministeriels Khmers du 18 Mars 1945 à 18 Mars 1970*, ed., Ministry of Information (Phnom Penh, 1970), pp. 123–24. Amid all the rumors circulating in Phnom Penh at the time, there was no evidence to support speculation of CIA involvement. Only a dozen U.S. officials—the skeleton staff of the newly opened embassy—were in Cambodia on March 18. They appear to have realized only a few hours in advance that Sihanouk's overthrow was imminent, according to descriptions given later privately of the drama of Sihanouk's fall.

25. Cheng Heng's message was broadcast the same day, March 18, 1970, over Phnom Penh Radio and published the next day, March 19, by Agence Khmère de Presse. Also see *Cabinets Ministeriels Khmers*, op. cit., p. 120.

Chapter 5

1. U.S. Mission in Vietnam, "Hanoi's Central Office for South Vietnam (COSVN): A Background Paper," (Saigon, July, 1969), pp. 1–2.
2. *Réalités Cambodgiennes*, no. 621 (Oct. 25, 1968), p. 21.
3. Agence Khmère de Presse, Oct. 2, 1968.
4. "Talk Between Lieutenant-General Lon Nol with Monsieur Nguyen Thuong, Ambassador of the Democratic Republic of Vietnam, and Monsieur Nguyen Van Hieu, Ambassador of the National Liberation Front," *Le Sangkum*, June, 1969; reprinted in *Documents on Viet Cong and North Vietnamese Aggression Against Cambodia*, ed., Ministry of Information (Phnom Penh, 1970), pp. 12–13.
5. Lon Nol, "The Vietcong and North Vietnamese Bases Along Our Borders," a "confidential report," *Le Sangkum*, Oct., 1969; reprinted in *Documents on Viet Cong and North Vietnamese Aggression Against Cambodia*, op. cit., p. 19.
6. Associated Press, April 16, 1970.
7. Associated Press, April 20, 1970. The dispatch said the Vietnamese youth had described what had happened in a written statement "obtained by a responsible authority and transmitted to the apostolic delegate in Saigon and to at least one major power's embassy here."
8. Official program, "Telle Est la Volonté Pour l'Abolition de la Monarchie, Spectacle Interprété pour la Jeunesse du Sauvetage National," April 11, 1970, p. 4.
9. Agence Khmère de Presse, May 11, 1970.
10. Tass, May 4, 1970.
11. Radio Peking, May 6, 1970. Sihanouk outlined his plans at a press conference on May 5 in which he proclaimed his government-in-exile.
12. "Joint Communiqué of the Indochinese Peoples' Summit Conference," Hanoi Radio, April 27, 1970. The conference was actually believed to have been held in the southern Chinese city of Canton.
13. U.S. Military Assistance Command, Vietnam, "Memorandum for Correspondents," no. 181-70, June 30, 1970, p. 1. The memorandum claimed that U.S. troops in Cambodia had picked up two-and-a-half times the number of weapons and fifteen times the amount of rice and ammunition found in Vietnam in the previous year. In actual figures, the U.S. command reported having captured 9,115 "individual weapons," such as rifles and grenade-launchers; 1,267 "crew-served weapons," requiring two or more men to fire; and 5,319 tons of ammunition.

14. Richard M. Nixon, "Address on Cambodia Sanctuary Operation," radio and television broadcast, June 3, 1970.
15. Information based in part on interview with Prom Thos, Cambodian secretary of state for commerce.
16. Ministry of Commerce, Food, and Transportation, "Direction du Commerce Extérieur du Cambodge Mois de Novembre 1970," Phnom Penh, p. 2. Ministry officials said Cambodia exported no rubber whatsoever after September, 1970.
17. Richard M. Nixon, Message to Congress, Nov. 18, 1970. (Italics mine.) Nixon also asked for another $100 million to compensate for the diversion to Cambodia of sums totaling this amount from aid programs for Taiwan, Greece, and Turkey.
18. Agence France Presse, Sept. 26, 1970; dispatch from Peking by Pierre Comparet.
19. Phnom Penh Radio, Oct. 4, 1970.

Chapter 6

1. See David A. Wilson, Politics in Thailand (Ithaca, N.Y., 1962), pp. 21–24.
2. Ibid., pp. 127–128.
3. See Donald E. Nuechterlein, Thailand and the Struggle for Southeast Asia (Ithaca, N.Y., 1965), p. 135.
4. The New York Times, April 5, 1968. The extent of Sarit's holdings was revealed in February, 1964, three months after his death, when his two sons by his first marriage filed suit in a Bangkok civil court, contesting his decision to leave most of his estate to his second wife. The court, on April 4, 1968, ruled the will was valid. A government investigating commission, set up in the furor of publicity surrounding the trial, ruled that he had misused government funds. The government later announced the recovery of the equivalent of $24.9 million from his estate.
5. Statistics supplied by the National Economic Development Board and the U.S. Embassy, Bangkok.
6. "Construction Industry in Thailand," a Bangkok World special supplement (Bangkok, 1969), p. 11.
7. Society of International Development, Panel on Impact of U.S. Military Spending, report, (Bangkok, Oct. 1, 1969), p. 6.
8. National Economic Development Board, Office of the Prime Minister, Summary of Current Economic Position and Prospects of Thailand Under the First and Second Economic Development Plans (Bangkok, Oct., 1966), pp. 4–5. Roads and highways in Thailand in 1950 totaled approximately 5,000 kilometers.
9. Pote Sarasin, "Stable Currency Matches Rapid Economic Growth," The Financial Times, London, Dec. 2, 1968, p. 13.
10. Thanom Kittikachorn, "The Administration of the Present Thai Government" mimeographed statement in Thai and English, March 25, 1967, p. 3.
11. The New York Times, June 22, 1968, p. 3.
12. U.S. Embassy, Bangkok, Economic Summary of Thailand, Aug., 1970 (unpaginated).
13. G. I. Kennecott, "The Trade Balance Issue," Standard Bangkok Magazine, Nov. 2, 1969, p. 5.

14. U.S. Embassy, Bangkok, *Economic Summary of Thailand*, Aug. 1970.
15. Thanom Kittikachorn, "Statement of Policy to Members of Parliament," delivered in Thai, written in Thai and English, mimeographed, Bangkok, March 25, 1969, p. 1.

Chapter 7

1. The English translation of the pamphlet was shown to this writer by an official in Nakhorn Phanom in April, 1969.
2. New China News Agency, Jan. 11, 1969.
3. See Donald E. Nuechterlein, *Thailand and the Struggle for Southeast Asia* (Ithaca, N.Y., 1965), pp. 134–36.
4. Voice of the People of Thailand, Dec. 31, 1968.
5. See National Economic Development Board, Office of the Prime Minister, *Thailand: Summary of Northeast Regional Development Strategy* (Bangkok, July 29, 1968). Later figures are based on interviews with Thai officials and U.S. Embassy analysts in Bangkok.
6. "The Prime Minister on ARD: Accelerated Rural Development Task in Thailand," a *Bangkok Post* supplement, April, 1968, p. 5.
7. "Thai People's Armed Struggle Develops Swiftly and Vigorously," *Peking Review*, no. 8 (Feb. 21, 1969), p. 13.
8. Lieutenant General Saiyud Kerdphol, speech before the Foreign Correspondents Club of Thailand, Feb. 29, 1968, p. 3.
9. *Ibid.*, p. 4.
10. *Ibid.*, p. 3.
11. "The Hill Tribes in Thailand and the Government's Attempts," unsigned and undated mimeographed copies, translated into English, published, and distributed by the Thai Government in 1968.
12. Transcript of press conference given by Praphass, July 17, 1968.
13. *Ibid.*
14. George K. Tanham and Dennis J. Duncanson, "Some Dilemmas of Counterinsurgency," *Foreign Affairs* 48, no. 1 (Oct., 1969), p. 114.
15. United Press International, Bangkok bureau files, Jan., 1969.
16. New China News Agency, Jan. 11, 1969.
17. *Ibid.*

Chapter 8

1. Thanom Kittikachorn, address to the Foreign Correspondents Club of Japan, May 17, 1968.
2. Agreement Respecting Military Assistance Between the Government of the United States of America and the Government of Thailand (Bangkok, 1950).
3. Quoted by David Wilson, "China, Thailand and the Spirit of Bandung (Part 1)," *The China Quarterly*, no. 30 (April–June, 1967), p. 161.
4. *Ibid.*, p. 164.
5. Donald E. Nuechterlein, *Thailand and the Struggle for Southeast Asia* (Ithaca, N.Y., 1965), p. 201.
6. Thanat Khoman and Dean Rusk, joint communiqué issued March 6, 1962, at the State Department, Washington, D.C.
7. Hearings Before the Subcommittee on United States Security Agreements and Commitments Abroad of the Committee on Foreign Relations, United

States Senate, Kingdom of Thailand, Ninety-first Congress, first session, part 3, Nov. 10–14 and 17, 1969, pp. 633, 748. Transcript of hearings includes figures through 1969. For 1970 figures, see U.S. Embassy, Bangkok, *Economic Summary of Thailand*, Aug. 1970.

8. Hearings, *op. cit.*, pp. 613–14 and p. 748.
9. *Ibid.*, p. 622.
10. *Ibid.*, p. 748. Also see *Economic Summary of Thailand, op. cit.*, for 1970 figures.
11. Hearings, *op. cit.*, p. 622.
12. *Ibid.*, p. 657. Apparently, the 1966 costs of these Thai troops were covered by oral agreement.
13. *Ibid.* The 1967 agreement for sending Thai troops to Vietnam also included the final stipulation that the United States "assist the Thai with the air defense problems by providing a battery of Hawk anti-aircraft missiles." This clause seemed to reflect Thailand's concern that North Vietnam or China might retaliate with air strikes for the cooperation that Thailand was offering the United States and South Vietnam.
14. *Ibid.*, p. 764.
15. *Ibid.*, pp. 842–44.
16. Thanom Kittikachorn, "The Administration of the Present Thai Government" (Bangkok, March 25, 1967), p. 15.
17. Louis E. Lomax, *Thailand: The War That Is, The War That Will Be* (New York, 1967).
18. *Siam Rath*, Dec. 26, 1967.
19. Thanat made this remark in an interview with the author in Wellington, New Zealand, during the thirteenth annual conference of SEATO.
20. Thanom Kittikachorn and Lyndon Johnson, joint communiqué, Washington, D.C., May 10, 1968.
21. *Bangkok Post*, March 30, 1969.
22. Transcript of statement by Nixon, Bangkok, July 28, 1969.
23. Transcript of press conference given by Thanat, Bangkok, July 29, 1969.
24. Transcript of statement by Robert J. McCloskey, Aug. 15, 1969.
25. Transcript of speech by Thanat before Foreign Correspondents Club, Bangkok, Aug. 19, 1969.
26. The U.S. Embassy in Bangkok and the Thai Government simultaneously released texts of the announcement.
27. Hearings, *op. cit.*, p. 655.
28. Transcript of English-language statement by Thanat, Jan. 4, 1970.
29. Society of International Development, Panel on Impact of U.S. Military Spending, report (Bangkok, Oct. 1, 1969).

Chapter 9

1. Arthur J. Dommen, *Conflict in Laos: The Politics of Neutralization* (New York, 1971), p. 22.
2. See Paul F. Langer and Joseph J. Zasloff, *North Vietnam and the Pathet Lao* (Cambridge, Mass., 1970), pp. 49–50, 224–25.
3. *Ibid.*, pp. 92–98. Langer and Zasloff cite March 22, 1955, as the date of formation of the Phak Pasason Lao. The word Lao, as in Laos, should not be confused with the Veitnamese word lao, meaning "worker," as in Lao Dong, or Workers' Party.

4. Ministry of Foreign Affairs of Laos, "North Vietnamese Interference in Laos" (Vientiane, 1965), pp. 20–22.
5. Paul F. Langer and Joseph S. Zasloff, *The North Vietnamese Military Adviser in Laos: A First-Hand Account*, Rand Corporation report (Santa Monica, Calif., July, 1968), p. 17.
6. *Ibid*, pp. 17–18. See also Langer and Zasloff, *North Vietnam and the Pathet Lao*, pp. 106–107.
7. Edwin T. McKeithen, "Life Under the P.L. in the Xieng Khouang Ville Area," U.S. Embassy (Vientiane, 1969).

Chapter 10

1. Report by the International Control Commission on the Incidents at Dong Hene," in *White Book on the Violations of the Geneva Accords of 1962 by the Government of North Vietnam*, Ministry of Foreign Affairs of Laos (Vientiane, 1966), p. 94.
2. Vietnam News Agency, Oct. 3, 1965.
3. Quoted in British Information Services, *Laos* (London, 1967), pp. 45–46.
4. New China News Agency, Aug. 20, 1966. In Chinese propaganda parlance, this statement is relatively mild. In a stronger warning, Ch'en might have declared that China would "not stand idly by" while the United States supported the Vientiane government.
5. Peking claimed that its missions in Pathet Lao territory did not need the sanction of the Vientiane regime, which it had ceased to recognize as the true "Government of National Union" after the coup of April 19, 1964. Peking retained its embassy in Vientiane on the grounds that it was accredited to the king.
6. New China News Agency, Dec. 4, 1962.
7. U.S. Embassy, Vientiane, "Army Attaché Press Background," undated, unsigned, and unattributed.
8. Ministry of Foreign Affairs of Laos, *White Book on the Violations of the Geneva Accords of 1962 by the Government of North Vietnam* (Vientiane, 1968), pp. 17–18.
9. *Ibid.*, p. 18.
10. Pathet Lao News Agency, Nov. 23, 1968.
11. Transcript of statement by Souvanna, Dec. 31, 1968.
12. Vietnam News Agency, July, 1969.

Chapter 11

1. Don Schanche, "Behind Pathet Lao Fight—Indianan for All Seasons," *The Sunday Star*, Washington, D. C., April 12, 1970, p. B-2. Schanche recounted his impressions and experiences with Buell in the book *Mister Pop* (New York, 1970).
2. Hearings Before the Subcommittee on United States Security Agreements and Commitments Abroad of the Committee on Foreign Relations, United States Senate, Kingdom of Laos, Ninety-first Congress, first session, part 2, Oct. 20, 21, 22, and 28, 1969, pp. 441–43. The record of the hearings includes the full text of the correspondence between Souvanna and Unger.
3. The agreement forbade the "introduction into Laos of armaments, munitions, and war material generally, *except such quantities of conventional armaments as the Royal Government of Laos may consider necessary for*

the national defense of Laos. . . ." (italics mine). See Protocol to the Declaration on the Neutrality of Laos, Article 6, signed in Geneva on July 23, 1962, by the foreign ministers or heads of delegation of fourteen countries represented at the conference.

4. Hearings (Laos), *op. cit.*, p. 369.
5. *Ibid.*, pp. 369, 409, 457–58.
6. U.S. Army Attaché Press Background, undated, unsigned, unattributed.
7. Hearings (Laos), *op. cit.*, p. 483.
8. Schanche, "Behind Pathet Lao Fight," *op. cit.*, p. B-2.
9. *Tokyo Akahata*, Jan. 7, 1970, interview with Souphanouvong.
10. Hearings (Laos), *op. cit.*, p. 569.
11. "Refugee and Civilian War Casualty Problems in Indochina," a staff report prepared for the use of the Subcommittee to Investigate Problems Connected with Refugees and Escapees of the Committee on the Judiciary, United States Senate, Sept. 28, 1970, Washington, D.C., pp. 26–27.
12. Richard M. Nixon, "Statement on Laos," March 6, 1970, p. 8.
13. Radio Moscow, English-language broadcast, March 15, 1970. The Soviet position still was more moderate than that of China, which edited out references to a political solution in its reports on the program and called the broadcast a "condemnation of American aggression" rather than "a search for a political solution," the term used by the Pathet Lao.
14. Vietnam News Agency, March 6, 1970.
15. Pathet Lao News Agency, March 9, 1970.
16. Agence France Presse, March 24, 1970.
17. *Ibid.*, April 10, 1970.
18. Text of State Department statement on Laos, Washington, D.C., Feb. 8, 1971.
19. *The New York Times*, Jan. 31, 1971, p. 1.

Chapter 12

1. Nguyen Van Tran, "Some Basic Problems to Be Settled in Order to Make Light-Industry Progress," *Cong Nghiep (Industry)*, Hanoi, Sept., 1970.
2. *Sankei Shimbun*, Tokyo, Aug. 7, 1970, morning edition, interview with correspondent Hiroshi Aikawa.
3. Radio Hanoi, February 8, 1971.
4. Extracts April 10 (?) to April 11 from notebook of unidentified North Vietnamese soldier, included as "document no. 4" in "Documents Illustrating Vietnamese Communist Subversion in Cambodia," Joint U.S. Public Affairs Office (Saigon, Oct., 1970).
5. *Bangkok Post*, Sept. 7, 1970, p. 7.
6. *Ibid.*
7. Truong Chinh, "Let Us Be Grateful to Karl Marx and Follow the Path Traced by Him," Radio Hanoi, Sept. 16–21, 1968.
8. See Welles Hangen, "The Russians in Asia," *The Atlantic*, 225, no. 11 (May, 1970), pp. 30–42.
9. Radio Moscow, May 9, 1970, anonymous commentary entitled "U.S. Aggression Against Cambodia and Mao Tse-tung's Policy."
10. New China News Agency, May 20, 1970, statement by Communist Party Chairman Mao Tse-tung, "People of the World Unite and Defeat the U.S. Aggressors and All Their Running Dogs."

11. Tass, July 15, 1970, "Statement of U.S.S.R. Supreme Soviet in Connection with the Spread of the Aggression of U.S. Imperialism in Indochina."
12. United Press International, April 17, 1970.
13. Richard M. Nixon, "Address on Vietnam and Southeast Asia," Oct. 7, 1970.
14. Vietnam News Agency, Sept. 17, 1970.
15. *Ibid.*, Oct. 8, 1970.
16. "Statement of the Government of the Republic of Vietnam on a Negotiated Settlement of the War in Indochina," Oct. 8, 1970.
17. Official transcript, "Vice President's Press Briefing En Route to Bangkok," 3:35 P.M., Aug. 28, 1970.

Selected Bibliography

Southeast Asia

BASTIN, JOHN; and HARRY J. BENDA. *A History of Modern Southeast Asia: Colonialism, Nationalism and Decolonization*. Englewood Cliffs, N.J.: Prentice-Hall, 1968.

BLACK, EUGENE R. *Alternative in Southeast Asia*. Foreword, Lyndon B. Johnson. New York: Praeger, 1969.

BRIMMEL, J. H. *Communism in South East Asia: A Political Analysis*. London: Oxford University Press, 1959.

CADY, JOHN F. *Southeast Asia: Its Historical Development*. New York: McGraw-Hill, 1964.

————. *Thailand, Burma, Laos and Cambodia*. Englewood Cliffs, N.J.: Prentice-Hall, 1966.

CENTRAL OFFICE OF INFORMATION, LONDON. *Vietnam, Laos and Cambodia: Chronology of Events 1945–68*. London: British Information Services, 1968.

COEDÈS, G. *The Indianized States of Southeast Asia*. Ed. Walter F. Vella; tr., Susan Brown Cowing. Honolulu: East-West Center Press, 1968.

————. *The Making of South East Asia*. Tr., H. M. Wright. Berkeley: University of California Press, 1969.

FIELD, MICHAEL. *The Prevailing Wind: Witness in Indo-China*. London: Methuen, 1965.

FIFIELD, RUSSELL H. *Southeast Asia in United States Policy*. New York: Praeger, 1963.

GIRLING, J. L. S. *People's War: Conditions and Consequences in China and South-East Asia*. New York: Praeger, 1969.

HALL, D. G. E. *A History of South-East Asia*. 3d ed., New York: Macmillan, 1968.

HAMMER, ELLEN J. *The Struggle for Indochina*. Stanford, Calif.: Stanford University Press, 1954.

HARRISON, BRIAN. *South-East Asia: A Short History*. London: Macmillan, 1957.

KAHIN, GEORGE McTURNAN, ed. *Governments and Politics of Southeast Asia*, 2d ed. Ithaca, N.Y.: Cornell University Press, 1964.

KUNSTADTER, PETER, ed., *Southeast Asian Tribes, Minorities and Nations*, vols. 1, 2. Princeton, N.J.: Princeton University Press, 1967.

MAO TSE-TUNG. *Basic Tactics*. Tr., intro., Stuart R. Schram; foreword, Samuel B. Griffith. New York: Praeger, 1966.

MYRDAL, GUNNAR. *Asian Drama: An Inquiry into the Poverty of Nations*, 3 vols. New York: The Twentieth Century Fund, 1968.

NIXON, RICHARD M. "Asia After Vietnam," *Foreign Affairs* XLVI, no. 1 (Oct., 1967).

PURCELL, VICTOR. *The Chinese in Southeast Asia*, 2d ed. London: Oxford University Press, 1965.

SCALAPINO, ROBERT A., ed. *The Communist Revolution in Asia: Tactics, Goals and Achievements*, rev. ed. Englewood Cliffs, N.J.: Prentice-Hall, 1970.

SCHAAF, C. HART; and RUSSELL H. FIFIELD. *The Lower Mekong: Challenge to Cooperation in Southeast Asia.* Princeton, N.J.: Van Nostrand, 1963.

SHAPLEN, ROBERT. *Time out of Hand: Revolution and Reaction in Southeast Asia.* New York: Harper and Row, 1969.

TRAGER, FRANK N., ed. *Marxism in Southeast Asia: A Study of Four Countries.* Stanford, Calif.: Stanford University Press, 1959.

WARNER, DENIS. *Reporting Southeast Asia.* Sydney: Angus and Robertson, 1966.

Vietnam

BODARD, LUCIEN. *The Quicksand War.* Boston: Little Brown, 1967.

BUTTINGER, JOSEPH. *Vietnam: A Political History.* New York: Praeger, 1968.

CENTRAL OFFICE OF SOUTH VIETNAM (COSVN). Resolution issued by 9th Conference, held in early July, 1969; copy captured by U.S. troops; tr., republished, Joint U.S. Public Affairs Office, Saigon, Nov., 1969.

DOMMEN, ARTHUR J. "The Future of North Vietnam," *Current History*, April, 1970.

FALL, BERNARD B. *Hell in a Very Small Place: The Siege of Dien Bien Phu.* Philadelphia: Lippincott, 1967.

————. *Street Without Joy: Insurgency in Indochina, 1946–1963*, rev. ed. Harrisburg, Pa.: Stackpole, 1964.

————. *The Two Viet-Nams: A Political and Military Analysis*, 2d rev. ed. New York: Praeger, 1967.

————. *Viet-Nam Witness, 1953–66.* New York: Praeger, 1966.

GIAP, VO NGUYEN. *Banner of People's War, the Party's Military Line.* Preface, Jean Lacouture; intro., Georges Boudarel. New York: Praeger, 1970.

————. *"Big Victory, Great Task."* Intro., David Schoenbrun. New York: Praeger, 1968.

————. *People's War, People's Army: The Viet-Cong Insurrection Manual for Underdeveloped Countries.* Foreword, Roger Hilsman; profile of Giap by Bernard B. Fall. New York: Praeger, 1962.

HALBERSTAM, DAVID. *The Making of a Quagmire.* New York: Random House, 1965.

HICKEY, GERALD. C. *Accommodation and Coalition in South Vietnam.* Santa Monica, Calif.: The RAND Corporation, P-4213, Jan., 1970.

————. *Village in Vietnam.* New Haven, Conn.: Yale University Press, 1964.

HILSMAN, ROGER. *To Move a Nation: The Politics of Foreign Policy in the Administration of John F. Kennedy.* Garden City, N.Y.: Doubleday, 1967.

HONEY, P. J., ed. *North Vietnam Today: Profile of a Communist Satellite.* New York: Praeger, 1962.

LANCASTER, DONALD. *The Emancipation of French Indochina.* London: Oxford University Press, 1961.

LE DUAN. "Under the Glorious Party Banner, for Independence, Freedom and Socialism, Let Us Advance and Achieve New Victories," *Nhan Dan,* Hanoi, Feb. 14, 1970; republished as "document no. 77" in *Vietnam Documents and Research Notes,* Joint U.S. Public Affairs Office, Saigon, April, 1970. Le Duan's treatise was also broadcast by Hanoi Radio, Feb. 16–21, 1970.

MECKLIN, JOHN. *Mission in Torment: An Intimate Account of the U.S. Role in Vietnam.* Garden City, N.Y.: Doubleday, 1965.

NGUYEN VAN TRAN. "Some Basic Problems to Be Settled in Order to Make Light Industry Progress," *Cong Nghiep (Industry),* Hanoi, Sept., 1970; republished in *Principal Reports from Communist Radio Sources,* Joint U.S. Public Affairs Office, Saigon, Oct. 17, 1970.

NIXON, RICHARD M. "Message to Congress," Nov. 18, 1970; "Report on Cambodia," June 30, 1970; speeches, May 14, 1969, Nov. 3, 1969, April 30, 1970, June 3, 1970, Oct. 7, 1970; Transcript of Guam briefing, July 25, 1969.

PIKE, DOUGLAS. *Viet Cong.* Cambridge, Mass.: MIT Press, 1966.

SHAPLEN, ROBERT. *The Lost Revolution: The U.S. in Vietnam, 1946–1966,* rev. ed. New York: Harper and Row, 1966.

————. *The Road from War: Vietnam 1965–1970.* New York: Harper and Row, 1970.

TANHAM, GEORGE K. *Communist Revolutionary Warfare: From the Vietminh to the Viet Cong,* rev. ed. New York: Praeger, 1967.

THOMPSON, ROBERT. *No Exit from Vietnam.* London: Chatto and Windus, 1969.

THOMPSON, VIRGINIA. *French Indo-China.* London: Allen and Unwin, 1937; New York: Paragon, 1967.

TRUONG CHINH. "Let Us Be Grateful to Karl Marx and Follow the Path Traced by Him," Radio Hanoi, Sept. 16–21, 1968; published as "document no. 51," *Vietnam Documents and Research Notes,* Joint U.S. Public Affairs Office, Saigon, Feb. 1969.

————. *Primer for Revolt: The Communist Takeover in Viet-Nam.* A facsimile edition of *The August Revolution* and *The Resistance Will Win;* intro., notes, Bernard B. Fall. New York: Praeger, 1963.

————. "Weaknesses, Shortcomings and Mistakes in Agricultural Cooperatives," *Nhan Dan,* Jan. 29, 30, 1969, published as "document no. 63," *Vietnam Documents and Research Notes,* Joint U.S. Public Affairs Office, Saigon, June, 1969.

ZAGORIA, DONALD S. *Vietnam Triangle: Moscow, Peking, Hanoi.* New York: Pegasus, 1967.

Cambodia

BOOKS AND ARTICLES

AMERICANS WANT TO KNOW. *Is Cambodia Next?* Washington, D. C.: Russell Press, 1967.

ARMSTRONG, JOHN P. *Sihanouk Speaks.* New York: Walker, 1964.

"Le Cambodge," *La Revue Francaise,* Jan., 1968. Entire issue devoted to Cambodia.

"Cambodge: Quinze ans d'indépendance," *Europe France Outremer,* Oct., 1968. Entire issue devoted to Cambodia.

CHANDLER, DAVID P. "Cambodia's Strategy of Survival," *Current History* LVIII, no. 340 (Dec., 1969).

————. "Changing Cambodia," *Current History* LIX, no. 352 (Dec., 1970).

CHAU SENG. *Les Élites Khmères.* Phnom Penh: Culture et Civilisation Khmères, Dec., 1965.

CHOU TA-KUAN. *Notes on the Customs of Cambodia.* Bangkok: Social Science Association Press, 1967.

COEDÈS, GEORGE. *Angkor: An Introduction.* Hong Kong: Hong Kong (Oxford) University Press, 1963.

DAUPHIN-MEUNIER, A. *Le Cambodge de Sihanouk.* Paris: Nouvelles Editions Latines, 1965.

GORDON, BERNARD K.; with KATHRYN YOUNG. "Cambodia: Following the Leader?" *Asian Survey* X, no. 2 (Feb., 1970).

LANGGUTH, A. J. "Dear Prince: Since You Went Away," *The New York Times Magazine,* Aug. 2, 1970.

LEIFER, MICHAEL. *Cambodia: The Search for Security.* New York: Praeger, 1967.

MACDONALD, MALCOLM. *Angkor,* 2d ed. London: Jonathan Cape, with Donald Moore, 1965.

PRUD'HOMME, RÉMY. *L'Économie du Cambodge.* Paris: Presses Universitaires, 1969.

SIHANOUK, NORODOM. "The Future of Cambodia," *Foreign Affairs* XLIX, no. 1 (Oct., 1970).

————. "How Cambodia Fares in the Changing Indochina Peninsula," *Pacific Community* I, no. 3 (April, 1970), Tokyo.

SMITH, ROGER M. *Cambodia's Foreign Policy.* Ithaca, N.Y.: Cornell University Press, 1965.

WILLMOTT, W. E. *The Chinese in Cambodia.* Vancouver: Publications Centre, University of British Columbia, 1967.

GOVERNMENT DOCUMENTS AND PUBLICATIONS—THROUGH MARCH 18, 1970

"Background Notes." Washington, D.C.: U.S. Department of State, July, 1969.

Bulletin Mensuel. Phnom Penh: Banque National du Cambodge, various issues from 1955 to 1970.

Cabinets Ministériels Khmers de 18 Mars 1945 à 18 Mars 1970. Phnom Penh: Ministry of Information, 1970.

Cambodge. Phnom Penh: Ministry of Information, 1962.

"Le Cambodge et la Chine." Phnom Penh: Ministry of Information, 1964. Pamphlet.

Cambodia and Its Industry. Phnom Penh: Sangkum Reastr Niyum Jan., 1967.

Kambuja Revue Mensuelle Illustrée. Ed., Norodom Sihanouk. Various issues from 1965 to early 1970.

KIM, M. TOUCH *Le Régime Monétaire et le Controle des Changes au Cambodge.* Phnom Penh: 1969.

Kingdom of Cambodia. *Achievements of the Sangkum Reastr Niyum.* Phnom Penh: Ministry of Information, 1963, 1964, 1965.

————. *Biographie de S.A.R. Le Prince Norodom Sihanouk.* Phnom Penh: Ministry of Information, Nov., 1965.

_____. *Cambodge: Terre de Travail et Oasis de Paix*. Phnom Penh: Ministry of Information, Oct., 1963.

_____. Constitution du Royaume du Cambodge. Phnom Penh, 1966.

_____. *Livre Blanc des Agressions Americano-Sudvietnamiennes Contre le Cambodge 1962–69*. Phnom Penh: Sangkum Reastr Niyum, 1969.

Ombre sur Angkor. Phnom Penh: Sangkum Reastr Niyum, Nov., 1968. Program of world premiere and synopsis of film by Norodom Sihanouk.

Le Sangkum. Political illustrated review directed by Norodom Sihanouk, fifty-four issues until Jan., 1970.

SIHANOUK, NORODOM. *L'Action de S.N. Norodom Sihanouk pour l'Indépendance du Cambodge, 1941–1955*. Phnom Penh: Ministry of Information, 1959.

_____. "Mon 'Anti-Américanisme,'" *Kambuja*, April 15, 1965.

_____. *La Monarchie Cambodgienne et la Croisade Royale Pour l'Indépendance*. Phnom Penh: Ministry of Education, 1961.

_____. *Notre Socialisme Buddhique*. Phnom Penh: Ministry of Information, 1965.

_____. *Open Letter to the International Press*. Phnom Penh: Ministry of Information, 1965.

_____. "Le Rejet de l'Aide Américaine," Phnom Penh: Ministry of Information, 1963.

_____. "Sommes-Nous de 'Faux Neutres'?" *Kambuja*, July 15, 1966.

GOVERNMENT DOCUMENTS AND PUBLICATIONS—AFTER
MARCH 18, 1970

Le Cambodge Économique. Semiweekly economic review edited by the Chamber of Commerce, Industry and Agriculture of Phnom Penh.

Cambodge Nouveau. Monthly illustrated magazine published by the Sangkum Reastr Niyum, Phnom Penh. First issue dated May, 1970.

Documents on Vietcong and North Vietnamese Aggression Against Cambodia (1970). Phnom Penh: Ministry of Information, 1970.

Hanoi Radio. *Communiqué* of Indochinese People's Summit Conference, April 27, 1970. Republished by Joint U.S. Public Affairs Office, Saigon.

"The Indochinese People's Summit Conference." Broadcast record published in *Vietnam Documents and Research Notes*, Joint U.S. Public Affairs Office, Saigon, June, 1970.

Joint U.S. Public Affairs Office, Saigon. Ten Documents Illustrating Vietnamese Communist Subversion in Cambodia. Saigon, Oct. 19, 1970.

LON NOL. *Message Radiodiffusé à la Nation*. Phnom Penh: Ministry of Information, Aug. 15, 1970.

Ministry of Information. *Communiqué* [regarding legality of Sihanouk's overthrow]. Phnom Penh: Sangkum Reastr Niyum, April 5, 1970.

Réalités Cambodgiennes. Weekly periodical published in Phnom Penh.

U.S. Army. "Cambodia Special," *The Hurricane*, Sept., 1970, authorized publication of II Field Force, Vietnam.

U.S. Embassy, Thailand. "Chronology of Developments Affecting Cambodia." Unclassified summary of dates and events, mimeographed, compiled by Frank Tatu, Bangkok, July, 1969, and June, 1970.

YEM SAMBAUR. Speech delivered at the Djakarta Conference, May 16–17, 1970. Phnom Penh: Ministry of Information, 1970.

Thailand

BOOKS AND ARTICLES

"Accelerated Rural Development," *Bangkok Post*, April, 1968, special supplement.

CHULA CHAKRABONGSE. *Lords of Life: A History of the Kings of Thailand*. London: Alvin Redman, 1967.

COLLIS, MAURICE. *Siamese White*. London: Faber and Faber, 1936.

"Construction Industry in Thailand," *Bangkok World*, special supplement, 1969.

COUGHLIN, RICHARD J. *The Chinese in Modern Thailand*. Hong Kong: Hong Kong University Press, 1960.

DARLING, FRANK C. *Thailand and the United States*. Washington, D.C.: Public Affairs Press, 1965.

INSOR, D. *Thailand: A Political, Social, and Economic Analysis*. New York: Praeger, 1963.

LOMAX, LOUIS E. *Thailand: The War That Is, the War That Will Be*. New York: Vintage, 1967.

MUSCAT, ROBERT J. *Development Strategy in Thailand: A Study of Economic Growth*. New York: Praeger, 1966.

NUECHTERLEIN, DONALD E. *Thailand and the Struggle for Southeast Asia*. Ithaca, N.Y.: Cornell University Press, 1965.

PHILLIPS, H. P.; and D. A. WILSON. *Certain Effects of Culture and Social Organization on Internal Security in Thailand*. Santa Monica, Calif.: The RAND Corporation, RM-3786, June, 1964.

POOLE, PETER A. "Thailand's Vietnamese Refugees: Can They Be Assimilated?" *Pacific Affairs* XL, nos. 3, 4 (Fall–Winter, 1967–68).

————. *The Vietnamese in Thailand*. Ithaca, N.Y.: Cornell University Press, 1970.

POTE SARASIN. "Stable Currency Matches Rapid Economic Growth," *Financial Times*, Dec. 2, 1968.

SIFFIN, WILLIAM J. *The Thai Bureaucracy*. Honolulu: East-West Center Press, 1966.

SILCOCK, T. H., ed. *Thailand Social and Economic Studies in Development*. Canberra: Australian National University Press, 1967.

SKINNER, G. WILLIAM. *Chinese Society in Thailand: An Analytical Survey*. Ithaca, N.Y.: Cornell University Press, 1957.

SOCIETY OF INTERNATIONAL DEVELOPMENT. Transcript of panel on "Impact of U.S. Military Spending." Bangkok: U.S. Embassy, Oct. 1, 1969.

TANHAM, GEORGE K.; and DENNIS J. DUNCANSON. "Some Dilemmas of Counterinsurgency," *Foreign Affairs* XLVIII, no. 1 (Oct., 1969).

THOMPSON, VIRGINIA. *Thailand: The New Siam*. 2d ed., New York: Paragon, 1967.

WILSON, DAVID A. *China, Thailand and the Spirit of Bandung*. Santa Monica, Calif.: The RAND Corporation, P-2607, July, 1962. Reprinted in *The China Quarterly*, nos. 30, 31 (April–June, 1967, and July–Sept., 1967), London.

————. *Politics in Thailand*. Ithaca, N.Y.: Cornell University Press, 1962.

————. *The United States and the Future of Thailand*. New York: Praeger, 1970.

WIT, DANIEL. *Thailand: Another Vietnam?* New York: Scribner's, 1968.

WOOD, W. A. R. *History of Siam*. Bangkok: Chalermnit Bookshop, 1924.
YOUNG, GORDON. *The Hill Tribes of Northern Thailand*. Bangkok: Siam Society, 1969.
YOUNG, KENNETH T. "Thailand and the Cambodian Conflict," *Current History* LIX, no. 342 (Dec., 1970).

GOVERNMENT DOCUMENTS AND PUBLICATIONS

"Economic Summary of Thailand." Bangkok: U.S. Embassy, Aug., 1970. Pamphlet.
Facts and Figures: An Investor's Guide to Thailand. Bangkok: Bangkok Bank Limited, 1966.
Government of Thailand. "The Hill Tribes in Thailand and the Government's Attempts." Mimeographed, unsigned, undated; distributed in 1968.
_____. "Summary of Current Economic Position and Prospects of Thailand." Bangkok, Oct., 1966. Mimeographed.
Handbook. Bangkok: Ministry of National Development, 1968.
National Economic Development Board. *Summary of Northeast Regional Development Strategy*. Bangkok: Prime Minister's Office, July 29, 1968.
SAIYUD KERDPHOL. "Communist Threat to Thailand." Mimeographed copy of speech to Foreign Correspondents Club of Thailand, Feb. 29, 1968.
Thailand Facts and Figures. Bangkok: Ministry of National Development, 1966.
THANAT KHOMAN. *Collected Interviews of Thanat Khoman*, vols. 1–3. Bangkok: Ministry of Foreign Affairs, 1967–69.
_____. *Collected Statements of Foreign Minister Thanat Khoman*, vols. 1–6. Bangkok: Ministry of Foreign Affairs, 1964–70.
THANOM KITTIKACHORN. "Address on the Occasion of the Anniversary of the Establishment of the Prime Minister's Office." Mimeographed copy of speech given June 28, 1968.
_____. "The Administration of the Present Thai Government." Bangkok: Prime Minister's Office, March 25, 1967. Mimeographed.
_____. "Introducing the 2509 Budget to the Constituent Assembly." Bangkok: Prime Minister's Office, 1965.
_____. "Statement of Policy." Mimeographed copy dated March 25, 1969.
U.S. Embassy, Thailand. *Economic Trends in Thailand*. Bangkok: March 30, 1970. Mimeographed.
U.S. Senate, Committee on Foreign Relations. *United States Security Agreements and Commitments Abroad, Kingdom of Thailand*, Hearings Before the Subcommittee on United States Security Agreements and Commitments Abroad of the Committee on Foreign Relations, Nov. 10–14 and 17, 1969. Printed for use of the Committee on Foreign Relations. Washington, D.C.: Government Printing Office, 1970.

Laos

BOOKS AND ARTICLES

BURCHETT, WILFRED G. *The Furtive War: The United States in Vietnam and Laos*. New York: International Publishers, 1963.
Chalermnit Press Correspondent. *Battle of Vientiane of 1960*. Bangkok: Chalermnit Press, 1961.

DOMMEN, ARTHUR J. *Conflict in Laos: The Politics of Neutralization*, rev. ed. New York: Praeger, 1971.

———. "Laos in the Second Indochina War," *Current History* LIX, no. 342 (Dec., 1970).

FALL, BERNARD B. *Anatomy of a Crisis: The Laotian Crisis of 1960–61*. Ed., epilogue, Roger M. Smith. Garden City, N.Y.: Doubleday, 1969.

FREDMAN, H. B. *The Role of the Chinese in Lao Society*. Santa Monica, Calif.: The RAND Corporation, P-2161, 1961.

HALPERN, J. M. *The Lao Elite: A Study of Tradition and Innovation*. Santa Monica, Calif.: The RAND Corporation, RM-2636-RC, Nov. 15, 1960.

———; and H. B. FREDMAN. *Communist Strategy in Laos*. Santa Monica, Calif.: The RAND Corporation, RM-2561, June 14, 1960.

JONAS, ANNE M.; and GEORGE K. TANHAM. *Laos: The Current Phase in a Cyclic Regional Revolution*. San Francisco: The RAND Corporation, P-2214, Feb. 2, 1961. Republished in *Orbis* (Spring, 1961), pp. 64–73.

LANGER, PAUL F. *Comments on Bernard Fall's "The Pathet Lao: A 'Liberation' Party."* Santa Monica, Calif.: The RAND Corporation, P-3751, Feb., 1969.

———. *Laos: Preparing for a Settlement in Vietnam*. Santa Monica, Calif.: The RAND Corporation, P-4024, Feb., 1969.

———. *Laos: Search for Peace in the Midst of War*. Santa Monica, Calif.: The RAND Corporation, P-3748, Dec., 1967.

———; and JOSEPH J. ZASLOFF. *North Vietnam and the Pathet Lao: Partners in the Struggle for Laos*. Cambridge, Mass.: Harvard University Press, 1970.

"Le Laos," *La Revue Française*, Oct. 1967. Entire issue devoted to Laos.

LEBAR, FRANK M.; and ADRIENNE SUDDARD, eds. *Laos: Its People, Its Society, Its Culture*, rev. ed. New Haven, Conn.; HRAF Press, 1967.

MANICH, M. L. *History of Laos*. Bangkok: Charlermnit Press, 1967.

SCHANCHE, DON. *Mister Pop*. New York: McKay, 1970.

SISOUK NA CHAMPASSAK. *Storm over Laos: A Contemporary History*. New York: Praeger, 1961.

SOUVANNA PHOUMA. "The Future of Indochina." *Pacific Community* I, no. 2 (Jan., 1970).

TOYE, HUGH. *Laos: Buffer State or Battleground?* London: Oxford University Press, 1968.

WOLFKILL, GRANT; with JERRY A. ROSE. *Reported to Be Alive*. New York: Simon & Schuster, 1965.

GOVERNMENT DOCUMENTS AND PUBLICATIONS

Central Office of Information, London. "Laos." Pamphlet no. R5489167. London: British Information Services, 1967.

McKEITHEN, EDWIN T. *Life Under the P.L. In the Xieng Khouang Ville Area*. No publisher or date listed. Publisher was the U.S. Agency for International Development, Vientiane, Laos, which produced a mimeographed edition in 1969.

MANN, CHARLES A. *4 Questions on American Economic Aid to Laos*, Vientiane: U.S. AID Mission, Nov., 1969.

Ministère du Plan et de la Cooperation, Commissariat General au Plan, Royaume du Laos. *Plan Cadre de Développement Économique et Social, 1969–1974, Priorité au Secteur Productif*. Vientiane, 1969.

Ministry of Foreign Affairs, Laos. *North Vietnamese Interference in Laos.* Vientiane, 1965.

————. *White Book on Violations of the Geneva Accords of 1962.* Vientiane, 1966.

————. *White Book on Violations of the Geneva Accords of 1962.* Vientiane, 1968.

————. *White Book on Violations of the Geneva Accords of 1962.* Vientiane, 1970.

NIXON, RICHARD M. "Statement on Laos," March 6, 1970. Released by U.S. Embassy, Laos, in mimeographed form.

U.S. Agency for International Development. *Foreign Assistance for the Development of Laos.* Vientiane: U.S. AID Mission. Published in cooperation with the Commission General of the Plan, July, 1969.

————. *United States Aid to Laos,* rev. ed. Vientiane: U.S. AID Mission, 1970.

U.S. Senate. *Refugee and Civilian War Casualty Problems in Indochina.* Prepared for use of Subcommittee to Investigate Problems Connected with Refugees and Escapees of the Committee on the Judiciary. Washington, D.C.: Government Printing Office, Sept. 28, 1970.

U.S. Senate, Committee on Foreign Relations. *United States Security Agreements and Commitments Abroad, Kingdom of Laos.* Hearings Before the Subcommittee on United States Security Agreements and Commitments Abroad of the Committee on Foreign Relations, Oct. 20–22 and 28, 1969. Printed for use of Committee on Foreign Relations. Washington, D.C.: Government Printing Office, 1970.

Index

Abrams, Creighton, 18, 34, 36
Accelerated Rural Development (ARD) program, 157–58, 162
Agence Khmère de Presse, 100–101, 108
Agnew, Spiro, 189
Air America, 233–34
Alor Star, 173
An Quang Pagoda, 26–27
Ananda Mahidol, 137–39
Angkor, 6–7, 68, 73, 129
Angkor Wat, 73, 133
Anglo-French agreement (1896), 10
Anglo-Siamese treaty (1904), 10
Annamite Cordillera, 5, 7–8, 195, 215
Anti-Communist act (Thailand), 154, 177, 179
Army of the Republic of Vietnam (ARVN), 17
Asian-African conference (1955), 46–48, 63
Asian and Pacific Council, 185
Association of Southeast Asian Nations, 185
Attopeu, 128, 224–25, 229, 239, 252–53
Auriol, Vincent, 44
Australia, 45, 120, 129, 177
Australian Embassy in Phnom Penh, 65–66
Ayudhya, 11

Ban Karai Pass, 216
Bandung conference (see Asian-African conference)
Bangkok, 5, 8–11, 137, 141, 146–48, 151, 153–61, 170, 172, 174, 176–79, 182, 184, 186, 187, 188, 189, 197–98

Barré, Jean, 108
Barthélémy Pass, 199, 216
Bartlett, Charles, 64
Bassac River, 118, 127
Batene, 222
Battambang Province, 7, 10, 66, 69, 78, 80; revolt of, 76, 78–81
Bavet, 33
Be, Nguyen, 23–24
Beck-Friis, Johan, 49
Bekker, Konrad, 190–91
Beng River, 222
Bhumibol Adulyadej, 139, 143–44
Binh, Nguyen Thi, 270–71, 276
Black, Eugene, 65
Bolovens Plateau, 216–17, 224–26, 228–30, 260
Boun Oum na Champassak, 206–8
Bowles, Chester, 65
Brezhnev, Leonid, 99, 266–67
Brown, George, 220
Buddhism: Mahayana, 14, 224; practices of, 74–75; Theravada, 14, 224
Buddhist uprisings (1966), 26–27
Buell, Edgar ("Pop"), 234–35, 242, 244
Bulletin du Contre-Gouvernement, Le, 85
Bunker, Ellsworth, 28, 33–34
Burma, 9–10, 61, 137, 172, 221; army of, 11

Cam Ranh Bay, 6
Cambodia, 4–8, 10, 14–15, 19–20, 22, 28, 32–34, 37, 41–133, 175, 179, 192, 199, 259; and China, 58; Communists in, 44–46; declared a Republic (1970), 133; Democratic Party in, 69–71, 77; economy of,